STRAWBERY BANKE

A Seaport Museum 400 Years in the Making

Strawbery Banke

A Seaport Museum 400 Years in the Making

J. Dennis Robinson

Published for
Strawbery Banke Museum
by
Peter E. Randall Publisher LLC
PORTSMOUTH, NEW HAMPSHIRE
2007

Book Design: Grace Peirce, J. Dennis Robinson
Jacket Design: Brown & Company, Portsmouth, NH

Peter E. Randall Publisher LLC
Box 4726, Portsmouth, New Hampshire 03802   USA
www.perpublisher.com

Distributed by
University Press of New England
Hanover and London

Library of Congress Control Number: 2007936026
ISBN10   0-9603896-2-8
ISBN13   978-0-9603896-2-9

FRONT END LEAF: Detail of Portsmouth, New Hampshire from the Navy Yard, Kittery, Maine, 1854, drawn and lithographed by Charles Parsons. (SBM)

REAR END LEAF: A Map of Portsmouth, New Hampshire, *An Old Town by the Sea* by Dorothy Vaughan and Harold G. Rundlett, copyright 1930, H. G. Rundlett. This is one of the first appearances of the name "Strawbery Banke" with the spelling later adopted by Strawbery Banke Inc., in 1958 at the founding of the museum. (SBM)

TITLE PAGE: Lithograph by E. Whitefield entitled *View of Portsmouth, NH on July 4th, 1873*. (SBM)

JACKET FRONT & BACK: Photographs of Strawbery Banke Museum by Ralph Morang.

DEDICATION

To Wanda Kenick
(1953–1977)
who stole inside the museum fence
with me one winter day, tap-danced, and sang
Button Up Your Overcoat
on the icy stage at the empty park
and was so very suddenly lost to us in spring

Also by J. Dennis Robinson

RICH WITH CHILDREN
The Birth of an Italian Family in America

JESSE JAMES
Legendary Rebel and Outlaw

WENTWORTH BY THE SEA
The Life and Times of a Grand Hotel

LORD BALTIMORE
Founder of Maryland

NEW ENGLAND
A Photographic Portrait

PORTSMOUTH AND COASTAL NEW HAMPSHIRE
A Photographic Portrait

CONTENTS

Acknowledgments

Creating this book would not have been possible without three people: Larry Yerdon, president of Strawbery Banke Museum, who boldly gave the project a green light on the day it was proposed and encouraged me to follow whatever direction the story required; Dr. Richard M. Candee, Boston University Professor Emeritus, who read and red-penciled every chapter as it appeared, then left clues and shouted warnings as I stumbled through four centuries of Portsmouth history; and Dr. Maryellen Burke, my wife, who read every word aloud back to me, researched, critiqued, argued points, gave praise and then, after two years of it all, announced that she was taking her week of vacation time to edit and proofread the manuscript once more. Other than paid staff and a Pulitzer, what else could an author require?

My special thanks to James L. Garvin, who not only offered his expertise as New Hampshire State Architectural Historian and a character in this story, but can still spot a typo in a footnote from twenty paces. Also my appreciation to Jan Harney who helped gather black and white photographs, and to my photographer friends, Richard Haynes and Ralph Morang, for their special color sections; to photographer Douglas Armsden whose rich black and white photographs still deserve their own volume; to publisher Peter E. Randall and his staff, including designer Grace Peirce; to my friend Mary Jo Brown for work on the jacket design; and to all those who created the imagery here. For those

OPPOSITE: *Fourth of July celebrants parade among the historic houses of Puddle Dock. (PER)*

who never read a word of my text, these pictures should tell the story just as well.

I am indebted to the busy staff at Strawbery Banke, including Peggy Sanders, Stacey Brooks, Tara Webber, Rodney Rowland, Courtney MacLachlan, Carolyn Singer, Bob Hogan, and everyone else who offered ideas, interviews, images, and time. And my sincere thanks to all those who read the manuscript along the way, for their wisdom and warning, including Greg Brackett, Tom Hardiman, John Mayer, Michael Huxtable, Peter Michaud, Richard Adams, Rodman Philbrick, David Sanderson, Thomas Watson, Thomas P. Kelleher, and Nancy Grossman. My thanks, as always, for use of the library facilities at Strawbery Banke, the Portsmouth Athenaeum, and the Portsmouth Public Library, and to the creators of Google and the Internet.

All history books are treasure hunts and the greatest enjoyment for the author is the discovery that happens along the way. I am indebted to all ten directors of Strawbery Banke for lengthy and candid conversations, and to all those who offered interviews, clippings, photographs, and suggestions. I was guided throughout this journey by the scrapbooks of Muriel Howells, the papers of Dorothy Vaughan, the "underground" manuscript history of Strawbery Banke by Thayer Cumings, and the theories of John W. Durel and Paige W. Roberts. My great appreciation to Dr. "Tad" Baker and my brother, Dr. Brian Robinson, for guidance in the Prehistoric, Contact, and seventeenth-century eras; to Cynthia Raymond and Marion Fuller Brown for information about the founding of The Guild of Strawbery Banke; to Jim Garvin and Richard Candee for tracking down the Howells-Decatur WPA proposal and map; to Sherm Pridham for his knowledge of Puddle Dock; to Sumner Winebaum for his persistent question, What about the Indians? and for material on his father, Harry; to Jonathan Hubbard for loaning the papers of Rosamond Thaxter; to long-time museum supporter Nancy Beck for frequent guidance and information on archaeologist Lawrence Straus; to Wendy Pirsig for material on her father, George Kimball; to Clare Kittredge and Mark Sammons for research assistance; and to Bob Pecunies for arriving at the eleventh hour with a box full of Puddle Dock memorabilia.

SPONSORS

Mary and Storer Goodwin Decatur
The Roger R. and Theresa S. Thompson Endowment Fund

FOREWORD

Thousands have visited the preservation project and out-door history museum called Strawbery Banke. Countless thousands more across the nation have heard the story told since its founding fifty years ago. The preservation com-munity, museum-goers, local residents, and the museum's volun-teers, trustees, and staff have followed the progress of the project with avid curiosity. Many have supported the project financially. Others have encouraged its growth by gifts of their time and knowledge. Still others have given artifacts to the growing collec-tion that is at the core of the exhibition program. In the fiftieth anniversary year, we take time to celebrate these people and their commitment to this project, and to consider the road traveled to get to where the Museum is today.

Yet, after all this time and all these people, Strawbery Banke is not finished. Very likely, it never will be. That quixotic char-acteristic is at the heart of this preservation endeavor. The fact that Strawbery Banke remains a work in progress is, in large part, why it continues to inspire such excitement and interest. It is the ongoing restoration and unearthing of new discoveries in these beloved buildings—below ground, in the research archives, and through oral histories—that continually shift, sharpen, and expand our understanding of the past. Members of the commu-nity come forward every year, offering new pieces of information that help us do our job—remembering those grand and ordi-nary people who lived here. Strawbery Banke is an organic and dynamic project, and its outcome belongs to all of us.

OPPOSITE: *The US Coast Guard's tall ship* Eagle *in Portsmouth Harbor as seen from Memorial Bridge that spans the Maine/New Hampshire border. (PER)*

This project began at Puddle Dock in 1958 with the dedication, foresight, and faithful service of a large and varied community. A great many of these early founders have fulfilled their service to the museum, some making it a focus of their lives. As we celebrate the first fifty years of Strawbery Banke, our hearts go out to them. We honor them here by telling their stories. We honor them best by continuing their work. A new, equally dedicated group carries on the work of Strawbery Banke. Drawn to these tantalizing tales and these grand structures, we know generations of Strawbery Banke enthusiasts will follow. They will never quite finish the job, but they will find great delight and wisdom here on the Portsmouth waterfront. And like its founders, and like us, they will find themselves both immersed in the four hundred year history of Puddle Dock — and part of it.

Lawrence Yerdon
President
Strawbery Banke Museum

OPPOSITE: *Role-player in the garden of the Governor Goodwin House with the Daniel Webster House in the background. Photograph by John Dunkle. (SBM)*

INTRODUCTION

Cities and towns have distinct voices, I'm convinced. Their neighborhoods, houses, and rooms tell tales; they hold deep impressions of their makers and their keepers. Like the kid in the movie who sees dead people, I hear buildings. You could call me a house whisperer. The stories are what interest me. The buildings are the stage on which the drama is enacted.

This volume may surprise a few who already cherish Strawbery Banke Museum. It is not, as many assumed I was writing, a detailed study of the old houses that make up the ten-acre museum campus. I'm afraid I do not speak architecture, nor am I fluent in the language of decorative arts. I don't know a Federal entablature from a Georgian highboy. The Piscataqua is rich with experts on these topics. Like many in the field of "narrative history" my training is in literature. So it is not surprising that when I first expressed the urge to write a history of Strawbery Banke, a former museum employee put it to me bluntly that I was "the last person on earth" who would ever be granted that opportunity. There was nothing unkind in this comment. I was simply not a museum professional.

But narrative writers work best when they start blank. What intrigued me, having lived thirty-something years in town and having written hundreds of essays on Portsmouth history, was how little I knew about Strawbery Banke. The museum, surrounded by a wooden fence, has always seemed a kingdom unto itself. It has its own name, its own streets, its own logo, mission, and staff. There was a haunting sense of separateness here. Before it was a museum, Puddle Dock was a neighborhood distinguished by its ethnic diversity and its poverty. It hovered on the edge of a gritty Red Light district. Before that it was the heartbeat of the city's maritime trade. Before that it was an isolated plantation surrounded only by a dense, dangerous forest.

The more I tried to assemble all these pieces, the more hazy and mysterious the South End waterfront appeared. Where exactly had the first Portsmouth settlers built the Great House in 1630? Why had they come? Where were the Indians? Where were the strawberries? How had the tidal inlet disappeared? What caused the hub of the city to become a "blighted slum" in the eyes of the federal government? Where did the displaced Puddle Dockers go when the neighborhood was confiscated under eminent domain? Strawbery Banke, for me, held as many secrets as Stonehenge. Each year as I passed through and around The Banke, its ancient cluster of buildings whispered louder and louder. Qualified or not, I was being called.

The questions that nagged me defined the research that followed. Local legend has it that Strawbery Banke was born when city librarian Dorothy Vaughan gave a rousing speech at the Portsmouth Rotary in 1957. She told me so herself. But the full story is more dramatic and complex and satisfying. The truth simply takes more time to read than a bumper sticker. There were rumors that an earlier "maritime village" plan had failed here. Turns out this was true. There are buildings, half a century after the museum was established, still awaiting restoration. I felt that Strawbery Banke, for all its decades of detailed self-analysis, has yet to come to terms with its traumatic founding years. The fiftieth anniversary of the museum in 2008 seemed a good time to dispel those ghosts. I asked permission to dig around, and permission was granted.

The result of my research, I see now, is really three books. The first is the history of Portsmouth as it swirls around this dynamic campus where the museum is located today. The second is the story of the people who birthed and raised Strawbery Banke Incorporated. The illustrations comprise a third book. Collecting and captioning and placing them where they belong was a trying process that added months of late night work. Many histories wisely skip this final step, but the pictures, for me, are as important as the words. I simply could not let them go. The photos of Richard Haynes, Ralph Morang, and Doug Armsden were playing in my head long before the first sentence here was composed.

The transition at Strawbery Banke from urban renewal project to a professionally-run museum was a tumultuous one. My job throughout has been to listen closely to these old buildings and to take good notes. I have left it to others, as best I could, to debate what all this means. I see Strawbery Banke Museum as a work in progress, constantly adapting its message to fit the times. My contribution has been to lay out in these pages what has transpired here over the last four centuries. Hopefully, with the full arc of its story revealed, the museum's future path will be easier to define.

For many readers, this book may serve as their introduction to the history of Portsmouth. For most of the last two centuries, this city has suffered from an inferiority complex. Local historians have long noted with pained regret that Portsmouth lost its economic edge early in the 1800s. After the demise of the West India Trade, they tell us, the city could not keep pace. It was quickly overcome by commercial seaports like Boston, Gloucester, Salem, and Portland, and later by manufacturing centers from Manchester and Dover to Lawrence and Lowell. Like the helpless heroine in a romantic play, Portsmouth fell into a swoon, if not into a coma. The opulent colonial mansions of the ruling aristocracy survived, but the rich people and their mannered society were gone forever—or so the story went. Sometime around 1823, at the bicentennial of the landing of its first white settlers, Portsmouth citizens let out a collective moan that still echoes through the empty rooms of its historic house museums. "I used to be a great town!" the ghostly voice cries. "I wish I were wealthy and important again."

Like so many of the people mentioned in this book, I fell in love with Portsmouth when it was still a gritty workingman's seaport. During my first visit here as a high school newspaper reporter in 1968, the coach warned our basketball team to stay close to the bus because Portsmouth was a "dangerous town." On a college outing here in 1972, I inadvertently brought my date to a topless restaurant. Living downtown a few years later, I saw a man stabbed in a bar fight just outside the door of my apartment. Yet throughout these tough times, Portsmouth was slowly re-inventing itself, as it has time and again. Thanks, in part, to the success of Strawbery Banke, Portsmouth came to realize that its past and its future were closely aligned. The more modern and streamlined other cities grew, the more appealing the preserved homes of colonial Portsmouth became. Today's walkable downtown with its cozy waterfront shops, theatres and fine restaurants owes much of its success to the historic environment all around. Business, I fear, does not always appreciate history, but take away all these old buildings and for many of us, you rob the city of its soul.

And with the current cultural and economic renaissance, I hope, Portsmouth will soon find a new and less depressing voice. Instead of the town that used to be great, it is poised to be rich and important again. But this time it will be rich in American history and important as a place where people can connect with our ever-changing past. Each generation defines itself against the generations it must follow, and we need places like Strawbery Banke where that measuring takes place.

I apologize in advance to the hundreds of museum staff, benefactors, and volunteers who will search this book for their own names and come up empty. I'm no Tolstoy. In a work of this scope, literary guidelines suggest, the fewer characters the reader meets, the easier it is to stick with the plot. I chose in the final chapters to follow the story of the museum's many directors. Each brought something unique. I chose not to include their photos, however, to avoid turning the text into a yearbook. Despite the buzz that surrounds any nonprofit institution where there is always more talent than money, I worked from a simple guiding philosophy. I believe that everyone who ever worked here did what he or she thought was best for Strawbery Banke. I see many heroes and no villains. They aimed high and, as inevitably happens when astronauts run low on fuel, life inside the space capsule sometimes got tense. That dramatic tension, for me, is what makes this story so interesting. The tension begins here in 1600 and never lets up.

I wrestled with the colonial spelling of the museum's name. The original settlement on the Portsmouth waterfront was called

"Strawberry Bank," but is spelled many ways in early records. The missing "r" in "strawbery" and the added "e" in "banke" were contrived by the colonial revival founders of Strawbery Banke Inc. In an effort to distinguish the museum from the seventeenth-century settlement, I have used the modern spelling "Strawberry Bank" for the original settlement or any other use of the phrase. Although this may seem counterintuitive, it was easier to standardize the past than to change the published name of the museum during its fifty years. So in this book—"olde" spelling equals new and modern spelling equals old.

It was a relief to discover through two years of study that nobody I read or talked to fully understands Strawbery Banke. It has, in the end, a certain Rorschach quality. People see different things here. The one thing everyone agrees on is that Strawbery Banke is not finished. The one characteristic most former directors used in describing the place is "potential." Even after half a century, Strawbery Banke vibrates with new possibilities. Asked in 1972 in which direction he thought the museum should go, director Ed Lynch quoted the Cheshire Cat in *Alice and Wonderland*. "That depends a good deal," he replied, "on where you want to get to."

Which reminds me of the time I presented a gift to historian Dorothy Vaughan on her ninety-fifth birthday. The mayor had just presented Vaughan with the key to the city when I stepped up to make my offering. I gave her an ancient sleeve of Portsmouth sheet music I discovered on eBay.

"Can I keep this?" Dorothy asked, her eyes bright and hopeful.

"That's Dennis," the mayor whispered to Dorothy. "He's one of our wonderful local historians."

"When he gets it right!" Dorothy said and grinned, not unlike the Cheshire Cat.

Getting this book right is no longer under my control. My time listening to sage, old buildings is over. This story of Strawbery Banke and its future, dear Reader, are now in your hands.

J. Dennis Robinson

1

OPENING CEREMONIEſ

Summer 1965

> *Somewhere among the dreaming spires beyond, a distant clock trills time upon its tongue and in the village a new day has begun . . . Let's take a walk through the wonderland of Portsmouth's ancient Strawbery Banke . . . where every exquisite detail is a portrayal so rich, so provocative that one stands almost rooted to the spot in the pure enchantment of its drama! . . . The dream has become a reality, the reality, a dream!*
>
> —The Merchant News, May 1965

Advance reviews were rapturous. Newspapers from the *New York Times* and the *National Observer* to the *Boston Globe* and *Toronto Star* trumpeted the event with over ten thousand lines of type. A million American school children read about the launch of Strawbery Banke in their classroom publication, *World News of the Week.* After seven years of planning and restoration, the ten-acre "colonial village" in Portsmouth, New Hampshire, was finally ready to open. The official ribbon cutting was scheduled for Memorial Day, 1965, but the project had already generated hundreds of press clippings since it was founded in 1958.[1]

The story was unique from every angle. For the first time a city, a nonprofit agency, and the Federal Housing Authority

ABOVE: *Door of the Stephen Chase House on Court Street (formerly Pitt Street) at Strawbery Banke. (SBM/DA)*

OPPOSITE: *Strawbery Banke "belles" in strawberry-print skirts pose near the Chase House. This volunteer group of tour guides welcomed visitors, including Lady Bird Johnson, during the opening years of the museum in the 1960s. Douglas Armsden photo. (SBM/DA)*

were working together to preserve historic houses. While "urban renewal" usually meant tearing down old buildings to build modern ones, Strawbery Banke Inc. managed to salvage over two dozen colonial structures from demolition. Two other historic buildings had been moved from other parts of town, and four more would follow. Most of the buildings stood on their original foundations in one of the oldest neighborhoods in the nation. Although the 1630 Great House was gone, the waterfront area had once been the hub of the state's only thriving seaport. But the Portsmouth maritime trade collapsed early in the 1800s and the waterfront neighborhood faded. By the middle of the twentieth century Portsmouth's Puddle Dock region—busy with dilapidated apartments, family shops, homes, and rusting scrap metal yards—was officially designated as a "blighted" and dangerous slum and targeted for destruction. With almost no financial backing and a poorly paid staff of two men, the grassroots volunteer group persevered. The original founders of Strawbery Banke were mostly downtown merchants. Their dual goal was to preserve Portsmouth heritage while attracting hordes of tourists to spend time and money in the once grand Port City. Simply put, according to *The Portsmouth Herald*, it was time to "sell the city," and judging from the media blitz in the spring of 1965, the dream was about to come true.[2]

The dream was to transform the Portsmouth waterfront into a northern version of the much-admired Colonial Williamsburg outdoor museum in Virginia. By 1965 Williamsburg had an annual budget of $13 million and its visitors poured an additional $18 million into the local economy, statistics that made Portsmouth merchants dizzy with anticipation.[3] But Williamsburg had a wealthy benefactor named John D. Rockefeller, while Strawbery Banke had local stockholders, most of whom purchased a single share of stock for $10. The most famous stockholder, President Dwight Eisenhower, owned a single ceremonial share. In true Yankee style, by aligning itself with a federal urban renewal project, Portsmouth preservationists were able to buy a used neighborhood for about $28,000, about $1,000 per preserved house—all of which needed costly work. Portsmouth's "multi-million dollar restoration project" was rich in dreams, not cash.

"You have ploughed unploughed ground," the founding

president of Williamsburg Kenneth Chorley told a gathering of Portsmouth businessmen in 1965, "and established a valuable precedent for this country's cultural future." But the kudos came with a warning: Strawbery Banke was more authentic, Chorley agreed, than other largely reconstructed historic villages. To compromise that authenticity would lead to failure. "Whatever you do," he said, "don't try to be another Williamsburg, or another Sturbridge Village. Just be yourselves, for yours is a wonderful opportunity."[4]

The opening celebration, one New Hampshire paper predicted, "will doubtless go down in Portsmouth history."[5] According to another writer, wandering through the restored seacoast village could transport visitors to "a sense of almost unbearable nostalgia."[6] But for some, the opening days at Strawbery Banke were a textbook case of selling the sizzle, not the steak.

"It was pretty bleak," Bruce Fuller recalled more than forty years later. "It was bare bones. The opening was a milestone, but a non-event."[7] Then a freshman at the nearby University of New Hampshire, Fuller was hired to write a series of upbeat newspaper

BELOW: *A Revolutionary War re-enactor mans his cannon at a public muster. The tall grass in front of the Jones House dates this image toward the opening of "the project" in the mid-1960s. (SBM/DA)*

Within sight of the North Church spire, Strawbery Banke Inc. slowly restored the boarded-up Puddle Dock neighborhood to create a maritime museum. Here (top) workers begin building the Dunaway Store that opened in 1967. Strawberry road signs attracted the museum's first tourists and volunteer guides offered tours in this surrey with a fringe on top. (SBM/DA)

features about The Banke leading to the Memorial Day opening ceremonies. He reported weekly to "Captain" Carl Johnson, "a rather intimidating man," the Strawbery Banke executive vice president and former acting commander of the U.S. Naval Base at the Shipyard. Johnson's office was located in the middle of the restoration project, Fuller recalls, in a "rundown, musty old place" surrounded by one boarded-up, weather-beaten building after another. Weeds grew thick between the battered buildings separated by fields of yellow ragweed and grass as tall as hay.

"True," a Strawbery Banke press release admitted in May 1965, "some of the structures have fallen onto evil days and are in poor repair, perhaps covered with ugly asbestos siding or simply left to weather."[8]

By 1965 over half a million dollars in federal funds had been spent clearing out five junkyards and removing forty-four "ugly new" houses and many outbuildings. More than one hundred families were also removed from the "substandard" dwellings, evicted under federal eminent domain legislation. Many of the "displaced" Puddle Dockers found housing in the South End nearby or were relocated to new garden-style apartments for the poor and elderly elsewhere in town. A federally funded brochure in 1966 described Portsmouth—along with Savannah, New Orleans, Chicago, San Francisco, Norfolk, and others— as "an outstanding example of a city's use of urban renewal to achieve historic preservation goals."[9] Almost half a century later, resentment against urban renewal in Puddle Dock and in other parts of the city still lingers.

"Even the skeptics will admit," the *Portsmouth Herald* announced in a special twenty-eight-page Strawbery Banke advertising supplement, "that tomorrow's dedication ceremonies signal the beginning of a new era in Portsmouth."[10]

It was true. Downtown Portsmouth blossomed over the next few decades from a gritty seaport to a popular cultural destination, trading topless bars for tasteful boutiques, restaurants, galleries, and theaters. While some still prefer those blue-collar days over the charming and gentrified city, no one doubts that Portsmouth re-invented itself with an eye towards preservation. The "Old Town by the Sea" had a longstanding reputation for its aristocratic colonial architecture, colorful folk tales, and

ABOVE: *Two "subminiature" candid prints from August 1965 show a folk trio with bass fiddle made from a trash can and a family walking among the unrestored buildings of the newly-opened campus. (SBM)*

ABOVE: *This sign posted at Strawbery Banke promised to link the past with the future.* (SBM/DA)

OPPOSITE: *The adaptation of this colonial hallway with its grand arched window into a twentieth-century bathroom hints at the enormous amount of restoration work still ahead. This picture of the 1796 Walsh House appeared in the first Strawbery Banke guidebook in 1966.* (SM/DA)

independent historic house museums. The media attention lavished on early Strawbery Banke simply put Portsmouth "back on the map"—and this time it stuck.

But in May 1965 the skeptics remained skeptical. Only the most visionary could have predicted that the city's broken-down South End waterfront would rise again. Not even the cluster of teenaged Strawbery Banke Belles in their strawberry-print gowns or the red, white, and blue bunting could disguise the forlorn looking Puddle Dock on opening day. Cloudy skies, scattered showers, and cool temperatures dampened the formal ceremonies and turned the plowed areas between the empty houses into pools of mud.[11] In fact, since 1958, only two of the thirty structures—the 1762 Stephen Chase House and the 1813 Governor Ichabod Goodwin Mansion—were restored in time for the "Phase One" Memorial Day kickoff. A few other buildings, cleaned and furnished by volunteers with almost no available budget, offered an art and architecture exhibit, a gift shop and old-fashioned "penny store" managed by Boy Scouts, plus live demonstrations of weaving, spinning, pewter work, furniture repair, candle dipping, crewel work, and rug hooking. Volunteers dressed in "authentic" costumes drove a horse and buggy through the streets. Strawberry shortcake, strawberry sundaes, and sodas went on sale. Fewer than a thousand curiosity seekers toured Strawbery Banke that first weekend, a total of eleven thousand during the first summer. Admissions in 1965 totaled $5,627.[12]

Attendance rose rapidly although progress on the campus was slow; only three more restored buildings opened over the next three years. But other large-scale historic projects had grown from equally small seeds. Even Plimoth Plantation, the outdoor museum honoring the Mayflower settlers in Massachusetts, the newspaper reminded readers, started out as little more than "a reconstructed stockade and a few dummies dressed to look like Pilgrims."[13]

Although New Hampshire's first documented European settler arrived in the region in 1623, just three years after the Mayflower landed at Plymouth, details here are sketchy. The first critical century of Piscataqua River history seems to defy a simple telling. The Portsmouth story remains, for most visitors, as a mish-mash of colorful events and characters forever tumbling

around in time like clothes in a clothes dryer. Famous figures from Captain John Smith to George Washington fall into view, then disappear amid a laundry list of local heroes and villains. The importance of Portsmouth history, for many, is the way it both mirrors the familiar textbook America, and simultaneously redefines America through its own cast of fresh and independent characters. During four continuous centuries, those characters lived in or passed by the riverfront neighborhood of Puddle Dock. Those who study this fascinating ten-acre chunk of land through time quickly discover that it functions like a geologist's core sample, revealing in its many layers, the dynamic growth of a changing nation.

The life of Stephen Chase makes a perfect example. His story is the Portsmouth story, richly complex, vaguely familiar, and surprisingly dramatic. So it makes sense that his Court Street home, among the finest surviving in the South

End, became the first restored structure at Strawbery Banke. Like many of the founders of the museum itself, Chase was a successful downtown businessman, except that in his era following the Revolution, the hub of Portsmouth business still revolved around the waterfront. Wealthy and progressive, Chase owned a store on the new Portsmouth Pier that jutted far into the Piscataqua River at the foot of State Street, just a few blocks from his elegant mansion. He also owned shares in two new bridges, one connecting Portsmouth to New Castle, the other linking the town of Durham with the seacoast at Newington. Fresh water from a spring three miles away ran into his Court Street home and more than two hundred others, via the high-tech wooden Portsmouth Aqueduct.

Born in 1742, the Harvard-educated son of a Harvard-educated minister from the tiny island town of New Castle, Stephen Chase was no chip off the old block. He was censured at school for stealing and blasphemy, before heading off to sea to prove his mettle. New Hampshire was still a British colony when Chase made his fortune at the height of the West India Trade. He married nineteen-year-old Mary Frost, a grand niece of Sir William Pepperrell of Kittery, Maine, the only New Englander granted the hereditary title of baronet by the British crown. They were peacefully raising a family when the famous Paul Revere rode into Portsmouth and incited local citizens to attack the king's fort at New Castle in December 1774. Chase's father was an outspoken Tory, but Stephen joined the rebel cause. When his father died in 1778, Chase moved his family to Portsmouth, just up the street from the William Pitt Tavern where John Hancock, the Marquis de Lafayette, and John Paul Jones reportedly mingled with local patriots.

It was a mariner from Kittery, not Stephen Chase, who built the house in 1762. It was also owned by a future Lord Mayor of London, England, and there is speculation that John Wentworth, the last royal governor of New Hampshire, hoped to make it his executive mansion. But the Revolution killed those plans, ending the reign of a powerful Portsmouth aristocracy. When Stephen Chase rented the house in 1779 he was one of the richest men in a new wave of Portsmouth patriots who rode the economic boom after the Revolution. In 1800 as timber values increased

TOP: *Legend says that, before merchant Stephen Chase leased this house, royal governor John Wentworth considered it for his use. Wentworth, however, was later driven to Halifax, Nova Scotia, as a Tory during the American Revolution.* (SBM/DA)

BOTTOM: *Furnishings purchased for the Chase House in the early days led to a controversy years later that eventually redefined Strawbery Banke itself.* (SBM/DA)

a thousand percent, Chase paid his taxes in lumber. The Chases ran a store selling everything from linens to rum, speculated in real estate, and raised six children in the elegant house. When George Washington toured the region in 1789, according to local legend, the first President stopped at the Chase house where he kissed the three Chase girls on the head before heading down "Pitt Street" to the Stavers Tavern and to visit the mother of his secretary Tobias Lear.[14] Stephen Chase finally bought the house in 1799, the year of Washington's death. When Chase himself died in 1805, the local court produced a detailed room-by-room inventory of every item in the house.

It was perhaps this inventory, more than any other single item, that helped launch Strawbery Banke into the mainstream of professional history museums. Such documents are rare when matched to a surviving home, and the inventory provided a freeze-frame of life among one elite Portsmouth family during a less familiar moment in American history. Restoring and furnishing the Chase House was a unique project and it attracted the museum's first "guardian angel." Nellie McCarty, a New York City socialite materialized out of thin air in 1962 with a gift of $100,000. McCarty made her offer to restore the Chase House after reading that William Perry, a key architect of Colonial Williamsburg, had volunteered his time to help design Strawbery Banke.[15] Semi-retired and in his 80s, Perry was drawn to the authenticity of the Puddle Dock architecture. Perry was simultaneously guiding the restoration on the Governor Goodwin Mansion at the opposite end of the campus. But it was ornate, hand-wrought wood carving in the Chase House that drew him and other famous architects to examine the exciting, new Portsmouth project. The eighteenth-century woodwork of Piscataqua carvers and joiners—many of whom worked on both ships and houses—ranks today among the finest in America.

To have both the beautifully appointed mansion and its 1805 inventory intact was amazing considering that so many New England homes of this era had been razed, stripped of their architectural elements or mangled by modern renovations. In 1882 a grandson of Stephen Chase presented the house to the city for use as an orphanage. When the orphanage moved to a larger facility around World War I, the Stephen Chase

ABOVE: *Decorative details built into the Chase House included this ornamented mantel and hand-carved newell post. (SBM and JDR)*

House fell into private hands until the arrival of Strawbery Banke Inc.[16] Records show the feverish rush, once Miss McCarty's funds were secured, to resuscitate the endangered treasure before opening day in 1965. The restoration work, everyone agreed, had to be top notch. Architect Perry feared that no one in New Hampshire was capable of such quality work until Strawbery Banke officials reminded him that it was Portsmouth workers who had built the house in the first place. Perry had insisted on using a Massachusetts contractor for work on the Governor Goodwin Mansion, paid for by the state of New Hampshire, at a cost of $135,000. To hire an outside crew for the Chase House too, Captain Johnson of Strawbery Banke told Miss McCarty, "might have unfavorable repercussions from a public relations point of view."[17] The work by a Portsmouth contractor, Johnson assured Miss McCarty, was "to be accomplished to the highest standards, with maximum fidelity and in the interest of complete authenticity."[18] Originally budgeted at $55,749, the Chase House restoration costs rose as Perry's management team uncovered one unforeseen change after another.[19] It was trial by fire for the early founders of Strawbery Banke who had attracted so much media attention that postponing the Memorial Day ribbon cutting was no longer possible. "We have many irons in various fires," Captain Johnson informed his only benefactor, "and things are far from quiet here at Strawbery Banke."[20] On May 22, with the Chase House nearly completed, Captain Johnson hired a landscaping crew for $2,040 to grade and plant the lawn, build walkways, plant a garden, and install trees and shrubs. You have six days to get the work done before the opening ceremonies, Johnson informed them.[21]

As the costs rose and eventually overran the budget, the amount of money available to furnish the Chase House dwindled. With no professional curator on staff, the choice of furnishings fell to a "house committee" at Strawbery Banke. With a copy

ABOVE: *The Chases lived in the style of a moderately wealthy merchant family as in this illustration No portraits survive, however, two important inventories do. (SBM)*

ABOVE: *Two visitors at the nascent "colonial village" during the opening days of Strawbery Banke in 1965. Although only two buildings were completely restored, the museum featured other nearby attractions as this freshly constructed sign post suggests. (SBM/DA)*

LEFT: *The Governor Ichabod Goodwin Mansion (c. 1813) is seen here on its original foundation on Islington Street before it was moved to Strawbery Banke. (SBM /DA)*

of the 1805 inventory in hand, the well-intentioned amateur historians searched the local antique shops for affordable furnishings. These items included a tall gilded Victorian harp, a number of imitation Chippendale chairs, long hanging drapes, thick rugs, a Windsor armchair with bamboo legs, and dozens of other items that were not on the inventory and came from later periods and, therefore, did not belong in the restoration.[22] In addition, the angel of the Chase House donated her prized collection of Parian ware, a set of low-cost faux-marble figures popular in the later nineteenth century, to be put on display. Whether she was on a distant cruise, convalescing from a series of operations or vacationing, Miss McCarty monitored the progress of her project. She made a special trip from her Fifth Avenue apartment to attend the opening day ceremonies in Portsmouth. During a private tour, she was delighted to see her pet project so beautifully displayed.

But history never stands still, not even in museum exhibits. Fresh interpretations, shifting attitudes, and newly unearthed facts continue to change our perceptions of the past. Within a few years, research at Strawbery Banke turned up another equally detailed inventory of the Chase House, this one completed soon after the death of Mary Chase in 1819. By comparing the two documents, it was possible to draw an extremely accurate picture of how the rooms of the Chase House had looked during the Federal period, a time quite different from the earlier Colonial period or the more familiar Victorian period at the end of the nineteenth century. To be perfectly authentic, or not to be—that was the question that nearly tore the young Strawbery Banke apart. Was it nobler to remove the items that did not belong in the Chase House restoration, or to suffer the criticism of museum professionals who might brand The Banke as just another artificial tourist attraction? Officials at Strawbery Banke took sides on the issue, dug in deeply, and the battle began. When the smoke cleared, "Captain" Johnson was gone and a new, young generation of college-educated historians were in charge.

The rift over the Chase House furnishings was not the greatest battle fought along the shores of Puddle Dock. Conflict here, as far as the record shows, has been as constant as the tides. But the changes have never been dull. Early explorers ousted Native Americans. Portsmouth's "Old Planters" pushed back against Puritans. Each generation took on the next wave of newcomers—witches and wolves, British landlords, Indian avengers, wealthy oligarchs, patriotic mobs, slave traders, bold seamen, poor immigrants, rich tourists, murderous sailors, publicity agents, WPA workers, real estate developers, junk dealers, published writers, ladies of the night, urban renewal bulldozers, and professional historians. Each has staked a claim and left a mark on Strawbery Banke.

BELOW: *A grinning steed pauses for a snapshot on Memorial Day 1965. This photo is the only image in the museum collection labeled "Opening Ceremonies." (SBM)*

Abenakise   Abenakis

Left Behind:
The Orphaned Plantation
1600–1635

No stirring central story enlivens the arrival of the first Portsmouth settlers. There is no Pilgrim diary or legendary Plymouth Rock. We lack a central character or plot like the adventurous John Smith during the starving years at Jamestown, Leonard Calvert founding a Catholic colony in Maryland, Roger Williams's flight to Rhode Island, or the Quaker William Penn's founding of Pennsylvania. The founding chapter of New Hampshire, by contrast, is vague and tattered or missing altogether.

The artistic flaw is obvious. Captain John Mason, the protagonist in this story and driving force behind the colonization of New Hampshire, dies off in the opening scene. It was Mason who dreamed the dream of a Piscataqua business venture after serving six years as governor of Newfoundland in the burgeoning New World. A soldier, sailor, mapmaker, author, and adventurer, Mason was the man who might have made a difference in settling New England. He was an entrepreneur who, despite lack of any significant return, continued to pour his considerable fortune into establishing a feudal empire in the land between the Merrimac and Kennebec rivers.

Mason and his partner Sir Ferdinando Gorges were important men in England. They were key members of an investment

ABOVE: *A detail of a ship from Captain John Smith's famous map of his 1614 voyage to New England. (JDR)*

OPPOSITE: *With contemporary illustrations of Native Americans unavailable locally, we rely on other sources. These are Wabanaki (Abenaki) natives as depicted at a French mission on the Saint Lawrence River around 1700. From Bibliotheque de Montreal. Illustration from Bibliotheque de Montreal (SBM)*

group made up of British nobles, mostly Royalists, a far cry from the familiar Puritans. The Council of New England smelled gold in the untapped region between Canada and Virginia. Gorges helped establish two private fishing outposts in New Hampshire at what is now Rye and Dover in 1623. These were disruptive times for the British government. King Charles I succeeded James I in 1625 and Mason was distracted for the next few years as paymaster and treasurer to the king's army in France and Spain. But after the war ended in 1629, Mason and Gorges combined forces to colonize the Piscataqua region. They eventually split their ownership, with Gorges taking Maine, while Mason focused on the tiny coast of New Hampshire and all its promised lands back to the mysterious "Lake of the Iroquois." In 1630–1631 Mason and Gorges sent a larger, well-equipped group of settlers three miles down the Piscataqua River to a new place they called Strawberry Bank, a name reportedly derived from wild strawberries found growing there. Start-up costs were high and returns were disappointing. The dynamic John Mason was preparing to board a newly built ship and join his growing colony as governor in 1635 when he suddenly died, leaving his young settlement without a guiding hand. The story of New Hampshire, from that very early point, became a tale told by orphans on scattered scraps of paper.

Before Strawberry Bank

Most books about early Portsmouth scarcely mention its original settlers except to chronicle the rare Indian acts of aggression here much later in the seventeenth century. The first major report from an Englishman seeing Native Americans in New England comes from Bartholomew Gosnold, who examined the coast from Maine to Massachusetts in 1602.[1] Spotting eight men in a "Biscay shallop with sail and oars," probably near what is now Cape Ann, Gosnold at first thought they were European fishermen in distress until the party of Indians came aboard ship.[2] One man in the group of Natives wore "Christian" clothing including a black waistcoat, breeches, shoes, stockings, and a hat with a band. The rest were naked except for short pants

ABOVE: *Detail of an engraving after Martin Pring's account of his voyage to the New World in 1603. A trained mastiff carrying a pike was employed to frighten off Indians. (JDR)*

made from seal skin and deerskins thrown loosely about their shoulders. The Indians gave a lengthy speech using some "Christian words" and drew Gosnold a map of the area using a piece of chalk. In memory of this initial close encounter with an obviously intelligent and adaptable new race, Gosnold named the location "Savage Rock."[3] Native Americans, despite their sophisticated culture would remain "savages" and "heathens" to many New England historians through the next three centuries. Their story remains largely untold to this day.

Martin Pring, who had traveled with Gosnold, was the first known European explorer to document a trip ten or twelve miles up the Piscataqua River in 1603. "In all these places," Pring reported, "we found no people, but signes of fires where they had been."[4]

Accounts by Pring and Gosnold were not widely distributed until 1625, just five years before the settlement at Strawberry Bank. The fact that Native Americans were rarely reported in the Portsmouth area, and did not attack and destroy the first European outposts here, is sometimes seen as evidence that Indians were never here at all. Prehistoric Portsmouth is often depicted as an empty landscape frozen in time. Well into the twentieth century, local historians imagined an unpopulated and lush region, along a breathtaking and swift river, waiting only to be discovered by white explorers.

We can be certain that Native Americans populated New Hampshire's coast, rivers, lakes, forests, and hills for twelve thousand years or more before European settlers changed everything. The oldest Native American occupation sites directly on New Hampshire's coast date to a little over four thousand years ago in Seabrook, when people were taking swordfish on the open sea, along with many other species. Earlier than this, the coastal sites are submerged below rising sea level. A mastodon tooth recently dredged up by a fisherman off the coast of Maine attests to this fact.[5] But we have ample evidence of their presence on the nearby streams and rivers.

A Paleo-Indian site discovered just across the Piscataqua from Portsmouth in Eliot, Maine, included artifacts recently dated to at least ten thousand years of age.[6] Archeological evidence from the last three thousand years proves that early Native Americans

Sassafras variifolium: **1,** fruiting twig; **2,** flowering twig.

ABOVE: *Martin Pring became the first known European to record his visit up the Piscataqua River. Pring was searching for sassafras, then considered a remedy for the "French Pox" or syphilis. (JDR)*

in this region were adept at building oversized, ocean-going canoes. Piles of shells or "kitchen middens" discarded by coastal Natives are more abundant after about three thousand years ago because sea level rose more slowly and the coastline looked more like it does today. Analysis of these trash heaps shows large cod bones among the many fish remains, in addition to seal and terrestrial mammals. Indians fished with great success using bone hooks and elaborate fishing weirs or nets strung across the rivers on poles. They ate scallops, clams, oysters, and lobsters found along the shore in the summer, then moved inland to hunt and trap birds and mammals living in the dense, local forests. Within the last millennium corn, beans, and squash were introduced. The native people that the first Europeans met were established agriculturalists. They cleared great areas of trees for farming, and foraged and thrived through thousands of brutal New England winters. Speculation about prehistoric life along the seacoast is made more difficult by the fact that the boundaries have changed significantly as the water level rose over millennia, pushing back the coastline and leaving the evidence of former occupation under water.[7]

If Indians were scarce in the founding days at Strawberry Bank, they had good reasons. Historians estimate that as much as eighty to ninety percent of the local Native population died of exposure to smallpox and other diseases carried by European visitors at the beginning of the seventeenth century. This "Great Plague" from 1616 to 1619 certainly decimated Piscataqua Natives as well in the years just prior to European settlement here. A few years later, in 1633, another wave of disease swept through the region. A rare reference in the local record notes that the infection came to Pascataquak, "where all the Indians (except one or two) died."[8] Surviving members of local tribes were in no shape for war and understandably wary of all white visitors. Sixteen tribes, according to white colonial accounts, gathered in a loose confederation under the leader known as Passaconaway, whose influence spread across an area even larger than John Mason's New Hampshire claim. Legends track the leader of the Pennacook Nation from Mount Agamenticus in nearby York, Maine, to the White Mountains, the Amoskeag Falls at Manchester, and into what is now the Massachusetts North Shore. According

ABOVE: *This Americanized depiction of Passaconaway in a Lowell, MA, cemetery honors, not the historic Native American leader, but the Christian legend of the "praying Indian." Renamed Saint Aspinquid, this mythical figure reportedly lived to the age of 122. The statue was created by the Improved Order of Red Men, a nineteenth-century fraternal organization. (JDR)*

to European historians, Passaconaway was guided by a spiritual vision that required he not harm white visitors within his realm. More likely, the Indian leader was being politically astute in his dealings with settlers. Whatever the motivation, for the half century following the arrival of New Hampshire settlers in 1623, with very few exceptions, peace reigned under Passaconaway's guidance. It was a purposeful and organized peace. Indians were canny traders who valued English, French, and Spanish trade goods, and feared the power of European weapons and their sometimes-unscrupulous owners. Whites were known to rob Natives or kidnap them to use as guides or slaves.

Early New Hampshire Natives visited the seacoast seasonally, preferring the falls of rivers when the fish were plentiful, and moving inland for the winter. Archaeologists have yet to discover a major Native camp site near where Strawbery Banke Museum stands today. Perhaps they were there, or perhaps the rocky shore, an extremely swift current, tall timber, and less than perfect farming soil atop thick ledges were undesirable. Where John Mason's settlers saw deep, navigable waters and a protected, highly defensible natural harbor, Natives may have seen less-desirable real estate. Equally possible, although no evidence supports this, Mason's Laconia Company settled, like so many other early colonists, in a spot that Natives had already developed. Assuming Piscataqua-area Indians followed the patterns of tribal groups in nearby Maine, they too had begun moving to a more agrarian lifestyle with the introduction of corn, bean, and squash crops to this area as late as 1,300 to 1,400 AD. This more stationary lifestyle, at least in southern Maine, means Indians had more well-defined village designs and a more sophisticated view of land ownership and property boundaries than historians have traditionally credited them with. Native women may have been more involved in Native government and clearly understood the treaties and sale of lands.[9]

New Hampshire's indigenous people traveled along its natural river highways. The rivers they named, adopted by English settlers, are often the only evidence of their long and wide-ranging occupation: Merrimack, Penobscot, Kennebec, Saddahoc, Cochecho, Saco. Portsmouth historian Ralph May wrestled with the derivation of the Abenaki name Piscataqua for decades. He

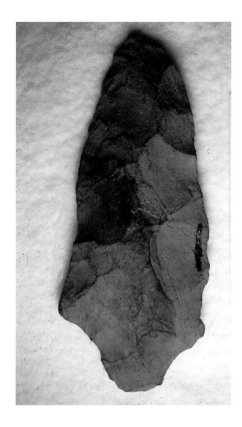

ABOVE: *Native American artifacts have been found in the Portsmouth waterfront area, but to date no Indian encampment has been discovered. (SBM)*

studied and rejected the theory that the name might have instead come from the Latin words "pisces" and "aqua," for the many fish found in its waters. May was disturbed to find more than thirty different spellings of the word in early documents, but was eventually satisfied that they all came from the same root words. "Peske" (some say "Beske") likely meant "branch" to Abenaki speakers, and "tegwe" could be "a river with a strong current."[10] The Piscataqua is one of the fastest-flowing navigable rivers in the world. It branches at a large tidal estuary, now called Great Bay, and is fed by five major rivers—the Lamprey, Squamscott, Cochecho, Bellamy, and Oyster Rivers—each with rushing rocky falls and each the site of ancient fishing grounds. Following the Piscataqua River that now divides New Hampshire from Maine, native travelers reached the Salmon Falls River, another rich fishing ground not far from the site of the region's first sawmill on the Great Works River built by the first Strawberry Bank settlers. At each spot where the Natives fished, the English established dams and sawmills, and eventually water-powered factories. And in every case, as crude settlements evolved into coastal towns, most of the fragile evidence of the "people of the Dawnland" was rapidly obliterated.

John Mason's World Vision

Ironically, it was trade with these now-forgotten Native Americans—and the hope of trade with the Chinese—that drew John Mason to plant his colony at Strawberry Bank in New Hampshire. Like his partner, Sir Ferdinando Gorges, Mason was convinced that their rivers in the New World were the gateway to the riches of the Orient. Gorges's search for a "northwest passage" had led him to fund Weymouth's exploratory voyage in 1605. When Weymouth returned with five kidnapped Maine Natives, among the first Indians ever seen in England, he presented three of them—Tisquamtum, Manida, and Skidwarres—to Gorges, who was then governor of Plymouth.[11] Gorges entertained, housed, and studied them for two years, presenting the Indians to the English court and rousing investors for New World exploration. His public relations campaign led, in part, to the creation of the

ABOVE: *Reconstructed Indian pottery artifact from Seabrook site dates from the Middle Woodland era of 100 to 600 AD. (UNH)*

OPPOSITE TOP: *Detail from earliest Piscataqua River area map from the 1660s showing Native American figure. (BAK)*

OPPOSITE BOTTOM: *University of New Hampshire students preserve early Native American site in Seabrook, New Hampshire, in 1975 prior to the building of the Seabrook Nuclear Power Plant. Photo by Jack Adams (UNH)*

London Company of investors who started Jamestown at Virginia in 1607.

The Plymouth Company, a second group of investors, was formed at the same time, but their early voyages to the north are mostly ignored by American history texts because they did not lead to "permanent" settlements. Run largely by Gorges, the Plymouth Company focused on exploring and exploiting the natural resources of Northern Virginia, later to become New England. Just months after its formation in 1606, Plymouth Company investors launched a small test ship toward modern Maine, much as NASA would launch a probe toward Mars. The voyage misfired, ending up in Puerto Rico. Gorges's group quickly launched another, bigger mission with 124 men, two ships and a prestigious leader named Sir George Popham. Unfortunately for Maine historians, Popham's group settled near the mouth of the Kennebec River in 1607, just three months after the southern group set foot at Jamestown. The Popham Colony survived just over a year, abandoning a sophisticated fort and leaving behind the body of leader George Popham, the only member of the group to die during the frigid winter.[12] But this failure did not kill Ferdinando Gorges's hope that he was on the right track. Before his death, Popham wrote to King James I saying that the local Indians had assured him there was a great large sea only seven days journey from their fort. Popham's stirring letter, written originally in Latin, claims, "This cannot be any other than the Southern Ocean, reaching to the regions of China, which unquestionably cannot be far from these regions."[13]

Whether Popham's sources were talking about nearby Sebago Lake, Lake Winnipesaukee in New Hampshire or the unlikely and very distant Great Lakes is unknown. While the idea of sailing up the Piscataqua to reach the Orient seems ridiculous today, it was downright logical to English entrepreneurs like Gorges and Mason, whose explorers had scarcely pierced the skin of the mysterious American continent, and whose Indian guides

ABOVE: *Samuel de Champlain passed by the New Hampshire coastline and the Isles of Shoals in 1605. (JDR)*

OPPOSITE: *The oldest surviving Anglo-American wall paintings can be found at the Warner House in Portsmouth. This image depicts two of four Mohawk sachems taken to London in 1710 where they met Queen Anne, not long before the house was built. (SBM/DA)*

spoke of great lakes to the west. When Henry Hudson discovered his giant Hudson's Bay deep in the Canadian wilderness the following year, he assumed it was the Pacific Ocean. It wasn't, but the game was on for the next wave of explorers.[14] Hudson did not find his Northwest Passage to the East, and the search continued to fire American exploration for two more centuries. Hudson's voyage did open a lucrative new English trade with North American Indians.

Following his Jamestown and Pocahontas adventures, Captain John Smith then toured the New England coast in 1614, stopping at Monhegan Island in Maine and charting the Isles of Shoals. His encouraging tales of abundant natural resources there excited British investors once again. John Smith's chief investor in his next three failed New England adventures was none other than the indefatigable Sir Ferdinando Gorges, part-owner of the as-yet-unsettled Northern Virginia territory. Smith, too, believed in the existence of an American passage to China and, with Gorges's help, he made three attempts to land his own New England colony. Because Smith named the Isles of Shoals "Smyth's Isles" and spoke favorably of the region, local historians have theorized that he may have been eyeing the Piscataqua River area for his colony.[15] Fierce storms, technical problems, bad luck, and French pirates crushed Smith's dogged attempts to colonize New England, and by 1616 Smith was back in England, his best days behind him. Smith's impact in America, however, had just begun. In 1616 his influential "Description of New England" was published with a detailed sketch of the region that, for British investors, was as good as a treasure map. The northern New World was moving from buzz to boom. European fishermen routinely worked the waters along the Grand Banks and the Maine coast, stopping seasonally at the Isles of Shoals, just ten miles from modern day Portsmouth, to dry and salt their valuable catch before the six-week voyage home. During the next few years, as Smith languished in London and the Plymouth colonists settled in Massachusetts, Ferdinando Gorges continued to set up faltering colonies along the Maine coast at Saco and Cape Elizabeth. His settlement at what became York was humbly named Gorgeana. By this time the great smallpox pandemic had killed four out of five Indians from Cape Cod to the Kennebec and set the scene for the white invasion.

The Plymouth Company was designed, not as a money-maker, but as a sort of early holding company for granted lands. Despite setbacks, Gorges convinced many of the original investors to try again. He created a new joint stock company chartered by the king and generally referred to by historians as The Council for New England.[16] The grants and patents issued in New Hampshire during this era are often vague and overlapping. John Mason named the shared land within his first charter "Mariana." It fell largely in what became Massachusetts and he did not attempt a colony there. For a few years all of what is now New Hampshire was co-owned by Gorges and Mason, who named it the Province of Maine. Without the funds to launch their own colony, the Plymouth Council authorized small private ventures including fishing settlements at Cape Neddick, Maine, and at Pascataway (also called Pannaway by the Indians) in 1623 under Scotsman David Thomson (also spelled Thompson). Thomson brought his wife Amais and a small crew to what is now Rye, New Hampshire. The Hilton brothers, William and Edward, some historians believe, established a second Piscataqua fishing colony at Dover Point, the same year. Others date the Dover settlement at 1628 in a controversy that has raged on for centuries.[17] Within three years, or perhaps sooner, Thomson moved to claim a large island in what was to become Boston Harbor and built the first house there. Thomson then suddenly and inexplicably disappeared, leaving New Hampshire's founding years in a perpetual fog.

While it is true that the first New Hampshire settlers came to fish, founder John Mason had very different plans for his colony at Strawberry Bank, established between the Thomson and Hilton fishing sites. Mason intended a faster, bigger return on his growing investment than any plantation or fishing camp could provide. On November 17, 1629,[18] Mason and Gorges received a vaguely defined grant to the land bordering "the rivers and lakes of the Iroquois," assumed today to be from Lake Champlain north to Lake Superior and west halfway to Lake Ontario. This land along these lakes in the "Laconia" grant also included a thousand acres on the seacoast of New Hampshire. The strange

ABOVE: *A portion of this post–Civil War era monument to Captain John Smith still survives on Star Island at the Isles of Shoals. The image at the top of the pedestal represents one of three "Turk's heads" the explorer reportedly severed in battle during the Crusades. (ATH)*

Plymouth merchants' fishing station Pascataway (N.H.), 1623   Matthew R. Thompson III

combination of seemingly disconnected tracts was possibly based on a seventeenth-century theory that the Lake of the Iroquois was the source of the Piscataqua River. Mason's settlement at Strawberry Bank was intended as the key trading post for goods, mostly furs, obtained at the "Lake of the Iroquois," transported down river to Strawberry Bank and exported to England.[19] Should Mason's men also find the elusive outlet to the Orient, all the better for New Hampshire's tiny seacoast.

Mason's Laconia Company lost no time in getting boots on the ground in New Hampshire. The short-lived company needed to quickly pay for, populate, and manage the new territory. Captain Walter Neale, an English army officer, reportedly arrived with eight or ten ex-military adventurers aboard the bark *Warwick* in the spring or summer of 1630. Neale appeared at the Royalist colony in New Hampshire the same year as the Great Migration of Puritans began in the Boston area not far away. As governor, Neale had wide-ranging powers. He set up operations at Pannaway Manor. David Thomson's fortified stone house, fish-drying operation, a small fleet of ships, the farm, and saltworks all appear to have been largely abandoned.[20] Possession is nine-tenths of the law, so the Laconia Company grant was quickly amended to include this area and the lucrative fishing posts at the Isles of Shoals.

Similar to Jamestown, but unlike the religious colony at Plymouth, Massachusetts, Strawberry Bank was fathered by former military leaders turned businessmen. History offers no painted portrait of Walter Neale, John Mason or Ferdinando Gorges, and only one image of Captain John Smith. They were all professional English soldiers and contemporaries, men of similar cut—adventurous, determined, ambitious, perhaps thuggish at times. With no other imagery available, it is fair to picture Walter Neale as a New Hampshire version of Miles Standish, the military protector of the Pilgrims at Plymouth a decade earlier. Nicknamed "Captain Shrimp" by one of his enemies for his short stature, Standish could be ruthless, and on one occasion, suddenly stabbed an Indian leader to death during a dinner meeting. Pilgrim diaries report that Standish visited David Thomson at Pascataway in 1623 and, soon after arriving in New Hampshire, Walter Neale called on the Puritans at Boston. Although he may not have been as short,

ABOVE: *Portsmouth's nineteenth-century historians reported seeing the original stone house foundation, well, and graveyard of New Hampshire's first founders at Rye, New Hampshire. The well and unmarked graves still survive, but their origin at Odiorne's point is still uncertain. (JDR)*

OPPOSITE TOP: *Fishing and fur trading were the dominant industries in the region during in the early seventeenth century until the rise of the timber industry. The low flat Isles of Shoals and Piscataqua islands were ideal for drying fish on wooden racks or "flakes." Sketch of Pascataway by Matthew R. Thompson. (PER)*

OPPOSITE BOTTOM: *The site of the confrontation at Bloody Point is today a picnic site and boat launch marked by a modern highway bridge and the currently unused Gen. John Sullivan Bridge (right) at the entrance to Great Bay. (JDR)*

ABOVE: *Captain Walter Neale of Strawbery Bank, like Miles Standish of Plymouth, was a military man. Standish was popularized during the nineteenth century in Longfellow's romantic poem "The Courtship of Miles Standish," seen here on a comic book cover from* Classics Illustrated. *(JDR)*

hot-tempered, and godless as Miles Standish, Neale likely dressed and acted the part of an ex-Tudor soldier. Sporting a bushy beard, ruffled collar, armor breastplate, sword, and helmet, he was likely a figure of authority in the earliest days when Strawberry Bank was little more than a single large house on the river surrounded by a dense and dangerous wilderness.

Neale was a dutiful employee of Mason and Gorges. Even as the first Strawberry Bankers were settling in, Neale got word that an English pirate named Dixey Bull was plundering an outpost in coastal Maine. Taking forty men in six boats, Neale rushed to Pemaquid, but "New England's first pirate" was gone. Neale was stranded in Maine without a wind to sail on for three weeks, leaving his own colony at Strawberry Bank defenseless.[21]

As the Dixey Bull incident implies, the greatest danger to most early New England settlements was not Indians or wild animals, but other white visitors from Europe. Justice in seventeenth-century America was harsh and could lead to lashing, tongue piercing, pillorying, jailing, ducking, branding, banishment, or even hanging. Puritans, like their contemporaries, practiced these strict rules as their numbers grew across New England. It was Gorges and Mason and their Plymouth Council itself that opened the door to the great Puritan migration by first granting settlement rights to the Massachusetts Bay Colony that would eventually swallow up their group's holdings in Maine and New Hampshire. Decades later, as Puritan influence in England grew during the rise of Oliver Cromwell, Puritan intolerance of alternative lifestyles in New England kept pace. Strawberry Bank settlers had scarcely built their communal Great House when Puritan agents at the Hilton settlement just up the river challenged Mason's right to establish another colony on the Piscataqua.[22] Both claims had been verified just days apart, in March of 1629, by the Council of New England, but the dispute did not reach critical mass until the summer of 1632 when each site had a military leader and a tiny army of its own. Walter Neale had been sent to establish a Royalist presence at Pascataway and Thomas Wiggin, a Puritan, had been sent from nearby Salem, Massachusetts, to occupy the Hilton site eight miles up the river. The Puritans had taken over the Hilton patent, which clearly overlapped the new Strawberry Bank claim. The two military agents threatened each other and then met with their tiny armies at "Bloody Point" in what is now Dover, just upriver from the shopping malls and "miracle mile" of Newington. It was High Noon on the New England frontier.

No blood was actually shed at Bloody Point. The hawkish name may be ironic, or purposely grandiose, but warriors Wiggin and Neale did not clash. Instead they compromised, splitting up the Piscataqua territory peacefully. Portsmouth historian Bruce Ingmire has suggested that this "non-battle" helped define the character of the region at a very early point in its history. Strawberry Bank was not going to be like the Massachusetts Bay Colony. It would be more tolerant and nonconformist, guided more by the will of an independent people than its intolerant Puritan neighbors.[23]

Besides acting as Mason's paid police chief and governor, Neale's real job was to extract something—anything—valuable out of New Hampshire as quickly as possible to appease its grumbling investors back in England. To that end in 1632, Captain Walter Neale and a small group plunged bravely into Indian territory toward the distant white peaks in search of the fabled Lake of the Iroquois.[24] How far they ascended into the White Mountains, New Hampshire's highest peaks, is unknown. The best report of their journey comes years later in a 1658 biography of Neale by a grandson of Ferdinando Gorges. Neale figured the journey toward the White Mountains to be ninety to a hundred miles from Pascataway, the temporary capital of Mason's colony. They traveled by boat and on foot and were just a day away from ascending the great mountain, Thomas Gorges reports, when they ran out of food and were forced to return. The explorers did help establish trade relations with the local Indians and they did bring back treasure. The men picked up beautiful "chrystall stones" but, being without horses, the explorers were forced to carry the heavy load on their backs. Returning to Strawberry Bank, Neale shipped the white crystals to the eager John Mason who had them quickly analyzed in London. They were worthless.

Other prospecting trips and mining expeditions were fruitless too. Mason had hoped for precious metals, but Walter Neale returned to England empty-handed in 1633, leaving behind, according to genealogists, only an illegitimate son with an

TOP: *Historians continue to debate New Hampshire's founding history, including the dates and landing sites. While Hilton Point and Odiorne Point are both recognized as 1623 landing sites with official state signs, no such marker commemorates the 1630 landing site at Strawberry Bank. (JDR)*

BOTTOM: *Walter Neale's party approaches the Crystal Hills of the White Mountains in New Hampshire in an artist's sketch from a 1923 Portsmouth history book for children. Whether Neale or Durham settler Darby Field was the first white man to reach the site remains in dispute. (JDR)*

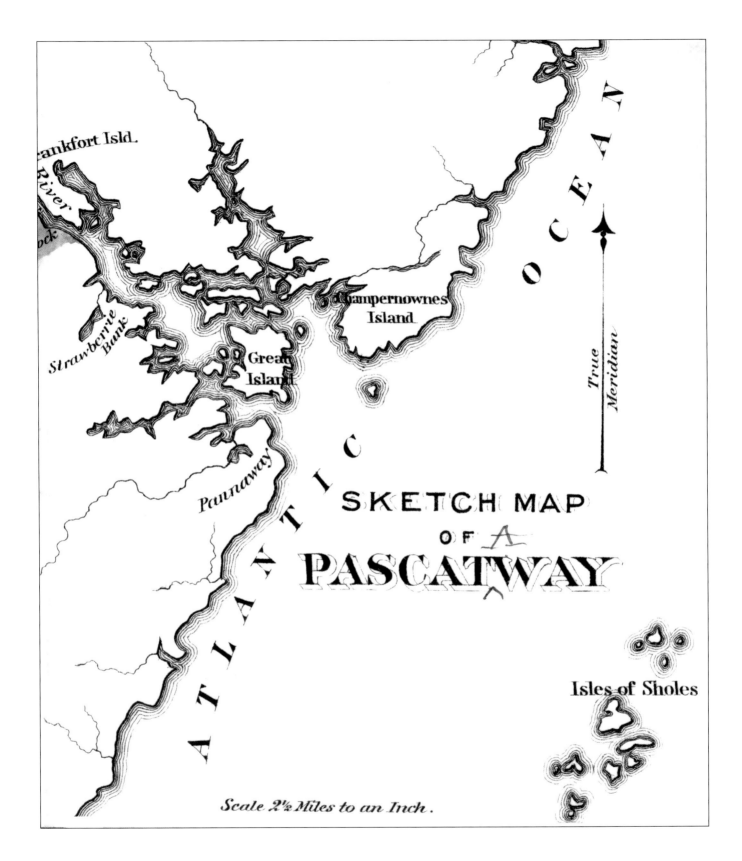

SKETCH MAP

OF A

PASCATWAY

Frankfort Isld.

River

Rock

Strawberrie Bank

OCEAN

True Meridian

Gampernownes Island

Great Island

ATLANTIC

Pannaway

Isles of Sholes

Scale 2½ Miles to an Inch.

unnamed Piscataqua mother. Mason, clearly frustrated with the lack of return from his colony, wrote to one of his agents at Strawberry Bank on May 5, 1634. He still clung to the hope of connecting New Hampshire and the Orient. "I have disbursed a great deal of money in ye plantacon and never received one penny," Mason said, "but hope if there was once a discoverie of the lakes, that I should, in some reasonable time, be reimbursed againe."[25]

His agent Ambrose Gibbons wrote back: "I perceive you have a great mynd for the lakes and I as great a will to assist you, if I had 2 horses and 3 men with me, I would by God's helpe soone resolve you of the cituation of it, if not to live there myself."[26]

The Great House

Reimbursement from the New Hampshire colony came too little and too late. Captain John Mason was becoming land rich and cash poor. He now technically owned three plantations along the Piscataqua at what is now Rye, Portsmouth, and South Berwick, Maine—all three thousand miles from his own comfortable home in Portsmouth, England. Each plantation had its own "great house."[27] The term, confusing to modern readers, refers to any large manor house usually occupied by the reigning landlord in a highly class-conscious society. Important English families lived in big houses and, although the largest dwelling was at Strawberry Bank, the phrase seems to have been used to refer to all three Piscataqua settlements interchangeably.

Just keeping track of his holdings was a painstaking process, with months lagging between reports. On December 5, 1632, Mason wrote to his chief business agent, Ambrose Gibbons, to confirm that "Pascattaway" (Rye), "Strawberry-bancke" (Portsmouth) and "Newichwannick" (South Berwick) were being managed, in order, by Mr. Edward Godfrey, Mr. Thomas Wannerton, and Gibbons himself. But by the time Gibbons received the landlord's letter and wrote back it was already July 13, 1633. Godfrey had left the fishing post at Rye and Wannerton had moved in there. Gibbons, with his wife and child and four men, plus nine cows, one bull, and thirteen calves, was running the bustling sawmill at South Berwick. Placing most of the settlers

OPPOSITE: *This map of sixteenth-century Pascataway appeared in a rarely seen pamphlet by local historian John Scribner Jenness (complete with spelling error) in 1878. (JDR)*

and the largest settlement just a few miles down river at Strawberry Bank may have been a miscalculation. The real action was further up river at South Berwick. As many as a hundred Indians, drawn to their seasonal fishing grounds at the Great Works falls, were now trading furs at the isolated new settlement there. In his follow-up letter, Gibbons did not even mention the operation at Strawberry Bank that, despite being the most populated of Mason's plantations, was exporting neither fish nor fur.[28]

Today our view of the central Strawberry Bank Great House in its founding years, with dozens of busy English immigrants, is as vague and dreamlike as Mason's imagined Indian lakes. One precious miniature sketch of the building survives on a hand-drawn map of the Piscataqua from the 1660s.[29] It shows a large two-story structure with two end chimneys separated by four peaked gables along the front of the roof. William Chadbourne, an early arrival, may have been hired by Mason to build the house before moving on to the sawmill at South Berwick, where he and his son Humphrey Chadbourne constructed their own manor around 1640.[30] These early houses were built of timbers squared by hand, probably oak, since that wood was familiar to skilled English carpenters. Initially, at least, the Great House would have been an all-purpose space with a large downstairs room similar to a medieval "great hall" that functioned as communal living space, trading post, and storehouse. Outside, records appear to indicate, was a small field to the east, a "Great Field" to the north and west, and an orchard on the south and southwest.[31]

No written description of the Great House at Strawberry Bank survives, but a look inside a 1640-era manor at Cape Elizabeth offers clues. Owner John Winter described his manor there as 40 by 18 feet with a large fireplace, an attached room near the kitchen, storage for twenty tons of casks, a steward's room, and a sizeable eating area. Each room had doors and locks. Of the two large chambers, one was big enough to sleep all the men working at what is still called Richmond Island.

"Every man hath his close bordered cabin [bunk], and I have room enough to make a dozen close bordered cabins more," Winter recorded. " . . . and in the other chamber I have room to put the ship sails into, and allow dry goods which is in casks."[32]

ABOVE: *The only known view of the "Great House" at Strawberry Bank comes from a 1660s map of the Piscataqua region in the British Museum. (BAK)*

Portsmouth's premier amateur historian, Charles W. Brewster, a nineteenth-century newspaper editor, summarized the 1631 emigrants as including about eighty "stewards, agents, workmen and servants."[33] These settlers arrived in stages, many indentured to work for a specified time. Brewster named the ten managing stewards in his book, *Rambles About Portsmouth*, then listed all the remaining men by surname, noting as an afterthought, that there were also twenty-two unidentified women. How many of these settlers actually arrived on the *Pied Cow* (often spelled "*Pide Cowe*"), Portsmouth's bland equivalent of the *Mayflower*, is uncertain.[34] Early settlers were often anything but settled, and moved to the next advantageous spot or left on the next available ship. Some of the "Old Planters" that Brewster mentions, research indicates, may have already been at Pascataway as early as 1623, arrived with Captain Neale, or as part of one of Sir Ferdinando Gorges's early Maine experiments, or showed up with his son Roger Gorges during his brief term as governor of the region. There was much more coming and going of settlers than simple histories assume, leaving genealogy enthusiasts in a maze with many false passages and dead ends. It is only as residents of the Great House moved to their own lands and houses that the founding families of Portsmouth can be better identified.

City memory is clearer about the physical location of the Great House than its appearance or function. It is not, as some Portsmouth visitors naturally infer, still standing within the ten-acre grounds of the Strawbery Banke Museum. It is not the brooding Sherburne House with its steep roof, pointed gables, tiny diamond-pane leaded windows, and central chimney that looks like the setting for a Nathaniel Hawthorne novel. Remnants of the 1630-era Great House, one of its chimneys and the southern wall, were still standing in 1695 when the Sherburne House was built, perhaps as close as a hundred yards away facing the nearby river. Historians generally agree that the Great House, the first European-built structure in Portsmouth, sat near what is now the southeast corner of Court and Marcy streets (formerly Pitt and Water streets), across from the modern entrance to Prescott Park near the Memorial Bridge that spans the river to Kittery.[35] The Laconia Company's original thousand-acre Piscataqua grant then covered much of what is now downtown

ABOVE: *Early twentieth-century artist's concept of the Pied Cow or the Warwick arriving in Strawberry Bank settlement. Few speculative images of the "Mayflower of NH" exist. (JDR)*

Portsmouth, including tall pine forests, salt water marsh, and two tidal ponds.

Strawbery Banke Museum today is literally in the "back yard" of the Great House. The area may originally have been used as an orchard. As the town evolved, this area became part of the Portsmouth South End neighborhood, later nicknamed Puddle Dock. The puddle, no longer visible, ran through what is now the flat, open area of the museum campus originally called "The Cove."[36] Filled in at the turn of the twentieth century, the cove once rose enough at high tides to allow a small boat to navigate into the South Mill Pond—providing one more good reason to locate Mason's "middle" plantation here.

For four years starting in 1631, John Mason was very good to his people at Strawberry Bank, at least from his vantage point far away. The Laconia Company equipped them with state-of-the-art armaments including brass canon and ample ammunition. Under Captain Neale, Mason's men quickly defended the mouth

ABOVE: *The possible site of the Great House is today occupied by the Oracle House (1702), moved here from another part of the city and privately owned. This lot borders Strawbery Banke Museum on two sides and faces the entrance to Prescott Park and the arrival point of the first Strawberry Bank settlers. (JDR)*

of the Piscataqua, setting up crude fortifications at Fort Point on Great Island (New Castle), later to become Fort William and Mary. Mason sent over a sketch of the sawmill to be built and later forwarded "8 Danes" to work the operation. Historians have argued over whether these "Danes" arriving aboard the *Pied Cow* and *Warwick* were Scandinavian citizens or valuable Danish cattle of a distinctive yellow color. Others believe the reference actually reads "hands," not "Danes." Whichever way, livestock thrived in New Hampshire. The sight of them grazing near the Great House on fields cleared of timber must have been all but indistinguishable from the view of an English manor back home. This pastoral view of Portsmouth, however briefly it lasted, is an important snapshot, now largely forgotten.

Early correspondence between Mason and his colonial agents follows a similar pattern. The colonists wanted things from England—fish hooks and lines, nails, spikes, locks, hinges, beds, leather, rugs, more men, wives, seed, malt for beer, farm logging tools, Indian trade goods, blankets, clothes—and Mason's investors wanted results. The language was polite, but insistent. "We hope you will find out some good mines," investor Tom Eyre wrote from England at the outset in 1631, "which will be welcome newes unto us."[37] Mason's Laconia Company was careful to itemize the cost of everything delivered, down to the shilling and pence. Distracted by failed attempts to hunt for precious metals and install vineyards to produce wine, the Piscataqua settlements consumed much and offered little in return. The disappointed investors began holding back supplies, asking for payment on demand in beaver pelts that quickly replaced money on the Piscataqua. Ambrose Gibbons, writing back in 1633, reminded his investors that a plantation could not be built on words. "Those that have bin heare this three year," Gibbons wrote, "som of them have nether meat, money, nor cloathes — a great disparagement."[38]

Despite the constant complaints from Gibbons at South Berwick, life at Strawberry Bank and Piscataway was better, certainly, than the early years at Jamestown or Plymouth where half the new colonists died. A precise and extended inventory of all three plantations made after John Mason's death in 1635 offers a look inside the great houses where everything belonged to the

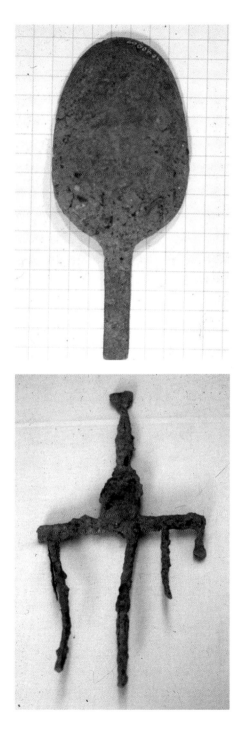

ABOVE: *Colonial spoon and fork utensils discovered in digs by Strawbery Banke archaeologists. (SBM)*

proprietor. The inventory includes scores of items, including: guns (161), swords (61), shirts (80), pairs of stockings (204), iron kettles (23), rugs (40), musical instruments (17), sugar (610 lbs), corn (140 bushels), pine planks (1,151), livestock (155 head), and Bibles (1).[39] The condition of these items, or whether they were to be used as trade goods, is not spelled out.

Mason had reason to be a good provider. Like his contemporary Cecil Calvert, Lord of Baltimore, who founded the first colony at Maryland at the same time, Mason was looking at a long-term investment in the New World that would make him and his heirs magnificently rich. Both men followed the advice of Captain John Smith and did not skimp when provisioning their colonists. Both men sent the most qualified settlers they could find, hoping to reward service now with land later. Both acted as absentee landlords. From humble beginnings they imagined an English province sprouting great profitable plantations, each with its own grand manor house and each run by a loyal baron much as it had been in England during the Middle Ages. Both Lord Baltimore and John Mason were Royalist sympathizers, owing their fealty only to King Charles I in England, and not to the Puritans soon to overtake the British throne. As proprietary landholders they would function much like kings themselves in America. In exchange for expanding the king's colonial territory in the New World and keeping out the French and Spanish, Mason and Baltimore and others could assign land, charge rent, write laws, dispense justice, and collect taxes on their own turf. Both men fully intended to travel to the New World once their colonies were up and running and to govern with a just and mighty hand. But both men died, and neither ever saw the colony he started.[40]

Lord Baltimore's son, who inherited his father's title, wisely stayed in England where he spent the next four decades of his life battling in the volatile English courts to retain his proprietary Maryland colony. During this period Charles I was beheaded, Puritan leader Oliver Cromwell came and went, and the monarchy was restored under Charles II. John Mason, on the other hand, built a brand new sailing ship and then died suddenly in 1635, leaving his New Hampshire colonists to their own devices and creating decades of legal wrangling for his descendants.

ABOVE: *George Calvert, Lord of Baltimore, first attempted to plant a fishing colony at Newfoundland, but found the winters too frigid. His son Cecil Calvert successfully established a colony in Maryland near the time when John Mason founded his plantation at Strawberry Bank. Neither Calvert nor Mason ever saw his successful settlement. (JDR)*

With its founding father, chief investor and corporate CEO gone, the New Hampshire colonists appealed to Sir Ferdinando Gorges for guidance and support, but he had his hands full in Maine. Stock speculation in Strawberry Bank and its sister plantations was as unattractive to British investors as Internet futures after a dot-com bust. By 1638 the Plymouth Council of New England and its Laconia Company speculators had turned off the lights and gone home. When stranded Piscataqua settlers begged the widow Anne Mason to keep her husband's venture alive, she curtly rejected them, then told Ambrose Gibbons to sell the swine in his stable to pay her lawyer's fees.

More letters went unanswered. Stockpiles dwindled. As one harsh New England winter bled into the next, the men and women of Strawberry Bank woke up to reality. The Lake of the Iroquois was a pipe dream. Their wealthy leader was dead. They were deep in the heart of darkness three thousand miles from home—and they were on their own.

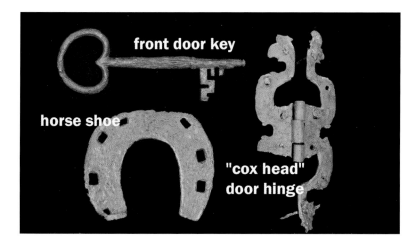

ABOVE: *An amazing array of seventeenth-century architectural and household artifacts have been discovered in a decade of excavation at the Humphrey Chadbourne site in nearby South Berwick, Maine. (BAK)*

Portsmouth at Rivermouth 1635–1700

Wild strawberries really did grow along the banks of the dark, swirling Piscataqua River in 1630 when the first influx of John Mason's settlers arrived. That is, at least, what the town fathers recalled more than two decades later in 1653 when they decided it was time to change the name Strawberry Bank to Portsmouth. By then under the thumb of Puritan rule, New Hampshire residents had to petition the general court at Massachusetts for permission to brand their new, more commercial, maritime identity. Indian names, still fine for rivers, were politically incorrect for growing towns seeking to link themselves with Mother England. Although Portsmouth would sometimes be called "Pascataway" for generations to come, the trend toward Anglicized names was strong in New Hampshire. All three sister plantations on the seacoast joined in. Hilton Point or Cochecho evolved to North-ham and eventually to Dover. Squamscott became Exeter. Winnicunnet became Hampton. Future counties on the Piscataqua—Rockingham and Strafford in New Hampshire and York in Maine—continued to Anglicize. Durham, Rye, Berwick, Newmarket, Newfields, Somersworth, Rochester, Kittery, Barrington, New Castle, Newfields, Newington, and others all owe their names to English places or personalities.

The name "Strawberry Bank" itself may not have been original. There has long been a Strawberry Bank manor at Cartmel

OPPOSITE: *The 1664 Richard Jackson House in Portsmouth is the oldest surviving house in northern New England. Saved by William Sumner Appleton in the early 20th century, it is still open to the public, owned by Historic New England. (SBM)*

Fel in Lancaster, England and a Strawberry Bank in Cumbria. The highest point in Nottinghamshire is still called Strawberry Bank. It is more than likely that at least one immigrant aboard the *Pied Cow* held strong nostalgic connections to one of these British locations.[1] Yet rather than look outward for the derivation of the name, generations of local historians have chosen to debate the precise location of the famous berry patch with the fervor of biblical scholars.[2]

Although abandoned by its original investors, Strawberry Bank survived and thrived in the seventeenth century. For a while the port of Portsmouth even kept pace with ports in Massachusetts to the south. The trick was finding something on the New Hampshire frontier worth selling back to Europe or bartering with neighboring colonies. Fishing and fur trading sustained the region temporarily when Mason's get-rich-quick schemes failed and his Northwest Passage to China did not turn up. But it was New Hampshire's virgin forests—when combined with fish and fur—that saved the day. Like tobacco and cotton in the south, trees became the cash crop that defined northern New England. The demand for more lumber and the rise of scores of water-powered sawmills, all but unknown in England, shaped the local economy and its politics. Trees and the land they stood on provided an economic incentive that helped New Hampshire break free of Massachusetts rule and, eventually, of English rule as well.

But before they could fly, or even walk, the orphans of Strawberry Bank had to learn to crawl.

Be Very Afraid

The wolf was literally at the door. Wolves were the first item on the lengthy agenda of Strawberry Bank town officials in March 1652. "It is generally agreed upon," the record states, "that every wolfe that hereafter shall be killed in this Towne: the partie shall have twenty shillings of the Town stock."[3] Ten years later under the protection of Massachusetts the problem seemed to have gotten worse and more complicated. The bounty for killing a wolf had risen to £5, but in order to collect from the town treasury, the hunter had to jump through a few legal hoops. The hunter

ABOVE: *This detail from the 1660 Piscataqua River map shows an abundance of wild animals, but to encourage investors and settlers in the New World, they appear more tame than intimidating. (BAK)*

"shall bring some of the next neighbours, where such a wolf is killed, to testify it was done in the town's bounds, and shall nayle the head of such wolf killed, upon the meeting house . . . "[4] The honor system was already a thing of the past.

Besides wild animals, and the possibility of pirates, Indians, marauding French or aggressive Puritans, there was the harshest of weather to fear. In 1638 as if by warning, just as the Laconia Company officially dissolved itself forever of any interest in New Hampshire, a major earthquake shook the walls of the Great House, knocking dishes to the floor.

The abandoned citizens of Strawberry Bank, many likely brought up in London or other bustling cities, were not wild game hunters. Most were neither farmers, fishermen, trappers, nor Indian traders. They were utterly dependent on England for clothes, shoes, gunpowder, weapons, tools, and basic supplies. They couldn't even make beer without imported malt. In many ways they were no closer to Nature than people today, yet they were wholly unlike us. These ancestors, according to seventeenth-century archaeologist Emerson Baker, would be almost as foreign to twenty-first century Americans as Martians. They spoke in unintelligible accents through decaying teeth. They were unfamiliar with modern sanitation. The men and women of the Great House did not believe in bathing for fear that immersing the body in water could be deadly. They did not swim. They did not drink water, but imbibed great quantities of beer, rum, and wine. They believed in the Devil as a living breathing presence on Earth. They believed, without question, that some people were born to be servants, while others were born to be kings and queens.

The one thing the original Strawberry Bank citizens share with post-9/11 Americans is fear. Without Captain Neale and his soldiers, they were sitting ducks for the dangers they assumed lurked just outside the door. Even the simple passing of neighbors at night could lead to high drama as when Susannah Trimmings filed this Portsmouth court complaint against Goodwife Walford in 1656:

> "As I was going home on Sunday night the 30th, I heard a rustling in the woods, which I supposed to be occasioned by swine, and presently there appeared a

ABOVE: *A cat, perhaps enchanted, prowls in the lane near a seventeenth-century home similar to the Jackson House in superstitious early Portsmouth. This illustration appeared during the 1923 city tercentenary in a book called* Some Three Hundred Years Ago. *(JDR)*

woman, whom I apprehended to be old Goodwife Walford. She asked me to lend her a pound of cotton; I told her I had but two pounds in the house, and I would not spare any to my mother. She said I had better have done it, for I was going a great journey, but I should never come there. She then left me, and I was struck as if with a clap of fire on the back; and she vanished toward the water side, in my apprehension, in the shape of a cat."[5]

According to her husband's testimony, when Susannah Trimmings arrived home her back was aflame with pain and her lower parts were numb. She could not speak and was scarcely able to breathe. Timothy Trimmings suggested that his wife was just experiencing "her weakness," but she insisted that the wicked Goody Walford had threatened to kill her. One neighbor attested to the fact that Susannah was definitely ill and her eyes looked as if she had been scalded. Neighbors took sides, one saying the whole story was a fantasy. Another said he too had seen a cat, and when he tried to shoot it, his gun, probably bewitched, had refused to fire.

The pervasive sense of dread and distrust in the Piscataqua settlements in the seventeenth century is best illustrated by the famous case of the "Stone Throwing Devil."[6] Stones rained on New Castle Island in the summer of 1682. For three months rocks tossed by unseen hands battered the New Hampshire home of George and Alice Walton and crashed through their small leaded glass windows. A torturing hail of stones followed George Walton into the fields, pelting his arms and legs, bruising the flesh. Walton, an elderly tavern keeper and planter, was struck full in the back. When he crossed from "Great Island" to the Portsmouth mainland by boat to report what was happening to him, a flying rock "broke his head."[7]

ABOVE: *The late seventeenth century in New England is best known through the pen of Nathaniel Hawthorne in novels like* The House of Seven Gables *and* The Scarlet Letter. *Published by Portsmouth-born editor James T. Fields, Hawthorne was among the earliest tourists to the Isles of Shoals where he stayed 10 days in the fall of 1852. (JDR)*

The mysterious flying stones came and went all that summer. As many as one hundred were reported in a single session, always focused on Walton or anyone who happened to be near him. Walton reported being struck as many as thirty or forty times. This incident of early "witchcraft" was studied by no less than Cotton Mather, author of the Salem witch trials a decade later. The account was published under the title "Lithobolia"[8] in London in 1698 by Richard Chamberlain, an eye witness to the events who had lodged at Walton's tavern. Chamberlain was also a lawyer for the Mason family who, decades after the death of John Mason, attempted to reclaim their family land.

Emerson Baker, in his in-depth study of the Stone Throwing Devil incident, offers compelling reasons why this was actually a battle about political power and property, not witchcraft. He explains why many of Walton's relatives and Portsmouth neighbors may have wanted to frighten or even murder him.[9] Walton was a wealthy landowner by seventeenth-century standards, influential, elderly, and a member of the detested Quaker faith. He was sympathetic to the Masonian proprietors, loyal to the British king, and defiant to Puritan leaders who were horrified by his sinful tavern. Walton, officials noted, had allowed his "heathen" Indian servant to bear the illegitimate child of a passing sailor under his roof—a child conceived on the Sabbath day.

Walton was the perfect example, from a Puritan perspective, of the very worst citizen possible, and the reason New Hampshire needed a strict Puritan government. In Massachusetts such a man could be stoned to death, or at least driven off. But in the Piscataqua settlements, independent iconoclastic men like Walton were just as likely to be important landholders and successful businessmen. Scholars often compare settling the seventeenth-century New England frontier to the taming of the American "Wild West" two centuries later. The comparison is apt. Although George Walton was no Ben Cartwright and Strawberry Bank was not the Ponderosa, we can trace familiar elements. Early New Hampshire involves the grabbing and defending of land, a host of colorful characters, clashing cultures, the rise of a few successful entrepreneurs, and the constant struggle to establish law and order in a wild and unpredictable environment.

ABOVE: *To seventeenth-century residents of Portsmouth, the devil was a very real character who might appear suddenly or influence events at any time. (JDR)*

Call Us Portsmouth

Unlike many failed colonists in New England, the orphans of Strawberry Bank did not all cut and run. Perhaps the rising chaos in England, as King Charles battled his own Parliament, made the woods of New Hampshire appear a little more desirable. Some stayed and laid claim to Mason's buildings, land, and property, valued at a total of £10,000 sterling, that they felt were owed to them.

With no help coming from Mason's heirs and with supplies running low, about twenty locals got together in 1640 and formed their own government. The document they devised, the Strawberry Bank Combination, has been lost, but it likely offered the same oath to God and to the King as the famous Mayflower Compact or the one signed in the nearby town of Exeter in 1639. Exeter, another early town, was founded by Reverend John Wheelwright and his followers who had been driven out of Puritan Massachusetts for heresy. Dover, during the same year, gave itself over to control by Massachusetts as did the settlement at Hampton. But Mason's former settlers clung to

a hope of independence. Captain John Mason himself had been strongly opposed to the expanding Massachusetts Bay Colony and its governor, John Winthrop, who had his eye on Mason and Gorges's "Royalist" territory in Maine and New Hampshire. Mason's death and later Gorges's death in 1647 made the takeover possible.

For a few moments Strawberry Bank, like Kittery, Dover, and Exeter, was an independent nation. The Combination created a new Pascataway governor, Francis Williams, and appointed former stewards Ambrose Gibbons and Thomas Wannerton as assistants. There was not much to govern. New Hampshire was "a mere wilderness, with here and there a few huts scattered by the seaside."[10] When Strawberry Bank agreed to come under the jurisdiction of Massachusetts in 1641, the three leaders of the short-lived independent republic became magistrates of the Massachusetts Bay Colony, but these original Strawberry Bank "founders" did not last long.

The arrival of a formal government in New Hampshire coincides with the arrival of African slavery. The governor himself, "Mr. Williams of Piscataquack," purchased the first

ABOVE: *A 1705 illustration from the British Public Record Office titled "Profile of Fort William & Mary on Piscataqua River" in New Castle, New Hampshire. It offers a rare early glimpse of the fishing village as well as the British fort (at right) that became the scene of an early colonial uprising in 1774. The letters refer to a key at the bottom of the sketch indicating items such as "the new made block house," officers quarters, town and church. (BAK)*

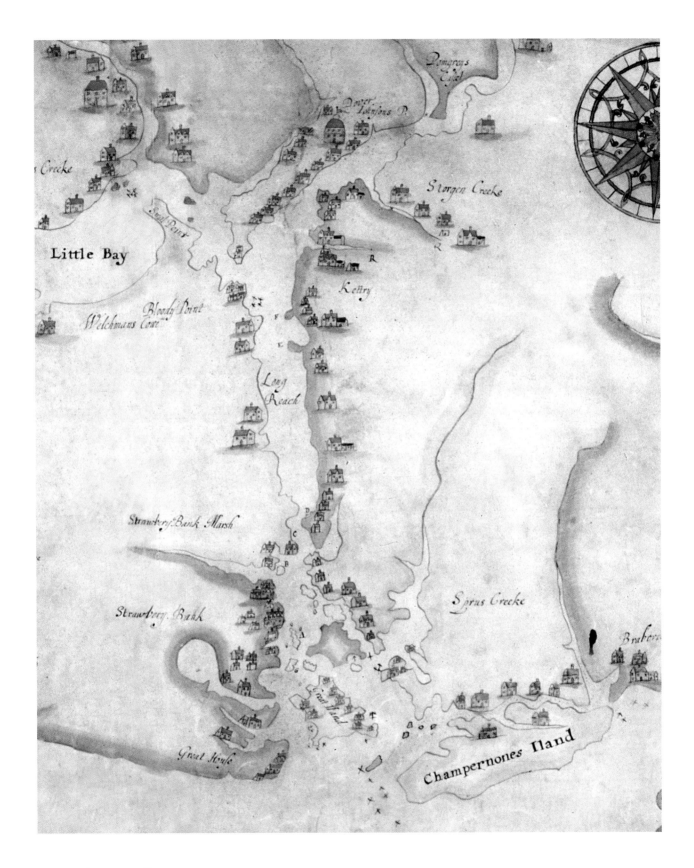

Little Bay

Snal Point

Bloody Point
Welchmans Cove

Long
Reach

Strawbery Bank Marsh

Strawbery Bank

Great House

Dover Tohnsons D.

Storgen Creeke

Kettry

Spras Creeke

Braberi

Champernones Iland

known enslaved Black in the colony, an unnamed African man from Guinea.[11] Williams was ordered by the Massachusetts Bay Colony to return the Negro man, not because the Puritans frowned on slavery, but because he had been "fraudulently and injuriously taken" from Guinea. That same year in 1645 Williams sold off his New Hampshire holdings and was last seen in Barbados three years later where he soon died.

Captain Thomas Wannerton, the most colorful of Portsmouth's first managers, lived in the Great House at Strawberry Bank. Reviled by the Puritans for his immoral ways, he traded briefly along the coast "wherever drink was easily got."[12] He was sued often and fined by the court in 1643 for striking his wife Ann with a stool. As one of the original investors in Captain Mason's failed venture, Wannerton certainly felt he deserved compensation for his service in the rugged New World. So in 1644, he packed up some of the provisions at the Great House, grabbed the cannon at New Castle, and sold it all to the French

OPPOSITE: *Detail from 1660s-era map of the Piscataqua River. This anonymously created map is a key source of information about early buildings and settlements in the region and resides in the British Museum (BAK)*

ABOVE: *This seventeenth-century marker at Point of Graves is a reminder of the European settlers who founded Strawberry Bank. Behind the tombstones the dock and warehouse are a reminder that enslaved Africans were traded here at the commercial waterfront as early as 1645. (SBM)*

at Port Royal in Nova Scotia. Legends says Wannerton was shot dead there while attempting to rob a house. That left only Ambrose Gibbons who had been somewhat successful running the trading post at South Berwick. Although he was "an honest, capable and faithful steward,"[13] Gibbons had by this time moved on to become a founder of a colony at nearby Oyster River, now the town of Durham and home to the University of New Hampshire. In a final blow to the local economy, steward Francis Norton, the attorney to Captain Mason's widow, secretly drove the hundred precious yellow cattle from Strawberry Bank to Boston, sold them each for £20 sterling, and did not return. And so, having been abandoned by their founder, the first wave of Strawberry Bank managers also abandoned the plantation.

Through much of the seventeenth century, the slow growth of the Portsmouth area was centered at New Castle near Fort William and Mary and toward Little Harbor and along Sagamore Creek. Early pioneers preferred the less dramatic Little Harbor entrance up the river along Sagamore, sometimes called "Witch Creek," where a few also settled. Not much was happening at the Strawberry Bank Great House just up the river, but the original three founders did plant the seed that would eventually shift the center of commercial attention in that direction. In 1640, the year of the Strawberry Bank Combination, the settlement had one Bible, no church, and no minister. So the founders officially set aside a plot of land or "glebe" of fifty acres designed to attract a minister to the wilderness outpost. Henry Sherburne and Thomas Walford, two of Mason's early stewards who stayed on, were appointed church foremen. A small church was apparently built in a back field at what is downtown Portsmouth today, an important first step in the expansion of the city waterfront neighborhood. The new Puritan government, however, did not like the region's first choice of an Anglican minister and drove him away.

Governor Winthrop intended nothing less than a complete Puritan takeover of the Piscataqua region and during Cromwell's reign, the Massachusetts Bay Colony pushed to redefine their borders and override Mason's claims. Initially the flow of Puritans in the Great Migration to northern New England did help protect the citizens of Strawberry Bank, who had effectively stolen Mason's holdings and did not want to give them back to his heirs. One of those heirs, grandson Robert Tufton Mason, came of age in 1650 and his early attempts to regain control of his family land were quickly thwarted by the Puritan courts. (Scholars today suggest that, in a strict legal sense, Captain John Mason did not really have solid legal claim to New Hampshire at all.) But the protection came at a heavy price. Puritan law quickly banned everything from drinking toasts to wearing long hair. Besides treason and murder, citizens could be put to death for idolatry, blasphemy, public rebellion, witchcraft, bestiality, buggery, bearing false witness, rape, "man stealing," and burning a house or ship. Even children could legally be put to death for cursing their parents.[14] During the 1640s, Puritans at Boston hanged their first victim of witchcraft. A pair of colonial lovers, although adultery was usually punished by whipping, were also hanged in the public square.

New Hampshire, however, resisted total assimilation from the start, exhibiting a kinder, gentler version of Puritan rule. Although Dover and Strawberry Bank were initially clustered with nearby Massachusetts towns into the new county of Norfolk, New Hampshire maintained its own local court. When Puritan law allowed only church-goers to vote on town issues, members of the "lower Piscataqua," who had no church, managed to get around that requirement. The "soft" takeover of the New Hampshire plantations, followed by a harsher domination of Kittery and York, opened the doors to an influx of Puritans along the northern coast. Puritans like Brian Pendleton, formerly of Sudbury, and brothers Richard and John Cutt from Wales began grabbing up land in Portsmouth, an area that then included the modern towns of Rye, Greenland, Newington, and New Castle. Their power and business success was often balanced by Royalist sympathizers like Henry Sherburne and John Pickering who had arrived in the 1630s, and also by the "Old Planters" and early fishing families, some of whom had arrived even earlier.

In January 1652 the town selectmen, including Pendelton, Sherburne, Pickering, and the town surgeon Renald Fernald, got together at George Walton's tavern on Great Island and "updated" the early written records of Strawberry Bank. Undesirable passages from the first twenty years of the colony were suppressed

ABOVE: *Although New Hampshire was temporarily governed by Massachusetts in the mid-1600s, Governor John Winthrop was never able to take over Mason's claimed lands. Maine, however, remained a part of Massachusetts until it achieved statehood in 1820. (JDR)*

and a new town book created. Historians have assumed the original documents were destroyed, but at least one local scholar has suggested that the first town book may have survived and could someday turn up.[15] It seems likely that the records were doctored to weaken the hereditary claims of Robert Mason, who was even then seeking restitution in the courts. The overt purpose was to define the fuzzy boundary between Strawberry Bank and Dover. The town fathers also confirmed forty-six land grants in the region that now included fifty or sixty families totaling about five hundred people. With seacoast land speculation on the rise and property rapidly changing hands, locals wanted legal rights to their land and houses. To the Masonians, they were all squatters. To the few surviving Native Americans, they were all usurpers.

The 1652 grants offer a snapshot of the ongoing Puritan land-grab superimposed over a map of the earliest Piscataqua pioneers. This was not going to be a feudal empire as Mason and Gorges had imagined, with annual quitrents paid to a powerful proprietor. Nor was New Hampshire going to be a colony of shared common farmland as in parts of England. New England was altogether different—a land of laws and fences and stone walls, with every man for himself. Piscataqua grantees received parcels as small as a few acres of salt marsh up to an area that is now the town of Greenland. In 1660, the year Cromwell died in England and the monarchy was restored, Portsmouth gave away an additional six hundred acres to ninety-one local men, women, and even to children. By this time the town finally had

ABOVE: *Portion of an ancient flintlock discovered by archaeologists during a dig at Strawbery Banke Museum. (SBM)*

a permanent minister in Reverend Joshua Moody. They also had a new church made out of sawn logs for a stronger defense. The church stood at the junction of what is now South and Marcy streets at the start of New Castle Avenue. This spot, then called Pickering's Neck, also included a sawmill and gristmill. These important new buildings were located, not at the populated Great Island, but just down the street from the ancient Great House, which had been home to the wealthy Puritan John Cutt since 1647. While granting out all its land to its citizens, Strawberry Bank also shifted its center away from the island and onto the new waterfront hub at what would become known as Puddle Dock.

Portsmouth also had its new name. Although named to honor its founder Captain Mason of Portsmouth, England, the change from Strawberry Bank helped separate the new and improved commercial seaport from its orphaned past. The first iteration of Portsmouth, the 1653 petition implies, was a mistake in need of correction. The plea to the Massachusetts General Court reads:

> And whereas the name of this plantation att present beinge Straberry banke accidentally soe called by reason of a banke where straberries was found in this place, Now your petitioners humble desire is to have it called Portsmouth, being a name most sutable for this place, it beinge the River's mouth & a good [harbour] as any in this land, & your petitioners shall humbly pray.[16]

Times change. Three hundred years later Portsmouth citizens created a corporation designed to preserve the history of their city on a ten-acre river front plot. At first they considered calling the nonprofit agency "Historic Portsmouth." In calling themselves Strawbery Banke Inc. instead, the group embraced the very title that the city founders had discarded. Preservation

ABOVE: *These stocks outside the Old Gaol in York, ME are a reminder of Puritan rule. Originally built in 1656, the building was replaced by a new jail in 1719, now one of the museum structures at Old York Historical Society. (MEB)*

LEFT: *Sketch of strawberries from an early Strawbery Banke Inc. brochure in the mid-1960s. (SBM)*

was becoming fashionable in 1958, but in 1652 the last place Portsmouth citizens wanted to look was backwards.

Turmoil and Transformation

The second half of the seventeenth century is arguably the most dramatic, most transformative, and least understood period in Portsmouth history. Accusations of witchcraft, deadly Indian raids, and the confusing legal wrangling among locals, the Bay Colony, and the heirs of John Mason all point to one fact—that the Piscataqua region and its abundant natural resources were worth fighting for. Fish, timber, and fur, as John Smith had predicted decades before, were as good as gold, and it is easy to forget that, while life on the Eastern Frontier seems primitive today, business was booming. Great fortunes were being made at the fisheries employing hundreds on the Isles of Shoals, and giving rise to influential men like Richard Cutt, John Cutt's brother, and William Pepperell, founder of the wealthiest colonial family in Maine. Shipyards were busy up and down the Piscataqua watershed that now powered up to two dozen local sawmills.

The economic value of these northern forests was well known to the Massachusetts government that currently controlled New Hampshire and Maine. England was starved for wood and without sawmills of its own. Bay Colony governor John Winthrop even rationalized the New Hampshire takeover as an effort to protect the forests from being spoiled by the locals. A 1660-era map of New Hampshire indicates fifteen commercial mills on the interior riverfront system and six more in nearby Maine. A key to this same map notes that "England's strength do lye unseen in rivers of the new plantation." By 1675 a total of fifty sawmills were producing, according to scholarly reports, anywhere from one to nine million board feet of lumber annually.[17] Contemporary readers might get a clearer picture by replacing the word timber with "oil."

The big money was in the mast trade where merchants like John Cutt thrived. Nothing could match the tall, straight New England white pine that reached three to six feet in diameter. Masts made from New Hampshire pine could last up to twenty

ABOVE: *Flat-bottomed gundalows were seen everywhere along the Piscataqua as early as the 1600s. A reconstructed gundalow was launched here in the early 1980s and functions today as a floating classroom. (SBM)*

years, many times longer than Norwegian-grown timbers. Felled at great risk by expert woodsmen, giant pines had to be dragged by powerful oxen that were sometimes worked to death. Trimmed logs for masts were floated down the dangerously rapid river and delivered to England in specially built ships. Mast logs were often stored in ponds located between Great Island and Portsmouth. A single tree worth £15 sterling as milled lumber could bring £100 as a replacement mast badly needed by the active British navy. By the end of the seventeenth century, Piscataqua loggers had to travel up to twenty miles inland to find valuable mast pines, and the search fueled New Hampshire's westward expansion under the coming dynasty of royal governors.[18]

As Cromwell's Puritan reign ended in England, Portsmouth was coming into its own as a port that, for a few years, rivaled Boston and Salem. Robert Tufton Mason, heir to his

ABOVE: *The launch of the 44-gun HMS* Falkland *on the Piscataqua in 1695 was ample proof that the region had evolved into a full-blown maritime community with its own supply of natural resources and skilled craftsmen. Painted by Geo. Campbell, owned by James A. Knowles. (SBM)*

grandfather's New Hampshire claim, eagerly assessed the operation at Portsmouth. In 1671 he reported that locals exported ten shiploads of tall straight pine trees for ship masts, ten thousand quintals of fish, several thousand animal pelts, ten thousand pipe staves, and sawn timber. The tidal rivers of the Piscataqua made it possible for ships to be built far up the many rivers. Ingenious "Yankee" shipwrights constructed flat-bottomed vessels miles into the forest, then dragged them to the river over snow-covered terrain in winter using up to a hundred oxen. More than a century before the Portsmouth Naval Shipyard was established, Piscataqua craftsmen had built two major British warships here, the 48-gun HMS *Falkland* (1690) and the 32-gun HMS *Bedford-Galley* (1696).[19]

By any measure Portsmouth had become a significant player in maritime trade. Despite English navigation acts banning trade with other nations, Piscataqua merchants were selling to Holland, Spain, and Portugal and had established solid connections in Boston, Nova Scotia, Virginia, and the West Indies. The king himself, according to one source, believed the Piscataqua River to be "of more concernment . . . to trade, present and future, than all New England besides . . ."[20] Robert Mason's claims to this region, in England at least, were considered authentic. Partially to give him a fair shake in the courts, New Hampshire was declared a separate colonial province in 1679, ending the total jurisdiction of Massachusetts Puritans and imbuing Granite State residents with the sense that they possessed, rightly or not, a particularly independent spirit.

The focus of this swirling international controversy now fell right at the doorstep of the ancient Great House at old Strawberry Bank. By royal decree, merchant John Cutt, who had moved into the Great House in 1647, was appointed president of the New Hampshire province, including the towns of Dover, Exeter, and Hampton. John and his brother Richard were the largest landholders in the region, with extensive property in the nearby towns and at what would become the center of the city of Portsmouth. President Cutt sent a message to the Massachusetts general court at Boston in 1680, thanking them reluctantly for "your care for us and kindness while we dwelt under your shadow." Cutt managed eight other councilors including his

ABOVE: *Major Indian raids at York, Dover, Oyster River, and elsewhere along the Seacoast forever changed the colonial perception of Native Americans, despite the first half-century of peaceful settlement. Richard Waldron, killed at the "Cochecho Massacre," was the ancestor of Jeremy Waldron, a twentieth-century founder of Strawbery Banke Museum. (JDR)*

son-in-law, Richard Waldron of Dover. The councilors were required by the official charter to "reconcile all Differanses if they can That Shall or maye arise betweene ye saide Roberd Mason & ye Saide Inhabitants."[21] This New Hampshire land dispute exploded two years later into the attack of the Stone Throwing Devil. Lawsuits dragged on well into the next century and, some might say, the aftershocks reverberate to this day.

The orphans of Strawberry Bank had grown up and some had become wealthy, but this was a terrible moment, many believed, to be cut loose from the Bay Colony. Britain was at war with France and New Hampshire was a vulnerable British colony, thousands of miles from the protection of the king. Native Americans, long peaceful under Passaconnaway's reign, now frustrated by oppressive European treaties and encroachment on their lands, had begun attacking colonial villages, sometimes under the influence of the French. Richard Cutt, who had organized the local militia and set up training exercises on the common at Great Island, died in 1676. Five years later, soon after his royal appointment as president of New Hampshire, brother John Cutt grew seriously ill. When Portsmouth citizens spotted a blazing comet in the sky, with their leader at death's door, many feared that God was displeased with the state of things on the

ABOVE: *William Dam's (1682–1712) log house is the only surviving garrison in Dover following Indian raids of the era. It was moved to the campus of the Woodman Institute in Dover early in the twentieth century where it remains on display to the public. (WOOD)*

Piscataqua. On March 1, 1681, the Council ordered a day of fasting and prayer, the origin of the former Fast Day holiday in New Hampshire. But despite their best efforts, President Cutt died a month later and was briefly succeeded by Richard Waldron. Soon after the demise of the Cutt brothers, the Indian threat increased. As historian Jeremy Belknap wrote a century later:

"All the plantations at Piscataqua were filled with fear and confusion. Business was suspended, and every man was obliged to provide for his own and his family's safety. Thus the labor of the field was exchanged for the duty of the garrison, and they who had long lived in peace and security were on their guard night and day, and subject to continual alarms and the most fearful apprehensions."[22]

Their fear was justified. For a brief time, New Hampshire slipped once again under the protection of Massachusetts, but there was nowhere to hide. Indians attacking at Sandy Beach, later Rye, killed twenty-one settlers in 1691. Much of the village of York was wiped out in 1692. Two years later ninety-four citizens of Oyster River were killed in a daylight raid. Ironically, the widow of President John Cutt became Portsmouth's best known victim. She and three workmen were surprised in the hay fields at her home and killed by a small Native raiding party in the summer of 1694. Ursula Cutt had moved to an isolated farm at "The Pulpit," two miles upriver, not far from modern day Atlantic Heights in Portsmouth. Remaining there, despite warnings of Indian activity, Madame Cutt and her workers were shot and scalped, and her hands cut off. Richard Waldron and his wife, who had planned to visit the Cutt farm that very afternoon, dodged a bullet.

ABOVE: *Following the era of Indian reprisals, white New England legends adapted the historic Passaconaway into the more acceptable image of Saint Aspinquid whose pacifism was explained away by his supposed conversion to Christianity. This image comes from a sign at the Saint Aspinquid summer lodgings in Ogunquit, Maine. (JDR)*

Images by

Richard Haynes

PREVIOUS PAGE: *A well-equipped kitchen at Pitt Tavern*

ABOVE: *The arched window at the Captain Keyran Walsh House*

A bed warmer and chair in the Walsh House kitchen

Early redware vessels

Pitt Tavern

Jackson House staircase

The lilac bush beside Wheelwright House

But his time was coming. In June 1696, Richard Waldron himself was brutally murdered; his hands were also cut off, as were his nose and ears during an Indian raid at Dover known as the Cochecho Massacre. Natives destroyed four of the five fortified garrison houses there. The final one still survives. Waldron had deceived the natives in a number of business and political dealings and they took revenge.[23] Within twenty-four hours of the Dover attack, fifty members of a raiding party fell on the residents of a small neighborhood called "The Plains" on the outskirts of Portsmouth. Fourteen men, women, and children were killed before news reached "The Bank" and armed men were dispatched. A fifteenth victim, scalped and left for dead, recovered. The Indians were pursued from The Plains to Breakfast Hill on the border of Greenland and Rye where four colonial captives were rescued. The Natives rowed out around the Isles of Shoals and disappeared.

ABOVE: *Scholars today know much more about the Native American practice of taking captives, many of whom were well-treated and survived. But the deadly raids of King Phillips War remained the focus of local history and fiction for centuries to follow. (JDR)*

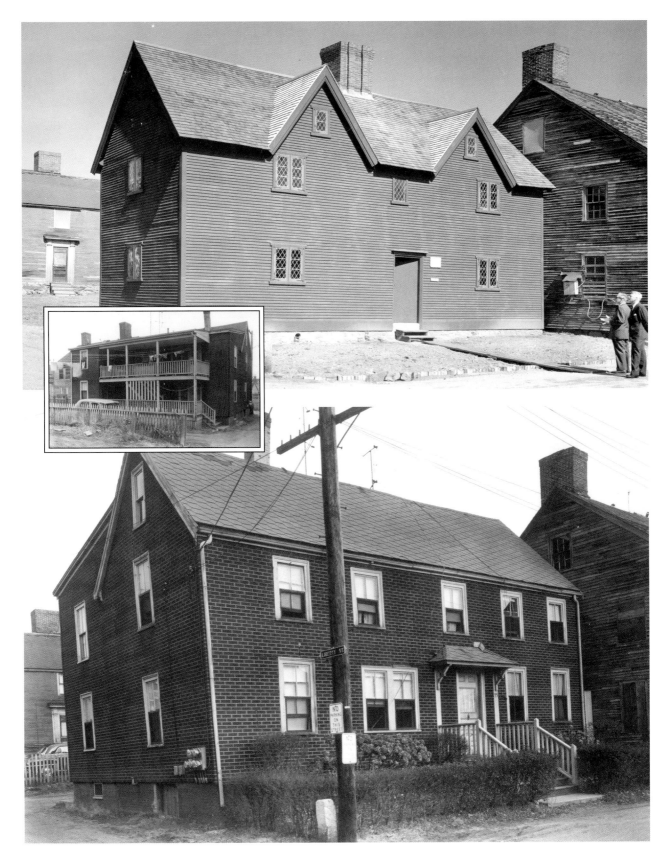

Early Urbanization

The deadly period of Indian reprisals, known today as King Phillips War, dealt the town of Portsmouth only a glancing blow. The waterfront, a growing center of commercial activity in Portsmouth by the end of the seventeenth century, was never attacked, not by the Indians or the French or by pirates. Tucked safely along the Piscataqua, it was held under siege but never raided by the British during the American Revolution and the War of 1812. It remained unmolested by German U-boats in World War II. The changes at Strawberry Bank—from plantation to museum—have all come from within. And here, on the verge of the eighteenth century, change began to accelerate.

By 1665, with the exception of the minister's glebe land, almost everything along the Portsmouth waterfront, from the South Mill to the North Mill, belonged to three men—Captain John Pickering, and Richard and John Cutt. As the population shifted away from New Castle to the mainland, the busiest area shifted to Pickering's Neck. Pickering had allowed the creation of a road through his property and toward the modern center of town, now Pleasant Street, in exchange for a piece of town land. A section of that road, now known as Marcy Street along the waterfront, passed a public burying ground set up by Pickering, today Point of Graves, the city's oldest cemetery. The Cutt brothers left lengthy wills subdividing their massive holdings among a host of relatives, splitting up their plantations like cells in mitosis. These divisions formed today's familiar urban network of roads and neighborhoods. Rye and New Castle and Greenland soon sheared off into separate townships, reducing Portsmouth almost to the 15.2 square miles it occupies today.

New Hampshire is often ignored in American history texts and its historians have long complained that the Granite State got off to a bad start. They blame the usurping Puritans, the King of England, the attacking Natives, and the litigious Masonians for stunting the state's economic growth at a critical point in history. In retrospect these misadventures may have saved Portsmouth from growing into another Boston. Instead of swelling and building, Portsmouth became a compact and closely-knit

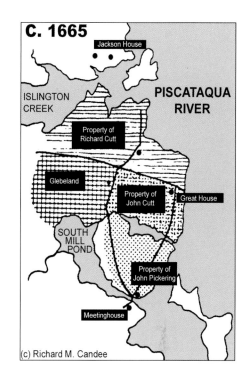

OPPOSITE: *The Sherburne House (c. 1695–1703) is the oldest house at Strawbery Banke Museum. Its exterior restoration from an apartment house (bottom) was a major accomplishment in the first years of the museum. The Drisco House to the right was not fully restored until the 1980s. The inset photo shows the back of the house before restoration. (SBM/DA)*

ABOVE: *By 1665 Portsmouth's waterfront was largely owned by three men—the Cutt brothers Richard and John, both Puritans, and the "Old Planter," John Pickering. A piece of little-used land further west called the "glebe" was assigned to the church. (RMC)*

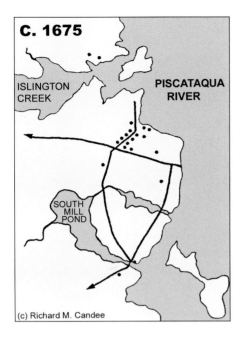

ISLINGTON
CREEK

PISCATAQUA
RIVER

SOUTH
MILL
POND

(c) Richard M. Candee

maritime community ideal for future preservation. Four centuries later, these major divisions are still visible to anyone walking through the city, a city that numbers little more than twenty thousand citizens at the dawn of the twenty-first century. And it is possible to discern the entire outline of American history along the edge of the Piscataqua. New Castle retains the look and feel of an early fishing village. The oldest surviving timber frame house in northern New England stands in Portsmouth just across Fresh Creek at what locals later came to call Christian Shore. Cooper Richard Jackson may have purchased the sawn timber for his 1664 home directly from the Cutt sawmill on the brook at the head of the North Mill Pond nearby. Jackson obtained his parcel in the 1660 Portsmouth land distribution and it remained in the Jackson family until preservationists saved it in 1924 and restored it for public view as the Jackson House beginning in the 1930s.

Many important buildings have been lost to the bulldozers of progress, the ravages of time, and the greed of scavengers. But inside each surviving house a hundred stories live. The 1631 Great House is gone, but its post-medieval descendant survives just inside the gates of Strawbery Banke Museum. The John and Mary Sherburne House at the corner of Puddle and Horse lanes is now the museum's most venerable structure, but in 1695 this timber frame house was among the new kids on the block as Portsmouth's South End neighborhood began to form on the acreage of John Mason's original plantation. John Sherburne's father Henry had been among the original stewards. John's mother Rebecca was the only daughter of founder Ambrose Gibbons, who successfully ran Mason's Indian trading post at Newichawannock. Abandoned into the frightening Piscataqua wilderness, Henry and Rebecca Sherburne thrived. They had eleven children including John. Over the next century Sherburnes would marry into the powerful Langdon, Wentworth, Penhallow, Jaffrey, Lear, Gilman, Atkinson, Brewster, Cutt, and Wendell families. Sherburnes would sail the world, attend Harvard, run a tavern, build mansions, fight in the Revolution, sit in the most prestigious pews, and lie in the most prestigious vaults at Queen's Chapel.

The next century transformed a failed river-mouth plantation into a wealthy British, then American social capital. And when it was all over, Portsmouth would forever mourn its halcyon days. That mourning, expressed as nostalgia, sparked the preservation movement that has kept the Sherburne, Jackson, and many more ancient homes standing. Eventually, when the great fishing and timber industries faded, Portsmouth turned to selling something new—its past.

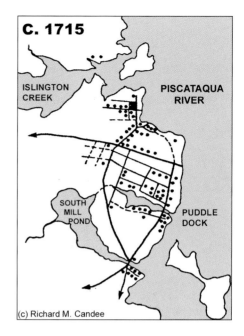

ABOVE AND OPPOSITE: *At first homes sprung up along Christian Shore and modern Market Street, but after the death of both Cutt brothers, two population areas evolved in the subdivided property north and south. Residents in the Puddle Dock area, eventually Strawbery Banke Museum, clustered around The Cove and the evolving wharves and warehouses. The glebe land that would eventually become downtown Portsmouth was just beginning to develop by 1715 on land leased to support the minister's salary. (RMC)*

ON THE WATERFRONT
THE 1700*s*

Oe word sums up eighteenth-century history in New Hampshire prior to the American Revolution— Wentworth. Three royal governors, all named Wentworth and all living in Portsmouth, dominated the political scene and shaped the state's social and economic development. Fifty years after the Wentworths crashed and burned, so did Portsmouth's waterfront settlement.

The rise of Portsmouth's small maritime empire changed the face of Old Strawberry Bank. As ship traffic increased, property along Water Street became too valuable for farming. Hundreds of sailing ships docked at long wharves that seemed to reach halfway across the Piscataqua. A tight network of prosperous merchants, linked by well-planned marriages, lived side-by-side with a growing population of skilled artisans who catered to the needs of the wealthy. The plantation of the Great House, first subdivided in the will of John Cutt, now divided again, and again. Each generation jostled for the best position near the busy docks within a small footprint of land.

By 1700 the shape of things to come in Portsmouth was already discernable in the outline of its early streets, paths, and rights-of-way. The center of town would eventually move inward toward the ancient glebe land, but for now the population clustered along the river. Farmers migrated further inland too, filling the lands cleared of trees as the lumbermen drove deeper into

OPPOSITE: *A crowd in Portsmouth's Parade (now Market Square) listen to the Declaration of Independence read from the balcony of the Old Statehouse. This artist concept is from a 1925 calendar. (RMC)*

the dangerous frontier. With barely eighteen miles of coastline, New Hampshire had no choice but to push westward, driven by its expanding population and the control of the Portsmouth ruling class under the Wentworths. Benning and his nephew John Wentworth eventually founded two hundred townships in New Hampshire and Vermont before the American Revolution swept the last British governor out of the neighborhood, and out of the nation.

For Portsmouth, the Revolutionary War was an economic opportunity. Although New Hampshire was at war with its best customer, shipbuilding was on the rise and locals profited from privateering, the legal looting of enemy ships. A decade after the war ended, business again boomed. By the time President George Washington visited in 1789, Portsmouth was at its peak. The original Strawberry Bank neighborhood was at the very heart of the city's greatest commercial success. This was the golden era that, although it faded quickly, still resonates in Portsmouth history and shapes the way the city defines itself even today. The boom also created a new middle class with a hunger for material goods that has come to define the American way of life.

Like Father, Like Son

In 1717 the first of three British kings named George appointed the first of three New Hampshire governors named Wentworth. More than three decades had passed since the brief rule of John Cutt from Strawberry Bank. Ten more of these "lieutenant" governors had come and gone, each overseeing the king's desire to populate and profit from the northern colonies and each seeking to grow wealthy in the process. Portsmouth-based lieutenant governors worked largely under the thumb of the governor of Massachusetts who technically reigned over the New Hampshire colony as well. John Wentworth's appointment, also largely ceremonial at first, focused the center of power in New Hampshire back at "The Bank." His own sturdy mansion was built there between 1695 and 1701 just over "The Cove," no more than a city block from where the Great House had recently fallen.

ABOVE: This image of Lt. Gov. John Wentworth was presented to the New Hampshire State House in 1874 and is a copy of another portrait. Whether it actually depicts John Wentworth or is an imagined portrait is not known. (NHDHR)

Long before John Wentworth's appointment as lieutenant governor of New Hampshire, this mansion proclaimed the importance of its owner. Likely the most significant structure in the growing neighborhood, the large, comfortable home was built with massive timbers of 12 by 18 inches, set around a central chimney that measured 13 by 10 feet at its base. The house was later decorated with the finest architectural details, including wainscot panels made from boards 35 inches wide. The Wentworth House demonstrated the union of two rising merchant families when John Wentworth married Sara Hunking, whose father purchased the extensive parcel of land from John Pickering during the first great subdivision of waterfront properties. After two years as a successful sea captain, John settled into the "wedding gift" home and the comfortable life of a merchant in the mast trade. Sara bore fourteen children here including Benning Wentworth, a future New Hampshire governor.

Sadly, the original Wentworth House is gone. So is the family wharf at The Cove, and the tidal inlet itself was filled in a

ABOVE: *This stately Puddle Dock home belonged to Lt. Gov. John Wentworth, founder of the family dynasty, and was the birthplace of Benning Wentworth. The building was demolished in 1926 (see Chapter 6) and portions sold to the Winterthur Museum. The site is currently a parking lot at Strawbery Banke Museum. (SBM)*

Captain Archibald Macpheadris built this house beginning in 1716 for his bride-to-be Sarah Wentworth, daughter of New Hampshire's Lt. Governor John Wentworth. Today the Warner House is the earliest extant urban brick mansion in New England. Engraving by Stow Wengenroth, 1961. (SBM)

century ago. Its loss, combined with the radically changed environment and the absence of wooden sailing ships and wharves, makes it all but impossible for modern-day visitors at Strawbery Banke Museum to connect this soothing, manicured waterfront with its busy commercial past. But unlike the mysterious Great House, ghostly remnants of the Wentworth mansion survive. Historians know how John Wentworth's house was built because it stood into the twentieth century when, in 1926, it was taken apart timber by timber and photographed. A local antique dealer scavenged the framing members and interior paneling and sold the pieces to the Metropolitan Museum of Art in New York, where the north second-floor chamber and two staircases were placed on display in the American Wing.[1] Other pieces were combined into a single room as a setting for American antiques at the Winterthur Museum in Delaware.[2] Portsmouth visitors to Strawbery Banke Museum, however, see only a parking lot where the governor's home once stood.

An even more stunning urban mansion from this era with Wentworth connections survives just up the hill to the north and is best known today as the Warner House. Its original owner, Captain Archibald Macpheadris, wisely chose, despite available timber, to build his house of brick. It is likely that Macpheadris admired the work of joiner John Drew while passing through Boston. Recently trained in London, Drew brought his sophisticated skills to Portsmouth where he settled and built a number of houses after finishing the opulent mansion for Macpheadris on the corner of Chapel and Daniel streets, just up from The Bank.[3] The Captain also admired Governor John Wentworth's daughter Sarah whom he married when she was just fifteen. Macpheadris cemented his connection to the ruling family by going into business with Sarah's older brother, Benning Wentworth, and serving on the Governor's Council. Benning later rented the house, known for its detailed woodwork and painted murals, before moving into his own larger estate two miles away.[4]

Lieutenant Governor John Wentworth was more politically astute than his forebears in managing the development of New Hampshire. When Massachusetts found itself without a governor from 1722 to 1728, Wentworth took the opportunity to strengthen his hold on his home province. He also learned to walk the delicate line between royal and colonial interests, making himself rich by keeping both sides satisfied. The Wentworths had a pedigree and were Royalists at heart, but they also kept deep connections to New England. To the colonists, Wentworth was a local boy. His grandfather, Elder William Wentworth, had arrived in Exeter in 1633 and his father Samuel received a license to brew and sell beer in Portsmouth in 1671. As a boy, John Wentworth may have cut his teeth on local politics while working in his father's busy tavern at Strawberry Bank where meetings of the Governor's Council may have been held.[5]

Wentworth continued to supply the king's navy with sturdy New Hampshire masts. He complained about his indirect access to the Crown while working to improve conditions for his colonial constituents. Colonists who felled a New Hampshire white pine that measured two feet in diameter or more could be fined up to £100. The king was taking all the best trees for himself, and this regulation, Wentworth said in 1717, "for want of a fair

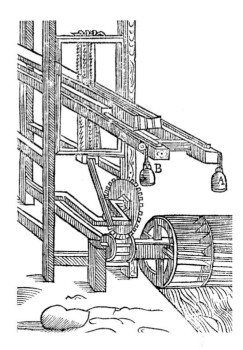

ABOVE: *The Piscataqua River tidal basin thrived as more and more sawmills appeared and settlers moved westward to clear forest lands. (RMC)*

representation to his Majestie is very hurtful and ruinous to many of his good subjects."[6] The White Pine Act of 1722 confirmed that every tree of appropriate size not located within a township was royal property. Each was marked with the three notches of an axe in the "broad arrow" insignia. Colonists responded angrily, sometimes with lawsuits, sometimes with violence. Wentworth's increasingly powerful merchant oligarchy even created "paper townships" that put the valuable timbers back on colonial turf. The resentment over royal control of the forests, historians have suggested, helped draw northerners into the approaching revolution.[7]

Although Lieutenant Governor John Wentworth died in office in 1730, his extended term inspired the formula that his son Benning later perfected—please the king, open new towns, hire your relatives, and grab what you can. Despite his inherited wealth, Benning was in imminent financial disaster when he was appointed Royal Governor to New Hampshire in 1741. A 1715 graduate of Harvard College,[8] Benning had followed his father into the timber trade. Like other Portsmouth merchants, despite strict Navigation Acts to the contrary, he even traded illegally with Spanish clients. When the British Parliament declared war on Spain, Benning stood at the edge of a bankruptcy that threatened to take his English merchant investors down with him. To keep Benning afloat, his influential friends helped him become New Hampshire's governor and the Surveyor of the King's Woods in North America, a lucrative post. The fox was now in charge of the hen house.

His eventual downfall was the result of taking the Wentworth formula to extremes. Over twenty-five years, Benning Wentworth expanded his influence and territory in proportion to his girth. His regal weight, along with other symbols of wealth and influence, are openly displayed in his only known portrait, painted at the peak of his power in 1760. By then he had the biggest house—a forty-five-room mansion at Little Harbor—and the youngest wife. He also had the most cronies on the payroll, with twelve out of thirteen advisors on the Governor's Council hailing from the Portsmouth area. Most were his relatives or had been appointed in exchange for business favors.

This is the Benning Wentworth best known to Portsmouth history—gouty, lecherous, haughty, ruthless to his enemies, pandering to the king, and gracious to his allies. It is an image seen through post-Revolutionary glasses in which all things English became all things Tory. Benning Wentworth has become, in retrospect, the New Hampshire version of the tyrannical George III.[9] His marriage in his sixties to Martha Hilton, a working-class woman forty years his junior, only makes the scandal more delicious. History forgets, however, that Wentworth was still very much an agent of the king. History also forgets that, with the death of his first wife and three children, the governor was a lonely man. His new wife, who survived to entertain President George Washington in the governor's mansion, had not been of high birth, but like her husband, she too was born into Portsmouth's waterfront neighborhood.[10]

Following his father's formula, Benning Wentworth served longer at his post than any other governor in colonial history and wielded more direct rule over his New Hampshire subjects than the king himself.[11] Pushed by Royal instructions and backed by his political machine, Wentworth transformed New Hampshire, driving new towns into the wilderness as far as modern Bennington, Vermont. When his own citizens broke the mast laws, felling and milling trees illegally, the official protector of the king's forest in North America winked and looked the other way. His own brother, Mark Hunking Wentworth, used his influence

ABOVE: *President George Washington, local reports say, went out of his way to visit Benning Wentworth's mansion and former wife during his tour of Portsmouth in 1789. (ATH)*

in the timber trade to become the richest man in the state. It was Mark Hunking's son John, another popular Portsmouth boy, who took over the governor's office in 1767 as the Revolution loomed.

A Tale of Two Taverns

The most dramatic depiction of eighteenth-century Portsmouth was filmed on a Hollywood sound stage in 1940. The movie version of Kenneth Roberts' novel *Northwest Passage* opens on the waterfront to a lush orchestral soundtrack. The year is 1757 and young Langdon Towne (played by Robert Young, best known as television's Marcus Welby, MD) has returned home after being expelled from Harvard. Towne finds his old drinking buddy Hunk Mariner (actor Walter Brennan of *The Real McCoys*) in the town pillory accused of "disloyal conversation" against a local king's official.[12] The two fictional characters retire to Stoodley's Tavern where they get into so much trouble that they are forced to flee the city. The real action starts when they bump into renowned "Indian fighter" Robert Rogers (played by Spencer Tracy) who abducts the Portsmouth pair into Rogers Rangers, a disciplined colonial militia on the march to Quebec.

Kenneth Roberts' novel and film depict Portsmouth as a refined social capital in colonial New England, the ideal jumping-off point for a tale about the harsh American wilderness.

ABOVE LEFT: *Despite his fame as an "Indian fighter" on the colonial frontier with his well-drilled Rangers, Robert Rogers was later branded a Tory and died in obscurity in England in 1795. (JDR)*

ABOVE CENTER: *Arthur Browne of Queen's Chapel in Portsmouth. (JDR)*

ABOVE RIGHT: *Rogers married Elizabeth Browne, daughter of the influential Rev. Arthur Browne of Queen's Chapel. She was 20. He was 29. In 1778, Elizabeth petitioned the New Hampshire General Assembly for a divorce on the grounds of desertion and infidelity. (JDR)*

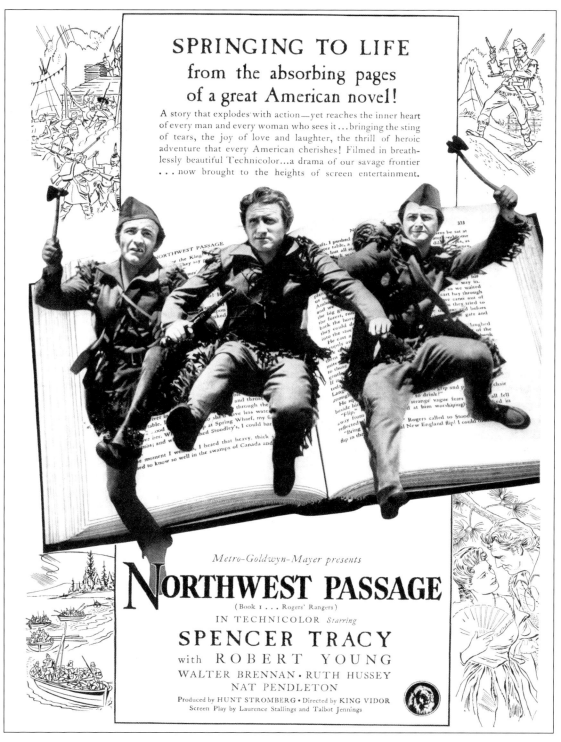

SPRINGING TO LIFE
from the absorbing pages
of a great American novel!

A story that explodes with action—yet reaches the inner heart of every man and every woman who sees it...bringing the sting of tears, the joy of love and laughter, the thrill of heroic adventure that every American cherishes! Filmed in breathlessly beautiful Technicolor...a drama of our savage frontier ...now brought to the heights of screen entertainment.

Metro-Goldwyn-Mayer presents

NORTHWEST PASSAGE

(Book 1 . . . Rogers' Rangers)

IN TECHNICOLOR *Starring*

SPENCER TRACY

with ROBERT YOUNG

WALTER BRENNAN · RUTH HUSSEY
NAT PENDLETON

Produced by HUNT STROMBERG · Directed by KING VIDOR
Screen Play by Laurence Stallings and Talbot Jennings

ABOVE: *The film version of* Northwest Passage *played as a patriotic call to arms for the military when it was released in 1940 just prior to the nation's entry into World War II. In Portsmouth, home of Stoodley's Tavern across the river from the Portsmouth Naval Shipyard, the film had special resonance. This Columbia Pictures promotion appeared in* Time *magazine. (JDR)*

A stickler for historical accuracy, the author knew that tavern-owner James Stoodley had actually served with Major Robert Rogers in the French and Indian War.[13] Rogers himself married a Portsmouth girl, the daughter of Reverend Arthur Browne of the prestigious Queen's Chapel. Reverend Browne, a key figure in the town's aristocratic Anglican Church, also presided over the nuptials of both governors Benning and John Wentworth.

Stoodley's Tavern, moved to Strawbery Banke Museum in 1965 from nearby Daniel Street, is the perfect vantage point from which to observe Portsmouth's reluctant transition from a colonial seaport into an American town. The change did not happen overnight as history texts often imply. New Hampshire men, for the most part, were happy to remain English citizens as long as they were treated with respect. The characters in *Northwest Passage* were fighting for England, not for the as-yet-unimagined United States.

James Stoodley eventually sided with the Patriot cause. By 1770 citizens unhappy with British rule were holding secret meetings at his tavern. In December 1774 Paul Revere galloped into Portsmouth to warn these same revolutionaries that the British were coming by sea to lock up the gunpowder and arms at nearby Fort William and Mary at New Castle. In blatant defiance of the king, at least four hundred locals raided the fort the next day, carrying off the guns and powder, and spiking the cannons. Unlike his friend Stoodley, Major Rogers cast his lot with King George, was imprisoned as a traitor, turned to alcohol, and died in obscurity in England. James Stoodley's son-in-law Elijah Hall eventually took over the tavern and, in a final irony, served with John Paul Jones aboard the warship *Ranger*, built in Portsmouth Harbor and named in honor of Rogers Rangers.

Another Portsmouth tavern, The Earl of Halifax owned by John Stavers, was built at what is now Strawbery Banke Museum in 1766 and is fully restored today. Stavers survived the Revolution by adapting to the radically shifting times. Born in England, Stavers was considered a loyalist by many. After the signing of the Declaration of Independence a local

ABOVE: *New Hampshire's first free colonial seal from 1775 shows the symbolic importance of the fishing and timber industries, and the traditional quiver of Indian arrows, often given by early colonists to show fealty to the king of England. (JDR)*

mob assembled outside the tavern. Stavers sent his servant James, an enslaved African, to drive off the mob. When one man tried chopping down the Earl of Halifax sign, James struck the man a "bad blow" in the head with an ax. Stavers was arrested and later released. James, according to oral tradition, was so frightened of reprisals that he went into hiding for days and was discovered up to his neck in water in a barrel in the tavern basement. John Stavers was released, but remained among "Persons of suspicious Character," even after he changed the name of his business to the William Pitt Tavern in honor of a pro-American member of the British Parliament. The tavern later catered to such famous American patriots as George Washington, Marquis de Lafayette, John Hancock, William Whipple, and General Henry Knox.[14]

Active public houses like those run by Stoodley and Stavers reflect, not only the shifting politics of the times, but eighteenth-century attitudes and customs as well. Taverns and churches were the gathering points for all classes of society—white, male, English society at least. Male groups from the Governor's Council to the secret Sons of Liberty and the Committees of Safety met in taverns. The nation's longest surviving Masonic Lodge was begun in Portsmouth and Masons later met on the third story of Stavers's tavern. Those same rooms were used for the exhibition of traveling shows, from legitimate plays and readings to the display of an African lion and an albino man. Slaves, male and female, were stripped, examined and sold at auction in these rooms.

Both Stoodley and Stavers kept slaves, a common practice in colonial New England, especially in wealthy seaport communities where African workers were considered a status symbol. By the start of the Revolution there were 656 enslaved residents in Portsmouth, more than ten percent of the population and ten times the number listed in 1708.[15] Historian Valerie Cunningham, creator of the Portsmouth Black Heritage Trail, has spent decades tracking and identifying the "invisible" members of the Stoodley, Stavers, and other Portsmouth households.

ABOVE: *After the signing of the state constitution became effective in 1784, the New Hampshire seal was changed to show a rising sun and a ship being built on the ways along the Piscataqua River. Although frequently updated, the current state emblem still reflects that post-Revolutionary change and notes the early focus on the Portsmouth region. (JDR)*

Enslaved worker James Stavers, she points out, was "caught in the cross fire" between white patriots and loyalists in the American Revolution. James was neither arrested nor tried in court for striking a white man with an ax. The legal controversy, later resolved, was between two white men "in these times of Jealousy & danger." As a Black man in the middle of the American Revolution, James simply had no voice at all.[16]

Goodbye Governor John

The New Hampshire version of the American Revolution, a story rarely heard outside the Granite State, differs markedly from the one told in nearby Massachusetts, largely because people in Portsmouth did not hate their royal governor. John Wentworth was young, handsome, intelligent, outdoorsy, and had the common touch. Unlike his uncle Benning, who after repeated attempts to turn the Macpheadris mansion (today's Warner House) into a gubernatorial headquarters, elected to isolate himself in a huge mansion two miles from town, John settled into a moderate-sized home on what is now Pleasant Street, halfway between the South End and the modern downtown area. Wentworth had attended Harvard in the same class as John Adams, who later became the second President of the United States. Wentworth then spent five years in England before returning to take over for his failing uncle.

ABOVE RIGHT: *Stoodley's Tavern was moved from Daniel Street to Strawbery Banke in 1965 to make way for a new federal building there. Attempts to reopen the building as a working tavern failed and it was adapted into an educational center 30 years after the move.* (SBM/DA)

Raised in New Hampshire, Wentworth was as staunchly opposed to the incendiary new British taxes as were the colonists themselves. Rather than simply protest, Wentworth worked at the problem from inside the government, using every drop of influence he had with his English supporters like Lord Rockingham and Lord Hillsborough to block, alter, or repeal the hated taxes that the governor knew were stirring his subjects toward rebellion. He worked overtime to keep down the local response to events like the Boston Massacre and the Boston Tea Party. Wentworth blamed Boston agitators for instigating unrest in his province. During his administration in 1771, Portsmouth voted to set up a house of correction "in which all idle and disorderly persons in the town should be confined to hard labor, agreeable to law."[17]

But all was not quiet in Portsmouth. That same year about fifty armed and disguised men suddenly appeared aboard the brig *Resolution* on the Portsmouth waterfront. Port collector George Meserve had seized the cargo belonging to Portsmouth merchant Samuel Cutt, suspecting that not all its cargo of molasses had

ABOVE: *Pitt Tavern, formerly The Earl of Halifax, was a key meeting place during the Revolution. Owner John Stavers ran his Flying Stagecoach to Boston from here. The building had long been adapted to residential use and was in disrepair when it became part of Strawbery Banke Inc. Photo from the Historic American Building Survey of 1961. (SBM)*

been accurately reported. Fearing trouble, Governor Wentworth had sent four guards from Fort William and Mary to secure the ship, but they were easily overwhelmed by members of what might be called the "Portsmouth Molasses Party." Anonymous men bore away forty or fifty hogsheads of molasses and returned the next day for more. A month later during an investigation into the incident, a witness for the admiralty was harassed by up to five hundred local citizens. The instant Wentworth heard of the mob action, he hopped into his coach and rode "unmolested" through the hostile gathering four times in a brave attempt to quell the angry crowd.[18]

"I never saw such an exasperated spirit in this Province," the governor wrote to the Earl of Hillsborough that year, yet he continued to stay the course.[19] During his administration Wentworth managed to expand and improve New Hampshire highways, founded Dartmouth College, and divided the state into counties. To further draw attention westward, Wentworth built a massive and elegant summer home on four thousand acres of woodland near modern Wolfeboro on what is now Lake Wentworth. The hip-roofed Georgian mansion measured over 100 by 40 feet. But Wentworth's expansionist dream faded quickly.

No royal governor, no matter how popular, could have survived the tsunami of anti-British emotion that washed over the Atlantic colonies. And John Wentworth was no saint. Like his Uncle Benning, he chose a controversial bride, inciting public scandal. Frances Deering Wentworth Atkinson married John Wentworth at Queen's Chapel just ten days after her first husband, Theodore Atkinson Jr., was buried there. Seven months later the church recorded the baptism of their son John Wentworth, who died soon after. The governor explained away the incident as a premature birth. Writing to the Earl of Rockingham he said that his parents had pushed for a hasty wedding, as had his Uncle Benning and even Colonel Theodore Atkinson, father of Frances's deceased husband. Perhaps explaining a little too hard, Wentworth appears to have suggested to his patron that his new wife suffered a miscarriage, "Sustain'd from Mrs. Wentworth's being frightened by the attack of a large dog."[20]

Frances was also Wentworth's cousin, making Colonel Atkinson now both his uncle and wife's former father-in-law, a fact not missed by Wentworth's detractors. Atkinson, who became Secretary of the Province, was a powerful merchant descended from the early Strawberry Bank settlers and his mansion, now lost, stood just across the street from the William Pitt Tavern. In 1773 the British press lampooned John Wentworth's nepotism by pointing out not only his close relationship to Atkinson through marriage to "Lady Wentworth," but also that Atkinson was New Hampshire's chief justice, president, and secretary of the Governor's Council and colonel of the militia.[21] But in Portsmouth, this was politics as usual for the Wentworth dynasty and no cause for alarm.

John Wentworth's fatal slip came in 1774 when he offered to assist his Massachusetts colleague Governor Thomas Hutchinson, also a native New Englander but a fierce loyalist. Wentworth hired a group of Wolfeboro carpenters to build housing to quarter British soldiers unwelcome in Boston. The *New Hampshire Gazette* got wind of the real purpose and published the story, damaging his public opinion. After locals stormed the nearby fort later that year, the handwriting was on the wall. When a mob threatened the governor at his own home the following year, he retreated to the relative safety of Fort William and Mary, where he spent his thirty-eighth birthday in April of 1775. The Wentworths sailed in the *HMS Scarborough* early that fall and spent the next five years in exile, always assuming they would return to Portsmouth after the war. Totally opposed to using arms against American colonists, Wentworth found himself an official enemy of the people, subject to execution if he ever again set foot on New Hampshire soil.

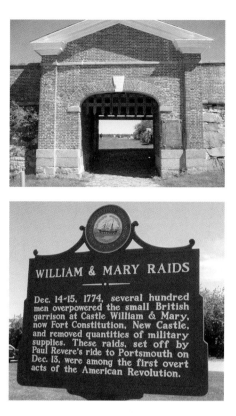

ABOVE: *Fort William and Mary as it looks today and a New Hampshire state historic marker proclaiming that the 1774 raids were among "the first overt acts of the American Revolution." Dorothy Vaughan, later president of Strawbery Banke, was among the state historians who wrote and designated these markers. (JDR)*

An American Seaport

The Revolution itself, like all American wars since, was something Portsmouth citizens read about in newspapers. In the first history of the city published in 1825, author Nathaniel Adams spent as much time recounting the impact of the weather and disease as the famous battles. He recalled deadly bouts of smallpox during the war, a flood that carried away Boyd's wharf, and a day in 1780 so darkened by ashes from a distant forest fire that the sun never appeared.[22]

It was the weather, in fact, that possibly saved Portsmouth from a very different history. In October 1775, British warships bombed and burned three-quarters of the defenseless town of Falmouth, now Portland, Maine. Expecting equal treatment, Portsmouth residents were panicked, but a sudden four-day storm prevented British ships from making the trip to New Hampshire's only seaport. General George Washington sent Brigadier General John Sullivan to beef up defenses in Portsmouth Harbor, but the attack never materialized. For security reasons the colonial capital of New Hampshire was temporarily moved inland to Exeter and later to Concord, forever reducing the city's political status. Curiously, according to *Adams' Annals of Portsmouth*, the town had avoided a similar fate three decades earlier. After the New England militia seized the French fort at Louisbourg at Nova Scotia in 1745, Piscataqua citizens were kept in "a state of fearful expectation for six weeks" when they learned that a large French fleet was coming to molest the city in revenge the following year. Colonel Theodore Atkinson, future father-in-law of John Wentworth, was then in charge of the local militia, which was no match for the approaching fleet. Suddenly a ferocious storm appeared, breaking up the fleet, sinking ships, and forcing the French to return home.

Adams makes no mention of the now-trumpeted Revolutionary War visits by Paul Revere, John Paul Jones, or Benjamin Franklin. Those tales grew out of the coming Colonial Revival in which locals struggled to weave Portsmouth into the fabric of popular American history. Nor does he refer to Portsmouth South Ender Tobias Lear who was President George Washington's

ABOVE: *Born in Portsmouth, Tobias Lear V was the son of a ship builder who worked on the ship* Ranger *for John Paul Jones and who is buried at Point of Graves. Lear served Washington off and on for sixteen years and was at his bedside when the first President died at Mount Vernon in 1799. Washington crossed through Puddle Dock to visit Lear's mother, Mary Storer, in the South End of the city during his 1789 visit. Lear was later the US consul to Algeria during the reign of the Barbary pirates. He committed suicide in 1816. His birthplace is an historic house museum in Portsmouth's South End. (JDR)*

secretary, accountant to his Mount Vernon farm, and tutor to his adopted children. Instead Adams prefers to describe the town celebration at the end of the war in 1783 when the statehouse was elaborately illuminated against a display of fireworks. His description of the 1788 parade following the ratification of the United States Constitution is among the most detailed passages in his book.[23]

Reading between the lines of Adams' chronicle it is possible to map the important areas of the expanding seaport. The city's first public executions, for example, were held far from the centers of population. Sarah Simpson and Penelope Kenny were hanged for infanticide in 1739 after the body of a newborn baby girl was found floating in a well. Both women confessed to separate crimes, but both said the baby in the well was not theirs. The scaffold was erected about a mile from the waterfront at what is now the South Cemetery. When Ruth Blay was executed for a similar crime almost three decades later, the gallows were in the same area of town. Portsmouth's prison and almshouse were set up closer to the evolving center of town, but located far back. A segregated "Negro Burying Ground" was also established early in the century in what was likely a potter's field at the outer edge of the glebe. Out of use by the end of the eighteenth century, the African cemetery disappeared as the town center was developed, and was rediscovered under Chestnut Street during a construction project in 2003.

The fact that Stavers Flying Stagecoach, the first regular direct service from Portsmouth to Boston, picked up and dropped off its passengers at the William Pitt Tavern beginning in 1761 indicates that "The Bank" was still an important destination point at this time. When Daniel Fowle set up the state's first newspaper office in 1756, he chose an office for the *New Hampshire Gazette* that was situated halfway between the waterfront and the evolving downtown.

The Constitution Parade of 1788 demonstrates that Portsmouth was beginning to see itself as a town made up of a number of important sections and inhabited by many types of people. Hundreds of proud workers marched in a procession organized by trade, from butchers, clock makers, and stevedores to ship captains, judges, and physicians. The festivities began with

ABOVE: *Tobias Lear's first wife Polly was his Portsmouth sweetheart. Polly became a close friend of Martha Washington when the two shared residence in Philadelphia. Polly died of yellow fever and, in a very rare exception to policy, George Washington reportedly attended the funeral. Lear's second wife Frances Bassett (seen here) was a widow and a niece of the Washingtons. When "Fanny" died soon after their marriage in 1796, Lear married another Washington niece also nicknamed "Fanny," who survived him. (TLWGA)*

ABOVE: *This image comes from the first American naval recruitment poster created by John Paul Jones to attract seaman to his voyage to Europe aboard the ship* Ranger *in 1777.* Ranger *was named for Rogers' Rangers. Jones returned to Portsmouth in 1782 and stayed a year while waiting for a second ship, also built by John Langdon who was among the first leaders of the new state of New Hampshire.*
(JDR)

simultaneous ceremonies at "all the churches," meaning the old South Meetinghouse, at North Church in the glebe area to the west, and at St. John's (formerly Queen's Chapel) on the hill north of the once dominant Strawberry Bank waterfront.

The march began, appropriately, at "The Parade" where the statehouse and North Church were located, then wound through the major areas of town. The waterfront, site of the Great House, had by now become the hub of commercial activity in the town and the area of largest population. It was still important enough to attract wealthy merchant Stephen Chase in 1779, but increasingly seen as the city's elder neighborhood. When Portsmouth citizens protested the Stamp Act in 1766, they headed instinctively to the waterfront and "Liberty Bridge" over The Cove at Strawberry Bank. When President Washington arrived in 1789, he did not come by boat, but marched up Congress Street (formerly King Street) to the statehouse in the central Parade. Washington visited with New Hampshire "President" John Langdon, who had built his mansion nearer to the evolving city center. Later during his four-day visit, Washington found his way to the waterfront, stopping at the home of businessman Stephen Chase, where he may have kissed the three Chase girls,[24] and on to the William Pitt Tavern nearby. Washington likely walked by or through what is now Strawbery Banke Museum to the South End. There he visited the mother of his secretary Tobias Lear, a nephew of John Langdon. The first President found his way to a boat on the waterfront and scouted the Kittery island that soon became the site of the nation's first federal navy yard. As if to close an open loop in Portsmouth history, Washington then paid a call to Martha Wentworth, former wife of Royal Governor Benning Wentworth, legend says, at her mansion at Little Harbor.[25]

Following the war the waterfront was busier than ever. From the rise of Sampson Sheafe's two-story overhanging warehouse in 1705 to the end of the eighteenth century, the evolution continued. Once divided into "The Bank" and "The Mill Dam," the waterfront had now grown into three distinct areas. The South End below The Cove became more residential. The Bank in the center grew longer wharves to accommodate the burst in international trade, while the North End became the town marketplace and an area for shipbuilding. Of roughly equal size, the three "neighborhoods" were designated as key locations for tax purposes by 1727. Each had a wide main road leading to the river, but evolved its own network of criss-crossing smaller roads. The minister's central glebe land, by contrast, was neatly divided in a grid pattern yielding fifty-one equally-sized lots. The result of Portsmouth's largely organic development is a unique and often confusing array of streets that charm pedestrians and frustrate motorists to this day.[26]

Many of the buildings surviving at Strawbery Banke Museum were built during the eighteenth century. Their evolving designs show what was happening architecturally across New England as Georgian construction made way for Federal designs, creating the generic "Colonial" style that future generations would long to return to. They were the homes of wealthy merchants as well as the specialists who lived around them. Portsmouth was home to ropemakers, sailmakers, blockmakers, blacksmiths, shipwrights, carpenters, silversmiths, furniture makers, muralists, portrait painters, and a separate society of slaves, freed Blacks, and servants.[27] By the end of the century a much wider range of occupations had evolved, and with them, a rising number of poor, unemployed, and dependent citizens.

Sandwiched between the very rich and the very poor, a new "middle" class was evolving. Wealth was no longer reserved for an elite lineage. In America, hardworking and resourceful citizens could earn their way to a comfortable living. By purchasing the right material goods—clothes, homes, carriages, furniture—and by affecting the appropriate manners, this middle group emulated their "betters" until they were virtually indistinguishable. The items they owned, this "material culture," would provide the focus of future collectors of decorative arts, scholars, and preservationists. As older fortunes failed and new fortunes were made, owning the "right stuff" became a defining characteristic in the new American class system, a system that was particularly important to the people of Portsmouth. Visitors in the eighteenth century often remarked on the highly evolved social systems here. Whether this was a town of sophisticates living in the boondocks or rural folk putting on airs depends on the mindset of the viewer. According to one observer, Portsmouth residents were notable

TOP: *Royal Governor John Wentworth was born in Portsmouth, and educated at Harvard with classmate John Adams. A victim of the times, he was driven out of New Hampshire and served as a royal governor to Nova Scotia with mixed success. (NHDHR)*

BOTTOM: *Lady Frances Wentworth Atkinson Wentworth was cousin and wife to John Wentworth. Her life was fictionalized in the historical novel* The Governor's Lady *by Canadian author Thomas Raddall. The novelist contacted Portsmouth librarian Dorothy Vaughan during his research. (JDR)*

"for their politeness in dress and behavior" and "have been thought to go beyond most others in equal circumstances, if not to exceed themselves, in their sumptuous and elegant living and things of like nature."[28]

The desire, as well as the possibility, of becoming one of society's elite led to the formation of a whole new class of consumers beginning at this time period. These consumers created a soaring demand for porcelain, silver, furniture, and other goods. Individual achievement, as evidenced by the ability to "buy stuff," eventually transcended blood relations to family dynasties like the Wentworths as the means to class stratification.[29]

Visitors after the Revolution were often less impressed. Portsmouth was smaller and less grand than ports at Salem and Newburyport. Critics sometimes wondered how the little port, with its drab stocky buildings and forlorn citizens, had gained such a notable reputation. By 1842 in Portsmouth, this consuming culture became a point of satire for a visitor to the home of Mrs. Cutt:

> She is one of those ladies who delight in displaying their own eccentricities and tastes and treasures to all who may have the honor of ten seconds acquaintance with her. She had us all over her house before we had been ten minutes in it, showing us old chairs, and china sets, and couches, pictures, and rooms, with complete history of their character as she called it.[30]

"New Hampshire is still in its infancy," one visitor commented in 1784, "and its capital Portsmouth is but a small insignificant place, not near so considerable as many of the towns in the other provinces which have not been thought sufficiently deserving of notice to be named here."[31]

As other cities expanded and modernized, Portsmouth seemed to fade in comparison, in the same way that the waterfront declined as the rest of the city grew. Having long considered

ABOVE: *He might have been hanged for treason for his role in the raid on a British armory, but John Langdon became instead, a wealthy shipbuilder, New Hampshire governor and a delegate to the Constitutional Convention.*
(JDR)

itself important, Portsmouth developed a sort of collective inferiority complex that often expressed itself as a zealous territorial pride. That pride, along with a salty combination of jealousy and entitlement, helped fuel the historic preservation movement in the twentieth century.

But to the Portsmouth residents at the close of the eighteenth century, this impending decline was in no way evident. On the crisp clear afternoon of February 18, 1796, a strange object hovered above the town. French aeronaut Jean-Pierre Blanchard's twenty-three-foot balloon made of silk taffeta was the shape of things to come. Three thousand spectators, more than half of the town's 5,339 residents, watched as the colorful balloon rose over the Assembly House on Vaughan Street. From this great height, passengers in a wicker basket could see a sophisticated modern seaport on the rise, with new bridges, wharves, and warehouses. Portsmouth had its own bank, two fire pumps, and a theater, and was building a fresh water aqueduct. On the waterfront, ships lined the wooden piers and tiny white sails were visible in the late afternoon sun, all the way from the Isles of Shoals and down the Piscataqua to Great Bay. Below Blanchard's balloon was a city of more than six hundred dwelling houses, of which only sixteen reached the towering height of three stories.[32] It was not a large American town, but it was growing and successful, and on the verge of great things.

But there was trouble in the wind. The following year would bring a devastating attack of yellow fever to town. A year later the city would drape itself in black to mourn the death of George Washington, who had become all but a god in the new nation. Fire, more war, and hard times loomed just over the horizon.

The occupants of Blanchard's floating car knew none of this, nor did they appreciate the view. The first aerial vision of Portsmouth was seen only by a cluster of four-legged farm animals, their distant cries drowned out by an enthusiastic military band. At the climax of the "Aerostatic Experiment" the great balloon shot upward as the gondola and its animal passengers broke free and drifted back to earth beneath a great red, white and blue parachute.

ABOVE: *Today the Gov. John Langdon mansion is one of three historic house museums in Portsmouth operated by Historic New England. (JDR)*

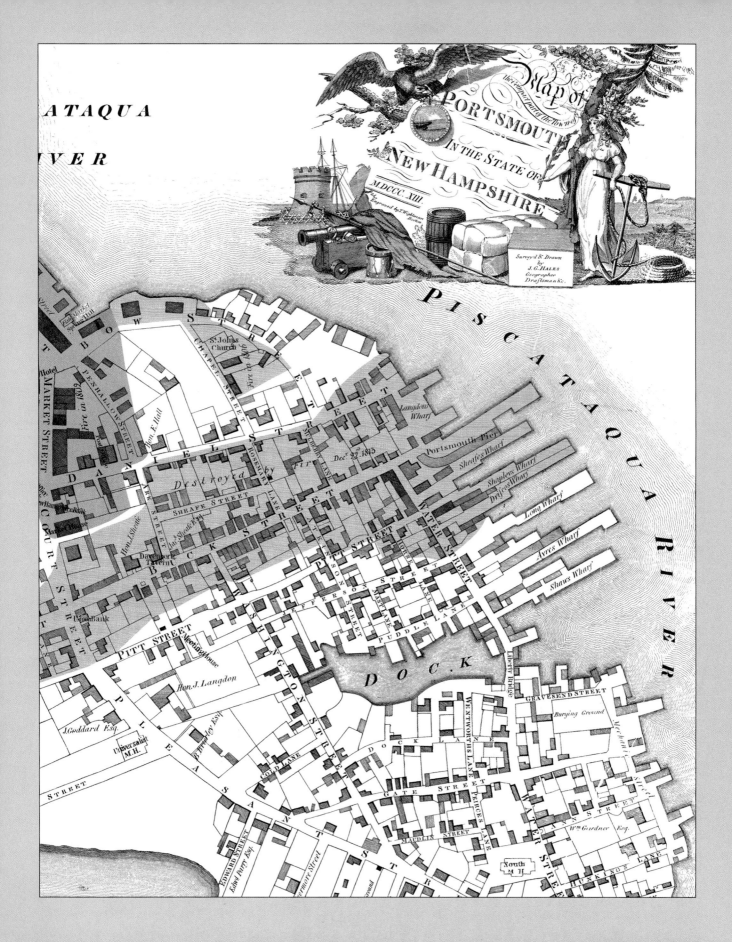

THE BIRTH OF PUDDLE DOCK
THE 1800s

The collapse of international commercial shipping along the waterfront was irreversible. Within a single generation the great trading port of Portsmouth went from boom to bust, as northern New England commerce gravitated to Boston. A generation later, the ruins along The Bank were just a reminder of lost greatness in an age of wealth and civility that grew ever greater in the minds of locals as the nineteenth century progressed. Author Thomas Bailey Aldrich later recalled:

> The crazy old warehouses are empty, and barnacles and eel-grass cling to the piles of the crumbling wharves, where the sunshine lies lovingly, bringing out the faint spicy odor that haunts the place—the ghost of the old dead West India Trade.[1]

Portsmouth, like many faded colonial towns, refused to let go of its ghosts. As the city declined, this proud past became an integral part of its self-image. Time and again throughout the nineteenth century, Portsmouth celebrated itself, reworking its founding facts and legends into a powerful canon of stories that served to remind locals that they were heirs to a once-great kingdom. The rotting docks and mansions were tangible proof that something significant had happened here and, even before the Civil War, the Old Town by the Sea began attracting curious visitors from industrial cities to the west. The more crowded

OPPOSITE: *The founders of Strawbery Banke initially used this 1813 map to determine what Puddle Dock buildings to preserve and interpret. This detail includes the urban renewal area that became the campus of the museum. It falls largely within the rectangle surrounded by Pitt (now Court), Washington, and Water (now Marcy) streets and Puddle Dock. The water area was later filled in. The wharves are gone and the river side of Water Street is now Prescott Park. (JDR)*

and polluted those cities grew, the more attractive the fresh air and crumbling history of the New Hampshire seacoast became. Through excursions to coastal towns like Portsmouth, modern city folk of every social class could not only enjoy summer recreation, but could travel through time by exploring old architecture and seaside forts.[2]

But progress in Portsmouth did not stop. It simply abandoned The Bank and moved on. Rising from the ashes of three major fires, downtown Portsmouth was soon back in business and, once connected to the outside world by railroad in the 1840s, became home to one of the largest breweries in the world. Although the timber trade was drying up (it moved east to Portland, and then to Bangor, Maine), shipbuilding continued along the Piscataqua. Directly across the river from The Bank, the once grassy Kittery islands now held a major federal shipyard.

Even the old waterfront, on closer examination, was far from stagnant. Now known to locals as Puddle Dock, the seventeenth-century Great House orchard had become the most densely populated neighborhood in town. Artisans who once served the wealthy oligarchy were supplanted by day laborers who were hired by the shipyard during bursts of work there, or fished, or manned the brewery shifts, taking any employment available. As immigrants flooded into New England in search of work and low cost housing, Puddle Dock grew even more crowded and diverse. By the end of the century, life along Water Street included a "combat zone" of at least a dozen notorious bars and bordellos.

As Portsmouth struggled to reinvent itself as a successful commercial city made of brick, the ancient wooden houses on the waterfront became both a nostalgic touchstone to the past and an embarrassing reminder that, perhaps, Portsmouth had fallen so far down that it could not get up again.

The End of the Beginning

The aristocratic "merchant class" planted during the Wentworth era was still thriving as the nineteenth century dawned. By 1800 just ten percent of Portsmouth's richest men still controlled half of the city's taxable wealth. But even during its economic heyday, New Hampshire's sole seaport did not impress one European visitor. "The population is small, many of the houses are dilapidated," he wrote, "and I saw a good number of women and children in rags, a sight I never before encountered in America. Yet there are some handsome houses."[3]

On June 12, 1800, under Massachusetts-born President John Adams, the federal government purchased a grassy fifty-eight-acre island on the Kittery side of the Piscataqua River, where George Washington had visited a decade earlier, just across from the busy wharves at The Bank. Kittery and all of Maine were then part of Massachusetts. The idea was to finally set up a series of naval shipyards for the "capacious building" of American warships to defend the young nation abroad. Other shipyards were planned at Norfolk, Philadelphia, Washington, Boston, and New York.[4]

The enemy du jour was France, again locked in battle with England. French ships also harassed American merchants in an undeclared or "Quasi-War" with Americans on the high seas. No longer under British protection, the few trading ships of the new nation were also easy targets for marauding Barbary Pirates. Worse, Her Majesty's Navy had taken to impressing American sailors abroad into British service. Congress hoped to survive on a small defensive navy including the ships USS *Congress* and USS *Portsmouth*, both of which had recently been built at Portsmouth. The new federal Navy Yard, although slow to start, helped keep the local economy afloat intermittently for the next two centuries.

ABOVE: *Isaac Hull was the first active commander of the Portsmouth Naval Shipyard in the early 1800s. Hull had been commander of* "Old Ironsides" *during its most famous battle and was in Portsmouth during the great fire of 1813. (JDR)*

When President Thomas Jefferson took action, business at The Bank suffered. His Embargo Act of 1807 banned American trade with Europe. The move was supposed to punish Britain and France for interfering with American shipping, but it simultaneously strangled Atlantic seaports. Ships and men lay idle as the impact of the embargo hit every element of an economy tied to building, fitting out, operating, and repairing merchant ships. The impact reverberated from the tip of the 340-foot-long Portsmouth Pier, through the half-empty warehouses, and into the homes of the artisans at Puddle Dock who now worked at far below capacity.

It was bad news at sea and bad news ashore. On Sunday, December 26, 1802, at 4 A.M., a devastating blaze suddenly disfigured the new face of the city. It started, by most accounts, in an old, wooden, gambrel-roofed building in the banking block in what is today Market Square and obliterated 114 stores and buildings along Daniel Street. In the central "Parade" only the North Church, the new custom house, and the statehouse were left standing. Then on Wednesday morning, December 24, 1806, the second blaze moved in from the Bow Street area, up Market Street and back toward the barely recovered square. Flames consumed even Queen's Chapel on the river, the former bastion of the Anglican aristocracy under the Wentworths. The South End was spared, but the sudden effort spent on the damaged downtown area helped shift attention permanently away from the waterfront. Residents began thinking of the South End as off

ABOVE: *Although much of the "compact area" of Portsmouth was devastated by three major fires, there was no loss of life. Victims suffered especially from robbers who plagued the victims by grabbing objects moved out of burning houses onto the streets. (JDR)*

ABOVE: *It is easy to see why this 1792 fire pumper was no match for the infernos that destroyed hundreds of Portsmouth buildings in the early nineteenth century. The old machine made in Philadelphia was later acquired by Portsmouth antiques dealer and bordello owner Charles "Cappy" Stewart (on right) seen in this rare photograph. (SBM)*

the beaten track and part of the city's past. As early as 1804 the new owner of Stavers Tavern was advertising his business in the local newspaper as "a little remote from the centre."[5]

The third and worst Christmas fire struck on Wednesday, December 22, 1813. It took out 244 buildings over fifteen acres along State Street—flattening the city like a bomb blast, from where the stone Unitarian Church stands today all the way to the Piscataqua River and out to the tip of the pier. Again the wooden structures of Puddle Dock escaped the fire as it burned its way to the river just a block away. The following year the New Hampshire state legislature, at the request of the Portsmouth town meeting, passed the Brick Act of 1814 "prohibiting the erection of wooden buildings of more than twelve feet high" in the downtown area. The downtown landscape of one- and two-story wooden buildings was slowly replaced by well-constructed, fire-proof brick buildings pressed tightly together and rising to four stories. "There are immense Buildings going forward," one downtown resident wrote in a letter, "and the Town is astonishingly altered."[6]

Meanwhile under President James Madison, the United States was again locked in battle with Britain. Even though British and French aggression had scarcely affected Portsmouth ships, New Hampshire was suddenly in the middle of "Mr. Madison's War." Wary of a new naval shipyard across the harbor at Kittery, British warships kept a close watch on the once-flourishing Piscataqua region during the War of 1812. Although they never dared attack, the damage was done. Within two years the value of New Hampshire exports plummeted ninety percent. Imports dropped nearly in half, fishing and shipbuilding suffered, and only small "coasting" vessels trading up and down the Atlantic stayed relatively successful. By the end of the war Portsmouth had lost its maritime edge and life on the waterfront would never be the same.[7]

Portsmouth's first historian Nathaniel Adams offers plenty of detail on the fires and the resulting Brick Law in his 1825

ABOVE: *Young Daniel Webster cut his teeth as a lawyer in Portsmouth in the early 1800s. Only one of the four houses he occupied survives and is now part of Strawbery Banke. (JDR)*

chronicle, but scarcely mentions the crippling War of 1812. Adams also fails to mention how Portsmouth's maritime community fought back—with privateers. Privately owned vessels swarmed over British supply ships with the official blessing of the United States government. Ten Piscataqua ships, mostly schooner-rigged with crews of fifty to one hundred men, made over four hundred profitable captures. While losses to Portsmouth ships amounted to $200,000, the return on investment for privateers was high. Just four privateer ships—the *Thomas*, *Fox*, *Hardy*, and *Squando*—brought in $2,250,000 worth of auctioned goods from fifteen of the captured prizes.[8] Many men struck it rich; some built fine new homes in town. But this was the last revenge for the old waterfront. When the privateering bubble burst at the end of the war in 1815, the Portsmouth economy popped too. When the nation's fifth president James Monroe visited Portsmouth in 1817, duplicating much of the ceremony afforded George Washington, this was a very different town. Attorney Jeremiah Mason's speech to the new president was less a cheerful welcome than a cry for help from a dying seaport.[9]

It is easy to say, for dramatic effect, that Portsmouth "came to a standstill" at this moment.[10] The end of foreign trade robbed Portsmouth of its primary means of support, but the wounds of fire and war were not mortal. So, like the orphaned settlers of John Mason's first plantation in 1635, Portsmouth citizens began casting about for something to sell. They raised capital by pooling their money, just as early British investors in the New Hampshire colony had done. A major attempt to construct a profitable salt works facility failed early in the century, as did an effort to revive the waterfront through whaling beginning in the 1830s. Despite the colonial revival view that the economy literally stopped in Portsmouth during this era, the rise of a little-remembered hosiery industry begun in 1830 indicates otherwise. By 1850 over one hundred knitting machines operating in town made Portsmouth the largest manufacturer of stockings north of Philadelphia.[11] Cooperative community efforts during this era also created a fresh water aqueduct, a downtown livery, a public bath, banks, a new private library, the Portsmouth Marine Society, new schools for boys and girls, and a number of charitable and social organizations. New bridges supported by business investors now

ABOVE: *Excavating around the Cotton Tenant House (c. 1835), Strawbery Banke Museum field school archaeologists recently turned up this coin. The rare East India Company "Quarter Anna" from the same era may have been dropped or possibly planted as a good luck token. (SBM)*

connected Portsmouth with New Castle, Dover, and Kittery, but times were still tough.

As in the days of the Old Planters, some citizens sought work elsewhere. Young people especially could see little future in a fading seaport and moved west or to Boston or to other pulsing industrial centers. Daniel Webster, who had cut his teeth for eight years as a young Portsmouth lawyer, was among the first to go after his downtown home burned. Many followed until, for the first time in its history, Portsmouth's slowly rising population finally dipped, from 8,082 in 1830 to 7,887 in 1840. Those who stayed were generally older and shared memories of Portsmouth's grander days. They escaped the economic depression, not by stagecoach or train, but by traveling backwards in time.

Remembering Better Days

On December 22, 1820, exactly seven years after his house in Portsmouth was destroyed by fire, Daniel Webster gave a stirring oration in Plymouth, Massachusetts. Webster's keynote address at the two hundredth anniversary of the arrival of the Mayflower was widely reprinted, and helped launch his own political fame. In his speech Webster laid the foundations for what is currently known as heritage tourism. Historic sites, he said, draw visitors with a special power and purpose. Gesturing toward the legendary Plymouth Rock, Webster called upon the "genius of the place which inspires and awes us." Then he continued:

> We feel that we are on the spot where the first scene of our history was laid; where the hearths and altars of New England were first placed; where Christianity, and civilization, and letters made their first lodgement, in a vast extent of country, covered with a wilderness, and peopled by roving barbarians.[12]

The speeches, toasts, and parades surrounding the Second Centennial celebration at Plymouth were part of an organized effort to draw attention back to New England and away from Virginia, Philadelphia, New York, and other historic locations. The movement to reestablish New England as the rightful

ABOVE: *Canopy over the imagined Plymouth Rock, a popular American heritage destination point. (JDR)*

"birthplace" of America grew up largely among elite Harvard graduates and Unitarian intellectuals. Jamestown might have seniority as the first permanent English settlement, they reasoned, but no southern or western location could hold a candle to the pure, unselfish, divinely-directed intentions of the Pilgrim fathers and mothers. Through the fog of two centuries, one small Separatist band of white English immigrants came to embody the fundamental characteristics of the ideal American. Their thrilling and well-documented story, however, picked clean of all its unsavory elements by patriotic historians, did not resemble the founding of Portsmouth or any other American settlement.

Portsmouth's Nathaniel Haven Jr. was among those early revisionist history makers who advocated the supremacy of historic New England. Haven was among seventeen children fathered by a prominent Portsmouth minister and had recently returned from Harvard. He managed a high-brow local newspaper, joined the newly formed Portsmouth Athenaeum, and was president of the local debate club.

Picking up on the Plymouth celebration, Haven's discussion group pushed for a similar two hundredth anniversary to celebrate the founding of New Hampshire in 1623. At the time, however, the most recent history of the state was a three-volume collection written by Dover cleric Jeremy Belknap in 1795. Neither Belknap nor his revered predecessor John Hubbard, author of a 1680 state history, knew about David Thomson's landing at Odiorne Point and little about Mason's colony at Strawberry Bank. Based on this, New Hampshire historians had initially assigned the state's "first founder" award to the Hilton brothers of Dover Neck. The question—who came first—was hotly debated and revived the rivalry between Dover and Portsmouth that began with the bloodless "Battle of Bloody Point" in the early 1630s. Fresh research in 1823 indicated that David Thomson of Pascataway had indeed arrived in the spring of 1623 before the Hiltons came to Dover (a claim historians still dispute). Portsmouth, therefore, won the bragging rights as the Plymouth of New Hampshire, even though the landing site is technically in Rye. Portsmouth also earned the honor of hosting the state's first major celebration of its own history.

ABOVE: *Portrait of Nathaniel Haven Jr. (1790-1826) who died young soon after spearheading the 1823 history celebration in Portsmouth. (ATH)*

Timed to match the supposed spring arrival of Thomson, the hastily organized festival on May 22, 1823, was a badly needed ego boost for a seaport with an uncertain future. Many of the state's top politicians and intellectuals were there, including Daniel Webster and his wife. About four hundred guests, aged twelve to eighty, attended a gala dance at "Centennial Hall" that evening, of which 293 signed a parchment scroll that still hangs on the wall of the Portsmouth Athenaeum. Festivities opened earlier that morning with an enormous formal procession passing through the principal roads of a town that now comprised thirty-seven streets and fifty-three lanes. The route included the expanding, elite neighborhoods along Middle and Pleasant streets, the commercial Market Street, and the evolving North End, as well as the central Parade. Conspicuously absent from the parade route was the old waterfront area, now commonly called Puddle Dock.

Masons in decorated aprons and full regalia marched under military escort to beating drums. At the North Church a capacity crowd listened to three hours of orations and choral music while gangs of enthusiastic boys set off so many "India crackers" that the day felt like the Fourth of July. That afternoon two hundred invited dignitaries dined on every known variety of fish at two long tables stretching the length of the second floor at Jefferson Hall above the brick market building. They toasted to great men

BELOW: *As early as 1823 Portsmouth was celebrating its historic past with patriotic parades. James H. Head sketched elaborate parade floats including this 1860s-era design for "Washington Crossing the Delaware" with live figures on a real boat drawn by oxen.* (ATH)

from local history and sang patriotic songs that very likely grew louder and more jubilant as the wine flowed. One surviving verse refers to the early occupants of the Great House in the early days of Strawberry Bank:

> Tom Wannerton he planted peas,
> And Humphrey Chadboure taters,
> Their children hopped as thick as fleas—
> Dear little chubby 'craters.[13]

Perhaps most important of all was the art exhibit that covered the walls of Franklin Hall from floor to ceiling with eighteenth-century portraits of the wealthy families of Portsmouth, many painted by the greatest artists of the era. For the first time members of the nineteenth century came face to face with the wealthy leaders of the faded merchant class. These were the men who razed the timber forests, built great ships, and fought at Louisbourg and in the Revolution. Here were the families from the era of the great Wentworth oligarchy, families that wielded political power, amassed fortunes, and built the fine homes that dotted the Piscataqua. These were English citizens of another age. Dressed in fine clothes, striking noble poses, and surrounded by painted finery, they appeared to live in a better time that was as distant and magical as Camelot. It was up to their descendants to keep the grandeur of these aristocratic days alive. Daniel Webster had made that point perfectly clear in his address to celebrants at Plymouth three years earlier when he said: "It is wise for us to recur to the history of our ancestors. Those who do not look upon themselves as a link connecting the Past with the Future, do not perform their duty to the world."[14] The gallery with its thirty paintings was so impressive that it was temporarily opened to the general public so that even the lower classes in town could see first hand what an important place Portsmouth used to be.

The 1823 Centennial also established the New Hampshire Historical Society, a group dedicated to preserving artifacts, documents, and stories of the past. From the beginning Portsmouth had to come to terms with its largely Royalist and commercial origins, so to keep pace with the founding myths of Plymouth, the rough and tumble merchant adventurers of the Piscataqua were imbued with more saintly and intellectual characteristics.

ABOVE: *Inspired by the 200-year celebration of the founding of Portsmouth, Nathaniel Adams wrote the first history of the city. His year-by-year* Annals of Portsmouth *appeared in 1825 during the decline of the West India trade. This portrait hangs in the Portsmouth Athenaeum that Adams helped organize. (ATH)*

Speaker Nathaniel Haven Jr. even referred to the founders of Portsmouth as "pilgrims" and described them as "men of profound learning, of unblemished morals, of heartfelt piety."[15] Although their depiction was largely fictional, the newly whitewashed Piscataqua pioneers served an important function in that they provided New Hampshire with both a copycat version of the Plymouth story and, if needed, an alternative canon of independent local heroes separate from Massachusetts.

Historian Nathaniel Adams concluded his two-hundred-year history of Portsmouth with a detailed eyewitness account of the 1823 festivities and a rousing chamber-of-commerce-style promotion for the economically challenged city. Yet for all its upbeat patriotic overtones, the 1825 *Adam's Annals* is filled with longing for lost fame, fortune, elegance, and power during the days of English rule. Adams is never more ebullient than when he eulogizes the town's aristocratic founders, whose portraits hung briefly at the centennial gallery and adorn the walls of the restored historic homes of Portsmouth today. Supreme among all Portsmouth citizens, he implies, was none other than John Wentworth, the town's last royal governor who topped the most-wanted list of treasonous Tories following the American Revolution. It is significant that Wentworth was seen, not as New Hampshire's greatest traitor, but as a brilliant, refined, amiable, visionary man who did his utmost to preserve the peace, but "was obliged to yield to the spirit of the times."[16] Wentworth went on to serve as governor of Halifax, Nova Scotia. Half a century had passed since Wentworth's expulsion, but Adams was old enough to personally recall life in those not-so-distant days. John Wentworth of Portsmouth died in Canada in 1820, the year of the Mayflower celebration. Also that year, as if in tribute, Wentworth's grand mansion in the wilds of Wolfeboro caught fire and burned to the ground.

Not everyone, however, accepted the romantic notion that the city's wealthy merchant class was worthy of adoration. John Lord, a professional history lecturer and writer born in Portsmouth in 1810, later described with distaste the way the seaport's "best people" struggled to emulate the privileged ways of English aristocrats. Lord saw historian Nathaniel Adams as a "semi-literary man" and the rich merchants of his era "who cultivated all the sentiments of inequality and exclusiveness which were supposed to belong to the higher classes in England." These pretentious Portsmouth men, Lord wrote in his unpublished autobiography, loved to attend luxurious dinner parties, drink wine and watered brandy, and to accumulate fine furniture, crockery and silverware—items that have since become the revered focus of modern museum collections. Everyone attended dull church services, Lord recalled, and most fell asleep during the sermon. Portsmouth's upper class was profane, avoided the theater, and had a total disregard for all forms of art. John Lord attended Portsmouth schools where he was routinely thrashed by the teacher, whose primary job, he says, was to train the next generation of "tyrants, liars, and hypocrites."[17]

Never one to mince words, Lord paints a striking picture of the local merchant elite in the early nineteenth century:

> No town in New England claimed to be more aristocratic. In no town was there greater pride in ancestors who were generals, merchants. In no town was society more exclusive and pretentious.[18]

For Haven, Adams, Brewster, and others living during the economic and historic doldrums, the fact that the greatest of days were admittedly over, made them even more hallowed and worthy of praise. Their apologetic and nostalgic version of Portsmouth history established the central tone that survives to this day. This "defensive" view of local history, according to historian John Durel, helped set the stage for the tourism industry that ultimately brought the city back to life. Talking about the "good old days" not only felt good, but it paid dividends.[19]

Tapping the Colonial Revival

This longing for a simpler, more genteel and orderly time grew stronger in the hearts of Americans as the Industrial Age grew louder, faster, and more polluted. The desire for a time before trains, factories, steam engines, and mass production expressed itself in what is now called the "colonial revival." This catch-all term describes an American fascination with all things old,

ABOVE: *No single character is more responsible for keeping Portsmouth history alive than newspaper publisher and writer Charles W. Brewster. His collected* Rambles About Portsmouth *offered glimpses of everything from witchcraft to slavery. (PER)*

ABOVE: *In the nineteenth century, the commercial market moved fully inland from the river to the rebuilt "compact area" that had once been the unpopulated glebeland. Market Square, seen here, was the hub of activity as tree-lined residential areas pushed west down Islington and Middle streets and away from the original settlement site at Strawberry Bank. (SBM)*

covering a wide range of expression in architecture, painting, sculpture, furniture, music, literature, fashion, and manners that exploded after the Civil War and continued into the twentieth century, and some believe, is still pervasive today. Scholars tend to assign the kick-off of the colonial revival to the burst of post-war patriotism kindled by the 1876 Centennial, but in Portsmouth, the sentiment was decades old by then. And no one stoked the nostalgic fires here more than Charles W. Brewster.

Born in Portsmouth in 1802, Charles Brewster was working for Nathaniel Haven Jr. at *The Portsmouth Journal of Literature and Politics* during the 1823 celebration. He purchased the paper from Haven two years later and, by his own admission, did little else during his life but raise nine children and put out the weekly news. Even his friends said he was dull, a man so fascinated by his historic hometown that he rarely traveled outside its hallowed boundaries. Shortly before his death in 1869, Charles Brewster calculated that he had walked the 2,300 feet from his nearby home to his downtown office and back for a total of 27,150 miles, a "beaten track compassing more than a circuit round the world."[20]

Between his duties as the *Portsmouth Journal* editor, printer, news reporter, and manager, Brewster wrote a sporadic column about local history. Those fifty years of essays were later collected into the two-volume *Rambles About Portsmouth* that remains the most influential source of Portsmouth history and lore to this day. Sometimes inaccurate, frequently romanticized, the gospel according to Brewster gave Portsmouth citizens faith in the born-again seaport.

Picking up the bones of Adams' dry chronicle of events, Brewster fleshed out the details of local history. He pored over forgotten documents, wandered through abandoned sites and ancient cemeteries, and interviewed elderly citizens back to the Revolutionary War, plumbing their memories for details that would otherwise be lost. His front-page newspaper essays ran the gamut from tedious details of seventeenth-century documents to stirring stories of witches, haunted houses, naval battles, murder, executions, yellow fever, smallpox, natural disasters, and Indian raids. It is thanks to Brewster that the raid on Fort William and Mary, the visit by Paul Revere, and the lengthy stay of

John Paul Jones—all largely neglected by the newspapers of the day—worked their way into the history of Portsmouth. Brewster's profiles of local celebrities and his attention to architecture led to the city's first published historic walking tour.

Relying heavily on the weighty leather-bound *Rambles*, Sarah Haven Foster published the delicate, pocket-sized *Portsmouth Guide Book* in 1876. Having seen similar portable guides during her tour of Europe, Foster adapted Brewster's 149 essays and Adams's *Annals* into an affordable street-by-street historic house tour that put the romanticized town history into the hands of tourists of both sexes. Asserting its seniority, New England began recasting itself into an historic destination as filled with stopping points as the capitals of Europe. Brewster's slightly racy version of the marriage of Benning and Martha Wentworth was recycled into Henry Wadsworth Longfellow's poem "Lady Wentworth," a poem that drew Victorian visitors to search out the Little Harbor mansion. Thomas Bailey Aldrich too borrowed heavily from Brewster for his bestseller *An Old Town by the Sea*. Brewster's detailed essay on local slavery even helped inspire the recent founding of the Portsmouth Black Heritage Trail toward the end of the twentieth century. And Brewster's tales pumped blood into the passionate heart of the preservation movement that founded Strawbery Banke Museum.

Relying on his journalistic instincts and a desire to sell newspapers, Charles Brewster made history accessible to the average reader just as the explosion of new middle-class Americans began to travel by train in search of rustic destinations. The seacoast on both sides of the Piscataqua offered attractive beaches, and soon it had a variety of summer hotels, ranging from tiny long-stay cottage rentals to the enormous Wentworth Hotel in New Castle that could accommodate over five hundred guests. Hotels with historic-sounding names like The Passaconaway, The Sagamore, and The Champernowne traded on the popular interest in the past. Early tourist brochures and newspaper advertising often quoted alluring lines from Brewster, or from poets John Greenleaf Whittier, Celia Thaxter, Longfellow, and others. Hotel managers, then as now, went to great lengths and expense marketing the dilapidated charm of the region. Hotel owner Frank Jones sent his managers to distant cities to drum-up summer business since wealthy guests might spend the entire season at a resort.[21] Portsmouth merchants, then as now, aggressively courted visitors by inventing special "old home" days in which the entire city was decked out in laurels, grand arches, signs, and flags. "The Return of the Sons" in 1853 was the first pro-active celebration of its kind designed to lure former citizens back to the city they had abandoned during its worst economic times. This early homecoming festival, with others that followed, helped brand Portsmouth—also the home of the nation's largest brewery—as a town that liked to party.

ABOVE: *Portsmouth's economy rose and fell with the building of warships in Kittery, affecting the livelihood of Puddle Dockers. A rare early image shows the USS* Franklin, *the largest wooden ship ever launched at the Navy Yard, leaving one of the nation's largest wooden buildings, the Franklin Shiphouse, in 1864. (SBM)*

ABOVE: *Due to its flagging economy after the War of 1812, Portsmouth lost many of its young residents to better jobs in the cities. Beginning in 1853, Portsmouth staged a series of homecoming events for its prodigal sons and daughters, decorating the city in welcoming arches, buntings, and flags. (SBM)*

Twenty-five thousand visitors arrived in the gaily decorated city in 1873 to celebrate a hastily organized two hundred fiftieth anniversary. Half a century after its economic crash, the invigorated tourist trade put a new spin on the past depression. Amid parades and fireworks, the mayor was "proud to know how much the success and enterprise that fill the West are due to the brave pioneering of the Portsmouth boys." Those lost sons and daughters had not abandoned Portsmouth after all, but had planted the ancient New Hampshire spirit in a new and distant land.[22]

Portsmouth, along with nearby York, Rye, and Kittery, managed to walk the fine line between selling itself as both a charming rustic village where time had stopped and a modern seaside resort. "Portsmouth is not, by any means, behind the times," one illustrated guidebook from this era claims. "It has lost much of its ancient commerce, but it is much given to modern ideas."[23] The pitch successfully attracted a diverse mix of visitors, from nearby urban day-trippers who built tent cities on the beach, to nouveau riche industrialists from as far away as Cleveland and St. Louis who filled the exclusive hotels. The historic seacoast package also appealed to wealthy Boston-area intellectuals who purchased and restored their own colonial mansions on the Piscataqua that they returned to annually, often creating ancestral estates for generations of visitors. It was these same educated "rusticators" who would become the strongest advocates for preserving the region's historic homes in the twentieth century and invest their dollars in the early survival of Strawbery Banke Museum.

Little has changed in a century and a half of marketing to Piscataqua tourists. The original advocates of Portsmouth as a historic destination point—mostly writers of tour guides, downtown merchants, and members of the hospitality trade—offered a two-pronged pitch. The town is both authentic, they argued, and unique. Sarah Foster introduced her portable guidebook by asserting: "The claims of Portsmouth to the notice of antiquarians are scarcely inferior to those of any city in our Union."[24] Comparing the city to its larger sister port in Maine, another guide reads: "There is an air of the old days of small-clothes and gold knee-buckles about the ancient place that is found no where else along the New England coast. Portland hasn't got it . . ."[25]

Not everyone felt the magic. One 1898 travel writer offered this less-than-flattering impression when approaching Portsmouth by boat:

> It seems as though the ghost of some old Colonial town had risen once more to bid defiance to the modern world, with its train of new ideas, before passing again into the misty sea of oblivion . . . On the rickety, worm-eaten wharves are old warehouses, which have an air of intense gloom wrapped about them—brooding over the glories of the past.[26]

But for many others the New England seacoast offered the American equivalent of a European tour with ruined forts, romantic lighthouses, and intriguing legends that attracted tourists of all economic classes. Middle- and lower-class visitors could explore the European-style streets, drink in the ancientness of a pre-Revolutionary social capital, and admire the Cinderella story of housekeeper Martha Wentworth who married the richest man in town. For the rich, there was something distantly elite here and a homey connection that seemed to whisper to them through the ages. The colonial revival worship of "antiquity" was, on one level, the desire by some for the return to a "purer" time when rich and poor, royal and plain, native and foreign all knew their place in a well-defined caste system. And despite the American dream of a nation founded on freedom and ruled equally by a democratic people, there was evidence all around that a distinctly white, British class system had been successfully transplanted into the heart of New England.

During a typical late nineteenth-century summer day, visitors of every ilk frolicked in the cold Atlantic surf, or paddled along the Piscataqua River or "kodaked" friends and family in front of historic sites. But at the end of the day, those who had not brought a tent or could not afford a guesthouse took the trolley back to their tenement or home. Others settled comfortably in for drinks and a late round of golf before dinner in an

BELOW: *Looking less than joyous in their wool bathing garb, seacoast visitors pose on the rocks near the beach. By the 1870s, with easy access by trolley and train, New Hampshire's seventeen-mile coast had already become a tourist Mecca. (SBM)*

elegant seaside hall, or took the carriage to their own summer estate. Every evening, through a complex and unspoken process of socio-economic self-selection, each visitor located his or her own kind and settled in for the night.[27]

The Rise of the Underclass

The existence of a "class system" was no more surprising in Victorian New England than it is in modern society. Portsmouth had handled its poor and indigent citizens since the mid-1600s through a system of almshouses, poor and work farms, detention centers, jails, charitable societies, church programs, and the kindness of strangers. But slowly there were more working poor, and soon great numbers of middle-class citizens, all of whom craved the promised fruits of life in post-Revolutionary America. They

BELOW: *A map showing buildings created during the era of the Brick Act in Portsmouth from 1814-1825. With the exception of a few buildings along Water and Court Street, it is evident that construction in the Puddle Dock area had stalled while the "compact area" downtown and to the north expanded. (RMC)*

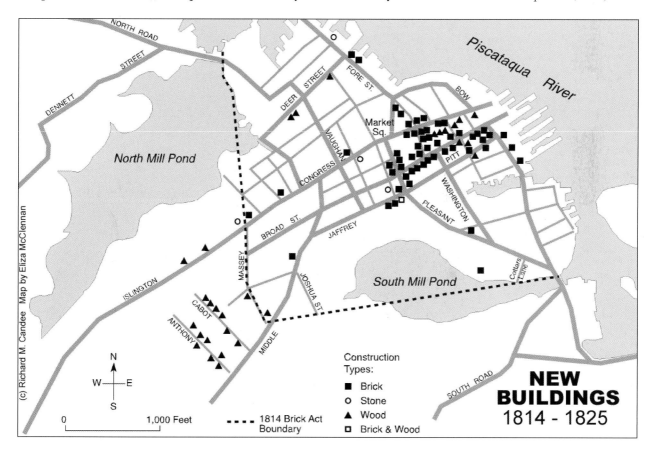

wanted to hold jobs, to enjoy life, to own things, to have rights, even to vacation and travel.

The first glimpse of a clash between these new classes and the wealthy elite erupted after the 1814 Brick Laws appeared. The act, passed after the three devastating fires, imposed heavy fines of $100 to $2,000 on anyone constructing flammable wooden buildings of more than one story within a downtown zone that stretched all the way to Puddle Dock. This rigid restriction, pushed through the state legislature by a few wealthy land owners in town, drew a hail of protest. Locals attempted to have it repealed, complaining that Portsmouth merchants and mechanics could not afford to build in brick and would "be obliged to sell their house lots to the rich citizens of this or some other town" or be driven to live elsewhere.[28]

The powerful merchant elite, battered by worsening economic conditions of the era, wanted to rebuild Portsmouth in brick because successful new industrial cities of the period were made of brick. Resistance to brick, they argued, was futile and only members of "the lowest grade of society"[29] could want to return to the past by continuing to build in wood. Members of the lower class resistance argued that the Brick Law was unconstitutional, and although it was not repealed for another decade, it turned out to be impossible to enforce. Some, mostly wealthy landowners, built in brick within the assigned zone, while others simply ignored the law and built in wood. Portsmouth, thanks in part to its own poverty, was not entirely rebuilt as a monolithic brick city, but retained much of its unique character.

From the outside not much seemed to change at The Bank through the nineteenth century. The three-story brick Shapley Town House, backing onto Strawbery Banke Museum from Court Street, is an example of a Brick Law building. Reuben Shapley, a successful local merchant, built what are actually two joined structures as an investment soon after he purchased the property in 1814. It sits today very near the presumed site of the Great House.

But the really big changes in this part of town had already taken place, first when the Great House plantation appeared, and then when the neighborhood divided and subdivided itself into increasingly smaller house lots. The shape of the original

neighborhood in 1700 was still recognizable two centuries later. But since that time, the quality of life in the city's oldest neighborhood changed radically. The rural environment with its vacant lots, large gardens, and minimal traffic evolved into a crowded urban setting with, not only more buildings, but more people crowded into buildings that were increasingly in need of repair. As the rest of the city expanded, each innovation in building and landscaping employed elsewhere made Puddle Dock look older. The neighborhood deteriorated in public perception too. It was not the idealized towering brick city of the future, but a wooden remnant of the past. Slowly Puddle Dock came to represent the

ABOVE: *Despite the demise of international trade, Puddle Dock retained its connection to the sea through the federally-owned shipyard directly across the river in Kittery. Here four old tars pose aboard the sloop of war USS* Mohican *in 1888. (SBM)*

worst real estate the city had to offer in location, style, convenience, attractiveness, and safety.

The name Puddle Dock first appears in local records as early as the 1780s, but grew in use as the neighborhood became more crowded and its elderly wooden buildings deteriorated. By the mid-1800s writers referred to this waterfront neighborhood in forlorn tones. "Puddle Dock was indeed, when the tide was out, a mere puddle," the *Portsmouth Journal* reported.[30] "You now reach Liberty Bridge," Sarah Foster wrote in her Victorian guidebook, "crossing the Dock now, alas! Puddle Dock, but beautiful and commodious once." After pointing out the original Lieutenant Governor John Wentworth house where Governor Benning Wentworth was born, Foster brushed off the ten-acre campus that makes up the museum today as historically insignificant. She said:

> Beyond the bridge the only site of interest is that of the Great House, which stood at the south-easterly corner of Court Street. Old houses there are, but they have no voices to tell what they were once, and the street is chiefly given up to low shops.[31]

The term Puddle Dock, like the name Strawberry Bank, apparently derives from a location in England. The Puddle Dock area of London was a muddy area used as a dumping ground for barges carrying garbage collected in the city.[32] There is no evidence that our Puddle Dock was an official dumping site for the city, only that the Dock tended to fill up with silt, garbage and probably pollutants over time. By late in the nineteenth century it gave off a rank odor and was too clogged even for travel by canoe. It was finally filled in with refuse and covered over in the early twentieth century when it became the site of a number of small private junkyards that appeared directly on top of the filled-in cove. Considered a natural business in the first half of the twentieth century, especially when scrap was needed for two world wars, the Puddle Dock junkyards also targeted the neighborhood for later urban renewal.

Thomas Bailey Aldrich, who lived briefly as a boy in his grandfather's stately home on the edge of Puddle Dock, returned to the city at the end of the century to take its measure for his

ABOVE: *A rare view of the 85-foot Liberty Pole on Liberty Bridge over the Puddle Dock tidal inlet. It was erected with great pomp on July 4, 1824 in memory of the Stamp Act resistance of 1766. It still stands today in Prescott Park. (SBM)*

ABOVE: *A century after Lt. Gov. John Went-*
worth built his home at Puddle Dock the tidal
inlet had become choked with silt and debris.
It was filled in soon after this photo was taken.
(SBM)

112   STRAWBERY BANKE

colonial revival book *An Old Town by the Sea*. He suggested in the 1890s that the view down Water Street to the Liberty Pole remained all but unchanged and said "the weather-stained, unoccupied warehouses are sufficient to satisfy a moderate appetite for antiquity."[33]

"What a slumberous, delightful, lazy place it is!" Aldrich wrote. "There is a mandragora quality in the atmosphere here that holds you to the spot and makes the half-hours seem like minutes."

But Aldrich was always of two minds about Puddle Dock. On first arriving back in his old neighborhood, Aldrich found the nostalgic view peaceful and comforting. He suggests that a man could sit for years on the old pier at the end of Court Street and drink in the river view—if only all the months were June, he adds, and the tides were always high. As his reverie continues, he looks more closely at the trash revealed by the receding tide. "A corroded section of stovepipe mailed in barnacles, or the skeleton of a hoopskirt protruding from the tide mud like the remains of some old time wreck, is apt to break the enchantment," Aldrich writes. Then after a quick trip to the Point of Graves cemetery nearby, he announces, "Let us get into some cheerfuler neighborhood!"[34]

Another glimpse of the fading waterfront comes from James T. Fields, the son of a Portsmouth shipmaster who died at sea. Fields would go on to become the second editor of *Atlantic Monthly* and, as a partner in Ticknor & Fields, the most celebrated publisher in Boston. Fields was born in 1816, when "the calm of closing day was already brooding over the town." After his father's death, Fields' widowed mother banned her two sons from exploring Portsmouth's waterfront. She willingly allowed young James to hike alone the many miles to Rye Beach in the next town, but "the ship-yards and wharves, attractive to every boy, became places of danger and distress in her eyes."[35] Fields was not allowed to join other boys who launched their boats into the rapid Piscataqua and was not even allowed to join a Sunday afternoon outing with his chums and their teacher. When the sailing boat with his classmates and teacher was caught in a sudden squall and all aboard perished, the obedient boy never challenged his mother again.

ABOVE: *Author Thomas Bailey Aldrich as a boy growing up in Portsmouth and Tom Bailey his semi-fictional alter ego from* Story of a Bad Boy. *Before writing* Tom Sawyer, *Mark Twain asked his friend Aldrich if he thought the reading public would confuse the two "bad boy" characters. Aldrich saw one as distinctly Northern and the other as distinctly a Southern boy. (JDR)*

The allure of the dangerous old Portsmouth waterfront appears in the juvenile books of other local authors. Aldrich, possibly tapping into the tragedy from Fields' childhood a generation earlier, offers a haunting incident in which one Portsmouth boy is swept out to sea on the swift current while his friends watch helplessly in *The Story of a Bad Boy*. Benjamin Penhallow Shillaber, another Portsmouth-born writer who became a successful Boston author and editor, continually returned to his youthful waterfront adventures. His "plaguey boy" Ike Partington, like the semi-fictional Tom Bailey, is forever getting into trouble, and is often seen in the company of Captain Bob, a retired sea captain who lives in a house shaped like a boat. Shillaber grew up in "a little hut on the river" at the North Mill Pond on the other side of town, but his accounts of risky playmates could easily come from days spent along the old wharves at Puddle Dock. In this scene Captain Bob tells a group of boys about the early days of another local sailor:

> He lived in Rivertown and was just like a muskrat for playing round the water. Why he'd tumbled into Swift River and been half drowned twenty times before he was a dozen years old, and scarcely ever went home a night with dry clothes on. His folks weren't very uneasy about him, and Joe used to say they acted as if they thought that one born to be hanged couldn't be drowned, and they let him go it.[36]

Both Shillaber and Aldrich built their fiction on the territorial battles among young Portsmouth boys. Shillaber pits neighborhood against neighborhood in a competitive sled race, while Aldrich recounts an epic snowball fight on "Slatter's Hill" with military precision. In one scene fifty Puddle Dock boys or "River-Rats" defend their fort against the North Enders hurling ice-covered snowballs packed around stones. The territorial rivalry, was as old as Portsmouth itself, Aldrich noted, although its origins were mysterious. He knew only that the North and South Ends of town harbored a "mortal hatred for each other, and that this hatred had been handed down from generation to generation, like Miles Standish's punch-bowl."[37] A century later, both the North and South End waterfront neighborhoods would be declared slums and few would protest their demolition by the cleansing forces of urban renewal.[38]

Aldrich revisited the clash of cultures along the waterfront in his 1877 short story "A Rivermouth Romance." Here an Irish immigrant working as a domestic in a wealthy family secretly weds an Irish sailor. The couple attempt to set up housekeeping in a shabby riverside apartment reminiscent of Puddle Dock, but the stereotypically drunken husband cannot resist the local pub. Order is restored when the heroine returns to her lowly station and the security of her employer's grand old mansion.[39]

Ironically, even as the name Puddle Dock took on an earthy negative connotation for those living outside its borders, the term "Strawberry Bank" was enjoying a revival. Celebrants at the 1853 homecoming frequently invoked the outdated term to signify a simpler pre-Industrial era that had passed by too quickly.[40] The more the phrase was employed in the nineteenth century, the more dreamlike its definition became. In an essay about the founding of Portsmouth, Charles Brewster imagines that Captain John Smith suddenly appears on the shores of Strawberry Bank. Smith then watches the years flow by as if seen through time lapse photography. It is a simple narrative device, but Brewster's nostalgic vision and colorful tales were an enormous influence on those who preserved historic houses in Portsmouth early in the twentieth century.

That same year Daniel Augustus Drown issued a volume of poetry entitled *Idyls of Strawberry Bank*, an homage to his native town. The book sold well through subscription, not because of the quality of its verse, but because Drown was "suffering in darkness and hopelessness of cure from a painful disease of the optic nerves."[41] Because of his disease, the author had been shut up in a dark room for twenty-four years, hidden away from light and people. Many of the poems focus on the author's Christian faith, his attachment to Portsmouth, and his strong desire to be released from pain through death. Using maritime imagery, Drown pictures himself in a sailboat leaving the bank of an earthly shore to find the more perfect bank of an eternal home. Alone with his pain, locked up with his boyhood memories, Daniel Drown's treatment of Strawberry Bank begins to sound more like a vision of heaven itself.

ABOVE: *Benjamin Penhallow Shillaber in his early years. The creator of the comic Mrs. Partington, Shillaber is distinguished as the first editor to publish a comic short piece by Mark Twain in his weekly humor magazine* The Carpet Bag. *(JDR)*

Why should I fear the ocean's foam?
Its waves but beat me nearer home;
Through stormy winds my bark assail,
She still outrides the boisterous gale,
And, bounding on her homeward way,
She nears the harbor, day by day;
And soon her sails will all be furled
Close by the shores of a better world.[42]

The more earthy Puddle Dock became, the more heavenly Strawberry Bank grew. By the turn of the twentieth century, as more immigrants arrived to occupy the low-cost housing along the waterfront, postcards labeled "Old Strawberry Bank" inevitably showed—never Puddle Dock—but photographs taken from the commercial brick area along Bow and Ceres Streets. Photographs along Water Street are hard to find as the Puddle Dock region began to attract a number of bars and bordellos, and a notoriety that, while known to sailors around the world, did not appear in any tourist brochures.

But this spot was neither heaven nor hell. Despite the literary allusions and scandalous whispers, life in nineteenth-century Puddle Dock was like that experienced by most American families of the era. Working class citizens, their lives largely invisible to history, came and went. While many of the houses on the outer ring of the neighborhood remained as single family dwellings, others were home to a parade of renters of diverse backgrounds—Irish, English, Canadian, Italian, Polish, Russian. Over time, as many of the original artisans moved on, new owners might divide up the house among family members. Downstairs shops were converted into additional living space. Rooms built to accommodate families were later leased to strangers. The old William Pitt Tavern, site of so much Revolutionary War history, was broken up into multi-family units. Grocer Leonard Cotton, a successful Portsmouth merchant, took advantage of the slump in land values and invested his profits in two tenements built in Puddle Dock in 1835, specifically for rental. This trend continued for more than a century until the early 1960s when, with one great swipe of urban renewal, the bustling waterfront neighborhood went silent.

OPPOSITE: *The climactic pre-Civil War snowball fight between North End and South End boys in Portsmouth as depicted in Aldrich's* The Story of a Bad Boy. *The territorial feud, according to Aldrich, had gone on so long that no one remembered its origin. The battle makes an apt metaphor for the dramatic 400-year struggle between opposing forces that seems to swirl around the 10-acre Puddle Dock site. (JDR)*

ABOVE: *Raised in the city's South End by the widow of a sea captain, James T. Fields became one of New England's most successful publishers. Friend to Dickens, Hawthorne, Whittier, Holmes, Longfellow, and other literary lions, he remained, at heart, a Portsmouth boy. (PPL)*

— 6 —

Red Lights and White Gloves 1900–1935

It is one thing to revere the past, quite another thing to preserve it lock, stock, and barrel. During the first third of the twentieth century, independent groups of concerned citizens saved five eighteenth-century Portsmouth buildings and turned them into historic house museums, setting the stage for the preservation of the much larger Strawbery Banke Museum decades later. It began, for the most part, as politically active women and men preserving the homes of famous local men—author Thomas Bailey Aldrich, Declaration signer William Whipple, and naval hero John Paul Jones. With nationally famous men in short supply here, the emphasis also fell on architecturally significant homes of lesser known wealthy merchants. Two more mansions, both connected with the faded Wentworth dynasty, were separately purchased and restored just as Americans were hitting the highways in a new wave of automobile tourism. These preservation efforts, for the most part, were driven by summer visitors and Portsmouth outsiders.

But back in Puddle Dock, things had gone from bad to worse. Catering to a hard-knuckle clientele from the navy yard, Water Street, running between Puddle Dock and the waterfront, became a high crime zone. Men fought in the alleys and a rash of robberies and murders infected the city. Brothel madams openly toured the streets promoting their latest teenage prostitutes. Although encircled by historic house museums, the city's oldest

ABOVE: *A Portsmouth door from Wallace Nutting's best selling colonial revival book* New Hampshire Beautiful, *published in 1923. Portsmouth promoted itself as the "City of the Open Door" in this era. (JDR)*

OPPOSITE: *Portsmouth's red light "madam" Alta Roberts and friends pose for a studio photo around 1900. Clockwise: William McGinnis (Ida's husband), Ida McGinnis (Robert's niece), Leona Hayward (Roberts' niece), Alta Roberts, man in bowler hat unidentified. Photo courtesy of Kimberly E. Crisp, a descendant of Mrs. Roberts. (KEC).*

and most rundown neighborhood gained a fearsome reputation even as wave after wave of immigrant families settled in to rented apartments there. Police, reportedly on "the take" from bordello owners, avoided the area after dark.

Images of decay, danger, and sin along the waterfront lingered in the public consciousness even after the red light district was broken up by government decree. Such images were in direct contrast to the romantic themes of the colonial revival that Portsmouth hoped to market to a burgeoning tourism industry. But they did verify the notion that the past had been a better place to live, especially after the horrors of the First World War. As Portsmouth and other Piscataqua towns preserved and restored more early merchant houses, the region hung onto its reputation for fine colonial architecture. But it was still a gritty riverside town in search of economic survival, and because only a minority believed there was any value in saving old buildings, many were lost.

Domestic Engineering

It all started with Mount Vernon. George Washington's Virginia farm was in near ruin by the 1850s when an unflappable group of women bought and restored the Washington estate, turning it into a public shrine on the Potomac. Following the traumatic Civil War and the abolition of slavery, American women continued their struggle for rights and independence. That struggle often expressed itself in good deeds and moral causes like the work of the Mount Vernon Ladies' Association, today the nation's oldest historic preservation group. The 1876 United States Centennial at Philadelphia drew ten million sightseers and generated a burst of patriotic spirit. Visitors were captivated by exhibits of modern machinery and saw, for the first time, the gigantic arm of what would become the Statue of Liberty. But one of the subtlest exhibits, a recreation of a simple early American kitchen, is said to have pushed the colonial revival in architecture and home furnishings into public awareness. This movement came to define and stereotype the images of New England that linger to this day.

ABOVE: *Jessie Varrell, owner of the Tobias Lear House from 1921 to 1935 standing in the doorway. Women from a variety of social groups and clubs were instrumental in saving historic houses in Portsmouth beginning in the early twentieth century. (WGTL)*

Along the Piscataqua, the preservation process had begun years earlier with the private restoration of Sparhawk Mansion in Kittery and the Governor Benning Wentworth mansion at Little Harbor. But these were wealthy residents reviving their own homes, not public museums. Thanks to its early home-coming events in 1853 and 1873, Portsmouth already had a jump start on this nostalgic trend. Depressed real estate values attracted intellectuals to the "shabby chic" homes along the New England coast. Architectural students made field trips to sketch the classic lines of local homes. Poets and folklorists inevitably included Portsmouth—along with Boston, Ipswich, Salem, Cape Ann, Newburyport, York, Hampton, Nantucket, and others in their anthologies of romantic colonial towns. The purity and perfection of design represented by these early homes was increasingly compared to the imagined purity of the nation's founders. The idea sparked at Mount Vernon, the creation of a patriotic house museum, offered the ideal marriage of male and female talents in an era when women's suffrage was on the rise. Men could focus on architecture and history and do the heavy lifting of restoration, while women often spearheaded the fundraising, ran daily operations, preserved oral traditions, and tended to the collection and upkeep of domestic artifacts. Be it ever so humble, there was no place like home—assuming the home had belonged

ABOVE: *In 1853 a South Carolina woman passing Mount Vernon by boat was "painfully distressed" to see its deteriorating condition. An energetic woman's group raised $200,000 to restore the building and purchased two hundred surrounding acres, kicking off an American restoration movement. The New Hampshire Society of Colonial Dames, founded in 1892, saved and restored the Moffatt-Ladd House in Portsmouth. Here a costumed group celebrates in the house garden. (COL)*

ABOVE: *A souvenir snapshot of Mount Vernon in Virginia as photographed by a visiting tourist in the 1930s. (JDR)*

to a famous patriot, a wealthy white merchant or aristocrat who had filled his richly designed mansion with finely crafted things. These fine eighteenth-century houses and decorative objects, rather than their "primitive" seventeenth-century forebears, came increasingly to define the past, even though it was a past in which few early Americans had actually participated. This was an elite past revived and extolled by an elite new class of American intellectuals who saw themselves reflected in the looking glass of history. This was particularly true in Portsmouth where members of the royal Wentworth oligarchy had set the bar especially high with their social airs, elegant Georgian homes, intricate interior woodworking, imported china, and handcrafted Piscataqua furniture.

The garden too enjoyed a rebirth in the colonial revival. Gardens were a fertile symbol of a more natural and orderly life before the onslaught of modern technology. They were deeply rooted in Christian theology. They offered clear organic links between England and New England traditions. And gardening was a safe territory for both sexes, a place where men and women could co-exist equally in an era leading to more significant woman's suffrage.

"One will scarce find a single old house in our town," R. Clipston Sturgis wrote about Portsmouth in 1899, "which has not its garden as carefully planned and as carefully protected from the casual passer-by as is their patio or dining-room."[1]

Sturgis, a Boston architect, "rusticated" in Little Harbor with other wealthy and influential Bostonians including Arthur Astor Carey, J. Templeman Coolidge, John Singer Sargent, Edmund Tarbell, Isabella Stewart Gardner, and others who showed interest in the region. Their interest in preserving Piscataqua architecture sometimes ran counter to Portsmouth progressives who wanted, like the city's founders and merchant class, to make money. "Many are lost," Sturgis wrote about the great homes of Portsmouth, "some have fallen into evil hands or evil ways; but the greater numbers are still in existence, and in most cases occupied by those whose families built them."

For Boston intellectuals, Portsmouth was a charming village easily accessible by train and trolley for even a one-day walking tour, although by 1900, no historic houses were open

to the public. For Bostonians, Portsmouth was populated by curious rural folk who, for the most part, neither understood nor cared about the gifts that history had lavished on them. And while it is true that Portsmouth locals did not come together early to save their architectural treasures, residents were highly aware that there was something special here. The proliferation of souvenir photographs and artifacts, guidebooks, parades, and social celebrations, even newspaper advertising from the turn of the twentieth century, all show that many in Portsmouth valued its reputation as an historic town, if only as a money-making scheme. Train timetables, insurance calendars, and pharmacy handouts from this era are crammed with pictures of historic houses and stories culled and abridged from Brewster's *Rambles About Portsmouth*. If Portsmouth citizens were not yet motivated to save old homes for public display, this awareness was "in the water" they drank daily.

ABOVE: *The garden of Mr. and Mrs. Barrett Wendell of Portsmouth, New Hampshire, appeared in the national magazine* The Mentor *in 1916. The Wendell family arrived in Portsmouth in 1640. (JDR)*

Like other towns in New Hampshire and elsewhere, Portsmouth had its share of women's groups. A chapter of the Colonial Dames, one of the national lineage organizations founded in the 1890s, opened here early. Members were required to prove their genealogical link to families that had arrived before the American Revolution, thus ensuring its members were largely of English origin. Chapters of the Women's Christian Temperance League and the Women's Civic League, along with a variety of church groups and civic clubs, were among those who successfully pushed for an end to the waterfront combat zone. Women founded the first cottage hospital, lobbied to become members of the Portsmouth Athenaeum, and conducted charitable work. In 1899 the Colonial Dames erected a monument to New Hampshire founder David Thomson at his 1623 landing site in Rye. But during the first decade of the twentieth century, Portsmouth history remained largely in the hands of men. The creation of the city's two Civil War memorials at Haven Park and Goodwin Park were largely men honoring men on land provided by other men.

Portsmouth women, in particular those of social standing and wealth, had not yet tried to replicate the work of the Ladies of Mount Vernon. They were still learning. It was not until 1895 that members of a Portsmouth current events club began wondering among themselves "whether the time might not be ripe for the formation of a modern well-organized women's club in Portsmouth." Searching in *Rambles* for an "unhackneyed" name, they discovered Bridget Graffort, daughter of Puritan merchant Richard Cutt, one of the city's earliest and wealthiest men. In 1700 Bridget Graffort had donated a large plot of her inherited land to the city for the creation of the first Portsmouth school. That philanthropic gesture by a powerful woman, members agreed, perfectly summarized their intentions.[2]

But the impact of the Graffort Club tended more toward arranging flowers than preserving buildings. The group did take a formal stand against the wearing of bird feathers in hats, but when a history committee was appointed, the group elected to study the architecture of ancient Vienna, rather than old Portsmouth. But even as a rehearsal of power, the Graffort women found "the discovery of unimagined ability, the exercise of which is a source of much joy." Simply by meeting, these women found

ABOVE: *Edith Greenough Wendell (at right) and her friends spirited a campaign that saved the Warner House in 1931. Mrs. Wendell was unsuccessful in finding a major benefactor to fund a 1935 attempt to create a maritime village restoration in the South End waterfront.* (WAR)

they had "broken down many of the walls of church and class prejudice."[3] The walls that came tumbling down, however, were all among white Christian women. It took a seasoned socialite from New York in 1908 to show Portsmouth how to make an old house into a new museum.

The Day Mark Twain Wore Black

In her memoir *Crowding Memories*, a chatty worshipful account of life with writer Thomas Bailey Aldrich, his wife Lilian Woodman Aldrich recalls how fate brought the couple together. After summering in New Hampshire's White Mountains in 1860, the young socialite stopped in Boston on her way home to New York. Attending a performance of Hamlet, she was swept off her feet by the handsome Edwin Booth. "That young actor will control my destiny," she told her sister Mattie.[4] A few weeks later the star-struck Lilian and her sister found themselves seated at dinner in a New York hotel with the twenty-seven-year-old Booth and his nineteen-year-old bride Mary Devlin. The three young women became close friends and devout groupies of the most famous actor in America whose only rival was his younger brother John Wilkes Booth.

The Booths spent the next year in London where their only daughter was born. As soon as they returned, Lilian pleaded with Edwin to introduce her to the young poet Thomas Bailey Aldrich, then a newspaper correspondent in the Civil War. Aldrich had arrived on the literary scene at the tender age of nineteen when his poem "Baby Bell," about the death of an infant, became an instant popular hit. "Show me Aldrich, please!" Lilian begged Booth during a New York party. Booth did as he was told and a union that would lead to Portsmouth's first historic museum was formed.

According to Mrs. Aldrich, the famous tragedian had by then become so addicted to alcohol that Aldrich and two other close friends shadowed Booth day and night to prevent him from sneaking a drink. Aldrich proposed to Lilian on February 21, 1863, the same night that Mary Devlin Booth died, leaving Edwin Booth a shattered widower with a two-year-old daughter.

ABOVE: *American's best known tragedian, Edwin Booth, was a close friend of Thomas Bailey Aldrich and his wife Lilian, a visitor to the Isles of Shoals, and brother of assassin John Wilkes Booth. (JDR)*

TOP: *Thomas Bailey Aldrich gained national fame at age 19 for his poem "Baby Bell," about the death of a child. This image comes from a newspaper article prior to the Civil War. (JDR)*

BOTTOM: *A very poor image, but the only one located showing Lillian Aldrich at the dedication of the Aldrich Memorial in 1908. It appeared in a local newspaper. (JDR)*

When the actor's brother assassinated President Abraham Lincoln two years later, Aldrich temporarily moved in with Edwin to help assuage his grief and shame. The friendship continued to the end when Aldrich, eventually editor of the prestigious *Atlantic Monthly*, served as a pallbearer at the famous actor's funeral.

The Aldriches entertained the toast of Boston and New York literati, from Harriet Beecher Stowe (whom Lilian despised), to author Bret Harte, painter James McNeil Whistler, poet Henry Wadsworth Longfellow, even Charles Dickens. When Aldrich invited a tawny-haired man in a sealskin coat to dinner, Lilian assumed the man was drunk by his strange slow drawl and tossed him out. "Why dear, did you not know who he was?" Aldrich asked.

"Mark Twain!" Lilian sobbed hysterically when she learned his name. "Mark Twain!"[5]

Despite being kicked out of the Aldrich house, Samuel Langhorne Clemens, aka Mark Twain, and Aldrich remained fast friends. Twain credited Aldrich's novel about growing up in Portsmouth, *The Story of a Bad Boy,* as an inspiration for his own Tom Sawyer. Twain described his friend as endlessly witty. "When he speaks," Twain once remarked of Aldrich, "the diamonds flash . . . He was always brilliant, he will always be brilliant, he will be brilliant in hell—you will see."[6]

When Aldrich died in 1907, his widow Lilian immediately instituted steps to turn her husband's boyhood home in Portsmouth into a literary shrine. The house was built in 1797 by William Stavers, the son of John Stavers who ran the Pitt Tavern next door. Both buildings are now part of Strawbery Banke Museum, as is the Stephen Chase House, two doors further west on Court Street. Aldrich called it "The Nutter House" after his fictionalized Grandpa Nutter in his genre-setting novel, *The Story of a Bad Boy.* In the 1880s the house had passed "into alien hands," according to an early museum brochure, and was used as Portsmouth's first "cottage hospital." Although Aldrich only lived there on and off during three childhood years, Lilian later recalled, "There was not an inch in the house or a spot in the garden that did not have a story to tell."[7] Aldrich was working on his *Story of a Bad Boy* during a summer visit to the house in 1868 when his own two boys, the "jocund sprites," were born.

The "Nutter House" on Court Street was used briefly as Portsmouth's first cottage hospital. It became the city's first historic house museum in 1908 and is now part of Strawbery Banke Museum. This view (top) shows the back garden and the "fireproof" museum building and its interior collection including the desk at which the novel was written. (SBM)

TOP: *On first meeting Mark Twain, Lillian Aldrich felt an immediate dislike for the noted author and kicked him out of her Boston home. The feeling was mutual. This image comes from her 1923 memoir* Crowding Memories. *(JDR)*

BOTTOM: *A sketch of Twain sent by the author to his friend T.B. Aldrich. In 1874 Aldrich asked Twain for a photo. Twain responded by sending one photo every day for two weeks until Aldrich begged him to stop. (JDR)*

Lilian Aldrich and her surviving son Talbot later raised $10,000 by private subscription to repurchase it. The rooms were restored to match the fictional home of the semi-fictional Tom Bailey prior to the Civil War, making it one of the first American house museums to turn back the hands of time for the entertainment and education of the public.

A thousand people gathered at the Portsmouth Music Hall on a sweltering hot day in July 1908 to dedicate the Aldrich Memorial. William Dean Howells, who had preceded Aldrich as editor of the *Atlantic Monthly* was among the dignitaries. It was Howells who had credited Aldrich, back in 1870, with the invention of "the American novel."[8] Howells, an enthusiastic world traveler, purchased a summer home at Kittery Point, Maine, in 1902 when he was 62 years old. Howells' descendants would play major roles in creating Strawbery Banke Museum later in the twentieth century.

Portsmouth Mayor Wallace Hackett introduced the one man in town who needed no introduction. At 73, still sharp and sarcastic, Mark Twain was internationally known for his shock-white mane of hair, his white hat, and crisp white suits. But this day, hot as it was, Mark Twain was dressed in a dark coat and hat. He had been warned by his family, he said, to wear black and act respectful for a change while dedicating the Aldrich Memorial.

"They seemed to think this was a funeral I was coming to, when in point of fact it is a resurrection and an occasion of joy," Twain told those gathered. "Aldrich's life was cheerful and happy. I knew him forty years. He was one of the brightest men it has ever been my pleasure to know."

Thomas Bailey Aldrich, above all, Twain later wrote, would have hated the pretensions of his own memorial ceremony. Twain certainly did, sweating in the stifling opera house in his black suit waiting for the "riff-raff" ahead of him to drone on. Later he toured the Aldrich Memorial, a shrine to a not-very-famous writer that Twain thought would appeal to one in ten thousand Portsmouth visitors. It was a shrine, more correctly, Twain thought, to Aldrich's impossible wife, Lilian. Twain watched her smiling joyfully in their carriage. Lilian was in her element, squeezed between the top-hatted state governor Curtis Guild and New Hampshire Adjutant General Cilley, a man aptly named—

Twain thought—festooned as he was in ridiculous epaulets, ropes and clusters.

Twain recorded his scathing thoughts that day in a journal, but insisted that his private scribbling be suppressed for another seventy-five years to protect his victims from his acid tongue. Twain's eager biographers, however, could not wait that long. The first of what would be many volumes of Twain biographies appeared in 1922, just a dozen years after his death. The book was called *Mark Twain in Eruption*, and it must have seemed that to Lilian Aldrich, who Twain described as: "A strange and vanity-devoured, detestable woman! I do not believe I could ever learn to like her except on a raft at sea with no other provisions in sight."[9]

"I conceived an aversion for her the first time I ever saw her," Twain wrote of Lilian Aldrich in his secret journal, "which was thirty-nine years ago, and that aversion has remained with me ever since. She is one of those people who are effusively affectionate, and whose demonstrations disorder your stomach. You never believe in them; you always regard them as fictions, artificialities, with a selfish motive back of them. Aldrich was delightful company, but we never saw a great deal of him because we couldn't have him by himself."

Twain did not harbor much more love for his first vision of Portsmouth. He hated the train ride on the smoke-belching Boston & Maine railroad where passengers were offered water from a battered tin cup in a bucket. The railroad cars, he suspected, were left over from the Civil War era. Instead of the venerable "Old Town by the Sea" that Aldrich had written of so lovingly, Twain saw a run-down whistle-stop on his own personal tour of the world. "A memorial museum of George Washington relics could not excite any considerable interest if it were located in that decayed town and the devotee had to get to it over the Boston and Maine," Twain grumbled into his diary after his 1908 visit.

Mark Twain was wrong. Although not the "literary Mecca" proclaimed in the *Portsmouth Herald*, the Aldrich Memorial drew a steady stream of curious visitors to Court Street during the early twentieth century as the long-surviving bad boy novel appeared in dozens of English and foreign language editions.

ABOVE: *Author William Dean Howells was among the first to praise Aldrich's "Bad Boy" novel as "a new thing" in American literature. The Howells family would later be central figures in the creation of Strawbery Banke Museum. (JDR)*

ABOVE: *A very early interior detail of the parlor at the Bailey Memorial reconstructed from details in the novel to mirror the room during the author's youth. (SBM)*

According to a 1912 report in the local newspaper, over a thousand visitors signed the guest book that July, many from elite cosmopolitan families.[10] A "fire-proof" brick building in the back garden housed a "treasure trove" of Aldrich artifacts, including the table on which the novel was written and a complete set of the author's first editions. The walls were hung with signed letters by Edgar Allan Poe, Washington Irving, Ralph Waldo Emerson, and other literary lions, as well as manuscripts, pictures, autographed poems, and books. Helen Keller signed "From a bad girl to a bad boy," and one of Twain's inscriptions read, "From your only friend."[11] Odd historic souvenirs such as a vase once owned by Benjamin Franklin filled a number of display cases. To find a more important museum, an early brochure boasted, the literary pilgrim would have to visit the Shakespeare Memorial at Stratford-on-Avon. Perhaps not, but the unstoppable Lilian Aldrich left Portsmouth with its first of many historic house museums.

Red Lights on Water Street

Another kind of museum was bringing more visitors to the Portsmouth waterfront. The "Museum and Emporium" on Four Tree Island boasted a stuffed alligator and other animal oddities imported by traveling sea captains. Exhibiting exotic objects was common practice in any seaport own, where even the Portsmouth Athenaeum offered a third-floor display case that included the bill of a sawtooth shark and the testicle of a whale. But only the isolated island Emporium, now a family picnic area near Prescott Park, boasted a stuffed cow with udders that dispensed beer when squeezed. The Emporium also had girls, young and beautiful, for sailors who could afford to entertain them. The fee for a boat ride to the island, according to local legend, was fifty cents out, and five dollars to get back.

Visiting "liberty parties" of as many as fifteen hundred sailors from military and merchant ships in Portsmouth Harbor appeared on the Portsmouth shore in a single evening. Before the construction of the Memorial Bridge from Kittery in 1923, most young men, some as young as fourteen, took the ferry from Kittery to the landing at the base of State Street. Their first sight,

after as much as a year aboard a cramped all-male ship, was the glitzy bordello called The Gloucester House at the corner of State and Water streets. One Portsmouth resident recalled visiting as a child:

> You never saw anything like it. There were mirrors on the ceilings and the rooms had little cubby holes, and I didn't know it at the time, but that's where the girls were. The house had a great big beautiful ballroom with a great big chandelier. There were red velvet curtains and paintings of bosomy nude women on the walls. It was really quite grand. [12]

Equally impressive was the house manager Mary Amazeen Baker, hard to ignore in her elegant dress, fur muff, ostentatious jewelry, and hennaed beehive hairdo. Baker and her husband ran their business, for tax purposes, as a saloon and ice cream shop, initially renting the building at the edge of Puddle Dock from none other than ale tycoon Frank Jones, who reportedly employed the Baker women to entertain visiting dignitaries at his nearby Rockingham Hotel. After Jones' death in 1902 the Bakers bought their building through Judge Calvin Paige, who like Jones, served a term as mayor of Portsmouth.

Corruption ran rampant along Water Street as oyster bars and saloons slowly replaced family grocery stores during the second half of the nineteenth century. By the early 1900s nearly a dozen houses of ill repute lined the waterfront along Puddle Dock and the South End. No documentation exists, but it appears that owners of the Union House, Clifton House, Asay House, Gloucester House, and others all paid bribes to sheriff Thomas Entwistle. A Civil War veteran, Entwistle was best known for capturing Louis Wagner immediately following the 1873 ax murder on Smuttynose Island. But arrests for sex trafficking were rare and fines were small. Mary Baker, renowned for the diamonds imbedded in her two front teeth, openly exhibited her newest employees by parading them through town in an open carriage. Another successful madam, Alta Roberts, known locally as the "Black Mystery" vetted her clients as carefully as the owner of an exclusive hotel, wore gold casings around her teeth, and was known for her generosity to the poor and homeless.

OPPOSITE: *Former bordello owner Alta Roberts poses in front of her former Water Street (now Marcy) establishment in 1933 at the age of 78, two decades after the closing of the red light district. Today, this building is the only former bordello still standing on the Portsmouth waterfront. Photo courtesy of the Kimberly Crisp collection. (KEC)*

The city's red light district was at its zenith in August 1905 when world attention focused on seacoast New Hampshire during negotiations leading to the Treaty of Portsmouth. The bloody Russo-Japanese War ended in "peace city" when top-hatted delegates from both nations assembled here at the suggestion of President Theodore Roosevelt. Although he never attended, Roosevelt won the Nobel Prize for his efforts and the city gained a public relations victory. But peace was never as profitable as war for the Portsmouth Naval Shipyard. With the shipyard now the economic engine of the Piscataqua, business had been off since the end of the Spanish-American War. Yet there was no slowing the influx of sailors and immigrants attracted to the low rents and high times at Puddle Dock.

By the summer of 1912, Portsmouth was in "a state of siege," according to the *Portsmouth Times,* over a series of unsolved daylight robberies. Families rushed to store household valuables in bank deposit vaults. Wives hunkered in upstairs windows with opera glasses scanning the neighborhood for thieves. Husbands bought shotguns in record numbers and filled them with rock salt to discourage midnight prowlers. Crime was on the rise everywhere. Portsmouth police marshal Thomas Entwistle and his patrolmen appeared unwilling or unable to bring order, but a series of violent crimes finally shocked the city into action.[13]

On August 10, the body of USMC private David H. Carlson, aged twenty-four, lay propped against the wall of the Asay House like a discarded puppet. His head, unsupported by a recently broken neck and a severed spinal cord, drooped to one side and both his legs were doubled up unnaturally beneath his body.

A passing sailor spotted him early Saturday morning and notified the police. Carlson, a well-liked marine just back from a tour of duty in Cuba, had reportedly gone "on liberty" with a significant amount of cash. He had, according to the men who knew him, an affinity for gambling. The dead marine's uniform, the newspaper reported, was immaculately clean. In his pockets police found only a knife, a dollar bill, and a full bottle of whiskey.

Initially Mr. and Mrs. Asay, owners of the brothel, denied ever seeing Carlson. But a female "inmate" of the house, the *Portsmouth Times* reported, told a Navy board of inquiry that

OPPOSITE: *Young sailors arrived at and departed from the Portsmouth Naval Shipyard by the hundreds. While on liberty they patronized the local shops, bars, and bordellos and were sometimes the victims of foul play. This group is reportedly on the deck of the USS* Constitution. *(ATH)*

ABOVE: *Patrolman William Carlton and son Ransom, born 1895, pose on Water Street circa 1899-1900. Carlton apparently lived across the street from junk dealer Jack Zeidman in Puddle Dock. (SBM)*

Private Carlson had indeed been inside the Asay House and gotten into a row with another marine who was a Portsmouth resident. A bartender at The Home, the saloon next door to the Asay House, testified that he had seen the body in the alley, but assumed he was just another Friday night drunk. The Portsmouth marine who admitted to pushing Carlson was turned over to Navy officials without a police trial.

On August 15, five days after the Carlson murder, the bloated body of what appeared to be a sailor, "evidently a Greek," was discovered floating on the Kittery side of the Piscataqua River. Twenty-year old John Costing, it turned out, had been a fireman on the USS *Hannibal*. It was not uncommon for sailors who fell overboard, many of whom could not swim, to disappear in the swirling Piscataqua. Costing's death went unexplained.

Four days later, the body of Army Private Reardon (also spelled Riorden), stationed at Fort Constitution, was discovered floating in the river at New Castle. Investigators initially concluded that Reardon was pushed off the New Castle bridge by marines. South End residents reported hearing a loud, angry group of men moving from the red light district on Water Street and up the New Castle road.

Reardon's death was ultimately ruled accidental, but the newspapers were quick to tally the score. A local fisherman discovered the fourth body in the river by the New Castle breakwater scarcely two days later. Private Everett Lesher, aged twenty-eight, had been missing from the USS *Southery* since August 10, coincidentally, the date of the Carlson murder off Water Street. Lesher's body was too decomposed to determine if he was a victim of foul play, according to the medical examiner. At least three of the four dead marines, the townspeople buzzed, had been under the influence of booze easily available in waterfront bars.

Local police appeared increasingly inept as each new death and robbery occurred. The South End summer crime wave churned up even more damning headlines for Thomas Entwistle's police force. In mid-August a woman was arrested on charges of "white slavery" and held on a heavy $5,000 bond. Constance Perry, twenty-five, was accused of luring a minor female from Dover to work in a Portsmouth brothel. In a rare public

acknowledgement of the city's sex trade, Ethel Duffy, aged fourteen, was interviewed on the front page of the *Portsmouth Times*. Mrs. Perry, she said, had given her a drink that made her dizzy and taken her to a Portsmouth bordello.[14]

"That day we were in a restaurant," Duffy told the newspaper, "and all the while the woman kept talking to me that if a man came to see us that night I should do what he asked me to."

And there was more. In one published instance a man "touched in the head" terrorized South End locals and fought off police for reasons unknown. In another, a group of marines were reported brawling, shouting, and using profanity near the South Mill bridge at midnight. They carried on for over an hour without police intervention. During this time, one marine was knocked senseless. A witness heard the group plotting to throw the man into the river if he did not recover. When a South End resident called out that he was going to notify the police, a marine

ABOVE: *"The Home" saloon stood on Water Street opposite Court Street. Painted signs advertise Frank Jones Cream Ale, a laundry, billiard room, and bottled goods. But locally, the building was said to be the last of a dozen houses of ill repute. Here in 1937 two men are surveying the land that became the ever popular Prescott Park. (SBM)*

threatened to "blow his head off" if the witness interfered. An anonymous South Ender wrote to the *Portsmouth Herald* on September 12:

> The residents of the South End pay their taxes, and naturally expect to have some police protection—but I'm sorry to say they haven't any whatsoever. Two policemen are kept on the upper end of Water Street for the protection of the dens of infamy that are allowed to flourish. They are given police protection, but the residents of this section of the city are forced to be annoyed by their dumpings after closing up time.[15]

The Water Street red light district did not disappear immediately, but the public had finally had enough. So had the administrators of the Portsmouth Naval Shipyard, who now learned that President William Howard Taft was planning a visit to the Kittery facility. With shipyard work at a near standstill and the region dependant on federal contracts, it was time to clean up the messy South End, and fast.

On September 21, the *Portsmouth Herald* announced the resignation of Marshal Entwistle in large bold letters accompanied by a front-page photograph, rare for that era. Entwistle received a laudatory farewell. But the very same day the *Herald* was forced to retract its story when Entwistle reported that, although the police commissioner had asked him to resign—he had not, and would not ever do so.[16]

The battle lines were drawn. Entwistle, the newspaper pointed out, a former member of the Governor's Council, had actually appointed the police commissioner who then requested his resignation. When Entwistle refused to go, the commissioner threatened to shut down the Water Street bordellos in retaliation. When Mayor Daniel Badger reluctantly made the Water Street bordellos a campaign issue in the upcoming election, Portsmouth's dirty little secret finally became a public issue.

"As Mayor of this city," Badger announced, "I call on you to close forthwith and permanently keep closed all houses of ill repute in this city, and to close forthwith and keep closed all places where intoxicating liquor is sold illegally."

ABOVE: *Police chief Thomas Entwistle was best known for jailing the Smuttynose murderer, Louis Wagner, in 1873. In 1912 he refused to resign during the closing of the waterfront combat zone that had thrived under his jurisdiction. This image is from the newspaper account of that event. (JDR)*

These *"before and after" images show dramatic changes on Marcy Street (formerly Water St.) during this era. The infamous Gloucester House (top right) was removed. Prescott Park now begins where the Walker Coal Company (at left) is seen in these photos. (SBM)*

Marshal Entwistle, then in his seventies, wrote a blistering attack on Mayor Badger. Was the city also going to shut down all the tobaccos shops, auto garages, newsstands, and drugstores too? Entwistle's comparison between prostitution and selling newspapers failed miserably with local citizens in an era of rising social reform. The memory of four dead marines in August was still fresh in the public mind. Badger easily won his re-election. Thomas Entwhistle quickly resigned, the major bordellos were closed, and Water Street was renamed Marcy Street. Whether it was named after a recent mayor or a former Portsmouth ship captain seemed not to matter. Either way, the "cleansing" of the Portsmouth waterfront had begun, but the moral stain proved difficult to erase. It lingered over the innocent residents of Puddle Dock for decades, even after the bordellos had been torn down and the street renamed. The stain would reappear as a "blight" that could only be eradicated, some believed, by the bulldozers of urban renewal.

Portsmouth's tough and tawdry reputation continues to fascinate. Modern tourists now follow costumed guides dressed as Victorian madams through the streets to hear tales of the city's underbelly. Robert McLaughlin, an early Strawbery Banke president and president of a downtown bank, self-published *Water Street: A Novel* in 1986. Dedicated to "several nameless gentlemen who reminisced," McLaughlin's book offers a seamy fictionalized account of sex, murder, rape, fire, drowning, money, exploitation, and revenge in the combat zone at the turn of the twentieth century—all stories the author says he heard while gossiping over the fence with South Enders.

The Wentworth Dynasty Restored

Portsmouth got into the historic house business very early. In 1845, long before the opening of Mount Vernon, the current owner of Governor Benning Wentworth's enormous mansion at Little Harbor was offering tours to the public. But the idea did not take hold until the arrival of Lilian Aldrich in 1908. Following in the footsteps of the Aldrich Memorial Association, five separate preservation groups soon adopted colonial Portsmouth

homes, all of which continue as museums today. Four of them were eighteenth-century Georgian houses with ties to the faded Wentworth dynasty. Each group tackled its project differently and was motivated by its own set of goals, but the results were much the same. They all spread the gospel according to Charles Brewster about the city's "golden era," when a few wealthy families reigned. Brewster's compelling bible of facts, misinformation, legend, hearsay, and personal commentary now took on physical form. Summer tourists and locals were finally able to step into these grand restored houses, wander into private bedchambers, gawk at the aristocratic finery, and see ancient family portraits not visible to the public since the city celebration of 1823. For a quarter, visitors saw how their betters, like the Moffatt family, had lived.

Captain John Moffatt arrived in Portsmouth as commander of a mast ship in 1723. As a successful merchant in the "triangle trade" with the West Indies, Moffatt exchanged fish, timber,

ABOVE: *An elegant merchant mansion, the Moffatt-Ladd House (1763) on Market Street was among the earliest historic houses restored for public view. It is operated today by The National Society of the Colonial Dames in the State of New Hampshire. The house is similar to the Treadwell House torn down in 1957 that sparked the preservation movement in Portsmouth. (COL)*

livestock, and masts for sugar, molasses, slaves, and cotton.[17] In a single voyage in 1755, Moffatt imported sixty-one African men women and children for auction.[18] Like Jonathan Warner and Mark Hunking Wentworth whose homes would also be preserved, Moffat was a major player during the royal Wentworth era. The house he built in the North End on Market Street in the early 1760s was the largest and most elaborate structure of its time, with a huge hall and ornate stairway at the entrance.

Moffatt very likely presented the house as a wedding gift to his son Samuel who sailed all the way to England to woo a descendant of New Hampshire founder John Tufton Mason. But Samuel soon went bankrupt. To avoid debtor's prison, he and his wife escaped to Barbados, leaving their two young children behind in the care of enslaved African members of the Moffatt household. The house was transferred through marriage, first to the Havens and then to the Ladds, a successful business family, whose descendants leased it in 1911 to the New Hampshire Society of the Colonial Dames. Founded in 1892, the Dames embodied a spirit and patriotic fervor reminiscent of the ladies of Mount Vernon. They quickly stripped the floors, painted the walls white, and adapted the Moffatt-Ladd House into a public museum following the colonial revival ideas popular at the time.[19] Their interpretation, as in other merchant house museums, would not include details of the owner's involvement in the slave trade until late in the twentieth century.

Meanwhile, over in the South End, another elegant hipped-roof mansion from the early 1760s was also being restored. The Wentworth-Gardner house too was built as a wedding gift, and the ornate hand-carved detail on its stairs, doors, and walls have been attributed to the same master woodworker who decorated the interior of the Moffatt-Ladd House. The house was purchased in 1915 by Wallace Nutting who, unlike the demure Colonial Dames, trumpeted his restoration work in mass-produced books, reproduction furniture, signed photographs, and advertising in national periodicals.

Wallace Nutting claimed to be neither artist nor historian, but rather "a clergyman with a love of the beautiful."[20] Swept up in the popular vision of the colonial revival, he saw heavenly perfection in a nostalgic view of the past. Born in Massachusetts

ABOVE: *Captain John Moffatt painted by John Greenwood around 1751. He married Catherine Cutt, grand-daughter of John Cutt, the first "president" of New Hampshire who owned the Great House on the Strawberry Bank waterfront. (COL)*

in 1861, Nutting was still an infant when his father was killed in the Civil War. His older sister died at age eighteen and his mother, descended from "New Hampshire stock," moved her son to rural Maine when their family home burned. Even as a child Nutting imagined himself as a preacher, but also worked as a clerk while taking classes at Phillips Exeter Academy in Exeter, New Hampshire, and at Harvard. As a result Nutting evolved as a man half evangelist, half entrepreneur.

Nutting kept Portsmouth on the tourist map by promoting his Wentworth-Gardner House among a chain of five house museums that he purchased, remodeled, filled with period antiques, and photographed. Sightseers could motor along the "colonial chain" of Wallace Nutting houses from Wethersfield, Connecticut, to Haverhill, Saugus, and Newburyport in Massachusetts, up to Portsmouth, New Hampshire. Even those who could not make the journey could own a piece of Nutting's "Old America" by purchasing any one of a series of photographs taken at his restored homes. Nutting posed women wearing colonial costumes in idyllic settings against the backdrop of grand houses like Wentworth-Gardner. An army of up to two hundred female "colorists" then hand-tinted the images and signed his name. Collectors, according to Nutting, gobbled up over ten million copies of his prints which are still avidly sought today.

It is difficult to overestimate the impact of Wallace Nutting's reinvented America on the public mind. Not since Currier and Ives, and not again until Norman Rockwell, would there be such a nostalgic vision of America, a vision that was echoed in the increasingly powerful medium of film. Behind the scenes, Nutting very quickly abandoned the costly colonial chain of homes and focused on his mass-market products. In 1918, as the nation plunged into the First World War, Nutting offered the Wentworth-Gardner House to the Metropolitan Museum of Art. They could either buy it whole, or carry it away in pieces to exhibit in New York, Wallace agreed. But the enormous publicity lavished on the house helped insulate it from destruction. William Sumner Appleton, the influential founder in 1910 of the Society for the Preservation of New England Antiquities (SPNEA), strongly objected to the destruction of the Wentworth-Gardner house. The *Boston Herald* announced in 1919 that "There will be

ABOVE: *Raised in Maine, educated at Phillips Exeter Academy and Harvard, Wallace Nutting gave up the ministry to restore a chain of colonial homes. His books, reproduction furniture, and tinted pastoral photographs sold in the millions. (RMC)*

ABOVE: *Restored by Wallace Nutting, the Wentworth-Gardner House (c. 1760) was then temporarily owned by the Metropolitan Museum and New Hampshire governor Charles Dale before it was saved by an independent organization. The Tobias Lear House, also saved, is in the background. This photo is from around 1916. (WGTL)*

INSET: *A posed female model photographed in the restored Wentworth-Gardner House by Wallace Nutting. Nostalgic images were colorized by an army of female workers and sold to a voracious audience for affordable prices. (WGTL)*

a sad gap in the string of jewels that almost nonchalantly adorns the old town of Portsmouth."[21]

Appleton's society stepped in to protect the Wentworth-Gardner house from being swallowed up by the Metropolitan Museum, but did not add it to the growing chain of SPNEA house museums that set the trend for colonial revival preservation techniques. He did purchase the 1664 Jackson House in Portsmouth's North End, the oldest surviving home in New Hampshire, and opened it in 1932. SPNEA later obtained the 1784 mansion of Governor John Langdon, the Portsmouth patriot who led the raid on the local fort that helped bring down the Wentworth reign in the American Revolution. But Appleton's overstretched group was unable to take on another project in 1919. The Wentworth-Gardner mansion, along with the home of Washington's secretary Tobias Lear next door, which hung in limbo for two decades until just before World War II, when they were adopted together by a new nonprofit association, the membership of which reads like a who's who of Portsmouth citizens and influential summer visitors.

The cluster of new house museums in Portsmouth during this era demonstrates an evolving national trend. Old buildings were increasingly considered worth saving, even if they had no association with a famous patriotic figure. Although the Wentworth-Gardner House had been built by Mark Wentworth—the son, brother, and father of three royal governors—its real value was architectural. Not so for the Tobias Lear house next door which was less important for its building design, but survived due to its link to the godlike George Washington. The Moffatt-Ladd House offered the best of both worlds. In addition to its architectural eminence, the house was home for sixteen years to William Whipple, one of three New Hampshire signers of the Declaration of Independence. Although they were savvy to its architectural and decorative arts value, the Colonial Dames never neglected to point out the hallowed "Whipple Tree," a towering horse chestnut in the garden reportedly planted by William Whipple in 1776.[22] Yet despite its double inoculation of architecture and patriotic lore, the "John Paul Jones House," another urban merchant mansion, almost disappeared in 1917. It was preserved at the eleventh hour, by an unmitigated lie.

ABOVE: *Scottish-born mariner John Paul Jones stayed in Portsmouth twice during the American Revolution, making him, arguably, the most famous resident in the city's history. (JDR)*

Whether John Paul Jones actually boarded at the gambrel-roofed house at the corner of Middle and State streets is unknown. The story, as usual, comes from Charles Brewster who claimed that Jones, a Scottish soldier of fortune, boarded with the Widow Purcell in 1777 while waiting for ship owner John Langdon to complete work on the *Ranger*. Jones, along with a reluctant crew of Piscataqua men, made history when he led a bold guerilla raid on the British Isles during the American Revolution. Jones returned to Portsmouth in 1782 and waited a year for Langdon to complete the *America*, the largest warship built in this country at the time. His host, again, may have been Sarah Purcell, a niece of Governor Benning Wentworth, who had married ship captain and merchant Gregory Purcell.

The legend was enhanced in 1900 when Jones' biographer Augustus C. Buell offered a delicious new footnote to history. According to Buell, five young women from Portsmouth sewed the first American Stars and Stripes ever seen in Europe as it flew over the *Ranger*. The white stars had been "cut from the bridal-dress" of young Helen Seavey herself, Buell wrote.[23] Buell's 1900 biography was filled with inaccuracies, but sold well and became a key source of information when Captain Jones himself reappeared five years later. In 1905, the mummified body of John Paul Jones was discovered in a lead coffin beneath the streets of Paris and shipped to Annapolis, Maryland, where it was later re-interred in a marble sarcophagus with great military pomp. That inspired the erection of a local monument to Jones in Kittery in 1906 by the Sons of Paul Jones.[24] Then in 1913, a group calling itself the Helen Seavey Quilting Party, attached a bronze plaque to the Widow Purcell's house commemorating the female side of the story, and resulting in the renaming of the house the John Paul Jones House. Buell's story, a New Hampshire version of the legend of Betsy Ross, was widely disseminated. Illustrations of the Portsmouth Quilting Party girls appeared in books, newspapers, and calendars.

The flag story turned out to be false. Buell had simply made it up along with the names of the women in the quilting party and scores of other invented "facts" in the book. But the popular legend attached itself to the house like a barnacle and the plaque remains on the side of the building, confusing visitors to this

ABOVE: *A re-enactor dressed as John Paul Jones poses on the steps of the Portsmouth Historical Society, also known as the John Paul Jones House. (PHS)*

day. Millionaire businessman Frank Jones, who kept his base of operations just next door in the Rockingham Hotel, had plans to demolish the old Purcell house and build a modern brick office block there for his Granite State Insurance Company. Frank Jones died in 1902, but the plan was resurrected by the tycoon's estate that auctioned off the house in 1917 "for wrecking purposes." Bids came in at $500, $800, $1,000, and $1,200. The winner was none other than "Cappy" Stewart, who had purchased his former waterfront brothel from the Jones estate. Now in the "antiques" business, Stewart had switched from selling young women to exploiting old houses that he dismantled for their decorative woodwork. He found a potential buyer in the Metropolitan Museum that was building its American Wing and looking for decorative colonial interiors. The situation looked grim for the noble 1758 house, its terraced colonial gardens, and carriage house, all surrounded by a curved cedar fence.

Mr. and Mrs. Woodbury Langdon III of New York City saved the day. A descendant of the prestigious Portsmouth family, the Langdons sometimes summered in the Governor Langdon Mansion just up the street. Elizabeth Elwyn Langdon apparently convinced her husband to purchase the building and land, for a reported $10,000, and donate it to the newly-formed Portsmouth Historical Society.[25] When the society put out a call for artifacts

BELOW: *This 1758 gambrel roof mansion was owned by merchant Gregory Purcell whose death left his widow in need of income. John Paul Jones reportedly rented a room here and his occupancy very likely saved the house from destruction in the early twentieth century.*
(JDR)

to fill the empty building, they were inundated with heirloom furniture, ancient dresses, toys, canes, guns, swords, ceramics, silverware, mechanical devices, photographs, portraits—so many items, in fact, that the group had to renovate the barn and extend the display area for its grand opening in 1920. A small room at the front on the second floor supposed to have been the lodgings of the man Augustus Buell dubbed "the Father of the American Navy," was filled with maritime trinkets and dedicated to John Paul Jones.[26]

The arrival of the Portsmouth Historical Society created a counterbalance to the "outside" influence of the statewide Colonial Dames, Wallace Nutting, Lilian Aldrich, and the Boston-based SPNEA. Although funded, initially, by the gift of a wealthy summer family, this soon became the closest thing in Portsmouth to a local museum run by local residents. It was dominated largely by male leaders, many with connections to the naval shipyard. Unlike the other houses, the Historical Society focused on all things Portsmouth, exhibiting a "grandmother's attic" of donated items without the thematic focus, the decorative arts taxonomy, the merchandising acumen, or the evangelical drive of its sister houses. This was, to put it simply, a museum of old Portsmouth stuff. The emphasis was more on whether the item was old, interesting, and locally-owned, than whether its owner had been a member of the aristocracy. Historical Society president Reverend Alfred Gooding expressed his personal vision during the opening ceremonies in the summer of 1920:

> It seems to me . . . that a society like this should not only seek to collect within the four walls of a building valuable memorabilia of the past, but that it should do what it can to preserve those ancient landmarks—buildings, trees, waterways and the like—which have long given distinction to a town like ours, but which, with the growing power of commercialism, are very apt to disappear.[27]

This, in a nutshell, was the preservation message that city librarian Dorothy Vaughan would deliver to the Portsmouth Rotary almost four decades later. Vaughan, who learned much about Portsmouth history from Rev. Gooding himself, was active in the Portsmouth Historical Society, across the street from the public library, before she became a founder of Strawbery Banke.

Invigorated by the opening of its historical society, Portsmouth held a lavish tercentennial pageant in 1923. Women, excluded from the formal parade a century earlier, now dominated the proceedings that the *Portsmouth Herald* called "a Dazzling, Inspiring Spectacle." A hundred women sewed the costumes. A hundred sopranos sang in the massive chorus. Thousands attended the three-day outdoor event that included a thousand cast members. The pageant, with its tableaux of living figures, was engineered to enact three hundred years of town history. Women dressed in flowing white robes symbolized Portsmouth; the attending members of her court representing Rye, Greenland, New Castle, Newington, Kittery, and the Isles of Shoals. No one represented Dover which, remembering the snub of 1823 and holding fast to the Hilton claim, celebrated its own three hundredth anniversary pageant.

Citizens of Portsmouth reenacted scenes from their history in a script written by Virginia Tanner, a Cambridge dancer and pageant dramatist, who was also a New Castle summer visitor. Tanner cut no corners in her pageant, produced on a $12,000 budget. Wigs were shipped in from New York. Performers came from the National Ballet in Washington, DC. Photos from the local paper show sleek muscular dancers in scanty Indian warrior

costumes flinging colonial maidens aloft in agile, exaggerated, Nureyev-style movements. There was a real stagecoach, animals, soldiers in Revolutionary War uniforms, a "Negro" chorus, and a parade of representatives from Portsmouth's Polish, Irish, Italian, Greek, and Chinese families. Children from every school in town marched by, then came veterans of World War I, the Spanish-American War, and the Civil War. It was pomp of the highest circumstance. Portsmouth, once again, was remembering its faded glory.

Festivals were fun, but many in Portsmouth remained uninterested in serious preservation of full-scale buildings, especially if they stood in the way of economic progress. The 1716 home of Archibald Macpheadris, considered one of the most impressive early brick houses in New England today, was next on the endangered list. Macpheadris built his grand mansion while courting the fifteen-year-old daughter of Lieutenant Governor John Wentworth. Her brother Benning Wentworth later sought to have it purchased as the royal governor's house. It then became home to merchant John Warner, a contemporary of John Moffatt and Mark Wentworth. In 1923, the same year as the Portsmouth Tercentenary, the new Memorial Bridge connecting Portsmouth, New Hampshire to Kittery was dedicated. The ingenious mechanical lift bridge elevated the entire road high enough to allow large ships to travel up and down the Piscataqua. This state-of-the-art bridge placed the Macpheadris-Warner House, just a hundred yards from the river, on the main drag where coastal New Hampshire and Maine connected. Motorists now arrived in Portsmouth not far from where the ferry had formerly delivered visiting sailors to the city's most prominent bordello, which was eventually torn down. Then in 1931, the owners of the nearby Macpheadris-Warner House offered the ancient brick mansion for sale. The prospective buyer was a local oil company that saw, not the most important historic treasure in Portsmouth, but the ideal site for a filling station.

The evolving preservation network snapped into action to protect the building, now known as the Warner House. By this time America was falling into a deep economic depression. William Sumner Appleton could not afford the $10,000 purchase price or the building upkeep. He encouraged the local

ABOVE AND OPPOSITE: *The construction of the lift bridge over the Piscataqua River in 1923 linked Maine and New Hampshire for hordes of new touring motorists. The bridge also allowed Puddle Dock residents to walk to work at the Portsmouth Naval Shipyard in Kittery. (SBM)*

Ranger chapter of the Daughters of the American Revolution, another national lineage group founded in the 1890s, to step up to the plate. They, in turn, contacted Edith Greenough Wendell, a Boston socialite, philanthropist, and Colonial Dame. Her husband, Barrett Wendell, was a Harvard professor and owned an ancestral home nearby in downtown Portsmouth. Mrs. Wendell managed to raise the funds and establish yet another small, tightly-focused, nonprofit house museum that promptly opened in 1932.

Shifting Views of History

The spinning wheel of the colonial revival that peaked in the 1920s was now grinding to a halt. Building new homes using the elements of colonial design was still popular, but thanks in part to the Great Depression, keeping the original structures standing for public display was proving to be incredibly costly. After thirty-seven years of saving historic homes, William Sumner Appleton was coming to agree with Wallace Nutting's assessment that it cost twice as much to restore a house as to buy it and twice as much to furnish it as to restore it.[28] A brave new world built from steel and glass had arrived. High rise apartments and industrial skyscrapers dominated America's expanding cities. Enormous suburban developments dressed in tin and asbestos were on their way. But along the Piscataqua, visitors could now escape into the past at any number of preserved house museums with a welcoming, if not historically accurate, open colonial hearth.[29] Amazingly, all the house museums of Portsmouth begun early in the twentieth century—Aldrich, Moffatt-Ladd, Jackson, John Paul Jones, and Warner—are still active today. The Wentworth-Gardner and Tobias Lear houses eventually declared independence from the Society for the Protection of New England Antiquities (SPNEA) and combined forces into a nonprofit museum association in 1940. Decades later SPNEA established two more Portsmouth house museums, at the 1784 Governor John Langdon Mansion and the 1807 Rundlett-May House.

Following in the footsteps of nine restored Portsmouth house museums proved to be both a blessing and a curse for the founders of Strawbery Banke Incorporated beginning in the late 1950s. All of the earlier organizations played a supportive role in the formative months of the Puddle Dock preservation "project." Their sheer existence was evidence that Portsmouth had a lot to offer historically. But they were ultimately poor role models — sometimes bickering and jealous, surviving on subsistence budgets, controlled by their benefactors, managed like tiny fiefdoms, prone to spotty research, suspicious of outsiders, and frequently class conscious. It is no wonder, in its early years before a professional curator or museum professionals, that Strawbery Banke furnished its first two houses with separate decorating "committees," operating more like a collection of independent houses than a single entity.

No one lived within the restored walls of these now-empty houses. The portraits never changed. The furniture rarely moved. Deceased family members were often represented by store mannequins dressed in period costumes. Children were required to look, but not touch, even in the reconstructed home of the rambunctious bad boy Tom Bailey. The Moffatt-Ladd house and Warner were rebuilt, one decorative object at a time, to correspond with ancient inventories that listed every item that had once occupied each room. Enormous expense went into putting

BELOW: *An all-male Portsmouth City Council, complete with spittoon, meets in 1921 under portraits of former city fathers. Centuries of patriarchy were about to end and by World War II Portsmouth would have its first female mayor. (SBM)*

old houses back the way they were, or the way their new museum keepers imagined they had been, so that visitors could better visualize better days.

Spawned by this romantic and worshipful view of the past, historic home museums of the Piscataqua stretched from Exeter, Dover, and Portsmouth in New Hampshire to South Berwick and York, in Maine. Together they formed a bulwark against the uncertainties of the future. Essentially anti-modern, they helped promote the theory, launched in 1820, that New England was the birthplace of America. With scores of other nostalgic public shrines, they helped identify New England with all things old, quaint, rustic, simple, honest, practical, and immutable. "Yankees," according to the stereotype, were hard working, thrifty, territorial, and resistant to newfangled notions, except those created through Yankee ingenuity. And no one loved the stereotype more than the Yankees themselves.

New Englanders were also typically descended from white, Anglo-Saxon, Protestant stock. Their historic houses can be seen, on one level, as an opportunity to indoctrinate waves of foreign immigrants into a morally superior system of American values through inspiring patriotic lessons, or what the Colonial Dames called "healthful instruction." Women, often charged with the moral education of their children, taught these lessons within these domestic museum walls. Rather than spread the American gospel abroad like missionaries on foreign soil, this homeland colonialism preached to the new immigrant arrivals on American soil. Strawbery Banke too would find itself preaching patriotism in what had been, before urban renewal, the city's most crowded immigrant neighborhood. Later, as the museum matured, the educational message would turn to a study of the ethnic and immigrant residents of Puddle Dockers themselves.

Strawbery Banke also inherited a tendency toward domestic discord from its older sisters. Forever strapped for cash and run by passionate volunteers with a variety of motivations, Portsmouth's dignified historic house museums were livelier behind the scenes. After the opening of the Warner House, for example, William Sumner Appleton wrote to praise founder Mrs. Barrett Wendell for "one of the most remarkable instances of preservation work in America." But to another leader of the Warner House, Appleton described Mrs. Wendell as "a dangerous woman" when it came to architectural restoration. She had "an inability to appreciate anything that isn't spic and span, neat and clean, lovely and beautiful, according to her own idea of what she would like to live with."[30]

This mild reproach only hints at the battle lines being drawn as preservationists evolved from amateurs, who simply loved the past and wanted to recreate it, to a profession in its own right. Mrs. Wendell, in the romantic tradition of the nineteenth century, saw the Warner House in emotional terms, as a place remote and heroic that she longed to visit. Appleton approached the restored building as an academic puzzle in which the latest research was displayed for the edification of visitors and scholars alike. These battles would only grow more complex and heated as the study of history branched into a variety of college degree fields including architectural history, social history, archaeology, and museum studies. The stakes grew even higher with the arrival of large outdoor museums like Colonial Williamsburg and Old Sturbridge Village. At Strawbery Banke, with more than two dozen houses to deal with, a schism quickly grew between the "Old Guard" who wanted a romantic colonial village and the "New Guard" that advocated a professionally run museum. Over the intervening decades, as preservationists fought to save ancient New England and squabbled among themselves, many great old Portsmouth buildings fell.

THE MARITIME VILLAGE IDEA 1935–1955

The idea for a ten-acre outdoor history museum in the Portsmouth South End did not simply fall out of the sky in 1957. The idea evolved, nourished for decades in the thick chowder of local history, enlivened by the colonial revival movement in New England, and preceded by generations of domestic house museums. Then, fully two decades before the appearance of Strawbery Banke Inc., two prominent men from Kittery Point engineered a brilliant plan. Tapping federal funds and local talent, they would turn the city's rundown waterfront into a national park.

A recently rediscovered 1936 blueprint proves this was a sophisticated, forward-thinking plan. It promised to provide skilled jobs for unemployed locals, restore nearly two hundred historic buildings, create local housing, preserve maritime traditions, and bring tourist dollars into a depressed economy. But this idea was too much for a government moving from a depression to a world war. Despite yeoman promotional efforts that reached all the way to the White House, their "maritime village" died on the drawing board. But it did not die in vain. The failed plan was later recycled into the original vision of Strawbery Banke in ways more deep-set than most people today remember.

But as the national park idea moldered, things were far from quiet in Puddle Dock. Two long-time Portsmouth residents, Josephine and Mary Prescott, had their own plan for beautifying

OPPOSITE: *During the 1930s two prominent Kittery Point men proposed a plan to restore Portsmouth's dilapidated waterfront to its 1800-era appearance. The "maritime village" plan failed and Portsmouth currently has no tall ship, but the buildings at Strawbery Banke survive. Here the USS* Constellation *lies in a quay in the Portsmouth Navy Yard in 1884. (SBM)*

The 1700-era home of Lt. Gov. John Wentworth was dismantled by former bordello owner "Cappy" Stewart in 1926. It was situated at Puddle Dock, now the parking lot of Strawbery Banke. These images (above and right) by the Metropolitan Museum of Art, that acquired portions of the interior, offer a rare view of a building during demolition. (RMC)

the waterfront. That plan, put simply, was to tear it all down. And when the Prescott sisters suddenly inherited almost three million dollars, they told their lawyer to turn their plan into action.

Win Some, Lose Some

Nothing fires the blood of preservationists like acts of wanton destruction. While the ladies of Mount Vernon successfully saved George Washington's estate, across New England, colonial treasures continued to disappear due to neglect, modernization, or in some cases—by preservation itself.

In 1924 the Metropolitan Museum finally got a piece of Portsmouth. Having failed to acquire and dismantle fine colonial rooms from the Wentworth-Gardner and John Paul Jones House, the museum purchased an exquisite paneled room and the staircase of the 1695 home of Lieutenant Governor John Wentworth from none other than former bordello owner Charles "Cappy" Stewart. For a fee Stewart dismantled the finest and most historic house in Puddle Dock, the birthplace of Governor Benning Wentworth. Portions of the house went on display at the Metropolitan Museum and at the Winterthur Museum in Delaware. The Metropolitan exhibit went a long way toward defining the progression of early American architecture, which now included an early Portsmouth building. But the building itself, sited at what is now the Strawbery Banke Museum parking lot, was gone forever.

Despite Wallace Nutting's proclamation that Portsmouth was "the most pleasing of all small shore cities," a great many architecturally significant buildings were already gone.[1] The list of lost Portsmouth structures included: the brooding Atkinson mansion on Court Street; the George Jaffrey house (1730) on Daniel Street; Franklin Hall (1814) on Congress Street; the Admiral Storer house on Middle Street; the Captain Thomas Manning house (early eighteenth-century) on Manning Street; Brewster-Hill house (c. 1750) on Hanover street; John Haven's house on Islington Street and one on Congress Street, as well as his father Reverend Samuel Haven's house (c. 1760) on Pleasant Street; the Greek Revival style Episcopal Chapel (1832) and the Old Court House (1836) on Court Street; the Bell Tavern

ABOVE: *Charles H. "Cappy" Stewart bought and sold Portsmouth antiques including the decorative interiors of fine colonial homes. The former owner of an oyster bar and Water Street bordello, Stewart was a shrewd businessman and a colorful character, seen here in the late 1930s. (SBM)*

downtown on Congress Street; the Piscataqua House (c. 1830) on Pleasant Street; the Universalist Church (1807) on Pleasant Street; Low House (1745) on Washington Street; the George Meserve house (1760) on Vaughan Street; the *New Hampshire Gazette* office (1756) on Pleasant Street; Supreme Court judge Woodbury Langdon's brick mansion (1785) on State Street; the "Stone Stable" on Fleet Street; the Old South Mill and the Old North Mill; Judge Sherburne house (1760) and Portsmouth's old "Gun House" (1808)—and many more structures. Still the buildings continued to fall.

Recognizing that American history was disappearing beneath the steamroller of progress, Congress passed the Historic Sites Act in 1935. Historic structures across New Hampshire were placed on the national endangered list by federally funded Works Progress Administration (WPA) researchers. Portsmouth topped the state list with the most at-risk historic buildings—so many, in fact, that the city's South End waterfront was considered for a new national park. But while Washington studied, tested, planned, and ruminated, two former Portsmouth schoolteachers were busy buying up and tearing down four city blocks in the former combat zone.

The Prescott Sisters Clean House

The story of how Josephine and Mary Prescott became millionaires while the rest of America suffered through the Great Depression begins at the edge of Puddle Dock around the time of the Civil War. Their father ran a small grocery store at 17 Water Street. Their elder brother, Charles W. Prescott, graduated from Boys High School in Portsmouth in 1869, and became the business protégé of William B. Trask, a wealthy merchant. How the two men met is unknown, but Trask did run a dry-goods store briefly in Portsmouth and in 1865, after moving on to Boston, Trask married Susie Walker, the daughter of the Portsmouth mayor.[2]

By 1877 the two men, Trask and Prescott, were partners in a highly successful retail business in Erie, Pennsylvania. Charles Prescott, like his two sisters, never married. He dedicated himself

OPPOSITE: *Despite its many historic house museums, Portsmouth lost a great many fine colonial structures. This mid-1880s picture shows a crew (at right) tearing down a house built by joiner Jonathan Low around 1745. It was deconstructed to make way for apartments that were later also demolished. (SBM)*

wholly to Trask & Prescott and lived with Susie and William Trask in their sprawling home in Erie. Both men invested wisely and grew increasingly wealthy. When Trask died in 1916, Charles and Mrs. Trask, both Portsmouth natives, continued to live in the Erie mansion.

In 1932 Charles Prescott, then seventy-nine-years-old and dying, entered an Erie hospital—and here the story takes a strange turn. Although he survived only a few days, Charles suddenly decided to leave the bulk of his nearly $3 million fortune to the Hamot Hospital in Erie. His deathbed will was handwritten on a sheet of notepaper—not by Charles—and witnessed by his doctor and nurse. In a faint childlike scrawl at the bottom of the page are the letters "C-h-a-r-l" followed by a large "X." Next to the signature someone wrote "his mark." Despite the strange conditions surrounding this will, which also gave two of Prescott's partners $100,000 each, it was accepted for probate by the city. Josie and Mary Prescott would receive the interest income from their brother's sizeable estate until their deaths, but no inheritance. An earlier 1927 will granting them most of his estate was thrown out.

The Prescott sisters, then living in a Portsmouth house purchased by their brother, decided to fight back. They selected Charles Milby Dale, a former Portsmouth mayor, as their attorney. Dale had come to Portsmouth during World War I, married a local woman and set up a law practice. Dale went to Erie with orders to break the alleged deathbed will. In a bitter encounter Erie lawyers argued that Charles Prescott's final wish was to support the hospital's charitable work with the poor. Dale argued that Pennsylvania law strictly prohibited dying bequests made to charitable institutions. The probate judge was forced to honor the earlier will, but appended a plea that the Prescott sisters might show charity to the city where their elder brother had earned his fortune and lived for half a century. They did not. Attorney Dale returned home triumphant with a court decision worth $2,752,693. His personal fee, it has been suggested, may have been a million dollars. Flush with cash, Dale went on to become a two-term governor of New Hampshire and a major investor in Portsmouth real estate. Dale was also dead set against preservation at Strawbery Banke and later did his best to scuttle the project.

Under the direction—critics say "under the thumb"—of Charles Dale, the Prescott sisters gobbled up waterfront properties and razed the old buildings. Eventually, only three structures, including a historic eighteenth-century warehouse that housed Cappy Stewart's antique shop, were left standing in what is now the beautiful Prescott Park. Whether the "spinster" sisters were motivated by community spirit or the desire to wash away the stain of the former red light district is unknown. The upper end of the park opened in 1939 just a few months before the death of Mary Prescott, aged eighty-four. Josie Prescott survived to age ninety-one and her will left Charles Dale almost totally in charge of completing her dream park. Dale invested both his own money and the Prescotts' in a dizzying array of properties in the South End and beyond.

In another odd twist, Dale became even more powerful when Susie Walker Trask died in 1936. The widow of the Erie millionaire donated a considerable sum to three charities in her hometown of Portsmouth, New Hampshire. Additional gifts of stock in Mrs. Trask's company, combined with shares already inherited by the Prescott sisters, gave Charles Dale—who represented all the Portsmouth parties—legal control of the surviving Pennsylvania company for years to come.

Although she had left Portsmouth behind at the end of the Civil War in 1865, and despite her fifty-year marriage in Erie, Susie Walker Trask decreed that her body be shipped back to Portsmouth for burial. Sixteen years earlier the body of Charles Prescott, her husband's partner, had taken the same final train ride from Pennsylvania to a Portsmouth cemetery. Whatever bond the two shared went to the grave with them.

Today thousands of visitors attend open air concerts and theatre productions in the expanded Prescott Park. The coal sheds, rotted wharves, tidal inlet, and warehouses are gone, replaced by lavish flower gardens and expansive green lawns. The income from the estate of Charles W. Prescott still supports the waterfront park, but he gets little credit for his inadvertent benevolence. A small engraved stone at the entrance to the park was dedicated in a quiet ceremony in 1939. It names, not Charles W. Prescott the millionaire son, but his father Charles S. Prescott, a farmer, grocer, and carpenter who brought his three children into

When sisters Josephine (opposite) and Mary Prescott (above) inherited nearly three million dollars, they used their windfall to buy up waterfront property and tear down buildings along Water Street. (ATH)

the rugged neighborhood on Water Street, then died mysteriously in an upstairs bedroom just across the street from where his memorial stone now stands. Josie Prescott, the last surviving member of the Prescott family, was born in that same house in 1858. But the house is gone. It was torn down—flattened like the entire waterfront neighborhood they grew up in—by the Prescott sisters themselves.

Back to the Boom Days

In sharp contrast to the Prescotts, historian Stephen Decatur and architect John Mead Howells saw Puddle Dock and the surrounding South End, not as a blot on the landscape, but as the ultimate historic spot. No other city in America, they argued to the National Parks Department in 1935, could offer an intact waterfront neighborhood dating to 1800. Rather than tear out the decayed wharves and warehouses, Decatur and Howells wanted to rebuild them. The plan called for the tidal inlet, filled in since the turn of the twentieth century, to be dredged back out to the way it had appeared when the first Piscataqua settlers arrived. Local artisans would then build four wooden vessels of various sizes—a barcantine, a flat-bottomed gundalow, a "snow," and a "pinky" —and float them in the restored cove. Up to 175 historic South End buildings were to be restored while seventy-five "ugly modern houses" would be removed from the "Restored Area" and clustered in the "Model Tenement" area nearby.[3]

Decatur and Howells left no detail unplanned. Motorists passing through the city center toward the new Memorial Bridge would suddenly find themselves driving by a neighborhood caught sometime between the American Revolution and the War of 1812 when Portsmouth was at the peak of its vitality. Tourists could not miss the rehabilitated maritime village because the plan called for traffic to be rerouted down widened streets. Lured into strategically placed parking lots just north of the Puddle Dock area, visitors could enter an impressive orientation building reconstructed from a surviving portion of the Old Statehouse that once stood in the center of Market Square under colonial governor John Wentworth.[4] There they would be invited to purchase

ABOVE: *Charles W. Prescott of Portsmouth became a millionaire working in Erie, Pennsylvania, and almost left his fortune there. His money, however, and his body were returned to Portsmouth after his death. (ATH)*

"strip tickets," redeemable at all seven of Portsmouth's independent house museums. By selling historic "Old Portsmouth" from a single location, Stephen Decatur argued, each house would attract more visitors and make more than a subsistence income. If the maritime village could draw just one-tenth of the existing summer traffic passing through Portsmouth to Maine—calculated at a million and a half vehicles—the South End restoration could pay for itself with ticket sales alone.

And there was more. The 1936 proposal called for a bridge leading to the city-owned Peirce Island, site of the nation's only intact earthwork fort, dubbed Fort Washington during the American Revolution. The site has since become a sewage treatment plant, and its archeological value destroyed. The planned Restoration Area also included the William Pitt Tavern, Point of Graves colonial cemetery, a revamped tidal mill, the restored "swing bridge," and the historic Liberty Pole, as well as the site of the 1631 Great House. Rather than create major new museum space, the Howells-Decatur plan emphasized what later became known as "adaptive rehabilitation" of old buildings into modern use, cleverly clustered around existing historic sites.

The proposal called for the entire portion of the town to be taken by eminent domain. All sixty-three property owners are listed in the WPA proposal with a plan for compensating them. An estimated two hundred fifty families lived in the "Restoration Area" during the Great Depression, most of them transitional renters subsisting on government relief checks. These residents were not, as some still suppose, longtime descendants of the original waterfront families. These families, according to Howells-Decatur should enjoy a much better lifestyle when relocated to the "Model Tenement Area" that included "parking, beautification, green swards, parks, playgrounds, etc., with a public square." The plan calculated that the income from rents in the beautified residential areas made the project "self liquidating," thereby amortizing all costs within twenty years. Unemployed poor citizens, the planners argued, should find work during the initial two-year renovation period, thus removing them from the federal dole. Best of all for historian Decatur, by restoring old homes and recreating early wooden boats and ships here, a host of fading maritime trades could be recaptured and passed on to

ABOVE: *Lawyer Charles M. Dale broke the Prescott will in Erie, Pennsylvania, and returned triumphantly to Portsmouth. Also a Portsmouth mayor and New Hampshire governor, Dale oversaw the creation of Prescott Park, demolished the Treadwell mansion on Congress Street, and vehemently opposed the Strawbery Banke project. (BCP)*

ABOVE: *A 1960-era aerial view of Prescott Park by Douglas Armsden tells many tales. The flat area in the foreground shows the filled-in tidal inlet leading to the scrap piles located along Newton Ave. across Marcy Street at what is now Strawbery Banke. The park was still incomplete at this time and urban renewal was about to begin. Point of Graves, the city's oldest cemetery, is visible to the left. The Liberty Pole is in the center across from the home of the Marconi family. The Sheafe Warehouse (bottom right) has been moved to its new location. (SBM/DA)*

future generations. As in the eighteenth century, the Portsmouth waterfront would again be home to blockmakers, sailmakers, joiners, blacksmiths, and the like, employed to reconstruct historic tall ships for the maritime tourism industry. Artisans would also be able to restore and purchase dilapidated homes in the area with government assistance. [5]

Designed to tap the flow of federal make-work projects during Franklin Roosevelt's "New Deal" administration, the Howells-Decatur plan received serious attention as early as 1934. A key member of the National Park Service visited Portsmouth and reported enthusiastically to his director. "I am convinced that such a development would rival Williamsburg in popularity," he wrote.[6] Portsmouth was frequently compared to the recently opened outdoor museum in Virginia. Both Portsmouth and Williamsburg had been important social and political centers before the American Revolution. Both had been provincial capitals, before the center of government moved elsewhere. Both had fallen on hard economic times. Due partly to this lack of prosperity, in both Portsmouth and in Williamsburg, many old buildings survived. The description of Williamsburg in an early guidebook as "a pleasingly decayed colonial city" exactly matched descriptions of New Hampshire's seaport. Creating this extraordinary outdoor museum in Virginia ultimately meant tearing down or removing five hundred "post-colonial" structures, restoring sixty-seven, and replicating another hundred buildings. Portsmouth, by comparison, was a modest proposal.

Fear of modernization prompted the creation of both Colonial Williamsburg and eventually Strawbery Banke. But Howells and Decatur were more interested in rejuvenating the existing waterfront. In 1944, ten years after his first proposal, still pushing the Portsmouth maritime village idea in a letter to President Franklin D. Roosevelt, Howells trumpeted the waterfront project as "greater than Williamsburg." Portsmouth was more authentic than the "recreated" Colonial Williamsburg, he argued, because it already existed and required only rehabilitation. This battle cry was recycled during the formation of Strawbery Banke Inc. in 1957, even though the later project was very different from the WPA concept.[7]

ABOVE: *Stephen Decatur Jr. was a naval officer best known for heroism against the Barbary Pirates and in the War of 1812. He was killed in a duel with another officer in 1820. (JDR)*

Two more capable champions could not have been found. Both Decatur and Howells had famous progenitors, one a naval hero, one a literary lion. Both came from well-known families, a condition that allowed them access into high society, but sometimes worked against them when attempting to rally Portsmouth locals. Both were summer neighbors at Kittery Point, just a short sail from Pepperell Cove around the Naval Shipyard to the banks of Puddle Dock.

Stephen Decatur, the fourth naval officer to wear that name, had big shoes to fill. His famous name has appeared on five United States battleships, eleven American cities and communities, and countless schools, streets, and buildings. The first American Decatur, a contemporary of John Paul Jones, served aboard a number of privateer ships in the Revolutionary War. His famous son, Stephen Decatur Jr., is best known for his valor in the War of 1812, and for defeating the dreaded Barbary Pirates. He was killed in a duel by another officer whom he had helped to court marshal years before. Since he died childless, the next naval commander in the family, a veteran of the Spanish American War, was descended from Decatur's brother. Stephen Decatur III grew up in Kittery and could trace his Piscataqua roots back to 1750 as part of the Storer and Lear families on his mother's side. The congenial old gentleman was most fond of fishing and hunting and never passed up an opportunity to show off his own private museum of naval memorabilia that he kept on display in the family homestead.

Stephen Decatur IV was born in Portsmouth in 1886 and, like the three Prescotts, graduated from the local high school. His darkest hour came in 1906, at Annapolis, when an incident of hazing reportedly took place in midshipman Decatur's dorm room. The resulting court martial case made national news. Decatur denied the charges and defended himself at trial, and although not convicted, he did not graduate with his class. Decatur served in World War I as a navigator on a destroyer and later ran his own manufacturing company. An avid historian and genealogist, Decatur discovered a collection of records of George Washington's household in an old family trunk, many written by his collateral ancestor Tobias Lear. Decatur published his study of the letters in his book, *The Private Affairs of George*

Washington, in 1933. The following year his father died at Kittery Point and Decatur, in collaboration with architect Howells, focused his attention on a visionary plan to restore the Portsmouth waterfront.[8]

John Mead Howells, meanwhile, was at work on a series of books for use primarily by serious students of early American architecture. Born in 1868, Howells was semi-retired, summering in Kittery and wintering in Charleston, South Carolina, by the mid-1930s. His career included a number of notable urban designs like the "Tribune Tower," headquarters of the Chicago Tribune. In 1931, he published *Lost Examples of Colonial Architecture*, a nation-wide picture study that included a number of Portsmouth buildings. Howells was working intensely on his influential photographic volume *The Architectural Heritage of the Piscataqua* (1937) even as he and Decatur were pushing their maritime village idea to the National Park Service.

Soliciting support for their "Portsmouth Project" in 1936, Howells wrote to the eminent American architect Ralph Adams Cram saying:

> I have worked for several years on this with the mayor of Portsmouth and Stephen Decatur, who is deeply interested in Portsmouth, and I think the Interior Department idea is to have Mr. Decatur present this personally to Mr. Roosevelt, because of his name and the President's interest in naval history.[9]

Howells had a prestigious name of his own. The only son of writer William Dean Howells, he was already successful in his own right when his nomadic father purchased a summer house at Kittery Point in 1902. Self-taught, witty, and gregarious, William Dean Howells originally hailed from southern Ohio. He was "discovered" and brought to New England, curiously, by Boston publisher James T. Fields who grew up on the edge of Portsmouth's Puddle Dock. Fields hired Howells to assist with his new magazine, *The Atlantic Monthly,* for which Howells and a former Puddle Docker, Thomas Bailey Aldrich, later served as editors.

Although the Howells's connection to the Piscataqua was less deeply rooted than the Decaturs', William Dean Howells

ABOVE: *Architect John Mead Howells, son of author William Dean Howells, wrote the well-known 1937 book* The Architectural Heritage of the Piscataqua *and organized an unsuccessful attempt with Stephen Decatur to transform Portsmouth's South End waterfront into a maritime village restoration project in the 1930s and '40s. (HOW)*

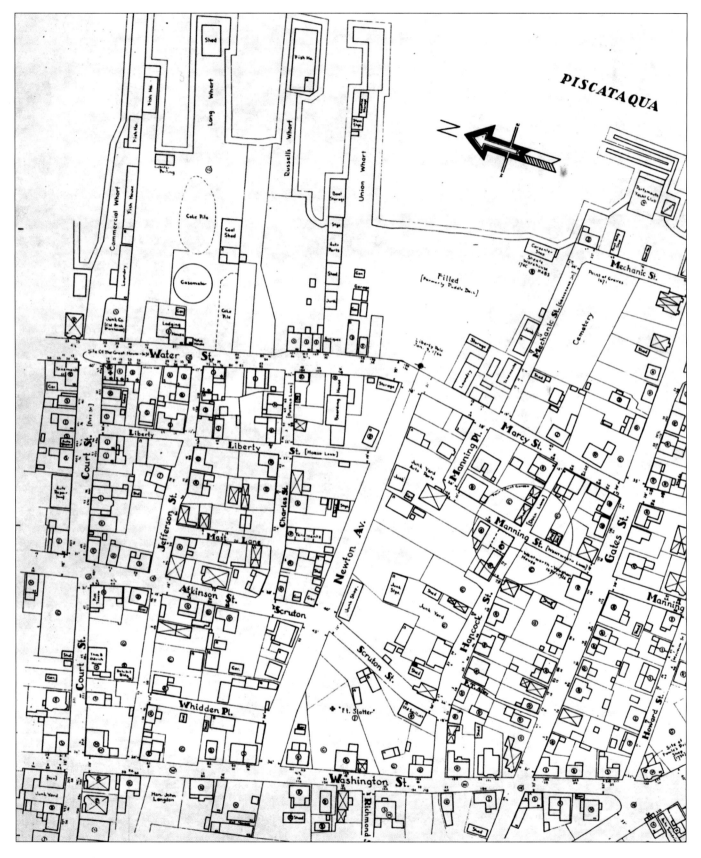

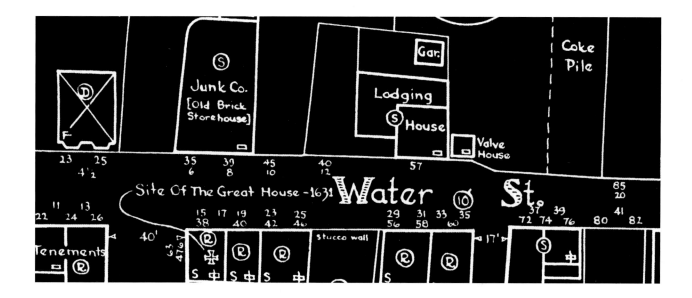

earned a favorable reputation among the locals.[10] He frequented the streets of Portsmouth, lectured at St. John's Church, loved riding the seacoast trolleys and gave books to the Kittery town library. Howells sometimes attended summer services at the Congregational Church in Kittery Point, just across the street from the historic Lady Pepperrell House which John Mead Howells later restored in 1922. When his father purchased another cottage at nearby York, John took over the Kittery Point house that included an impressive library built in a former horse stable. But the famous author still visited his grandchildren at Kittery until his death in 1920. One of those grandchildren, William White Howells, was destined to marry the woman who, as much as any other individual, orchestrated the founding of Strawbery Banke Museum.

High Tide, Ebb Tide

When Congress passed the Historic Sites Act in 1935, hope for the Howells-Decatur proposal blossomed. The Act summed up the very essence of the Portsmouth project when it promised "to provide for the preservation of historic American sites, buildings, objects, and antiquities of national significance. . .for the inspiration and benefit of the American people."[11]

ABOVE: *Examination of the 1936 map shows a clear awareness of the historic sites in the Puddle Dock area, including the site of the 1631 Great House (seen here), the Liberty Pole, the John Wentworth House and Point of Graves. (NHHS)*

OPPOSITE: *A detail of the 1936 Howells-Decatur WPA proposal for the South End waterfront. The plan did not create a museum, but instead proposed to restore many buildings to create a working waterfront as it might have looked in 1800. (NHHS)*

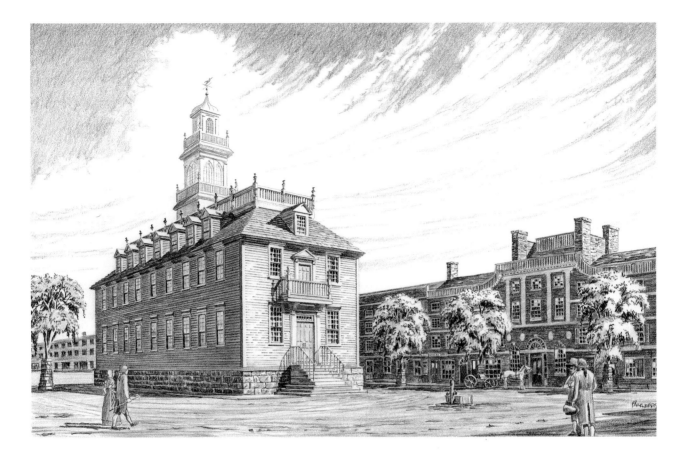

But John Mead Howells quickly suspected that the Interior Department did not have pockets deep enough to rehabilitate an entire city sector. Appealing to the financially strapped New Hampshire seaport was simply wasted energy. "In Portsmouth there is nothing," he told William Sumner Appleton in 1935, "the last of the aristocracy is falling—it is a town of tradespeople and politicians without interest in old houses."[12]

But the rollercoaster ride had just begun. The National Parks Service was intrigued. Portsmouth made its way onto the top ten list of potential park projects, and by 1936, it was among the top three sites in the nation slated for investigation, along with Annapolis, Maryland, and Nachez, Mississippi.

"It seemed for just a fleeting moment," according to preservation historian Charles B. Hosmer, Jr., "that the plan would work—that the National Park Service could get the money and the personnel to go into Portsmouth with a restoration program."[13]

Howells and WPA research architect Donald Corley toured the South End to gather data for a "base map" in order to define the precise boundaries of the Portsmouth Project. There was even talk that the National Park Service might purchase an historic house in Portsmouth to use as its headquarters during further research. Howells received a copy of the "Map of the Proposed Restoration at Portsmouth, N.H." from Corley in December 1936. The blueprint outlined every building along Marcy Street from top to bottom, extending to Washington and Gate streets, and as far up Pleasant Street as the Governor John Wentworth house (site of the current Wentworth Home). Every building in the area was marked by symbols indicating which were to be restored, saved, removed to the tenement area or demolished. Howells enthusiastically sent a copy of the blueprint to his colleague Ralph Adams Cram, who was himself a seacoast New Hampshire native born in North Hampton. The restored old Portsmouth, Howells wrote, would become "a splendid American picture."[14]

BELOW: *President Franklin D. Roosevelt made a whistle-stop visit through Portsmouth to the Portsmouth Naval Shipyard in 1940, passing down Daniel Street and right by Puddle Dock. Frank Hersey photo. (SBM/DA)*

Nothing happened quickly. Aware that federal funds were tight, John Mead Howells moved to his backup funding plan early in 1937. Colonial Williamsburg had found, in John D. Rockefeller, Jr., a primary source of capital. Rockefeller eventually contributed a major portion of the $25 million required for Virginia's enormous outdoor history museum. Portsmouth, Howells told his old friend Edith Wendell, needed its own Rockefeller. Mrs. Wendell had quickly located the $10,000 required to buy the Warner House five years earlier, but this giant project was another thing altogether. The 1936 WPA proposal based on Howells-Decatur called for a total budget of $2.5 million, just one-tenth of the Williamsburg tab. Plan B of the proposal suggested that private seed funding of about $650,000 was adequate to get the job started. Howells suggested gently to Mrs. Wendell early in 1937 that she might want to try contacting automaker Henry Ford for the money. Ford had spent as much as Rockefeller building his own historic Greenfield Village museum not far from his Michigan home. But Mrs. Wendell was unable to get more than a polite form rejection from Ford's secretary, which she quickly forwarded to Howells.

"I suppose we can hardly blame him," Howells responded. "We will have to carry on some other way." Howells was more disappointed with Roosevelt, a former Secretary of the Navy who had been known to vacation along the Piscataqua. Of the President, then moving from a national depression to a world war, Howells complained to Wendell, "Except for matters of their own policies I fear this administration is largely promises."[15]

Howells must have been especially frustrated when he learned that on April 10, 1940, while making a pre-war tour of the Portsmouth Naval Shipyard, President Franklin Roosevelt passed right by the proposed maritime village site. In his third and final visit to Portsmouth, Roosevelt rode in an open car up Daniel Street, past the historic Warner House and across the Memorial Bridge, one hundred yards from Puddle Dock. After just fifty-five minutes in the region, Roosevelt boarded his yacht *Potomac*, just across the river from the waterfront neighborhood, and sailed into history.[16]

ABOVE: *Three wooden eagles have topped the Liberty Pole at Puddle Dock since 1824. The original sculpture hangs in the Portsmouth Public Library. This latest version was carved by Ron Raiselis, the cooper at Strawbery Banke for over two decades. The "beehive" carving below includes thirteen balls representing the original colonies. (CER)*

Captain Mayo and the WPA Brigade

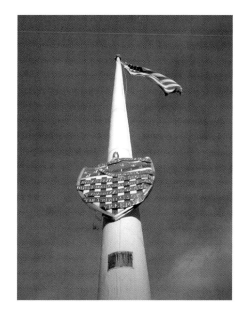

Howells, Decatur, and the Prescott sisters were not the only people with a historic vision for pre-war Puddle Dock. The ancient Liberty Pole site, seen today in modern Prescott Park, was then under consideration as a possible New Hampshire state park. Arthur I. Harriman, an amateur Portsmouth historian, was so passionate on the topic that he drew the attention and assistance of Ralph Adams Cram and William Sumner Appleton. Harriman served as advisor to the Liberty Bridge State Park committee in the 1930s, reminding the governor and all who would listen that Portsmouth residents had turned this spot into hallowed ground when they defied the Stamp Act there in 1766, nine years before the American Revolution.[17] Like the 1774 raid at Fort William and Mary, the Liberty Pole story had become a critical incident in a growing canon of patriotic colonial revival tales that attempted to place the largely-forgotten Portsmouth story within the mainstream of American history. New Hampshire not only participated in the national story, locals claimed, but sometimes led the way.

WPA researcher Donald Corley, perhaps unwisely, included Harriman's emotional commentary as the opening salvo in a 1937 update of the sophisticated Howells-Decatur proposal as it continued to circulate around Washington. Cobbling passages from nineteenth-century writers like Brewster, Foster, and Aldrich, Harriman rambled wildly in his introduction to "the finest harbor in the world." His sometimes inaccurate, ungrammatical, and archaic-sounding tour of the South End began and ended at his beloved Liberty Pole site, a site little remembered outside the boundaries of Portsmouth, if even there. Harriman opined:

> Where could be found the length and breadth of our land a shrine that from which radiated so early the true spirit of Liberty? By patriots whose ardor, by their action, not by words alone, but by immortal deeds. Heroes who rallied around this sacred shrine, whose loyalty figured so prominently in the birth of our nation.[18]

ABOVE: *A wooden shield was added to the Liberty Pole in 1857. The shield is dedicated to the nation's "emancipation from tyranny" on July 4, 1776. It includes thirteen stars and thirteen stripes. The shield has been replaced once. (JDR)*

In marked contrast to Harriman, Portsmouth's next pre-war preservationist worked with mechanical precision. A naval disbursing officer transferred to the Portsmouth Naval Shipyard, Captain Chester G. Mayo appeared on the scene early in 1937. John Mead Howells was then completing his book on Piscataqua architecture and seeking funds for his maritime park while attorney Charles Dale was buying up waterfront property for the Prescotts. Dale's incredible purchasing power in a depressed real estate market both intrigued and frightened many locals. Dale was also president of the New Hampshire State Senate about this time and soon after a member of the Governor's Council. Like so many newcomers, Captain Mayo fell under the spell of "The Old Town by the Sea" and agreed to manage a newly formed Historical Reconstruction Committee. Organized through Portsmouth Rotary, the committee was, on one level, a means to monitor Dale as he began buying, moving, and demolishing old Portsmouth buildings. Mayo pulled together an advisory group that included all the major players—Dale, Mayor Marvin, Appleton, Howells, *Portsmouth Herald* publisher F.W. Hartford, historian Ralph May, Mrs. Wendell, and Mrs. John Templeman Coolidge who owned the former Benning Wentworth mansion at Little Harbor.[19]

Organized and efficient by nature, Mayo knew that, before his committee could make decisions about restoring Portsmouth, he needed data. In order to gather data, he needed a system. Mayo turned naturally to the city assistant librarian Dorothy Vaughan, then in her early thirties and a storehouse of local historical information. Vaughan had distinguished herself in 1930 at the age of twenty-six by condensing the history of Portsmouth into a large detailed map. Her map was subtitled "Olde Strawbery Banke," a phrase the young writer recycled almost three decades later when she presided over a nonprofit corporation with the same distinctive spelling. Vaughan had assisted John Mead Howells in preparing the captions for his photographic book on Portsmouth architecture. She also assisted noted author Kenneth Roberts with research on his historical novel *Northwest Passage* and worked with writer Lois Lenski on her book about New Hampshire's legendary Ocean Born Mary. Vaughan was a Colonial Dame, an avid collector of photographs of historical portraits, a freelance writer for SPNEA, and her mother Mary was the librarian at the Portsmouth Athenaeum. Vaughan agreed to chair Mayo's subcommittee on buildings. Her assignment was to identify all the historic buildings in the South End worthy of attention by the Restoration Committee. Howells provided Vaughan with a copy of the 1936 WPA "blueprint" for his maritime village project. Vaughan eventually submitted 232 buildings for analysis. To evaluate them, Mayo designed a five-part scale for rating each structure based on its age, historic value, physical appearance, architectural style and surrounding environment.

Mayo's goal, ultimately, was to create a system from which the entire city could be methodically restored, or possibly to help attract private funding for the Howells-Decatur plan. It included a rating scale, not entirely unlike the one used decades later by federal agencies to identify substandard housing for urban renewal. But the Dale-Prescott demolition project was already in gear and Vaughan's volunteer group was falling behind schedule. Mayo requested more help from the WPA. A federal representative reviewed the work of the Restoration Committee and found it not of sufficient quality, but the agency was already tapped out with work in the historic seaport at Salem, Massachusetts, and unable to offer assistance. Mayo turned instead to state WPA officer Eugene Clark who was headquartered in nearby Durham. In the spring of 1938, Clark got approval for a group of researchers, mostly out-of-work men and University of New

BELOW: *The Liberty Pole is visible here down Newton Ave. looking toward the Piscataqua River at what is now Prescott Park. Scrap yards evolved on the flat filled area that was once the Puddle Dock tidal inlet, seen here around 1935. (SBM)*

Hampshire architecture students, just as Dale was threatening to raze an old warehouse to make way for Prescott Park.

With historic buildings already falling—thirty of those identified were lost during the years that the Restoration Committee deliberated—the new team of WPA researchers dove into the Rockingham Country deeds and documents on file in Exeter. Others worked with Vaughan to index all the key historic books relating to Portsmouth. The crew generated so much paperwork that the next problem was where to store it all. But in the fall of 1938 Captain Mayo was transferred to the Brooklyn Navy Yard. The Portsmouth Restoration Committee sailed on, but without Captain Mayo at the tiller, it faltered and eventually collided with the approaching world war like a canoe against a battleship.

Letters between Eugene Clark and Dorothy Vaughan show that they were still digging for information about Portsmouth houses well into 1940. Questions of who had lived where and when often went unanswered, and decisions about the historic "value" of buildings, despite acres of paper, often came down to guesswork. Struggling with one fuzzy detail, Clark wrote to Vaughan in January, 1940: "I am sorry to leave the question so much in the air . . . but I think this is an example that will show you the difficulties that we encounter in determining identity of houses, even when the chain of land ownership is without question."[20]

After three years of work, the results of the WPA study, including a few artistically sketched maps of Portsmouth, was trimmed down to an exhibit held in Ballard Hall of the University of New Hampshire. The exhibit closed four days later. The paperwork found its way into various state and federal filing cabinets. Dorothy Vaughan kept a copy of the WPA project in the local library where it has been used, on occasion, by residents searching for the history of a newly purchased home. The maritime village idea died slowly. In 1944, John Mead Howells suggested in yet another letter to President Roosevelt that the Portsmouth restoration plan might make an ideal post-war recovery project. The White House response, in a nutshell, was that they had heard it all before.

In his sweeping two-volume study of American historic preservation in the first half of the twentieth century, Charles

Hosmer chalked up the failed New Hampshire waterfront restoration efforts to red tape and short-sighted government programs. Hosmer concluded that, in Portsmouth, "the real leaders had to come from outside the community."[21] It was outsiders like Mayo, Decatur, and Howells, who spearheaded preservation efforts, while insiders like Charles Dale and the Prescott sisters preferred outright demolition of old buildings. This had been largely true during the creation of the city's independent house museums as well, with preservation efforts spearheaded by outsiders and summer visitors like Lilian Aldrich, Edith Wendell, the Colonial Dames of New Hampshire, Wallace Nutting, Woodbury Langdon, and William Sumner Appleton. While a few passionate local figures like Arthur Harriman, Reverend Alfred Gooding of the Portsmouth Historical Society, and Dorothy Vaughan were active in the preservation movement, they were exceptional among a generally apathetic public and without the financial resources or important political and social connections required to initiate real change. Even with the assistance of the WPA, Portsmouth citizens were not yet up to the task of preserving historic structures on a grand scale. Once created, Strawbery Banke would come to depend heavily on the largesse of a few benefactors who usually lived out of town.

Despite public malaise, the *Portsmouth Herald* continually published lengthy articles on Portsmouth history during the 1930s and with added patriotic gusto through the 1940s. While reporting on the WPA research in 1938, one unnamed *Herald* writer restated the popular colonial revival belief that the city's ancient charm "cast its welcome spell of rest and contentment over the all too hurried visitor." After recycling the story of the strawberries found along the colonial banks of the Piscataqua, the writer offered this editorial:

> There is an increasing realization that the wealth of New Hampshire comes in a very large part from tourist trade. The completeness of historical information and anecdotes [by the WPA] will add to tourists' interest and it is hoped that it will also increase local interest and pride in preserving old structures and the ancient character of Strawberry Bank and Portsmouth.[22]

The Coming War on Puddle Dock

Despite its failure, the Howells-Decatur proposal gave voice to the idea of a historic waterfront park. Twenty years later, it became the core of the Strawbery Banke Inc. plan. But the 1936-1937 WPA proposal also contained a ticking time bomb. The report referred five times to the waterfront neighborhood as a "slum," a term that would be applied to Puddle Dock often in the two decades before the neighborhood was emptied of its entire population by urban renewal.

This powerful four-letter word carried both political and moral implications. The term described the poor and crowded neighborhoods that appeared in many American cities early in the twentieth century during a burst of immigration. Drawn to jobs in urban factories, foreign-born workers and their families often could find shelter only in poorly built tenement buildings. A "slum," as defined by the federal government in the early 1930s, was seen as an area of substandard housing. But it was also a potential "social liability" to the nearby community. Substandard living conditions, it was generally believed, bred substandard people. Slum housing was often characterized as unsanitary, overcrowded, lacking light and fresh air, unsafe and run-down, and its occupants were often poor, transitional, and ethnically diverse.[23]

In Lawrence, Massachusetts, for example, tenement housing for thousands of immigrant textile workers was so dense that some areas rarely saw the light of day. Federal standards designed for cities like Lawrence, or Boston and New York, were also applied to the relatively tiny neighborhood in Portsmouth. WPA studies showed that the little New Hampshire waterfront area contained a cluster of families on relief, living in broken-down buildings not far from commercial junkyards. Color-coded city maps generated by federal surveys rated each city block based on detailed research. Each block was defined by the number of housing units, the number of occupants per unit, the number or absence of flush toilets and hot water faucets, the age and value of each house, the number of homeowners versus renters, and the race of its occupants. The "blighted" Puddle Dock neighborhood contained, not only the oldest houses in town, but the core

OPPOSITE: *The last remnant of a once thriving seaport, the Sheafe Warehouse (c. 1705) was designed so that flat-bottomed gundalows could easily transfer goods. Fear for the destruction of the last of the warehouse buildings helped spark the preservation work of Chester Mayo. "Cappy" Stewart used the building to store his antiques. The building is seen here around 1935 in its original position near the current Peirce Island Bridge and in a nineteenth century sketch (insert) by Sarah Haven Foster. It stands today in Prescott Park. (SBM and PPL)*

ABOVE: *This photograph of Puddle Dockers, often reproduced in museum materials, has sometimes been misinterpreted. The photo was sent to Sherman Pridham, then on active duty in World War II. The liquor bottle in the hands of his brother Zeke was a symbolic gesture. It was being saved for a toast to celebrate the soldier's safe return from the war. (SBM)*

RIGHT: *On an outing Dickie Tibbetts, Joan and Doris Finnigan of Puddle Dock pose for a "special effects" picture. (PEC)*

population of the city's "negro" and Jewish residents, as well as a widely diverse range of foreign immigrants.

If slums produced bad people, housing reformers believed, then conversely, good housing could produce good people. The sweeping solution was embedded in the Howells-Decatur plan that would not only restore 175 homes, but move residents of seventy-five newer buildings into more attractive garden-style housing blocks. But how could such sweeping change be made? The plan stated:

> It is proposed that the State of New Hampshire, or the City of Portsmouth, take over the area by right of eminent domain, by an act condemning these properties on the ground of unsanitary conditions, just as any slum area is condemned elsewhere.[24]

The planners were mostly concerned, not with the residents of the South End, but with the sixty-three people who owned real estate in the proposed restoration area. Buying up their property cheaply was critical to the success of the project. When architect Ralph Adams Cram asked Howells in 1936 whether he should keep the Portsmouth Project under his hat, Howells replied:

> There is no secrecy I can see about the whole matter, except the important one of not having it generally known in such a way that it might start stiffening of real estate prices among all the many little holders in that region, a good many of whom have become Italian and Hebrew immigrants but the remaining Yankees would be quite equal to the occasion also.[25]

Puddle Dockers never knew what almost hit them. The families most affected by the plan to return Portsmouth to its seafaring heyday were left entirely out of the loop. Historian Paige Roberts says such upper class planning of lower class destinies was typical of reform movements that attempted to help poor slum residents for their own good. Roberts writes:

> The deliberate exclusion of Puddle Dock inhabitants and the assumption that their displacement was necessary characterized improvement plans for Portsmouth's

ABOVE: *Puddle Dockers collected family photographs for a neighborhood reunion in 1982. A number of images showed children riding on a local pony. (PEC)*

waterfront section over the next two decades. Throughout the eastern United States, it became the norm to ignore the human cost of the proposals that tore up and dispersed neighborhoods, separated families, and obliterated small businesses.[26]

Puddle Dockers themselves often tell contradictory, but always colorful, tales of life in the first half of the twentieth century. They recall a tight-knit neighborhood where people left their doors unlocked and there was always a free meal and shelter for any wandering newcomer. Jewish families tended to socialize with each other, but mixed freely with longtime locals and with a variety of ethnic immigrant neighbors. "There was no animosity in any way, shape, or manner," Jack Zeidman recalled. "Nobody was envious of the next guy, that's for sure. And nobody had that much money that they could be envious of."[27]

Born in 1904, Zeidman inherited his father's Puddle Dock junkyard. The Zeidman family was among the largest property owners in the area, with even more square footage than Cappy Stewart. The family name appears nine times in the Howells-Decatur plan. Zeidman recalled Jewish families swimming at "Palestine Beach" near Peirce Island in the South End, dancing at a downtown club, and all-night parties at Hampton Beach. But when pressed during a 1977 interview, he remembered "some pretty rough characters" living in Water Street boarding houses that rented rooms for $10 a month. Public drunkenness and fighting, he remembered, were common place. Zeidman said he got his first taste of gin as a boy while drinking with Cappy Stewart and a local policeman during Prohibition. "This was the tough area of town," he admitted, but no tougher than "up the Crick" along Bartlett Street where the Irish lived, or in the city's Italian North End at Deer Street.

Jack Zeidman easily agreed that his family's sprawling junkyards piled with wrecked and rusting cars did nothing to enhance the public image of Puddle Dock. "Too bad scrap is such an ugly thing," he noted. "It's ugly looking and dirty and messy to handle. It ain't beautiful." But it was a good living, he added. Scrap sellers provided important access to recycled precious metals both during and between the war years. In 1929, his father had three

ABOVE: *Two young Puddle Dockers, identified as Dottie Westgate and Gloria Trueman, pose in what former residents universally describe as a safe and tightly-knit community. (PEC)*

thousand tons of scrap then worth $60,000. When prices suddenly plummeted at the onset of the Great Depression, he was forced to sell it for $15,000 to pay off overdue bank loans. But as the war loomed, the shipyard moved back into high gear, demand for scrap rose—and so did the Puddle Dock junk piles.

Six small grocery stores operated in Puddle Dock during World War II, each eking out a subsistence living for a family living above or beside the small store. No imagination is required to visualize life inside these typical family-owned shops because a perfectly restored version is open again today at Strawbery Banke, painstakingly reproduced right down to the labels on the cans and boxes that line the shelves. Although Bertha and Walter Abbott opened their "Little Corner Store" in 1919, museum curators stopped the history clock here between 1941 and 1945. The Abbott Store, therefore, offers twenty-first-century visitors a peek into a typical "mom and pop shop" during the war that transformed America. The permanent exhibit also provides a freeze-frame of the Puddle Dock neighborhood on the verge of its final decade.[28]

The Abbots exemplify the waterfront community in transition. Walter's father had been a rigger during the Age of Sail. Bertha was descended from a Nova Scotian fishing family. They married in 1896. She worked as a laundress, and he labored on the railroad until they opened their store soon after the red light district closed nearby. The building was already a century old when they purchased it and went through many renovations. The Abbotts and their children entered the store from their attached house through the candy room where they sold sweets in a large glass case. They shared the neighborhood with four junkyards, a bakery, two shoe shops, lots of residential homes, a restaurant, and a number of gardens. The Abbott house and store were listed in the Howells-Decatur proposal as worth just $1,800 in 1937.

When Walter Abbott died the following year in 1938, Bertha relied on her granddaughter for help in the store, but the granddaughter moved away when America entered the war in 1941. With all five of her grandchildren serving in the military, Bertha Abbott turned to a sixteen-year-old Puddle Dock boy named Leslie Clough who took on the lion's share of the work, rising two hours before school and returning to work during lunch and

ABOVE: *Louise Pridham with son Sherman, one of her thirteen children. Sherm grew up in Puddle Dock and fought in World War II. He returned to the neighborhood, worked at the shipyard, and raised a son, also named Sherm, who later succeeded Dorothy Vaughan as city librarian. (PEC)*

RIGHT: *Abbott Store employee Leslie Clough (on right) and other Puddle Dockers shovel snow on Jefferson Street circa 1940. (SBM)*

BELOW: *Walter Abbott in his "Little Corner Store" in Puddle Dock around 1937. The store is now fully restored as it appeared in the World War II era. (SBM)*

immediately after classes. Clough lived in the house with Bertha Abbott and stayed eight years until 1949. Similar tales of extreme interdependence and neighborliness are not uncommon in the tightly defined area bordered by Washington, Court, Hancock, and Water streets. What outsiders considered a slum, Puddle Dockers considered a safe haven.

Most Americans who lived through World War II recall rough times of rationed food, restricted travel, limited resources, and hard work. In Puddle Dock, such sacrifices were already standard living. In fact, life actually improved for many here, as war once again boosted the Portsmouth economy. Men unemployed a decade before now easily found work at the shipyard that, visible from Puddle Dock, was just a short hike over the Memorial Bridge to Kittery. Fully twenty-five percent of the men of Puddle Dock not in military service found work "on the Yard." Pumped up with federal money, the shipyard went from producing two submarines annually to an astonishing thirty-two submarines per year at its peak during the war. Insulated by poverty and reputation, Puddle Dock functioned like a small island with its vegetable gardens, easy access to fish and other seafood, its own scrap yard economy, and a well-defined social network, built from decades of living with few resources. More women went to work, and three of the rising number of neighborhood widows, including Bertha Abbott, were now in charge of the corner grocery shops.[29]

Unlike most American cities, Portsmouth elected a woman to its highest office during the war years. Mayor Mary Dondero, whose daughter Eileen Foley would eventually hold the same office, feared the city was about to be cut off from federal monies on which Portsmouth had become so dependent. Dondero, an Irish-American, married a first-generation Italian-American from the North End neighborhood. Anticipating tough times she warned locals in her 1945 inaugural address:

> It is a deadly serious task of reshaping and remolding the city of Portsmouth for the betterment of its present citizens and the boys and girls on the fighting fronts, who, please God, will return to us . . . I think that we should

put our heads together and learn just what aid we can secure for postwar rehabilitation.[30]

The new mayor was right. The real impact of the war on Puddle Dock came after the victory celebrations when the shipyard predictably cut back production and soldiers returned home. Swelled almost to bursting by the influx of residents during the booming war economy and addicted to government programs, Portsmouth and surrounding towns like Elliot and Kittery were now potentially in worse economic shape than during the Depression. Puddle Dockers had found it difficult to get bank loans for home mortgages during the war because their proximity to the Yard made them a "security risk." Now with so many new houses built on the outskirts of town to accommodate the exploding population, banks told Puddle Dockers that there was even less value in restoring rundown, inner city buildings. Bertha Abbott, like others, found that it was cheaper to tear down an apartment

BELOW: *Picture shows the launching of the USS* Parche *July 24, 1943. The war economy actually improved life in Puddle Dock. Jobs were plentiful at the Portsmouth Naval Shipyard just across the Piscataqua River in Kittery, where workers set records in submarine production during World War II. (PNS)*

building that she owned rather than repair it. She gave up the Little Corner Store in 1950 at the age of seventy-seven.

Sherm Pridham, who later succeeded Dorothy Vaughan as the city librarian, remembers the catch-22 of life in post-war Puddle Dock. Pridham's childhood home is now the Shapley-Drisco House exhibit at Strawbery Banke Museum, restored precisely as it appeared during his boyhood there in 1954. Walking through the reconstructed version of his family's rented living room today, Pridham notes that in his time, the house was always cold, not comfortably heated. It was dark, too, he says, even "Dickensian." Pridham remembers that his father, a former shipyard worker returning from World War II, wanted to improve conditions in their rented house. His father asked the landlord to paint the old house, but the landlord refused. Pridham vividly remembers what happened next.

> My father went down [to the landlord], and said to him, "I'll tell you what—if you buy the paint, I'll paint it." And the landlord said, "If you do, I'll have you in jail." You see, the landlord wanted it valued low, otherwise he'd pay more taxes, and as he told my father, then he'd have to raise our rent.[31]

It was through national legislation, designed to improve post-war living conditions for families like the Pridhams, that Puddle Dock eventually met its demise. The Federal Housing Act in 1949 made federal grants available to communities that wanted to clear and prepare land for redevelopment. The community had to put up only one-third of the cost; the rest was provided by the federal government. Communities were required to create an active planning committee and had to agree that, once rehabilitated, the neighborhood would not be allowed to slide back into its blighted and deteriorated condition. This was the genesis of the urban renewal program that had such a profound effect on American cities over the next few decades. An update to the Federal Housing Act in 1954 allowed that not all buildings had to be torn down, but might be restored or conserved as part of urban renewal.

Immediately following the war, the Baby Boom generation joined the cluster of children who ranged through their turf in

ABOVE: *The last generation of Puddle Dockers were the first of the Baby Boom generation born just after World War II.* (PEC)

Puddle Dock, rarely venturing into the hostile "South Ender" territory two blocks away. Sherm Pridham's family was the first on the block to own a television. He recalls neighbors sitting in chairs outdoors watching the TV through the Pridhams's living room window. He points out the narrow alley between the 1795 Drisco House and the 1695 Sherburne House that he and his friends dubbed "Batman's Cave." Like so many generations before, roving bands of kids played games in the streets and explored the waterfront. Bad boys and bad girls clashed in the traditional snowball fights and pretended to navigate junked cars through imaginary worlds. By 1955, with the Cold War and Communists replacing the Nazi threat, the Portsmouth Naval Shipyard was developing a new generation of nuclear-powered submarines. And just across the street from the Pridhams, the Marconi family had recently moved into their dream house on a piece of land across from Prescott Park. It was not their land for long. Years later, it would belong to the federal government, as America began a campaign to rid itself of "dangerous slums" like Puddle Dock.

Children outside Gould's Market on Charles Street around 1915, another family-run business in Puddle Dock. Proprietor Georgie Gould, a colorful local character, was half sister to Bertha Abbott whose Little Corner Store was located just two blocks away. (SBM and PEC)

THREE STRONG VOICES
1955–1958

Legend says Strawbery Banke Inc. was formed almost magically when librarian Dorothy Vaughan gave a rousing speech at the Portsmouth Rotary in June 1957. She warned business leaders that the Old Town by the Sea was dying. Bowling alleys, honkytonks, and stores with plate glass windows and neon signs were rapidly replacing grand colonial homes. Pretty soon, she said, Portsmouth would look like Main Street, USA. Citizens rallied, and when urban renewal threatened to wipe out the city's most historic neighborhood at Puddle Dock, preservationists stepped in to create an outdoor museum out of twenty-seven historic buildings spanning two full city blocks.

That is the short version of the story, the one repeated endlessly in the local newspapers and tourist brochures for half a century. But the full story of the museum founding is even more interesting—richer with important characters, filled with twists and turns, and the source of endless controversy. It is the story of a neighborhood preserved, and at the same time, destroyed. It is also the story of how two local women and one man from Washington, exercising very different types of power, called many citizens to rise up and take action.

Portsmouth was still a Navy town in the 1950s and the Portsmouth Naval Shipyard was its largest employer. Downtown merchants were solidly focused on serving visiting submariners,

OPPOSITE: *Muriel Gurdon Seabury Howells (center) was born in New York and summered in Portsmouth, New Hampshire, as a child. Married to noted anthropologist William White Howells, she was later instrumental in creating, administering and funding Strawbery Banke Museum. (HOW)*

shipyard workers, and their families, rather than the trickle of seasonal visitors. Today's assortment of live theaters, boutique-style shops, art galleries, and fine restaurants were unknown. A collection of diners, movie houses, clothing and hardware stores, and hard-knuckle bars dominated.

In the 1950s, Portsmouth also became an Air Force town. What began as a small municipal airport on the outskirts of town grew into a massive 4,365-acre facility that swallowed large tracts of land in Portsmouth, Newington, and Greenland through aggressive federal purchasing and eminent domain. The first B-47 bombers arrived at the new Strategic Air Command base in 1954. Pease Air Force Base swelled the local population and fueled the economy until it was closed suddenly in 1991. Today, back in local hands, it has become a high-technology industrial park. But during the rise of the Cold War, with Portsmouth Naval Shipyard busy producing nuclear-powered submarines, the region was as dependent on the federal government as it had once been on the West India Trade. If the federal money ran out, many warned, New Hampshire's only seaport would be left high and dry. As usual, the economy, not historic preservation, dominated Portsmouth as the Baby Boom era dawned.

ABOVE: *Dorothy Vaughan lived in Penacook, New Hampshire, until her family moved to Portsmouth when she was 12 in 1917. (NHHS)*

Dorothy and Muriel

The two women who championed the Strawbery Banke renaissance were from different worlds. Muriel Howells and Dorothy Vaughan might never have crossed paths if not for their shared love of history and their shared horror at the destruction of downtown colonial houses. Neither woman was Portsmouth-born, but both arrived in the city as young girls, made her presence quickly known, and fought tirelessly for historic preservation into her ninth decade.

Dorothy Mansfield Vaughan was born in Penacook, New Hampshire, in 1904. She won her first fight at age five, she once told a *Boston Globe* reporter, when the boy next door tried to take one of her toys. "I said no and whacked him on the head," Vaughan recalled. "I've been fighting and scrapping ever since."[1]

The Vaughan name features prominently in Portsmouth history. Wealthy William Vaughan was among the early merchant aristocracy. A judge, military major, member of the Governor's Council, and a slave owner, he was buried at Point of Graves near Puddle Dock in 1719. His son, George Vaughan, preceded the first John Wentworth as lieutenant governor of New Hampshire. Initially Dorothy Vaughan believed she was descended from these colonial leaders, but eventually discovered that her family tree was rooted elsewhere.

She was twelve years old in 1917 when her father took a job at the shipyard and moved Vaughan, her mother and her two brothers, Donald and Oscar, to Portsmouth. In 1921, while still in high school, she became a page at the Portsmouth Public Library. The following year, she officially joined the staff as third assistant librarian, tenaciously working her way up the ladder from the children's room to the reference desk, to first assistant librarian, and finally to head librarian by 1945. Although she was unable to go to college, Vaughan attended classes and eventually earned state certification as city librarian.

"I was there for fifty-four years," Vaughan joked at her ninety-fifth birthday party as the mayor presented her with the key to the city. "When I was head of the Portsmouth Library, my mother was head librarian at the Athenaeum. We had power!"[2]

ABOVE: *A young Dorothy Vaughan poses in front of the Rockingham Hotel where, decades later, she presented her famous speech on preservation to the Portsmouth Rotary. (NHHS)*

Vaughan's power was well earned. She read voraciously and, in her early years, asked endless questions of the reigning local historians like Reverend Gooding and Ralph May. She became an accomplished writer and, even today, her New Hampshire history articles exhibit the exuberance, wit, bluntness, and conversational style she expressed in person. She possessed a photographic memory, and could recall dates, names, addresses, and even phone numbers, more than half a century after studying them. What she lacked in education and worldliness (Vaughan did not get her driver's license until she was seventy), she made up for in energy. She never married, and by her own admission, rarely said no to a request for her time, which she usually volunteered. Her annual salary after twenty years at the library was still under $3,000.

Although there was little income to be made as the city's preeminent history researcher, Vaughan leveraged her ubiquitous presence into a career. She gave time to literally every historic house museum in town, serving as a trustee on many boards, creating exhibits, and writing essays. A long time Girl Scout leader, Vaughan marshaled her young troops like a volunteer army. As the gatekeeper of local information, she became a key source for newspaper, radio, and magazine reporters, who, in turn, featured her in scores of published articles. As a leader in the New Hampshire Historical Society and the New Hampshire Library Association, her reputation spread across the state in articles with titles like "Ask Dorothy," "Dorothy Vaughan Has the Answers," "A Woman of History," and in her later years, "The Woman Who Saved Portsmouth."

Heaped with public praise, especially after the founding of Strawbery Banke, Vaughan was most proud of an honorary doctorate from the University of New Hampshire in 1965. From that year on, she meticulously edited her title in all publications from "Miss Vaughan" to "Dr. Vaughan." Reporters who neglected her title often received a sharp rebuke. Entire generations grew up under her reign at the public library where Vaughan was both revered and feared. She inspired such loyalty that, when the city manager attempted to retire Vaughan at age seventy, enraged city council members tried to change the state's retirement laws. One councilman even threatened to quit over the ruling.

ABOVE: *City librarian Dorothy Vaughan became president of Strawbery Banke Inc. during its formative years and lived to age 99. She is seen here posing in the Portsmouth Public Library where she worked for 53 years.* (NHHS)

For nearly three decades after her retirement Dorothy Vaughan retained her influence over Portsmouth history. As a "living encyclopedia of Portsmouth lore,"[3] she acted as a bridge between the nineteenth and twenty-first centuries and her memories became dogma. But as an "old school" historian, like Charles Brewster before her, Vaughan often accepted anecdotes and legends as facts, especially if those accounts placed the aristocratic families of Portsmouth in a heroic light. And she often dismissed and distrusted trained historians who did not accept her "heroification" of her beloved Portsmouth forebears. Those who doubted or defied her interpretation of history might find themselves denied access to further interviews.

"She's also one of the most entertaining raconteurs you'll ever run into," a city council member and history buff once noted. "Dorothy has a way of telling stories about people from the past as if she were telling you neighborhood gossip."[4] Vaughan never tired, for example, of recounting the tale of the young women of Portsmouth who sewed their petticoats into a flag for John Paul Jones. Jones, according to legend, carried the Stars and Stripes aboard the warship *Ranger* while attacking the British Isles in 1777. Even though the author of this story that first appeared in 1900 was dismissed by serious historians, Augustus C. Buell's account was accepted by Vaughan as gospel. A brass plaque affixed to the side of the John Paul Jones House in 1913 repeated the story, and that, Vaughan concluded, was that. Teachers, tourists, school children, and newspaper reporters accepted and perpetuated her romantic story without question year after year, decade after decade.

Strawbery Banke's second "Originator," Muriel Gurdon Seabury Howells, was born in White Plains, New York, in 1910, and arrived in Portsmouth in 1918, a year after Dorothy Vaughan. Howells, however, had direct Seacoast connections and was descended on her mother's side from the Shapleigh family that arrived in the Kittery area in the seventeenth century. Her grandfather, Reverend Henry Emerson Hovey, was rector for twenty-five years at Saint John's Episcopal Church on the hill where two Wentworth royal governors are buried. Her uncle, Charles Emerson Hovey, was a Portsmouth war hero killed in the Philippines. A fountain honoring his memory stands at the entrance to

ABOVE: *Muriel Howells as a girl. Her maternal grandfather served as rector of St. John's Church in Portsmouth. A fountain in Prescott Park is dedicated to her uncle. (HOW)*

Prescott Park. As a child, Muriel and her three sisters frequently visited her grandmother who lived on State Street, just a block up from Puddle Dock.

Despite their proximity to the neighborhood, Muriel's family had little contact with Puddle Dock prior to the 1950s. She remembered shopping for antiques at Cappy Stewart's store with her husband in the 1930s, but she had no friends there when growing up. There were "huge great big piles of smashed cars and metal and rubber tires—just a sea of them," she once said. It was not a place she visited. The closest family connection was her grandmother's beloved maid, Bertha Askew, who lived for a time on Gates Street near Puddle Dock. Howells recalled that the first money she ever earned was a quarter Bertha paid her for a sewing project. "She made us all happy for many, many, many years."

Howells recalled exploring the Warner House and the Moffatt-Ladd House as a girl. She was especially drawn to the attic "garret" of bad boy Tom Bailey at the Aldrich Memorial, where she picked flowers in the backyard garden and pressed them in a book. Howells had a few mischievous Portsmouth memories of her own. Two years before her death at age ninety-two, Howells described the winter practice of "punging" in which children jumped onto the back runners of horse-drawn sleighs and carriages to catch a free ride. She fished off the pier at the coal wharf, and once had a dawn picnic of boiled snails discovered along the river at Little Harbor Road. She recalled playing with Oscar Vaughan, Dorothy Vaughan's younger brother, and at age eight, she survived being run over by a car while riding her bicycle down Junkins Avenue near the hospital onto Pleasant Street. "It's all smashed but the bell," she told her grandmother, arriving home after the accident, shaken and covered in grease. The car had passed directly over her, crushing the bicycle. "It was an absolute miracle, and I know it was a miracle," Howells said.

But Muriel Howells mostly recalled being a good girl. Her grandmother, widow of the church rector, instilled in her the belief that privileged families should perform "good works" for the poor. She made cookies for inmates of the Kittery Naval Prison and sang Christmas carols there. When one prisoner became outraged at the wealthy holiday "do-gooders," a plucky nine-year-old Muriel convinced the angry inmate to join them all in the caroling. She sold fundraising tags on the city sidewalk for Portsmouth Hospital and credits that experience with giving her the courage to walk up to strangers and solicit their help. It was a skill she later used in soliciting support for Strawbery Banke, creating the board of overseers, starting The Banke Guild, and serving as a museum trustee. "I've always been grateful that I had that experience," she recalled. "If I went into a soiree in Budapest, I was able to take care of myself and go up to anybody."

Muriel was married to the noted Professor William White Howells for seventy-three years. He was the son of architect John Mead Howells, author of the 1936 maritime village proposal, and grandson of writer William Dean Howells, a close friend of Mark Twain. After working with the Red Cross in World War II, Muriel became involved with the Boston Museum of Fine Arts and politically supported the ouster of Communist-hunter Senator Joseph McCarthy. As her husband gained fame as a Harvard anthropologist, the couple traveled widely, collecting data in the Solomon Islands. In the 1960s and 70s they worked together on a long-term study taking one hundred seventy thousand measurements of three thousand human skulls found at sites throughout Europe, South Africa, Asia, and the Pacific. But they returned like migrating birds to summer at the Howells' compound on the coast at Kittery Point, Maine.

The Final Straw

The destruction of one Portsmouth colonial house in particular pushed both Dorothy Vaughan and Muriel Howells over the edge at the same moment. From the outside, at least, the stately, three-story Jacob Treadwell House on Congress Street was very similar to the Moffatt-Ladd mansion preserved by the Colonial Dames. Inside, the layout of the sumptuously paneled rooms and the grand stairway were reminiscent of the Governor Langdon museum preserved by SPNEA nearby. Congress Street, the main road leading into the heart of the city, was still known as King Street when Charles and Mary Treadwell built the imposing structure for their son Jacob around 1765. Standing

ABOVE: *Muriel was married to her husband, Harvard anthropologist William White Howells for 73 years. Both were key benefactors to the museum. Mr. Howells was the son of architect John Mead Howells and grandson of writer William Dean Howells, all of whom summered at Kittery Point. Here Howells (on left) examines archaeological finds at an excavation in Puddle Dock with Strawbery Banke overseer Francis W. Hatch of Boston in the 1960s. Photo by Muriel Howells. (SBM)*

at the very top of Middle Street, it marked the turning point for every arriving visitor, from George Washington and the Marquis de Lafayette to the Russian and Japanese delegates who negotiated the Treaty of Portsmouth in 1905. Encircled by an elegant wooden fence, the Treadwell was a fixture of the city until the spring of 1956 when workmen began tearing it down. Charles M. Dale, the million-dollar attorney to the Prescott sisters and by this time a former governor of New Hampshire, owned the Jacob Treadwell mansion. After razing the historic building to the ground, Dale replaced it with a squat, flat-topped, modern bowling alley, now a restaurant and office suites.

Sickened and horrified, Dorothy Vaughan watched the demolition through the window of the Portsmouth Public Library directly across the street. She knew the building intimately, having researched its history for John Mead Howells, who gave the house an extended four-page coverage in his 1937 book *The Architectural Heritage of the Piscataqua*. The Jacob Treadwell House had been living on borrowed time, due in part to Dale's penchant for flattening old buildings. Almost two decades before its destruction—as Dale was clearing land for Prescott Park and John Mead Howells was planning a restored maritime village—Howells anticipated the demise of the old colonial when he wrote: "It is to be regretted that this splendid house, directly on the busy corner of a through route for motor traffic, is a danger to its being preserved indefinitely." And despite her protests in 1956, Dorothy Vaughan was powerless to save it.[5]

How John Mead Howells, then approaching his ninetieth year and living in New York, felt about the loss of the Jacob Treadwell House is unknown, but his daughter-in-law, Muriel, was moved to action. In October 1956, she wrote a lengthy letter from Kittery Point to Albert Wenberg, director of the Portsmouth Planning Board. Why not institute zoning laws, she suggested, that could prevent the destruction of more historic buildings? Howells offered examples of zoning laws recently passed in Boston, South Carolina, New Orleans, and Williamsburg. She sent Wenberg a newly published government brochure on how to establish a historic preservation district. Portsmouth had long maintained a national reputation among tourists for its fine buildings, she told Wenberg, but "it will never achieve fame

for the buildings it has put up in the place of the historic buildings it has torn down."[6]

The city planner wrote back in sympathy. He agreed with her that Portsmouth might be losing its colonial character to plate glass windows, asbestos siding, bowling alleys, parking lots, gas stations, cafeterias, and sporting goods shops. But there was not much he could do. Few citizens seemed to mind. Just five people had complained to him in the last six months, Wenberg reported. "Only one of these letters were [sic] written by a Portsmouth resident," he said.[7] The message was clear. Despite her longtime love for Portsmouth, Mrs. Howells paid her taxes in another town and another state. Even with the Howells name, expertise, and reputation, on this side of the Piscataqua River, she was just another tourist.

Michael Hugo-Brunt was a tourist too. A professor of architecture on sabbatical from the University of Hong Kong, he visited the New Hampshire seacoast in the winter of 1956-1957. Hugo-Brunt was studying the architectural impact of a British colony as it evolved into an American city. Dorothy Vaughan assisted in his research. Hugo-Brunt had intended to write about the city of Philadelphia, but like so many before him, he fell under the romantic spell of old Portsmouth, and he became concerned with the way Portsmouth was allowing its colonial houses to be swept away. Pointing out the site of the recently demolished Treadwell mansion, Vaughan certainly told the visiting professor how Charles Treadwell met and courted Mary Kelley in 1724. The story comes directly out of *Brewster's Rambles*, Vaughan's favorite book. Like the tale of young Lady Wentworth or the women sewing the Ranger flag, it translates a message of a resourceful female thriving in a male-dominated society.

Mary Kelley, the legend goes, was the daughter of a wealthy English couple who suffered a reversal of fortune after coming to the fishing village of New Castle, New Hampshire. Brewster writes:

> Mary's wardrobe was so limited, that a boy's jacket was worn by her for one winter for lack of suitable clothing. But nothing discouraged, she knit nets enough for the fishermen to buy her a new dress, and by industrious application she placed herself in the light of a better fortune.[8]

Images by

Ralph Morang

PREVIOUS PAGE: *Good fences made good neighbors on crowded Puddle Dock*

ABOVE: *Visitors opt for life in the slow lane*

RIGHT: *Junior role players on Puddle Lane*

FAR RIGHT: *July 4th sack races*

FACING PAGE: *Children gather for the July 4th parade*

FACING PAGE TOP: *Hundreds of luminaria light the way at Candlelight Stroll*

FACING PAGE BOTTOM: *Horses ferry visitors to Candlelight Stroll*

ABOVE: *A re-enactor recalls mid-winter traditions*

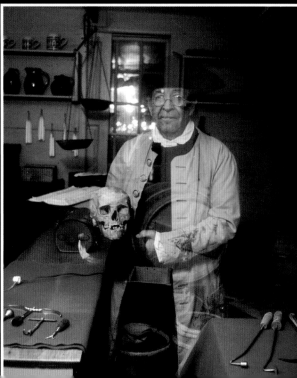

TOP: *Displaying new inventory at the Shapley shop*

ABOVE LEFT: *Abraham Lincoln returns for Independence Day*

RIGHT: *"Dr. Hall Jackson" at Ghosts on the Banke*

FACING PAGE TOP: *Sarah Goodwin's gardens*

FACING PAGE BOTTOM: *Colonial re-enactors in full regalia*

Evening falls at the Abbott Store

TOP: *The original Portsmouth preservation movement initiated by Vaughan and Howells did not immediately envision a colonial village. It began in protest of "modernized" colonial structures with asphalt siding, plate glass windows and neon signs. The Samuel Hart House (c. 1710) on Market Street, for example, (in center) was raised a full story with others to create more commercial space. Here it is occupied by Pope's Café offering rooms and beer on the site of the modern Sheraton Harborside Hotel. (RMC)*

BOTTOM: *Another 1705- era house originally built by Nathaniel Rogers was raised ten feet in 1871 on Congress Street. (SBM)*

Wearing her new dress, Mary attracted the sailor Charles Treadwell of Ipswich, Massachusetts. With her profits from knitting nets, the couple purchased a new house. Unwilling to fall back into poverty, Mary convinced her husband to open a store in Portsmouth that she managed with amazing skill. They eventually purchased land with their profits and built a beautiful home for each of their three children. The romantic tale of Mary's rise from life in a fishing hut to owner of four downtown mansions perfectly fit both Hugo-Brunt's architectural interests and Vaughan's colonial revival taste.

Before his departure in January 1957, Professor Michael Hugo-Brunt was asked to address the members of the Portsmouth Rotary about his research. Donald Vaughan, Dorothy's brother, was in charge of finding interesting speakers for the weekly Thursday Rotary luncheon. "DON'T LET THEM DESTROY YOUR CITY!" Hugo-Brunt told Vaughan and the Rotary early in 1957. Over the next four decades, she told this story often.

> I wanted to hear his talk, to see how he thought we could save our city. I asked my brother Don if I could go and hear the lecture, and he said, "No, . . . women don't go to Rotary, it's a men's club and you know that! I did know, but I wanted to hear the young man from Hong Kong. I harped on the subject until my brother finally asked the Rotarians if he could bring me to the meeting. It took a lot of doing, but finally I was approved, and I heard the very exciting talk on my favorite subject—Portsmouth.[9]

Five months later, on June 20, 1957, the short, middle-aged librarian found herself at the podium, scanning the all-male audience at the Rockingham Ballroom. She wore a pink suit and a straw hat trimmed in rosebuds. She was nervous. Stuck without a speaker for Rotary, Don Vaughan asked his sister to pinch hit. Dorothy taunted her brother, reminding him that women were not allowed to speak at Rotary. "This one does," Don Vaughan replied. "Give 'em hell."

"I decided to lay it right on the line," Vaughan later told historian Ray Brighton, "and tell them what Portsmouth was throwing away each time a house was torn down or a piece of furniture was sold out of town."[10]

She did not have to look far. The noisy, smoke-filled bowling alley she passed while walking just one block from the public library to the Rockingham luncheon was enough to fire her blood. Vaughan focused her brief speech on the creeping Cold War threat against the "American Heritage." "Evil forces are all about trying to destroy the American Way of Life," she told the assembly after they had all pledged allegiance to the flag and sung a patriotic anthem, and bowed their heads in prayer. She continued:

> No where in America is there more of this thing . . . The American heritage drips off the eaves of our houses, hangs from our trees, and is in the brick sidewalks under our feet . . . We feel it when we enter the doors of our historic homes, and we can see it everywhere, yet, it is slipping from us, day by day, and being replaced by ugly store fronts, "joints," and honky tonks.[11]

It was a powerfully subtle tactic, linking the erosion of local architecture to the infiltration of Communism in a city dependent on income from a Navy shipyard and an Air Force base. With its unique aristocratic character watered down and replaced by bland generic buildings, Portsmouth would soon look like "Main Street, USA," she warned the group.

Vaughan was on dangerous turf. The men in the room owned many of the businesses she was indicting. But the canny librarian knew where she was going. After telling a few stirring tales about her favorite Portsmouth families, Vaughan slipped back to her theme. Colonial Williamsburg, she said, was attracting "millions" of tourists each year, while historic Sturbridge Village in Massachusetts could draw ten thousand paying visitors each Sunday. The history dripping from the eaves of Portsmouth houses, was liquid gold. As if scolding a classroom of unprepared school children, many of whom she had once tutored at the library nearby, she concluded:

> It seems to me that Portsmouth is missing the boat, and losing a lot of money by not being "Aware of our Wares" and I mean our American Heritage . . . I'm doing what I

can at the Portsmouth Public Library by collecting and preserving all historic records . . . so that if we go forward with the Restoration of Colonial Portsmouth, we will have something to steer by. I'm doing all I can— what are you doing?

Trumpets did not sound. The clouds did not open. The gist of the now-famous speech did not find its way into the local newspapers. Vaughan made no suggestion of turning Puddle Dock into an outdoor museum. Her pep talk was emotional, not specific. Her appeal, like that of Reverend Gooding at the opening of the Portsmouth Historical Society next door in 1923, was for an embargo against change. Vaughan too advocated preserving Portsmouth's colonial character city-wide by saving structures, artifacts, even trees. Michael Hugo-Brunt, Captain Chester Mayo, Stephen Decatur, John Mead Howells, Charles Brewster, Edith Barrett Wendell, William Sumner Appleton, Arthur Harriman, Ralph May, Thomas Bailey Aldrich, Sarah Haven Foster, and many others had issued this call before. Vaughan channeled their collective voices, and, in 1957, Portsmouth listened to her.

Vaughan's speech, according to Portsmouth attorney Jeremy Waldron, "was well received, and like other speeches, might well have been filed away in the members' minds and forgotten." When it was over, Waldron recalls today, James Barker Smith suddenly grabbed the young lawyer's arm. Smith, who owned the Rockingham and Wentworth by the Sea hotels, immediately saw the connection between history and increased tourism. Smith announced to Rotarians that he and his attorney, Waldron, would act as a committee of two and look into ways to promote historic preservation. Smith then assigned Waldron to look for a spot best suited to saving historic homes and "like a dutiful attorney," Waldron searched. Puddle Dock, he soon concluded, was the likely location.[12]

"It scares me now to think I dared to address that august group and tell them we were destroying our heritage," Vaughan recalled many years later. "My talk may not have been very good, but it was effective. It turned the tide."

Dorothy Vaughan threw down the gauntlet. She challenged a select group of community-minded businessmen to leap up

OPPOSITE: *These two images show the Captain Lewis Barnes house before (top) and after (bottom) its renovation into a service station on Islington Street, just down the road from the Treadwell Mansion and Portsmouth Public Library. These same images from the Historic American Building Survey were used by Dr. Richard Howland as an example of architecture butchered by commercial use. After seeing them, Muriel Howells asked Howland to come to Portsmouth. (RMC)*

and save their imperiled city from the dragon of mediocrity. But besides a few suggestions about street signs and urban beautification, Vaughan did not tell them how to slay the dragon, restore the damsel, and collect the economic treasure. She did not tell them how, because she did not know.

The Man from Washington

Muriel Howells, meanwhile, was on a quest for practical solutions to preserving Portsmouth. Rebuffed by the city itself, she continued to read up on historic zoning in other locations and wrote directly to city planners facing similar problems elsewhere. Then in May 1957, while attending the annual meeting of the Garden Club of America in Chicago, Howells found her champion. Concerned with both the conservation of land and of buildings, the Garden Club invited Richard Howland, president of the National Trust for Historic Preservation, to speak to the gathering of five hundred women. One of Howland's slides showed an attractive colonial house on Islington Street in Portsmouth, New Hampshire, not far from the demolished Jacob Treadwell House. Howland followed that with a slide of the same Portsmouth building, butchered and converted into a filling station. Only one original window survived. The audience reacted with a collective groan.

"Five hundred women went—ugh!" Muriel Howells recalled years later. "And after 499 women had gone up to him [Howland] and said how marvelous he was, and what a good talk it was, I went up to him and said—'Portsmouth's my baby! When can you come up—free!' "[13]

Richard Howland told Muriel Howells that, coincidentally, he would be leaving his Washington, DC, office to visit another site in New England in two weeks. He agreed to swing by Portsmouth to "see if it was worth saving." Based on his research to date, Howland had his doubts. On June 22, 1957, just forty-eight hours after Vaughan's address to Rotary, Richard Howland got his first auto tour of Portsmouth and, according to Howells, he was "astonished at what was left behind turquoise vinyl. He'd

ABOVE: Dr. Richard Howland, originally of the National Trust (right), talks with Kittery historian Joe Frost during a Strawbery Banke Inc. overseers meeting in the 1960s. Photo by Muriel Howells. (SBM)

say—that was a wonderful house—but it looked like something awful to me."[14]

Howells arranged a brief but critical encounter at the Moffatt-Ladd House between the president of the National Trust and George Kimball, the incoming president of the Portsmouth Chamber of Commerce and owner of a downtown clothing store. Besides Howells, Howland and his assistant, and Kimball and his secretary, only the president of the Colonial Dames and a woman serving iced tea in the garden attended the intimate gathering. James Barker Smith, president of the Rotary, failed to show up. Kimball and Howland discussed strategies for getting a Portsmouth restoration project off the ground. A week later, Howland sent a letter to Kimball that spelled out, for the first time, a winning battle plan that would not only lead to the creation of Strawbery Banke, but would help Portsmouth citizens redefine the future of the city. First, Howland pushed for the creation of historic zoning in Portsmouth and sent Kimball the same how-to booklet that Muriel Howells had given the Portsmouth city planner the year before. Second and most important, Howland told Kimball to form a city-wide citizens group dedicated to historic preservation. Business leaders, historic house museums, and wealthy preservationists should unite and work together, Howland said. Only then, after demonstrating their mutual concern and dedication, would Portsmouth be eligible to raise larger sums of money from private donors and government agencies. Howland also agreed to return to Portsmouth, to address both the Rotary and the general public.[15]

The pieces were now falling into place. On October 24, 1957, the Rotary committee inspired by Dorothy Vaughan presented its findings at the weekly luncheon. Attorney Jeremy Waldron led a panel that included Muriel Howells, Jim Smith, and Chamber secretary Helen Kelly, who had attended the private meeting with Howland and Kimball months before. After searching the city and visiting other historic museums, the group proposed creating a "colonial village" on the waterfront at Marcy Street. The economic potential for the city, Waldron urged, was greater than Williamsburg and Sturbridge Village. Waldron cited four incentives for moving ahead—economic gain through tourism, the cleanup of "subpar" housing and junkyards in the

ABOVE: *George Kimball was the first Portsmouth businessman to meet with Dr. Richard Howland during a tea at the Moffatt-Ladd House in 1957. A clothing store owner and then president of the Portsmouth Chamber of Commerce, Kimball became an early convert to the cause of historic preservation (PIR)*

COLONIAL SPEAKER — Dr. Richard H. Howland of Washington, D.C., president of the National Trust for Historic Preservation, will speak on assistance in planning for a Colonial village here on Thursday. He will address the Rotary Club at its meeting that day, and at a Chamber of Commerce sponsored meeting at 8 p.m. in the Rockingham Hotel.

ABOVE: *Notice in the* Portsmouth Herald *clipped by Muriel Howells in her Strawbery Banke scrapbook. Howells accumulated a total of eighteen scrapbooks covering the first thirty years of the museum's history.* (SBM)

South End, the fact that the restoration project could eventually become self-supporting, and the need for a community project that might unite the city. Muriel Howells made another plea for historic zoning while other panelists made less sweeping suggestions, such as using Girl Scouts as tour guides, putting up historic markers, and dressing Portsmouth bus drivers in Paul Revere-like uniforms.[16]

Unlike the secretive Howells-Decatur plan, the colonial village idea immediately hit the newspapers. A *Portsmouth Herald* editorial endorsed Waldron's idea to stop destroying old buildings. Through "cool indifference," the editor said, the city was squandering its architectural treasures "like a wastrel going through his frugal father's inheritance." Locals fell into three camps, the editor suggested—those who did not care about old buildings at all, those who wanted to save every scrap of the past, and those who wanted Portsmouth to grow its industry without killing its culture. Waldron's plan should please them all, the *Herald* said, by creating a dedicated area where historic buildings could be relocated rather than razed. The editorial also reinforced Waldron's concept that the colonial village would include only authentic historic Portsmouth buildings. "Shoddy reproductions are not contemplated," he wrote.[17] This fundamental principle of restoring, rather than reproducing buildings, an idea echoed in the Howells-Decatur Plan, would become a controversial issue in years to come.

With the topic gaining attention, the Rotary asked the city to create an official advisory group to study the colonial village idea. Rotarians suggested that every major community history, service, and fraternal organization should be contacted immediately to join a non-budgeted, volunteer committee. As the 1957 holiday season approached, Mayor Andrew Jarvis, a fan of preservation, asked the city manager to send letters to fifty-three organizations. Forty local groups agreed to sign on. The American Legion eagerly sponsored a high school essay contest with a $25 prize entitled "Why a Colonial Village Will Be a Benefit to Portsmouth."

True to his word, National Trust president Richard Howland returned to Portsmouth on February 6, 1958, just as the colonial village idea was gaining public attention. Muriel Howells and her husband picked him up at the Boston airport and rushed him to the Rotary luncheon at the Rockingham attended by Mayor Jarvis and the entire Portsmouth City Council. After prayer and the pledge and a rousing chorus of "My Country 'Tis of Thee," Rotary President Jim Smith introduced his special guest, Dorothy Vaughan, as "the most prominent historian of Portsmouth." Then, thinking quickly, he introduced Muriel Howells as "the most prominent historian of Kittery," which caused Howells to burst into laughter. Then the largest crowd in Rotary history to date fell silent as the man from Washington spoke.[18]

It was one thing for the local librarian, a woman who did not drive a car and rarely traveled outside the city limits, to predict tourism profits, but it was quite another to hear that prophesy from the nation's number one expert. Founded in 1949, the National Trust was created specifically to assist in preservation projects across the country. So when Howland called Portsmouth "a gold mine," both "metaphorically as well as realistically," people perked up.[19] He said that historic preservation was hard work. Even the Ladies of Mount Vernon had struggled to save the home of George Washington. But Portsmouth was by no means struggling alone, he said. Cities had faced similar problems preserving their heritage. Old buildings situated on important land could simply be moved to a new location. People have been moving buildings for centuries, Howland said, since the time of the ancient Greeks. This comment plucked the heartstrings of Portsmouth mayor Andrew Jarvis, who was of Greek descent. Following a standing ovation for the speaker, Jarvis rushed up to tell Professor Howland about his own recent trip to Greece. City councilor Donald Margeson, who would become a major force in the early years of Strawbery Banke Museum, left the luncheon wide-eyed. "Why I had no idea the economic aspects of all this," he told Mrs. Howells.[20]

But even as he was wooing Portsmouth, Howland was being charmed by his Kittery hosts. Following Rotary, Howland quickly toured the historic Sparhawk Mansion in Kittery Point, then caught a twenty-minute nap before the Howells whisked him to a closed-door meeting of the Chamber board of directors. By the time he was back in Kittery, Mrs. Howells had run him a hot bath in an antique clawfoot tub, where Mr. Howells delivered up

ABOVE: *Attorney Jeremy Waldron was among the first downtown businessmen to respond to the call for preservation and has continued to support Strawbery Banke ever since. Here Waldron (right) talks with museum overseers Bertram K. Little (center) and Clifford A. Waterhouse at Puddle Dock. Photo by Muriel Howells. (SBM)*

a whiskey sour and a plate of lobster tails with Russian dressing. The three enjoyed a quiet dinner before the Howells drove their guest back to the Rockingham Hotel where, despite a snowstorm, the ballroom was filled to bursting. With every available chair set out, visitors stood around the walls. At least six *Portsmouth Herald* staffers were in attendance.[21]

This time the professor showed slides, went into greater detail, and stirred even more emotion among over two hundred locals. Portsmouth, Howland told them, was the only city he could name with such rich historical resources and yet no plan for developing and exploiting those resources. Even little Tombstone, Arizona—a town two hundred fifty years younger than Portsmouth—had gone from a ghost town to a tourist destination, doubling its income, by creating a heritage plan, he said. The man from Washington ticked off city after city that had passed historic zoning laws. Such restrictive laws were constitutional, Howland assured his audience by quoting Supreme Court Chief Justice William O. Douglas: "It is within the power of the legislature that the community should be beautiful as well as healthy, spacious as well as clean, well balanced as well as carefully patrolled."[22]

Howland hammered away on the economics of preservation, quoting tourism statistics from the latest issue of *Time* magazine. Restoring an entire neighborhood would make tourists stay longer and spend more money, he said. If twenty-four tourists a day brought in an average of $100,000 a year, how much would a thousand daily tourists bring to Portsmouth—or ten thousand? He suggested incorporating a community group and selling shares of stock to raise funds. He suggested restoring some early buildings to provide housing for Navy and Air Force personnel, or office space for companies and nonprofits. He talked about urban renewal projects in which historic buildings had been recycled for public use.

People around the country were watching Portsmouth, Howland said, since Portsmouth was so rich in historic resources. And what was Portsmouth doing? Portsmouth was tearing down mansions like the Treadwell House and turning them into bowling alleys!

OPPOSITE: *Now converted to condominiums, the Rockingham Hotel was once owned by nineteenth-century ale tycoon Frank Jones and later by James Barker Smith. Portsmouth Rotary meetings were held here during the 1950s when Smith was a Rotary leader. A number of key Rotary speakers here in 1957 inspired Strawbery Banke Inc., including Michael Hugo-Brunt, Dorothy Vaughan, Jeremy Waldron, and Richard Howland. The John Paul Jones House is next door (to the left) and the former Portsmouth Public Library and the demolished Treadwell House were one block away. (SBM)*

After another standing ovation, Mayor Jarvis addressed Howland, speaking in Greek, "We have no key to the city of Portsmouth, it's an open city. But I have a present for you from Greece." When the mayor presented his gift, Howland thanked him by also speaking in Greek. The mayor, according to witnesses, was enraptured and pledged that he and the city council were behind the colonial village idea one hundred percent. In a single day, the man from Washington had fused together support from city government, the chamber of commerce, Rotary, local media, and two hundred local residents—and left them with working plans and a pledge that the National Trust was there to help guide them.

"The whole day was the most professional and personal triumph for Dick," Muriel Howells wrote to her family the following day.[23] She was right. Richard Howland too had fallen under the colonial spell of Portsmouth, and told Howells he actually found it difficult to leave. Returning to Washington the following day, Howland wrote to his hosts that he felt "a warm glow of some accomplishment and sensed that something very vigorous is developing out of the great interest that you and a handful of others have generated." [24] He was right too. Just nine months after Howland's brief visit to Portsmouth—Strawbery Banke was born.

OPPOSITE: *This map appeared in the original stock prospectus for the recently-formed Strawbery Banke Inc. in the summer of 1959. According to treasurer George Kimball, the organization had $3,184.79 in assets and $47,780 in promised, but unpaid, donations.* (SBM)

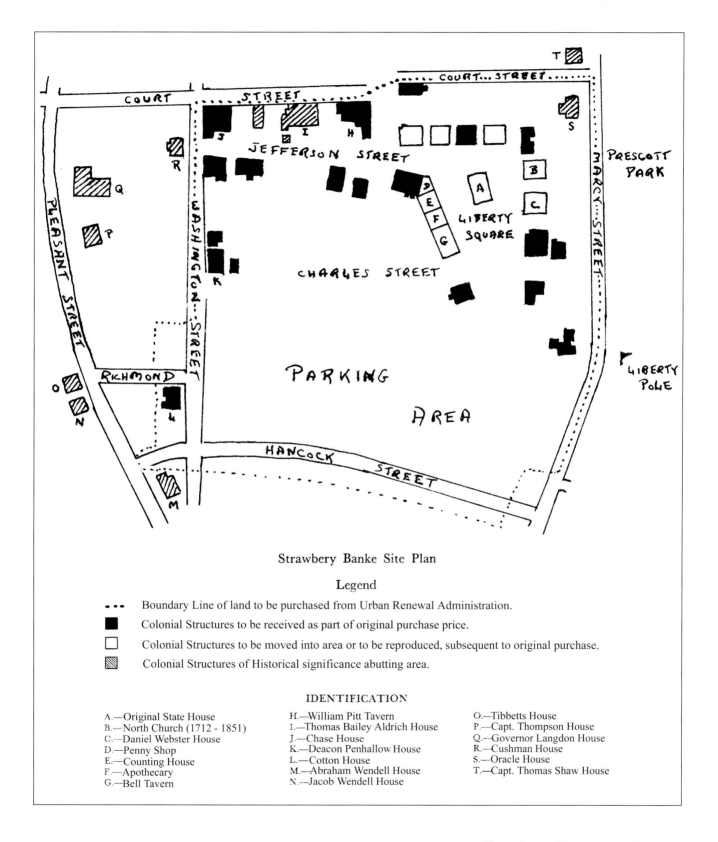

Strawbery Banke Site Plan

Legend

- - - Boundary Line of land to be purchased from Urban Renewal Administration.

■ Colonial Structures to be received as part of original purchase price.

□ Colonial Structures to be moved into area or to be reproduced, subsequent to original purchase.

▨ Colonial Structures of Historical significance abutting area.

IDENTIFICATION

A.—Original State House
B.—North Church (1712 - 1851)
C.—Daniel Webster House
D.—Penny Shop
E.—Counting House
F.—Apothecary
G.—Bell Tavern

H.—William Pitt Tavern
I.—Thomas Bailey Aldrich House
J.—Chase House
K.—Deacon Penhallow House
L.—Cotton House
M.—Abraham Wendell House
N.—Jacob Wendell House

O.—Tibbetts House
P.—Capt. Thompson House
Q.—Governor Langdon House
R.—Cushman House
S.—Oracle House
T.—Capt. Thomas Shaw House

STRAWBERY BANKE, INC. 1958–1965

Be careful what you wish for, the old saying goes, or you may get it. After rallying public support to save old buildings in Portsmouth, the newly-formed Strawbery Banke Inc. soon found itself in possession of twenty-seven ramshackle structures desperately needing repair. Even more historic houses, pulled from their ancient foundations, were headed toward the evolving waterfront campus.

Nothing in the dawning days of the museum happened easily. The band of preservationists had to convince federal officials to rethink their definition of urban renewal itself. Strawbery Banke volunteers pled their case to city councilors, to reporters, to stockholders, and to taxpayers. Moving ahead required rewriting New Hampshire law. Moving ahead meant uprooting families who, to no one's surprise, did not want to go.

America was moving ahead too. In the seven formative years before the museum opened its doors, three presidents occupied the White House. The Beatles unseated Elvis Presley. American bombers lifted off from Pease Air Force Base en route to Viet Nam.

Through all that, the colonial village that nobody really thought would happen—happened. Portsmouth was now poised to become a player in the expanding heritage tourism industry. The city was now "aware of its wares," in the words of Dorothy Vaughan. History had become a commodity, but how to get this

OPPOSITE: *Early members of the Guild of Strawbery Banke gather in the garden of the John Paul Jones House. Cynthia Raymond, a founder, stands in the center. Margaret Smith, owner of the Rockingham Hotel next door and the Wentworth by the Sea Hotel is at the far right. This image comes from the collection of Dorothy Vaughan. (SBM)*

ABOVE: *By the late 1950s and early '60s most Portsmouth residents still saw the past nostalgically as in this "Good Olde Days" annual sale at Kimball's clothing store on Market Street. Owner George Kimball, an early advocate of Strawbery Banke, is in the front with the handlebar mustache. (PIR)*

new product to the market was anyone's guess. And so, with little knowledge and even less cash, like the Piscataqua pioneers before them, the founders pushed ahead.

The creation of Strawbery Banke, the record shows, was a deeply grassroots effort. It required countless thousands of volunteer hours from carpenters, painters, and electricians, masons, business owners, teachers and students, society wives, shipyard workers, historians, politicians, and anyone else who could lend a hand. It became, as its founders had hoped, a project that pulled together the Portsmouth community and put the city back on the national map.

Taking the Plunge

The early months of 1958 were critical. Rising to Dorothy Vaughan's challenge and armed with Richard Howland's advice, the Colonial Portsmouth Committee began planning the campaign to revive Puddle Dock. But another army was already there. The site had been under consideration as an urban renewal project since 1954. "No place in New Hampshire is more in need of redevelopment than this particular section of Portsmouth," Portsmouth Housing officials declared in 1954, "and no place in the state would be better suited for a modern housing development."[1]

The federal plan was to demolish all the existing structures in a four-acre portion of the neighborhood, then turn the property over to a redeveloper who would build "garden apartments." The target area was expanded to eighteen acres and then, after protest by local residents, reduced to nine and a half acres. The final size of the Marcy-Washington Streets Urban Renewal Project was roughly that of Strawbery Banke Museum today. Uncle Sam had earmarked $835,000 for urban development in Portsmouth as part of an effort to clean up "blighted" areas all across the nation. To access the federal funds, however, the city was required to cover one-third of the total—$278,334 of taxpayer money. So far nothing had been done and the urban renewal money was due to expire at the end of 1958 unless Portsmouth could come up with an alternative plan.

ABOVE: *Puddle Dockers objected to reports that characterized their neighborhood as a "slum," but were largely powerless to make quick improvements to rented properties considered substandard by the local housing authority. (SBM)*

RIGHT: *Known affectionately as "Gilley's" after a longtime employee, this custom-made lunch cart, seen parked here in Puddle Dock in the early 1960s, is still in operation in downtown Portsmouth. (SBM)*

On February 19, less than two weeks after Richard Howland's visit, members of the Portsmouth Housing Authority (PHA), which managed urban renewal funds locally, met informally with the Portsmouth Planning Board. Federal plans to develop the Marcy-Washington Street area, known locally as Puddle Dock, had hit an impasse, the group was told. The plan was unworkable. People in Portsmouth simply could not afford the new apartments that would replace the demolished old buildings. Apartments were then renting for $85 to $110 a month. Based on high construction costs, studies indicated that these new garden apartments could not make a profit at that rate and might stay vacant at higher rents estimated to reach $185 to $215 per month. The housing authority, in light of this study, refused to offer mortgage insurance. Any developer taking on the project could lose his shirt.[2]

There were still ways to keep the federal dollars from leaving town, according to Edward Abbott of the Portsmouth Housing Authority, who was also a Portsmouth Rotary officer. The land, once taken by eminent domain and cleared, could be used for single-family or low-income homes. It could be used commercially or as housing for the elderly. Or—the land could be used, Abbott suggested, for a colonial village. Attorney Jeremy Waldron then took the floor and pitched his new idea to city planners. The major roadblock to a colonial village, he said, echoing the concerns of Howells and Decatur two decades before, was that Puddle Dock property owners might increase the asking price for their land and buildings. Sweeping change could be accomplished by combining federal funds and federal authority with a radically different Portsmouth idea.

The status of the urban renewal project was high on the list of topics when the mayor's new Colonial Portsmouth Committee met for the first time on March 26, 1958.[3] City Councilor Donald Margeson, a downtown furniture store owner who lived in an historic home on the edge of the deteriorating South End, was appointed chairman. George Kimball of the Chamber, who owned a downtown clothing store, chaired the finance subcommittee. Jeremy Waldron was at point for legal issues and Dorothy Vaughan headed research. State Senator Cecil Humphreys of New Castle agreed to handle legislative issues, a post that would

soon face a serious crisis. Muriel Howells, who usually wintered elsewhere, temporarily took a back seat, appearing only as a member of the publicity committee chaired by a newcomer, Mrs. Marston Fenwick. But Howells had been careful to invite the editor of the *Portsmouth Herald* to a party at her home and, soon after, the newspaper began publishing an upbeat series of articles on historic Portsmouth houses written by Mrs. Fenwick.

With a few niceties out of the way, the group began to draw the battle lines. City Manager Robert Violette made it perfectly clear that Portsmouth had a lot more on its plate than preservation. A bridge to Peirce Island, new voting machines, school and sewer projects, salaries, and another low-rent housing site were already in progress. Keep in mind, Violette warned the colonial village proponents, that the project would not only cost the city more than $250,000, but it might also fill up with historic buildings that could not be assessed for future taxes. Watching the sparks fly, Edward Abbott of the Portsmouth Housing Authority made it clear that his agency could not act as a go-between for the colonial village group and the city. They had to agree to move ahead together, and fast, or let go of the Federal Housing Authority windfall. The group voted unanimously that the city should notify the FHA of their new restoration plan for Puddle Dock and keep the money allocated towards Portsmouth. Aware that they had to quickly separate from the city and form an independent organization, the members then turned to a discussion of potential names for their nonprofit corporation. Dorothy Vaughan submitted a list that included Historic Portsmouth, Port of Portsmouth, Colonial Portsmouth and Maritime Portsmouth. There being no other business, after nearly three hours the group adjourned its first meeting at ten P.M. The die was cast.

The name "Strawbery Banke," with its quirky faux-colonial spelling, was apparently not on the table at the first meeting. It most likely came from Ralph May, an original member of the committee and author of the book *Early Portsmouth History*, published in 1926. All of Portsmouth's key nineteenth century historians including Adams, Aldrich, Brewster, and Foster had employed the modern spelling "Strawberry Bank" for the original settlement. Despite a variety of spellings used in early

ABOVE: *Hotel owners James Barker Smith and his wife Margaret were early and enthusiastic supporters of Strawbery Banke Inc. (SBM)*

records, Ralph May fixed on a particular spelling that, he says, was recorded in the town records in August 1643. Documents from that era display a wide variety of spellings, but Dorothy Vaughan borrowed May's version for her 1930 historic map of Portsmouth. It seems more than likely that the two collaborated on the choice and, by the next meeting, the group was called Strawbery Banke Inc.[4]

Phase one—getting the money—was a slam-dunk. Always eager for federal funds, Portsmouth residents came out overwhelmingly in favor of floating a twenty-year city bond for $200,000. Dozens of historic and social organizations spoke in favor of the bond at a May 26 public hearing, but were careful not to jump the gun by connecting the bond issue with the colonial village plan. The immediate issue on the table was blight, not preservation. Only a single "lone wolf" raised his voice in opposition. Louis Heney of Jefferson Street objected to his neighborhood being called a "slum." People were trying to fix up their homes, he said, but there were too many taxes and doctor bills to pay. "Just give us time," he pleaded, but time was running out as one prominent citizen after another testified in favor of the bond issue. Dr. Lester Whitaker, who often made house calls in Puddle Dock, told members of the public hearing that some of the structures he visited there were "just not fit for human living." Whitaker was also a member of the Colonial Portsmouth Committee

Phase two—getting the city to hand over the cleared land—proved more difficult. The Colonial Portsmouth Committee, riding the tide of public approval and now officially known as "Strawbery Banke," immediately appealed to the city to be placed at the head of the list of potential Puddle Dock developers. Strawbery Banke chairman Donald Margeson, who was also a city councilman, made his first request on June 8, the very day that the city council approved the $200,000 city bond. A fellow council member suggested politely that it was "pretty early in the game" for the group to be asking for land, since Strawbery Banke had not yet incorporated, had no bank account, and their project had not yet been approved by the Federal Housing Authority. The city had not even discussed what to do with the potential land once it was cleared. Didn't the city need a school or a

ABOVE: *Neighborhood children pose for a picture taken by Strawbery Banke executive vice president Captain Carl Johnson during the urban renewal of Puddle Dock. (SBM)*

shopping mall instead of more historic houses? Mary Dondero, a councilor and former Portsmouth mayor, called the Strawbery Banke request an act of "colossal nerve."[5] The honeymoon, short as it had been, was already over.

In October, following Richard Howland's advice, Strawbery Banke Inc. began seeking pledges for public stock in its not-for-profit organization at $10 per share. This "historic event" was intended to capitalize the corporation up to $300,000, but preservationists warned that this was really a charitable contribution; anyone who expected to make a profit should invest elsewhere. Sales were not brisk. Within a year the organization had raised little more than $50,000, but still the message was clear. As the supportive *Portsmouth Herald* noted, Strawbery Banke intended to "pay its own way."[6] And even if the restoration effort fizzled, the city and the federal government could still achieve their primary goal—the extermination of blight in the South End. A total of 387 members, most of them Portsmouth residents, signed the papers and Strawbery Banke Inc. became official on November 19, 1958.

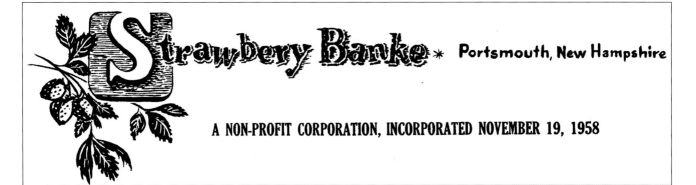

Then a legal squall appeared out of nowhere and threatened to sink the project. Although the Federal Housing Act of 1954 allowed urban renewal funds to be used for conservation and preservation, New Hampshire law did not. State law required that every structure within an urban renewal project had to be demolished, regardless of its historic value. In this early phase, the colonial village plan was primarily focused on moving endangered buildings from other locations to the cleared waterfront land. But at least half a dozen Puddle Dock houses were then

ABOVE: *The first Strawbery Banke Inc. stationery from 1958 and 1959 included this header with a photograph of the 1664 Jackson House (not seen here), a building that was not part of the Puddle Dock area of town. (SBM)*

considered worth saving, and tearing them down, Strawbery Banke officials agreed, was a bad way to kick off a preservation project.

A delegation was quickly dispatched to Washington, DC, to meet with New Hampshire's Republican Senator Styles Bridges. The minority whip and a member of the Senate for three decades, Bridges listened carefully to the Portsmouth predicament. Then, according to Harry Winebaum, an early Strawbery Banke founder who attended the meeting, Bridges was informed by his aide that there was nothing to be done. This was a law in the state of New Hampshire and could only be changed in the state legislature. The senator, however, used his influence to convince New Hampshire lawmakers to clear the way for the colonial village. "I don't give a damn," Bridges reportedly told his aide. "I'm from a little state. I get almost nothing. I want this to happen. You make it happen."[7]

On March 3, 1959, State Senator Cecil Humphreys, a Strawbery Banke founder, proposed a bill to the New Hampshire legislature. Among the largest democratic bodies in the world with over four hundred members, the New Hampshire House of Representatives is not known for speed. The revised New Hampshire law (RSA 205), specifically designed to pave the way for Strawbery Banke, permitted the restoration of buildings within an urban renewal project, bringing New Hampshire law in line with the federal legislation. It passed nine days later.

Although federal Urban Renewal officials were excited about the Portsmouth plan, they were not convinced it was workable. As a precaution, they hired a tough Boston appraiser named Bill Ballard to check out the Strawbery Banke project. Ballard met with the committee at Donald Margeson's house at the head of Marcy Street where the old Gloucester House bordello once stood. "What's in it for you, Don?" Ballard suddenly asked the group president. "Well, I live right on the corner of the project," Margeson reportedly said, "and it will improve my neighborhood." Ballard nodded. "Good, Margeson, good," he said.[8]

At first, Ballard was dubious of the grassroots colonial village plan, Jeremy Waldron remembers. He knew he was being set up as the "fall guy" whom Washington could blame if the project was approved and failed. But after visiting six other outdoor

Incorporated 1958

ABOVE: *An early Strawbery Banke Inc. "crest" depicting an anchor, crown and seashell. Dorothy Vaughan's 1930 historic map of Portsmouth (see rear endpaper) previously included similarly drawn crests of the Vaughan, Peirce, Wentworth, Whipple, Goodwin and Pepperrell families. Deeply interested in genealogy and Portsmouth's aristocratic founding families, Vaughan originally believed she was descended from seventeenth-century Portsmouth roots. (SBM)*

history museums, Ballard surprised Strawbery Banke planners with a thumbs-up recommendation. Ballard's report pointed to key reasons why the Portsmouth project could succeed. It would be, he said, the most "pure" of all the heritage museums, because the houses to be saved and moved were real Portsmouth buildings, not replicas. He was impressed that the project was to be located on a real New England waterfront and he urged the reconstruction of the Old Statehouse, of which a small portion still survived, to become a key element in the village. If Strawbery Banke succeeded, Ballard added, it would eventually pull up the economic status of the entire Portsmouth waterfront. Every one of these key points had been outlined in the 1936 Howells-Decatur plan.

In July 1959, after "marking time" for months, the group learned that Uncle Sam had finally approved their plan to purchase cleared land in the South End. With the exception of more than a dozen historic buildings already on site, federal urban renewal agents agreed to tear down Puddle Dock and sell the land to the Portsmouth preservationists. But first, Portsmouth itself had to agree.

Into Stormy Waters

Federal acceptance of Strawbery Banke as the potential redeveloper of Puddle Dock brought on a waterfront battle that threatened to wreck the entire project. Evelyn Marconi, the wife of a local fisherman, fired the first salvo. The Marconis had recently purchased a home at 138 Marcy Street, built in the 1930s by Charles Dale across from the evolving Prescott Park. Now it was inside the targeted urban renewal area. In a letter to the *Herald*, Marconi implied that taking homes by eminent domain was a practice better suited to the Nazi Gestapo and the Russian secret police than to Uncle Sam. "People could not sleep at night for fear of the knock on the door that would change their whole lives," she wrote. [9] Attending an early planning meeting, Marconi dug in her heels. "I'm not moving for Strawbery Banke, no matter what happens," she said.[10]

Charter Issue

CAPITAL STOCK CERTIFICATE

Strawbery Banke, Inc.

This is to Certify that *Rosamond Thaxter* is the owner of *Ninety-two* share(s) of capital stock of *Strawbery Banke, Inc.*, issued this *1st* day of *June* in the year *1961*.
Attention: The share(s) represented by this certificate are limited to one vote per share, are non-dividend paying, and if to be transferred for a consideration, must first be offered to the corporation for purchase at the original price of *Ten Dollars* per share.

A NON-PROFIT CORPORATION

Dorothy M. Vaughan
PRESIDENT

Robert E. McLaughlin
TREASURER

Former governor, former mayor, and Prescott Park attorney Charles Dale also joined the fray. Dale, who had unwittingly sparked the colonial village movement when he demolished the Treadwell Mansion three years earlier, now came out swinging against urban renewal. Representing a group of Puddle Dock property owners and his own real estate interests there, Dale told the Portsmouth Planning Board that the restoration project was "a pig in a poke" that would "chew up some little people" in the South End.[11] The planning board responded by tabling the zoning issue once, twice, three times, thus preventing the Portsmouth Housing Authority from bringing the project to the city council, whose approval was needed to request the federal funds.

ABOVE: *As advised by Dr. Richard Howland, Strawbery Banke Inc. issued stock certificates to capitalize the nonprofit company to purchase and redevelop the urban renewal project in the Puddle Dock area. Stockholders were initially granted one vote per $10 share purchased. This system was later abandoned in a controversial change. (HUB)*

Rare behind-the-scenes photographs show a radio and telephone fundraiser inside a former shoe shop. A window display includes a model of the proposed colonial village and the 1813 map of Portsmouth. One sign reads: "Once lost, historic buildings will never be recovered. Yet as long as they stand there is hope . . ." Another sign notes that Strawbery Banke Inc., will "create a new industry here—tourism based on the romance of the past." (SBM)

"If they try to take a man's home, the place to fight is the front door,"[12] Dale announced at an October meeting as a growing crowd of spectators cheered. Dale then accused several council members connected to the nonprofit group of a conflict of interest. In response, city councilor Donald Margeson and three others resigned their posts at Strawbery Banke Inc. in order to vote in favor of the project. Librarian Dorothy Vaughan took over for Margeson as president, a post she held for the next five formative years.

On November 18, 1959, approaching the first anniversary of Strawbery Banke, Inc., Portsmouth residents finally had their say. An estimated 580 people turned up at the local high school to air their views at a public hearing. Opinion favored the colonial village plan by a ratio of four to one, the *Herald* reported. South Enders were the only dissenting voices. Those who lived outside Puddle Dock were happy to see the neighborhood transformed.

It was all over but the voting. After legal squabbles and parliamentary wrangling, the city council voted to approve the Strawbery Banke plan on December 8 by a margin of five to two. One council member abstained. Mary Dondero, who was hospitalized and missed the final vote, remained convinced that Strawbery Banke proponents planned to profit off the poor citizens of Puddle Dock. "No one with a heart could do such a thing," she said.[13]

Profit, however, was not an issue for Strawbery Banke. From its founding days, the focus was always on financial survival. Despite criticism that the city had turned over its urban renewal windfall to greedy private investors, federal and city funds could be used only for "blight removal." The fledgling organization was about to receive title to roughly ten acres of bulldozed land and twenty-seven dilapidated old buildings. No Rockefeller or Ford had come to the rescue in the Howells-Decatur era. No major philanthropist appeared now with the millions of dollars needed to build, promote, and maintain a seasonal outdoor museum of this size. The total income from all shares of Strawbery Banke stock sold to date, ex-Governor Dale pointed out derisively, was not enough to restore a single Puddle Dock house.

Just before Christmas in 1959, as a show of good faith, Strawbery Banke presented the Portsmouth Housing Authority with a check for $5,482 for the Marcy-Washington Streets Project area. PHA director Edward Abbott accepted the deposit for a neighborhood that, so far, was still standing and still occupied. The balance of the $27,000 purchase price would not come due until it was cleared and emptied five years later.

The money for the down payment on Puddle Dock was earned in a single night. Two months earlier, with the project still caught up in the machinery of local politics, Strawbery Banke Inc. held its first gala fundraiser. It was a splashy affair for little old Portsmouth when the Hollywood film *John Paul Jones* premiered at the ornate Colonial Theatre in Market Square. Tall, dark-haired Robert Stack was an unlikely choice to portray the diminutive, red-haired Scotsman Paul Jones, who had twice lived in Portsmouth during the Revolution. Stack had just appeared in the pilot of his popular television role as "Untouchables" special agent Eliot Ness, and the city buzzed with anticipation that Stack would be among the "galaxy of stars" attending the opening night fundraiser. Others hoped to see co-star Bette Davis. Neither star materialized, but Davis sent her husband Gary Merrill instead. Merrill, who had co-starred with Davis in the classic film *All About Eve* and was on the verge of a Hollywood divorce, acted as master of ceremonies. He shocked and delighted Portsmouth's elite by appearing onstage in a tuxedo with short pants. Singer Jerry Vale performed, a Scottish highland band marched, and New Hampshire Governor Wesley Powell and his wife were among the luminaries at the festive Strawbery Banke coming-out party.

But glittering charity events were rare in this small Yankee town. Accustomed to pinching pennies and bootstrap economics, Strawbery Banke Inc. under President Vaughan had, as yet, no clear budget or fundraising strategy. There was the ever-present hope that a sponsor with deep pockets might be drawn to the increasing news coverage or to the continual letter-writing and public speaking campaign by Muriel Howells, Vaughan, and others. But for the most part, the strategy followed the survival plan used by all the historic house museums in Portsmouth—an endless cycle of charity tea parties, dinner parties, garden parties, charity auctions, and card parties. Much of this work began early with the formation of the Guild of Strawbery Banke, a separate nonprofit woman's group created to help fund the restoration project.

OPPOSITE: *A premiere of the swashbuckling film* John Paul Jones *starring Robert Stack marked the first major fundraiser for Strawbery Banke Inc. and led to the creation of the Guild. Although the stars did not attend, actor Gary Merrill hosted the event at the Colonial Theatre in Market Square. This advertisement comes from an authentic 1959 movie book distributed to cinemas by Columbia Pictures.*
(JDR)

HALF HIS CREW LOST...HIS SHIP IN FLAMES – AND THEN HIS SHOUT RANG OUT:
"I HAVE NOT YET BEGUN TO FIGHT!"

For the first time all the true-life excitement of America's incredible sailor of fortune!

SAMUEL BRONSTON Presents

John Paul Jones

FILMED IN **TECHNIRAMA**® COLOR BY **TECHNICOLOR**®

STARRING
ROBERT STACK · MARISA PAVAN · CHARLES COBURN · ERIN O'BRIEN
Guest Stars MACDONALD CAREY · JEAN PIERRE AUMONT · DAVID FARRAR
PETER CUSHING · SUSANA CANALES And a Special Appearance by BETTE DAVIS as Catherine the Great
Produced by SAMUEL BRONSTON · Screenplay by JOHN FARROW and JESSE LASKY, Jr. · Directed by JOHN FARROW · Music by MAX STEINER

Now on Warner Bros. Records at stores everywhere –
The thrilling "John Paul Jones" sound track album!

FROM WARNER BROS.

The Guild, which raised over half a million dollars for the cause over the next two decades, essentially began at the *John Paul Jones* movie premiere. Five prominent women, including Muriel Howells and Cynthia Raymond, then married to Captain Alan B. Banister, commander of the Portsmouth Naval Shipyard, volunteered to make dozens of strawberry-shaped corsages and boutonnieres. The decorations were given out in the theater lobby to anyone who purchased stock in Strawbery Banke Inc. When one of the five founding women donated $10 to cover the cost of wire, cotton, paper, and other supplies, the others matched her contribution. After the film event, with $40 in the "kitty" and their supply of leftover paper flowers, the group asked Dorothy Vaughan for permission to begin their own organization. Their goal, initially, was to restore one of the Puddle Dock houses.[14]

But Portsmouth locals feared falling under the wing of the wealthy ladies of Rye, Kittery Point, and York. When the women asked the fledgling Strawbery Banke board of directors for some seed money to increase their inventory, the request was denied. At first "rejected and resentful," the group kicked in their own money and became an independent nonprofit corporation. The Guild of Strawbery Banke purchased more items with a strawberry theme, then juried and sold hand-made strawberry crafts on consignment. Margaret Smith, wife of Rotary president James

BELOW: *The Guild of the Strawbery Banke functioned as a separate nonprofit agency and volunteers opened a number of gift shops throughout their thirty-year history—including the Conant House, the Reuben-Shapley House, the Kingsbury House on State Street and the Dunaway Store. (SBM/DA)*

History, Incorporated

Drawings by Norman Laselle

Barker Smith, joined next. Smith offered the group the use of her two hotels, the Rockingham and Wentworth by the Sea, for the group's first two sales.

Cynthia Raymond, now in her nineties and still an active supporter of Strawbery Banke, recalls that the initial sale netted the group $67.54. One of the ladies was assigned to be the banker for the group. "She was so excited and thrilled with our success," Raymond recalls, "that her big Cadillac ran off the road—fortunately not too far from her home. She didn't dare leave the cash in the car, so she carried it home and told [her husband] about that before she told him about the car."

It Takes a Village

Besides money, the major problem with the colonial village idea from the start was that no one knew exactly what the idea was. _Portsmouth Herald_ editorials implied that Strawbery Banke was a one-stop solution to the destruction of the city's architectural heritage. Editor Robert Blalock, whose name appears among the founders of Strawbery Banke, Inc., was the likely author. The two-fold purpose of the colonial village, the _Herald_ continually noted, was to sell the city's heritage to tourists by collecting old buildings, "now wasting away from neglect or fated to fall under

ABOVE: _This sketch from a 1959 stock prospectus shows the original colonial village idea borrowed from Colonial Williamsburg and Sturbridge Village. It includes the reconstruction of an imagined downtown Portsmouth circa 1800, including a wooden version of the original North Church, a duplicate of the Portsmouth Athenaeum, and possibly Stoodley's tavern. The Old Statehouse is the center and was a key element of the plan. (SBM)_

the wrecker's hammer"[15] and moving them to the South End. Strawbery Banke founders quickly assembled a wish list of the most historic and endangered buildings, and these homes were featured at length in an ongoing column in the *Herald*. Readers began to see Strawbery Banke as the future drop-off site for any old building that stood in the way of progress.

President Vaughan, however, had an even grander vision. She imagined a full-scale recreation of the city's central Parade as it might have appeared soon after the American Revolution. She had watched the slow modernization of downtown Portsmouth and likely assumed that the historic buildings that remained would all eventually be butchered into ugly storefronts or torn down and replaced by "lesser" structures. By providing a campus for unwanted buildings, the colonial village might, inadvertently be hastening the modernization of Market Square. Cleared of all but a few "historically significant" buildings, Puddle Dock provided Vaughan with the perfect opportunity to re-do the city center as she had always dreamed of it. A talented storyteller, she was drawn to save or duplicate buildings that had been lived in or visited by the most heroic and romantic characters in Portsmouth history. Her plan for Strawbery Banke was a true colonial revival as depicted in Brewster's *Rambles*. She described her goals this way during an early fundraising speech:

> Our plans call for a recreation of old Market Square in 1790, with the Old State House sitting in the middle of the cobblestone square—with a reproduction of the old three-decker North Church with Daniel Webster's home close by—and a row of shops and stores, printing office, sail loft, etc. on the north side of the state house. We look forward to the day when a replica of the *Ranger* will be tied up at the nearby dock and gundalows will ply up and down the river. . . We are looking through our rose-colored glasses, and we hope you can see through [them] too . . . and some fine day we shall be picking strawberries on the bank again![16]

Vaughan had this early view sketched onto notecards and presented it in booklets promoting the sale of stock certificates. Her written proposal to the corporation called for this work

to be completed within five years. In addition she planned to reconstruct the colonial Bell Tavern, restore an apothecary shop, a counting house, a drygoods store and a "bric-a-brac" shop. Besides Paul Jones' 1777 sloop of war *Ranger*, Vaughan pictured a recreation of the Revolutionary era "flying" stagecoach, and the 1851 clipper ship *Nightingale*. The entire site was to be landscaped and an educational and touring program put in place. Lastly, the exterior of all the surviving buildings in Puddle Dock were to be restored—a task that still continues after fifty years.

The idea to focus a maritime project around the original Portsmouth statehouse came directly from the Howells-Decatur WPA plan.[17] John Mead Howells, however, was opposed to making copies of old architecture. His maritime village, he declared, was "better than Williamsburg," precisely because it used only original buildings, many "*in situ*," with others moved around strategically like pieces on a chessboard. Jeremy Waldron had adapted the "no shoddy reconstructions" rule into his 1957 colonial village plan. Yet planners knew from their research that the most popular outdoor museums of the time—Williamsburg,

ABOVE: *While reproducing the entire Market Square area quickly proved too ambitious, the idea of a patriotic park was still being considered through the 1960s and beyond. Adapting the 1959 plan (see previous sketch) architect William Perry of Boston provided this design. It now incorporated the Daniel Webster House (left) and Gov. Goodwin Mansion (right) with the imagined Old Statehouse in the center. The Tyco Visitor Center, dedicated in 2005, sits roughly at the same spot today. (SBM)*

Old Sturbridge Village, and Mystic Seaport, in particular—were all largely restorations, and Plimoth Plantation was a complete reconstruction. Preliminary marketing of Strawbery Banke reflects this mixed message of a village both historically authentic and yet imaginary and idealized.

Howells and Decatur had also stressed the need for a vital "living museum" with most buildings owned or leased by commercial and residential tenants. This steady source of income was critical to the WPA plan that imagined, not a museum, but a self-sustaining project that would repay all invested funds. Vaughan adapted but downplayed plans to populate the new campus with renters. The WPA proposal to hire Puddle Dockers as temporary paid workers, to divert traffic around the village, or to partner with existing house museums were not adopted into the Vaughan proposal. It was not even clear at this time how many Puddle Dock buildings would survive. Reports and letters from this period set the number at anywhere between six and thirty-three.

But despite sometimes fuzzy and even conflicting goals, Strawbery Banke Inc. had instant media appeal. The fairy tale transformation of Puddle Dock from ugly duckling to a beautiful swan was tailor-made for the media. The "slum" angle proved irresistible to headline writers. As early as May 1959, months before the city approved the project, the *Christian Science Monitor* published a large photograph of the Marcy-Washington Street site dominated by a scrap pile. The headline read "Portsmouth Slum Clearance Marks New Era." It was a view, true as it might be, that ex-Puddle Dockers saw repeated in the press for decades to follow. The city was, at last, back in the national spotlight, but the focus, according to the *Monitor*, was on "a blighted rectangle of junk yards and shabby tenements."[18]

Portsmouth was good news for Washington too. The bootstrap, community-driven effort gave federal officials a whole new spin on what had been, until Strawbery Banke, an often unpopular policy of demolition and modernization. From its final federal approval on July 23, 1960, government officials labeled Marcy-Washington as the "nation's most unique urban renewal project."[19] This was the first time in the United States that historic preservation was the primary reason for an urban renewal project. *The New York Times* offered frequent reports on the Strawbery Banke

ABOVE: *Carl A. Johnson (center), retired from the Portsmouth Naval Base at the Shipyard, served as the executive vice president of Strawbery Banke Inc. from 1962 to 1972, the longest term of any museum administrator to date. He is seen here with New Hampshire Gov. Walter Petersen and Portsmouth Mayor Eileen Foley. (SBM)*

village and Vaughan fielded interview requests from writers at *Yankee Magazine, The Boston Sunday Globe*, the Associated Press, *New Hampshire Profiles, The Saturday Evening Post*, and a host of other newspapers and magazines across the nation. *Woman's Day* featured Portsmouth in a special issue dedicated to America's "Treasure Towns." An official six-state study approved plans to include Portsmouth on an upcoming Heritage Trail tour of New England. As in the peak era of the colonial revival, upbeat stories about historic Portsmouth were published widely. So even before the first tourist arrived or the first building was razed, Strawbery Banke was putting the city back on the map.

President Dorothy Vaughan too gained national attention. Reporters inevitably focused on her 1957 speech to the Portsmouth Rotary as the sole origin of the waterfront renovation. Kudos flowed in from across the city and the state, culminating years later in a breakfast at the White House, an entry in *Who's Who*, a visit by Lady Bird Johnson, the key to the city, and an honorary doctorate from the University of New Hampshire. Still at work as city librarian, Vaughan found her volunteer time stretched to the limit with Strawbery Banke interviews, meetings, research, fundraisers, and award banquets. So when the retiring assistant commander of the Portsmouth Naval Base offered himself as the group's first paid administrator in July 1961, no one stood in his way. Strawbery Banke Guild founder Cynthia Raymond, whose husband was a former shipyard commander, admits she probably floated the idea past Captain Carl Johnson and likely "talked him into it."[20] Captain Johnson agreed to serve for an annual salary of $5,000.

Like Captain Chester Mayo, who coordinated the survey of historic Portsmouth in the 1930s, Johnson ran a tight ship. He kept a precise calendar, adhered to timetables, and corresponded in a formal style, with color-coded copies of his every memo forwarded to the appropriate agents and filed in quadruplicate. With no formal job description, Johnson took on every task that needed to be done with military precision, coordinating with the Portsmouth Housing Authority, the city, and Strawbery Banke, Inc. as the urban renewal process slowly cleared the junkyards and unwanted buildings from Puddle Dock. Without Johnson's fierce loyalty and strict attention to bureaucratic detail,

ABOVE: *Strawbery Banke president Dorothy Vaughan and benefactor Judson Dunaway inspect the John Clark House (later Wheelwright House) prior to its restoration. (SBM)*

it has been suggested by one of his contemporaries, Strawbery Banke might never have opened in 1965. And it was this same approach, in part, that brought the group to its greatest crisis four years later.[21]

A Moving Experience

The ink was scarcely dry on the Puddle Dock agreement when Strawbery Banke began receiving calls to save more historic buildings in Portsmouth. First came the Daniel Webster house, which was threatened by another urban renewal project on the north side of the city. This was actually the fourth and final house Webster occupied during his formative years as a lawyer in Portsmouth. He stayed initially in a bachelors' quarters upon his arrival in 1807; that site was demolished in the twentieth century.[22] In 1808 he rented the historic Meserve House, site of an early Stamp Act riot, and that building was later torn down to build a parking garage. The house Webster then purchased for his family on Pleasant Street burned in the fire of 1813, so, in 1814, the Websters moved into a modest two-story house on High Street. By this time Daniel Webster was already making a name for himself in Massachusetts,

ABOVE: *Burned by arsonists, uprooted from its Hanover Street site, and trucked through the city streets, the Daniel Webster House awaits its new foundation at Strawbery Banke. The Goodwin Mansion is in the background. Photograph by Carl Johnson. (SBM)*

and he was gone from Portsmouth by 1817. The surviving house, therefore, was dear to the heart of Dorothy Vaughan because it was the only remaining proof that the famous Mr. Webster had lived here. It became a vital "anchor" building in her idealized colonial village plan of the 1960s.

The sight of the Daniel Webster house wheeling through the center of Market Square on its way to the South End was the first powerful evidence that the Strawbery Banke preservation movement had begun. The building made the three-quarter mile trip in a single day, squeezing through one tight corner with a clearance of only an inch and a half between a utility pole on one side and a residence on the other. Newspaper reports played up the drama of the move, noting that the house was rescued just a few feet from the wrecking ball. Shortly before the move the building was damaged by an apparent arson attempt, but local fire fighters arrived in the nick of time.

The move was further complicated when ex-governor Charles Dale blocked a request by Strawbery Banke to temporarily store the building in an unused portion of Prescott Park until the urban renewal clearance was complete. Although the park area donated by the Prescott sisters belonged to the city, Dale threatened to sue the fledgling organization over the matter. Dale also rebuffed a second historic building, the Folsom-Salter House built by Portsmouth privateer Titus Salter. Owners offered to sell the elegant mansion to Strawbery Banke for a dollar, but with no place to store the building Vaughan was forced to turn it down. Later the owners were convinced not to demolish the Salter House, though it was moved across Court Street to its present location. The Daniel Webster crisis was solved when ex-Puddle Dock junk salesman Jack Zeidman agreed to temporarily store the building on his property.

"In past days," editor Ray Brighton wrote on the front page of the *Portsmouth Herald* in November 1961, "if a business needed room to expand, it simply bought adjacent properties, regardless of their history, and brought in the wreckers to remove the old structures. But that's not the rule here anymore."[23] Brighton was referring to still another historic house offer. Bowing to the rising preservationist movement, a furniture store owner voluntarily agreed not to raze the Governor Goodwin mansion, built during the War of 1812, if Strawbery Banke agreed to immediately take it away so he could expand his business. Suddenly a new crisis was in play.

Born in South Berwick, Maine in 1794, Ichabod Goodwin typifies the rise to power of many Portsmouth merchants in the nineteenth century. Sent off to sea to "prove himself" as a young man, Goodwin saw that the local shipping trade was in decline and invested his future in the high-tech railroad industry instead. His instincts paid off. Goodwin married his Portsmouth sweetheart Sarah Rice, grew wealthy, bought his three-story mansion on Islington Street, went into politics, and was governor of New Hampshire during the critical opening year of the Civil War. When Abraham Lincoln issued his first call for Union troops, Governor Goodwin set an example by donating his personal funds to equip the New Hampshire Regiment. Sarah Goodwin left a poignant picture of American life in her diaries.

With no funds and no place to store another huge building, Strawbery Banke was unable to consider taking on the Governor Goodwin Mansion. But the mansion had friends in high places. Former Portsmouth Mayor Andrew Jarvis, who had formed the city committee from which Strawbery Banke evolved, was by this time a member of the New Hampshire Governor's Council, a descendent of the advisory group formed in the Wentworth era before the American Revolution. Jarvis suggested to Governor Wesley Powell, a staunch supporter of Strawbery Banke, that the state of New Hampshire could buy the building and move it to the colonial village. But when Powell asked his newly formed New Hampshire Historical Commission members about the idea, they turned it down flat. The Historical Commission had been formed in 1959, Powell was told, to define the state standards for historic preservation—not to salvage individual buildings with taxpayer money.

Still, Governor Powell, who had grown up in Portsmouth's South End, showed surprising interest in the Goodwin Mansion and persisted in finding a solution. Strawbery Banke leaders were nervous about taking on another building and waffled, until state officials gave them a twenty-four-hour deadline to make a decision. Fearing that the state might "wash its hands of the whole matter and put the blame on us,"[24] Strawbery Banke leaders

ABOVE AND OPPOSITE: *Ichabod Goodwin was New Hampshire governor during the Civil War and loaned his own funds to supply the troops called up by President Lincoln. His wife Sarah Parker Rice Goodwin was an avid diarist whose writings offer nineteenth-century insights from a woman's perspective. (SBM)*

Stoodley's Tavern (top) as it appeared on Daniel Street. The Revolutionary War era building was moved to make way for a federal building and post office in 1965. It is seen (middle) passing the Warner House museum (bottom) on its way to Strawbery Banke. Project founders hoped to revive the tavern with grog and "serving wenches," but it was adapted decades later into an education center. Two of the snapshots are by Captain Carl Johnson. The bottom image by Paul Marston shows the tavern on its new foundation. (SBM and SBM/DA)

agreed to accept the building as long as the state could agree to move it twice, first to a temporary site and then to The Banke. Against the recommendation of its own Historic Commission, the governor and his council approved a budget of $134,000 to move and restore the building. In announcing the plan Governor Powell noted that the historic Goodwin Mansion was not only the home of a famous New Hampshire governor, but it was also a house in which the mother of a governor had once worked as a maid. The odd reference was to Mrs. Mary Powell, the governor's own mother, who had once served as a housekeeper in the Goodwin Mansion.[25]

In February 1963, workmen removed the third story and roof of the Goodwin Mansion in three portable chunks, dismantled the three chimneys, and divided the lower portion of the structure into two large pieces. Photos of the mansion being wheeled through the city appeared in the newspaper alongside a picture of the first Puddle Dock house being taken apart by urban renewal contractors. Amid all the demolition, restoration, and house moving, Edward Abbott of the Portsmouth Housing Authority was busy contracting new multi-story apartments for elderly and low income residents, some of them refugees from Puddle Dock. Change was in the wind. In Washington, DC, President John F. Kennedy was photographed reading a copy of a new federal booklet entitled "Historic Preservation Through Urban Renewal" that trumpeted the breakthrough Strawbery Banke project. At the same moment in Rockefeller Center in New York City, a model of Portsmouth's upcoming colonial village went on public display.

Pictures of the new three-dimensional model appeared repeatedly in the *Herald*, accompanied by artist's conceptual drawings by architect William G. Perry of Boston. Perry, then eighty years old and in semi-retirement, was best known as the designer of Colonial Williamsburg, and his frequent presence in Portsmouth gave the project, to some, a distinguished glow.[26] Portsmouth architecture, Perry theorized, was unique in the nation because skilled local ship carpenters had worked on many of its finest buildings, creating features seen nowhere else. Portsmouth had advantages over Colonial Williamsburg, Perry said, even though the Virginia project had relied on millionaire sponsor John D. Rockefeller. It was "really a lot better" for Portsmouth to raise

ABOVE: *A salvage carpenter inspects one of four wrought iron balconies saved from the Samuel Ham / Levi Woodbury House (1809) demolished by the Portsmouth Housing Authority in 1961. Strawbery Banke rescued many architectural fragments in Puddle Dock, the North End, and elsewhere, creating a significant collection as part of its early preservation efforts. (SBM)*

ABOVE: *Three Strawbery Banke belles point out the sights to a group of young servicemen at the Liberty Pole. The playground area at Prescott Park in the background is currently the site of the flower garden display. (SBM)*

the money itself, he told a local reporter. "That way there is a lot more civic pride in what is accomplished," Perry said.[27]

Such comments from the renowned architect dovetailed perfectly with Vaughan's love of all things old, her passionate conviction that Portsmouth had a "special flavor," and her life-long distrust of wealthy outsiders, often the very outsiders whose largesse kept her colonial village solvent. Many years later and well into her nineties, Vaughan noted that "keeping Portsmouth old" was critical to its economic success, and she railed against the "millionaires, multi-millionaires, and billionaires coming into town."[28] Her dream for Portsmouth, ultimately, was to freeze time and attract tourist cash, while retaining local autonomy and low tax rates for a predominately blue-collar population. "One of my prime objects in life," Vaughan told a reporter in 1982, "is to see that the flavor of Portsmouth is kept. Portsmouth is not like St. Louis, San Francisco, Boston, or Newburyport. It has its own flavor, as distinct as strawberry is from chocolate and vanilla."[29]

Strawbery Banke brought in the Boston firm of Perry, Shaw, Hepburn, and Dean in 1963 to design the new colonial village. They suggested a scaled-down version of Vaughan's recreated

Market Square, centered around a surviving fragment of the colonial statehouse that had not yet been moved to the Puddle Dock campus. As the work progressed, Vaughan took every moment she could to wander the evolving site and compliment the workmen. "Sometimes I wake up in the middle of the night," she said, "and I start thinking about Strawbery Banke, and have to pinch myself to believe it's true."[30]

Carpenter Norman Clark may have pinched himself one morning when he arrived to find about a hundred broken windows in the empty Puddle Dock buildings. Vandals had had another busy night. A former milkman and apartment manager, Clark had accepted the post of maintenance worker at the as yet unopened historic site. Despite low pay and long hours, Clark stayed on for twenty-five years, repairing the ailing houses from foundation to roof.

"He didn't know a thing about old houses when he started. Neither did anyone," says Strawbery Banke restoration carpenter John Schnitzler, who apprenticed with Clark beginning in 1977. "Those guys learned as they worked. Eventually, they could do anything," he says today. Schnitzler often heard the story of the hundred broken windows and how, back in the mid-1960s, Clark had patiently cleaned the putty from each window pane, replaced and re-glazed the glass, and re-hung every old frame. He was reluctant, however, to tell his boss that, as a bad boy of eight years old, he himself had been among the vandals who had smashed the windows with rocks in what he then thought was an abandoned part of town. Schnitzler has been "paying penance" ever since, he says.[31]

By the summer of 1964, anticipation of the colonial village had reached fever pitch. Tourists, lured by years of advance publicity, came to visit what continued to be an active construction site filled with boarded-up weather-beaten houses. Restoration was well underway at the 1762 Chase House, the grandest of the Puddle Dock homes, thanks to the $100,000 gift from The Banke's first major donor, Nellie McCarty of New York City. The Chase House and the Goodwin Mansion, then being renovated by the state of New Hampshire, were the only two buildings that would be ready for tours by the opening of Strawbery Banke in 1965, a full year away.

ABOVE: *From its initial days the buildings of Strawbery Banke have been an inspiration to visiting artists and photographers. (SBM)*

Locals complained of being "shut out" of the project site that was a target for vandals and a lure to "winos" and "hobos." Attempts to secure some of the more valuable construction areas with a $5,000 metal fence brought accusations that the former neighborhood was now being run like a private club for its wealthy new owners. Jeremy Waldron, now secretary of the group, promised that the waiting game was almost over, and reminded Strawbery Banke critics that the nonprofit corporation still did not yet have official title to the land and buildings. Tapping into the increased public energy, Waldron announced a new $125,000 capital fundraiser and marshaled an unpaid army to ready the project for opening day. Comparing Portsmouth to Sturbridge Village, he projected that the city might see a total of a million paying visitors at the new colonial village by the 1980s. With each visitor spending up to $10 per day, he implied, the impact could be mind boggling.

"This is no longer a dream," Waldron told the *Herald*. "Strawbery Banke is everyone's project. . . we'll need furniture, we'll need services, we'll need money. . . As of right now the Strawbery Banke office is ready to list any volunteers, whether it's to help with landscaping, painting, or anything else."[32]

In July 1964, to whip up local enthusiasm for the 1965 opening, the town celebrated Strawberry Days with strawberry shortcake, strawberry punch, and strawberry ice cream. The Strawbery Banke belles, dressed in hoop skirts decorated in a strawberry print, marched with soldiers from the Marines, Navy, and Air Force. Incoming governor John King showed up for a symbolic strawberry planting ceremony in Puddle Dock. Guild member Muriel Howells offered her favorite strawberry recipes to the newspaper. Strawbery Banke staff posted strawberry-shaped road signs around the city, and the Guild of Strawbery Banke offered an expanded inventory of strawberry-related gifts. The Guild, which had already opened gift shops in the Chase House and the Aaron Conant House, now expanded further. Organized as a separate nonprofit agency, the women of the Guild paid $18,000 to purchase the endangered brick Kingsbury building about a block from Puddle Dock. With the help of architect William G. Perry, the ladies independently restored the early nineteenth-century building, privy, barn, and coach house,

ABOVE: *A pewter craft display during opening days in the mid-1960s. (SBM)*

adding a third gift shop and offices. Alert to future expansion, the group trademarked the Strawbery Banke name.

On September 24, 1965, William Slayton, commissioner of the Urban Renewal Administration, flew from Washington, DC, to hand-deliver the official paperwork to Dorothy Vaughan. Having paid the balance on the $28,686 due, Strawbery Banke Inc. now owned the cleared land and its twenty-seven surviving buildings. Slayton said that Portsmouth had proven urban renewal could "preserve as well as demolish."[33]

But before the museum could open, there was one more building to move. Stoodley's Tavern stood exactly where the city's modern new post office and federal building were going. Linked to visits by Paul Revere, Rogers Rangers, and John Paul Jones, the tavern was best known for its appearance in Kenneth Roberts's novel and film *Northwest Passage*. Regardless of the fact that Roberts was writing about an earlier tavern that burned in 1761, Stoodley's was on Dorothy Vaughan's "must save" list. She had researched the tavern for the author thirty years before. Gutted and reshaped into a series of commercial shops, the ground floor of the surviving pre-Revolutionary tavern had little to offer, but the second and third floors retained many early details.

Vaughan made a strong personal appeal for Stoodley's, vowing to return the tavern to working order with maids serving grog and chowder. Despite its ongoing stock sales and capital campaign, the group quickly managed to raise $23,000 to transport the building to a new foundation a few blocks away on Hancock Street, across from the recently moved Goodwin Mansion. The original moving date had to be postponed for two days when workmen realized that disconnecting power lines for the job would shut down voting machines during a November 1965 election. Transplanting Stoodley's Tavern was a smooth operation, but there were still three more Piscataqua buildings on the endangered list ready to be moved. One would arrive, one would not, and the third would hover in limbo, inciting a controversy that changed the way Strawbery Banke defined itself.

ABOVE: *Costumed volunteer directs visitors to a craft display in an unrestored building. (SBM)*

Portsmouth vs. Portsmouth

Surprisingly little is known about the final days of Puddle Dock. Despite hundreds of published articles on the arrival of Strawbery Banke, not a single newspaper reporter was on hand to document the slow exodus of residents from the ancient neighborhood. Many of the 109 families were poor and lived in rented apartments.[34] Most left quietly, accepting their fate and the $100 in moving expenses offered by the Portsmouth Housing Authority. Powerless against the combined force of their landlords, the city, and federal urban renewal, they packed their belongings and dispersed. Some found their way to other South End homes or downtown apartments or moved in with relations. Most moved willingly and without incident to the new apartments built by the Portsmouth Housing Authority.

The *Portsmouth Herald* limited its coverage of the actual urban renewal to a few captioned pictures of buildings being wrecked by a crane with a clamshell bucket. Research has so far turned up only a single publication from outside the seacoast region that offered a glimpse of the unfolding human drama. A roving reporter from the *New Hampshire Town Crier* talked over the fence with one Puddle Docker. George Ayers was willing to be photographed in his yard "full of rubbish" outside an "old house hidden by asphalt siding." (Today it is the Captain Keyran Walsh House at Strawbery Banke.) Ayers, who had rented the house for sixteen years, said he did not know when he was supposed to vacate, but most of his neighbors had already gone. Ayers wife, who was hard of hearing, said she refused to leave without taking the flowers from her garden. The cover of the article showed Strawbery Banke executive vice president Carl Johnson posed against a wall map of Puddle Dock like a military general planning an air raid.[35]

Many residents, like junk dealer Jack Zeidman and his wife Ida, later felt their lives improved after urban renewal. Long-time Puddle Docker Mae Johnson agreed. She moved up to Court Street after being evicted from her "blighted" house in the spring of 1962. Johnson had left school at age twelve and worked ironing clothes and linens at the neighborhood laundry. In fifty-five years on the job, her salary increased from twenty cents

an hour to $1.65. Separated from her husband, she raised one son alone, always refusing to accept charity or "go on the county." When her son returned home after World War II, they bought a house on Washington Street in Puddle Dock.

"They didn't give us much money for those places," Johnson told a Strawbery Banke historian years later. "The house was old . . . It was coming to the stage where you had to have a full bath and you had to have a furnace, and I couldn't afford that."[36]

"I missed it when I moved out of my house," Johnson said. The impact of losing her home and neighbors all at once was so great that Johnson did not venture back to Puddle Dock, scarcely a block away from her new home, for fifteen years. Speaking in a thick Portsmouth accent rarely heard any more, she waxed nostalgic about a life of hard but honest work among close friends. Asked what was special about life in Puddle Dock, at first

ABOVE: *The Leonard Cotton House (c. 1750) on Washington Street as seen through a nearby junkyard. Widely distributed for decades, this image and others like it seemed to symbolize the "trash to treasure" urban renewal project. Puddle Dockers considered this a staged and unfair depiction of the neighborhood in a publicity campaign that focused on building exteriors and scrap piles. (SBM)*

Johnson said she did not have the words to express her feelings. Then, gathering her thoughts, she offered a heartfelt epitaph for a time and place lost forever: "We just seemed to cling together, that's all. Nobody seemed to want to hurt somebody else. We could do things for somebody else—well, that was good—and they'd do it for you too."

Not everyone left quietly. "I kept saying—'This can't happen. This is America,'" Evelyn Marconi recalls today, the emotion as close to the surface as it was nearly half a century ago. "We were supposed to be low income morons, but we weren't."[37] Marconi still believes that the city and the federal government "singled out" residents of Puddle Dock and took their land because they were poor and without a legal voice. She agrees that the junkyards were an eyesore, many buildings were in shambles, and that real estate values were low. But she wonders if it was an accident that so many of the city's Jewish residents lived in Puddle Dock.

Marconi received notice in 1962, soon after the birth of her fourth child, that she and her family were required to vacate the house they purchased on Marcy Street. It was to be taken by eminent domain as part of the blighted slum neighborhood. After ignoring an $11,000 offer by the city for the house, she hired attorney Charles Dale who issued a "no salvage" order to stop the bulldozers at the front door. Marconi later sued the city and won an undisclosed sum, but still lost her house to the forces of urban renewal.

"I stayed over there with my little baby and watched them tear my house down," she says. "And I watched local people go in and steal my chandeliers and pull up my hardwood floors."

The memory of the lost neighborhood lingers. The impact, according to one former resident, was like a neutron bomb that obliterated the population but left the buildings standing. Worse, for former residents, the restored buildings seemed to be more important than the people who had occupied them. When Dorothy Vaughan described the opening of the colonial village in 1965 as "making the area respectable once more," ex-Puddle Dockers winced. Repeated press release photos of fashionable Strawbery Banke Guild members contributed to the South End perception that the neighborhood was now in the hands of a wealthy and intellectual elite. Others, Marconi included, placed

a share of the blame on the small group of Puddle Dock absentee landlords, who by refusing to paint and upgrade their shabby apartments, had forced the area into slum conditions. Resentment festered as the federal government adopted photographs of the Marcy-Washington junkyards as evidence that the urban renewal program cared deeply about historic preservation.[38]

Politicized by her battle over urban renewal, Evelyn Marconi went on to serve ten years as a Portsmouth city councilor and assistant mayor, then ran one more successful campaign while in her late seventies. Her coffee and chowder shop just down the street from Strawbery Banke is nationally known as a meeting place for conservative Republicans. As a measure of her influence, during a 1992 campaign swing through New Hampshire, President George Bush publicly apologized for failing to make his traditional stop at Marconi's riverside shop.

"I don't blame Strawbery Banke," she says today after years of watching the South End thrive and historic Portsmouth prosper from a growing tourist trade. "They were only the redeveloper. "It was the federal government and that urban renewal—something I still believe is unconstitutional."

Recently, Evelyn Marconi says, she received a surprise visit from a "former elected official" at her coffee shop. Her one-time political rival leaned forward and in hushed tones said, "I just want to apologize to you for everything we did to you and your family." The apology, though a long time in coming, was gratefully accepted.

ABOVE AND OPPOSITE: *Evelyn and Geno Marconi and family outside their "dream" house on Marcy Street, prior to its demolition. The family lived in one side and rented the other side of this twentieth-century colonial-style home. It was removed under eminent domain during urban renewal in keeping with plans for the incoming historic restoration project. (MAR)*

SHIFTING FOUNDATIONS 1965–1975

Strawbery Banke burst to life in 1965 after a long eight-year gestation. In retrospect, the troubles that quickly followed were simply growing pains, but at the time they came as one crisis after another. Creating and parenting "the project," as it was first known, required very different skills. At first, founders followed the money, completing whatever task was able to attract funding. But it was not long before the dream of a reconstructed colonial village came up against the daily demands of running a ten-acre summer attraction with only two year-round staff members. There were, as one contemporary put it, too many generals and too few soldiers. Promises were made, but could not always be kept.

The Originators were up against more than local discontent. Attitudes toward historic preservation were shifting across the nation. Due partly to the devastating effect of urban renewal itself, Americans were waking up to the need to save important sites and structures. In 1966, a year after Strawbery Banke opened, the National Historic Preservation Act established sweeping legislation. This federal act expanded the definition of what was "historic" and created a process to prevent the wholesale destruction of old neighborhoods in the name of urban renewal. At the same time too, a whole new generation of college educated professionals appeared on the scene. Young historians, archaeologists, museum curators, nonprofit managers, and preservation experts

OPPOSITE: *Greeted by Beverly Armsden, left, visitors arrive to tour the renovated Gov. Goodwin Mansion. Across Hancock Street, Stoodley's Tavern is visible through the doorway. Both buildings were moved from other parts of town to Strawbery Banke in the 1960s and placed on new foundations. (SBM/ DA)*

brought energy and expertise to the expanding preservation field.

America, too, was on a youth-driven trajectory. Student protests against the undeclared war in Viet Nam shut down the University of New Hampshire and disrupted the building of a nuclear power plant in nearby Seabrook. When Greek tycoon Aristotle Onassis tried to build an oil refinery at nearby Durham Point, with an oil offloading depot at the Isles of Shoals, local citizens elected to keep the environment intact and rejected the multi-million dollar project. Jobs grew scarce as gas prices climbed. Talented artists, craftspeople and performers from the Woodstock generation were increasingly drawn to a gritty Port of Portsmouth that seemed to be on the verge of a cultural revolution.

A growing "back to the earth" movement revived lost pioneering skills and drew inspiration from early folk traditions. Long-haired, tie-dyed researchers recorded the oral histories of their elders in search of times gone by. At the same time, rebellious Baby Boomers questioned the largely white, patriarchal approach to American history, upturned social, sexual, and racial stereotypes, and taunted long-held views of American citizenship and patriotism. Strawbery Banke opened its doors in celebration of one American Revolution only to find a new revolution in the

BELOW: The dream of creating a patriotic colonial village continued through the 1960s. When a new professional administration arrived at Strawbery Banke in the 1970s, the emphasis shifted to the Puddle Dock neighborhood and to exploring its maritime heritage. This image is from "Spring Hill," site of the tugboats and restaurant "deck" area today on Ceres Street. (SBM)

air. And inside the walls of historic Puddle Dock, to paraphrase folksinger Bob Dylan, the times were a'changing too.

Drifting at High Speed

The Piscataqua is a powerful river, as anyone who has navigated these waters knows. Tides pull one way and then another with such force that large ships often wait for slack water before venturing into the harbor. Small craft, from Indian canoes and colonial fishing shallops to fiberglass kayaks, have long followed a timetable defined by a river with the efficiency and speed of a commuter train. Those who choose to fight the tides do so at their own risk. It is a time-honored tradition in Portsmouth to go with the flow.

The founders of Strawbery Banke did have one navigational aid: a $10,000 report from a Boston public relations firm. The consultants studied seventy other historic sites, surveyed five hundred Portsmouth residents, analyzed five thousand national nonprofit agencies, and conducted exhaustive interviews. "The job is not impossible," the experts concluded, but raising millions of dollars, attracting public opinion, and restoring an entire neighborhood was a Herculean undertaking. The report advised the founders to stop selling stock and build a membership base with a $10 annual fee. It suggested creating a Board of Overseers to offer advice, to hire a public relations firm, to greatly expand the size of the board of directors, and to actively solicit funds from wealthy summer visitors living from Rye to Kennebunkport. Strawbery Banke should target families with the same last names as the first seventeenth-century settlers, the 1964 report said, and focus the campus around a visitors' center reconstructed to look like the Old Statehouse. The 1964 report offered dozens of recommendations, but noted that the organization, already stretched to its limits, did not have the resources or the people to implement them.[1]

With this consulting plan, little capital, and lots of raw ambition, the small group of colonial village founders had followed the flow of urban renewal money into Puddle Dock. The first two houses opened at Strawbery Banke in 1965, the Chase House and the Governor Goodwin Mansion, were both funded

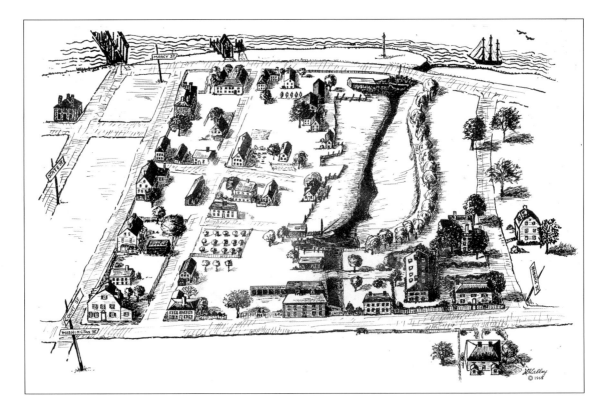

ABOVE: *By 1965, as seen by this illustration, founders still hoped to dredge out and restore a portion of Puddle Dock cove. Plans to reconstruct a small wharf and ship near the Liberty Pole were not realized. Plans remained active, however, to reconstruct the Old Statehouse (bottom right in sketch) near the corner of Hancock and Washington streets. The Dunaway Store had not yet been conceived here. (RMC)*

by outside sources. And despite the contention that the group was paying its own way when it purchased the cleared waterfront land, the $200,000 city bond and $227,000 worth of road and sewer improvements that followed were paid for by Portsmouth taxpayer dollars. With few detractors, Portsmouth citizens agreed that the primary work of Strawbery Banke was to keep its head above water, bring in hordes of tourists, and save old buildings. Easier said than done.

With three buildings moved to Puddle Dock, the tally now stood at thirty key structures. Although renovation of the relocated Stoodley's Tavern and Daniel Webster House languished, Strawbery Banke continued to receive calls to save more endangered buildings on its secure campus, which locals came to see as the "parking lot of history." In 1966, its second year of operation, Strawbery Banke announced that it was adding three more buildings to its growing collection.

The 1750 Sparhawk Mansion, first on the list, was already in desperate shape. A wedding gift from Sir William Pepperrell to his daughter, the nineteen-room mansion included a massive

central hall so grand that it was used as the setting of a film in 1949.[2] Unable to maintain the rambling, uninsulated mansion, the owners were forced to sell off the contents and woodwork room by room. In 1965 Rosamond Thaxter of Kittery Point, a Strawbery Banke director, donated $5,000 to preserve what was left of Sparhawk, and promised an additional $20,000 for its restoration. Thaxter was well known as the granddaughter and biographer of the much-loved local poet Celia Thaxter from the Isles of Shoals. The media trumpeted the good news that Sparhawk would soon "become part of The Banke."[3]

The actual plan, according to Captain Johnson, was to salvage the best carved interior woodwork from Sparhawk and reassemble it inside Stoodley's Tavern. The "extensive similarity" between the two buildings, Johnson wrote to Miss Thaxter and architect William Perry, would not harm their claim to historical authenticity. "True, we will be creating a composite house," Johnson admitted, "but it will be a distinguished one."[4] In an early attempt at "adaptive restoration," Johnson made a yeoman effort to locate an outside company to lease the restored Stoodley's and run it as a restaurant. No one, in the early days of the project, was willing to take the risk. So after removing a few carved panels and other items, Johnson used a portion of Rosamond Thaxter's money to hire a wrecking crew. In 1967 workers

ABOVE: *A farewell view of Sparhawk Mansion in Kittery Point is seen in this candid photograph by Captain Carl Johnson from 1963. Strawbery Banke managed to save architectural elements from the structure, but plans to incorporate those pieces into Stoodley's Tavern and create a restaurant were later abandoned. (SBM)*

delivered the remains of Sparhawk Mansion to the flames, in the donor's forlorn words "like an old worn flag."

Every bank in the city, it seemed, now wanted to get rid of an old building to build a parking lot. Late in 1967, the Portsmouth Savings Bank offered the Joseph Whipple House on State Street to Strawbery Banke. The extraordinary Georgian mansion, a sister to the Moffatt-Ladd House, was free for the taking. Strawbery Banke offered to pay $30,000 if the bank would leave the building at its current site. When Portsmouth Savings declined the offer, Rosamond Thaxter used her influence to have the National Trust for Historic Preservation in Washington, DC, send off a stern letter to the bank president suggesting he "give thoughtful consideration" to preserving the house. When Strawbery Banke was unable to accept the building, the Portsmouth Historical Society considered moving it one hundred yards to the lawn of the John Paul Jones House. Eventually, a private company trucked the Whipple House to a new location, Portsmouth Savings got its parking lot, and the building, although divided into apartment units, was saved.[5]

The Banke had more public success with its next project. Dover businessman and philanthropist Judson Dunaway donated $71,000 for the recreation of a "country store" fashioned after his own father's shop in West Virginia. To erect the new structure, Banke officials had to execute a tricky maneuver. They announced that one of the Puddle Dock buildings previously thought to be of historic significance was actually newer than originally determined and could be torn down. The Dunaway Store was then built on the same "historic site" on Marcy Street and equipped with authentic furnishings purchased from a wrecked nineteenth-century country store in Sudbury, Massachusetts. Architect William Perry's saltbox design seemed to blend with the colonial surroundings.

The opening of the Dunaway Store was a bigger event in Portsmouth than the launch of Strawbery Banke itself. On June 10, 1967, a sweltering hot morning in New Hampshire, First Lady Claudia Alta Taylor Johnson touched down at Pease Air Force Base at 10:45 A.M. With the national media in tow, a motorcade whisked "Lady Bird" Johnson through Portsmouth to the spot, according to the press, where "those English pilgrims"

ABOVE: *Sparhawk Mansion door salvaged by Strawbery Banke, Inc. (ARM)*

had landed 337 years before. Indeed, the reconstructed Dunaway Store stood only yards from the assumed site of the 1631 Great House. Johnson said the setting was reminiscent of her father's grocery store in Kamack, Texas. An estimated fifteen hundred well-wishers stood by as Johnson, dressed in a three-piece lime suit, became the first paying customer of the Dunaway Store. She purchased three spools of thread—beige, white and red,—a piece of penny candy and two Victorian children's books, for a total of $2.31.[6] Accompanied closely by Secretary of the Interior Morris Udall and a phalanx of local dignitaries and secret servicemen, Johnson visited the nearby Sherburne House before she moved on to Maine for a lobster dinner. The First Lady's whistle stop visit likely captured more headlines across the nation than the dozen presidential visits to Portsmouth that preceded her.[7]

Two days after Lady Bird's visit, Strawbery Banke accepted responsibility for the restored South Meeting House just up the hill on Marcy Street, which was owned by the city of Portsmouth. Built in 1866 as an election hall, the structure had briefly served as the first African American meeting place in the city. Although it was technically too "modern" for the 1830s cut-off date set for the Puddle Dock project, it stood on the site of a much earlier church and meeting house in the South End. Dorothy Vaughan had imagined a church with a steeple within her colonial village landscape. With no funds to reconstruct a replica of the North Church as originally planned, this building would have to do.

Again the directors drifted towards a new benefactor. Funds to repair the battered building came from John Elwyn Stone, a descendant of Revolutionary War hero Governor John Langdon. Following surgery at Portsmouth Hospital on "Hospital Hill," Elwyn could see the Old Meetinghouse spire from his recovery room window. Elwyn noticed that the clock on the tower across the South Mill Pond did not move. He originally planned just to repair the clock, but that required first straightening the steeple. Stone decided to finance the entire job. Former Williamsburg architect William G. Perry was called in once more, this time to renovate the Old Meeting House. In 1967 Strawbery Banke leased the building from the city for ninety-nine years.

One year later, The Banke also announced the opening of "The Parsonage," built downtown on Pleasant Street in 1790

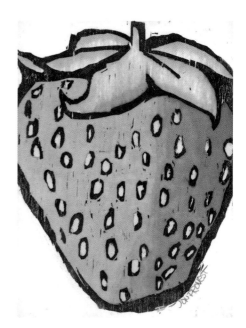

ABOVE: *Strawberries were ubiquitous in the opening years of "The Banke." Depicted here is a large painted berry signed by Jon Provest. (SBM)*

Johnson & Johnson: In 1967 First Lady "Lady Bird" Johnson, seen here with Captain Carl Johnson, became the first customer at the newly-built Dunaway Store. Partly due to controversy over the design (model seen on right), no major structure was built at Strawbery Banke for the next forty years. Portsmouth Herald *Photo. (SBM)*

for the early ministers of the North Congregational Church. Bequeathed by Mrs. Wendell Lord, the house and gardens were exhibited, not as a colonial restoration, but simply as the former owner had left them. Although these projects spread the word about The Banke and preserved Portsmouth buildings, the fledgling museum seemed to lack a central purpose. An increasingly disjointed array of exhibits and events were all packaged under the symbol of a bright red strawberry. Although rejected by early settlers in 1653 in favor of the name Portsmouth, the ubiquitous berry had all but become the raison d'etre for the settlement itself. A 1960s Strawbery Banke brochure posits what might be called the "fresh fruit" theory of New Hampshire's founding. It claimed:

> The City of Portsmouth, N.H. was born in 1630 on a hillside thick with wild strawberries. Spread over the river banks like a deep crimson carpet, the fragrance of these berries attracted a sea-battered sailing vessel into the mouth of the Piscataqua River. The passengers, starved for fresh fruit after a two month diet of hard tack, cask water and salted beef, eagerly went ashore.

From the perspective of its core founders and executive vice president Captain Johnson, however, Strawbery Banke was making enormous strides for a "boot-strap" operation. Dorothy Vaughan, now vice president, continually referred to Puddle Dock as a former slum that was now worth over a million dollars. This approach, juxtaposed against the unending call for more money and the high society balls, tea parties, art shows, chamber music concerts, and antique auctions offered a confusing image in the largely blue-collar town. Was The Banke poor or rich? Did it belong to Portsmouth or to a cultured aristocracy from out of town? Elegant Strawbery Banke Guild members in mink wraps and children collecting pennies for historic renovation formed an odd counterpoint to the many empty, boarded-up buildings.

"The local population to a large degree has never really accepted The Banke," a *Portsmouth Herald* editorial noted, "partially because it felt crowded out by the way it was made an 'in thing' with the well-heeled in the other environs."[8]

ABOVE: *Lady Bird Johnson at Dunaway Store dedication in 1967. Portsmouth Herald Photo. (SBM)*

Tourists, although generally enthusiastic, did not always believe the waterfront project lived up to the media hype. An Ohio visitor found the city downtown little more than "a bunch of junkie looking stores." The "much-talked-about" Banke, he complained to the newspaper, was "too slow and patched up, dusty, and too many shacky places that haven't been touched."[9] The Banke's failure to save the Sparhawk Mansion brought accusations that the whole preservation effort was "a complete farce."[10] Critics asked openly, with so many buildings left to restore, why the reproduction of a West Virginia country store got first priority. By adding the Dunaway Store, one *Herald* reader complained, Strawbery Banke risked turning into "a sort of Early American Disneyland."[11] It was a claim the founders took seriously. Disneyland, although the most successful theme park in the nation, was anathema to the founders. Fear of building anything "new" became so deeply engrained in the corporate consciousness that the museum did not add another major building for four decades.

Drifting from one exciting goal to the next, the Puddle Dock "project" was beginning to look, from the outside at least, like a ship without a compass. More than anything now, the Originators wanted to finish Phase One of their plan as designed by William Perry's architectural team from Boston. The final step was to reconstruct New Hampshire's original statehouse at the end of a long mall between the Daniel Webster and Governor Goodwin houses. Built smack in the middle of the downtown Parade in 1758, the pre-Revolutionary building had miraculously survived all three Portsmouth fires. The Declaration of Independence had reportedly been read from its balcony in 1776, the same balcony from which President George Washington addressed Portsmouth's citizens in 1789. The aging building was broken up and removed from Market Square in 1836. Only a portion of the eastern third of the statehouse was known to have survived; it stood a few blocks away. The state of New Hampshire purchased that structure in hopes of restoring it. By 1969 it was being used as a warehouse for the state liquor commission.

After years of political debate, Commander Cecil Humphreys, who as a state senator had orchestrated the change in urban renewal law that saved Strawbery Banke a decade before, finally managed to push a $35,000 resolution to save the building through the New Hampshire general court. The surviving chunk of the statehouse was moved the short distance from Court Street to the Strawbery Banke campus.

The trouble, besides the lack of funding and the small portion of the building left standing, was that no one knew exactly what the Old Statehouse looked like. Designers inevitably turned to an artist's rendition of the building drawn in 1902 for a Portsmouth guidebook. That drawing was created "according to the testimony of many old people, who can remember it distinctly."[12] But those old people had certainly seen the building in its declining years, after it had lost a cupola, roof balustrade and other attractive exterior features. To make matters worse, a 1970 study by an undergraduate at Boston University suggested that the Court Street building was probably not part of the Old Statehouse at all. And so the building sat at Strawbery Banke—and sat—for the next 20 years.

In its well-publicized drive to be the most "authentic" colonial village in America, with real buildings on their original foundations, The Banke set its own bar impossibly high. Damned if they acted, damned if they didn't, the board of directors at The Banke tabled the Old Statehouse project year after year. In 1983, a new study reversed the 1970 thesis. The rotting timbers at Strawbery Banke were indeed part of New Hampshire's original colonial statehouse. But by then the world had turned. A whole new professional management team had adopted a different plan that did not include an imagined patriotic mall. The timbers of the statehouse were later numbered, dissembled, preserved, stored in a metal trailer, and moved to a parking space not far from the golden-domed state capital in Concord where, through many failed attempts at resurrection, they lay a'moldering.[13]

ABOVE AND OPPOSITE: *Built on the site of the 1731 South Meeting House, the 1866 "Third Ward Hall" served as school and public function hall. Black citizens celebrated Emancipation Day here in 1882. It served for 25 years as the Portsmouth Children's Museum. It was restored in the 1960s by a Strawbery Banke benefactor. (SBM)*

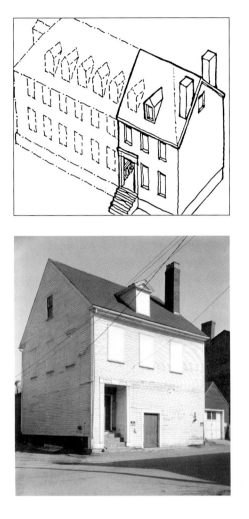

Handwriting on the Wall

Quietly and methodically, a precious few of the historic buildings at Puddle Dock underwent an amazing transformation. With "glacial speed," according to one contemporary trustee, Strawbery Banke brought the mid-eighteenth century Wheelwright House and the late-nineteenth-century Walsh House into full restoration.[14] The Reuben Shapley and the Gookin houses followed, restored by the Guild of Strawbery Banke, along with the restored exterior of the 1695 Sherburne House, the only seventeenth-century building on the museum grounds. Although only six restorations were open to the public by 1970, the quality of the work, and the meticulous research behind it, showed an emerging professionalism at The Banke. Work progressed only when a generous philanthropist could be found and, it was clear that at this rate, restoring the entire campus to this high standard would take decades to complete.

To fill in the blank spaces and please the increasing number of annual visitors, The Banke relied on a patchwork of strategies and outside support. Guild members scrubbed and converted the Aaron Conant House, named for an early stagecoach driver, into a makeshift souvenir shop before opening their own office in the Kingsbury House nearby. Members of the fraternity of Masons considered adopting the William Pitt Tavern where the state's first Masonic lodge had begun. The Shapley Townhouse, built of brick at the end of Horse Lane soon after the fire of 1813, was hastily converted into an art gallery. Volunteers from the Piscataqua Garden Club developed floral areas at their own expense. "Fifty-one percent of the work is landscaping," designer William Perry noted in a special Strawbery Banke issue of *New Hampshire Profiles* in 1967. Perry suggested planting a small orchard, constructing fences and walkways, and beautifying trouble spots with horticultural details that would bring "an element of surprise" to the campus.[15] The old "tidal inlet was outlined in willow trees and stones in an attempt to help tourists visualize the missing cove that had attracted John Mason's settlers. Dorothy Vaughan suggested a plan to revive the sport of lawn bowling to draw competitive teams to the yawning empty space.

While Captain Carl Johnson coordinated the missions of these disparate troops, Strawbery Banke's second employee saw to the museum-quality historic restoration. James L. Garvin joined the two-person staff fresh from college in 1963, with the open-ended title of "general administrative assistant." His first job was to free up the Captain by typing all official correspondence on a 1912 Oliver typewriter. Garvin, an engineer and art historian, received $50 a week, a rate that, he recalls with "a perverse pride," made him the lowest paid member of his college graduating class. He was allowed to board in the Shapiro House as the removal of the last "nonhistoric" houses and scrap metal yards continued all around. After dark, Garvin acted as night watchman, rousting teens, vagrants, and drunks from the boarded-up buildings of the empty neighborhood. In one *Portsmouth Herald* feature, the future Strawbery Banke curator discovered a litter of feral kittens while attempting to rid the area of an infestation of rats.[16]

"We had high hopes for restoration of our buildings, but absolutely no plan for interpretation or education," Garvin wrote years later. "Strawbery Banke's eventual restoration was then to be based largely on a detailed Portsmouth map of 1813; nothing in the area was to date from after 1830."[17]

Garvin, then aged twenty-four, took a leave of absence in 1967 to attend graduate school at the prestigious Winterthur program in Delaware. It was during his absence that the reconstructed Dunaway Store was completed and a late nineteenth-century blacksmith's shop was added to the campus. These buildings, Garvin notes, "signaled trouble" because, by strict interpretation, they were not on the 1813 map and, therefore, did not belong in Puddle Dock. The rift between a professional interpretation and the ever-changing vision of the founders continued to widen.

Trouble came, in part, from the new Strawbery Banke Overseers, who met for the first time in 1965. The group, as conceived by Muriel Howells, included prestigious and talented volunteers who agreed to watch over and guide the young corporation. Tapping her ability to boldly solicit strangers for charity, a skill she had learned in the streets of Portsmouth as a child, Howells signed on thirty of the best and the brightest. Admiral Samuel Eliot Morison, the renowned naval historian and biographer of

ABOVE AND OPPOSITE: *The surviving portion of the Old Statehouse (see sketch) was moved a few blocks from Court Street to the campus of Strawbery Banke during this era, but no action was taken to adapt it into a visitor center. (SBM)*

John Paul Jones, agreed to serve, as did "country arts" collector Bertram Little and James Biddle, curator of the Metropolitan Museum of Art. Dr. Richard Howland, whose lecture helped inspire the project in 1958 and who was by now a director at the Smithsonian Institution, came aboard as did Henry Francis du Pont, founder of the Winterthur Museum. Hotelier Jim Smith, historian Ralph May, and donor Rosamond Thaxter were among the local names. Howells' brain trust included recognized experts in archaeology, landscaping, crewel work, herb cultivation, marketing, fine arts, American history, architecture, and antiques. Thayer Cumings, an advertising executive from New York recently retired to the Seacoast, accepted the job of chairman.

If the board of directors acted as parents, the Overseers were the kindly, sage—and hopefully wealthy—grandparents. The Guild of Strawbery Banke, to extend the metaphor, acted more like generous aunts or godmothers, providing added income and encouragement where necessary. There were also twelve hundred stockholders who met annually. Voting stockholders approved the action of the board, who managed the two paid employees and a host of vendors and volunteers. Somewhere within this organizational chart hovered a handful of influential donors whose contributions paid for restorations and public programs.

Despite this unwieldy administration, local opinion held that Strawbery Banke was still run by a small and wealthy elite. These Originators, with the exception of Dorothy Vaughan, were all downtown businessmen. Although this group rotated titles—president, secretary, treasurer and vice president—the same faces appeared in the news year after year. Their motivation from the start had been to preserve history in order to drive paying customers into the city. And their marketing plan worked. Paying visitors to Strawbery Banke increased to over thirty thousand in the first five years of operation, and then doubled in the next decade. But despite millions of tourist dollars spent in the region, like most cities of this era, the downtown area continued to suffer as one shopping mall after another moved into the outskirts of town.

The Overseers gathered biannually to examine the latest developments, drink tea, listen to the president's report, and then cloister themselves for a rousing discussion of the health of the organization. Their annual notes to the board of directors

ABOVE: *Wheelwright House, formerly known as the John Clark House, was among the early restoration projects organized by a volunteer committee. (SBM)*

TOP: *Today Strawbery Banke is known for its historic gardens and scholarly approach to horticulture. Initially thought of as landscaping or beautification, the gardens have become an integral part of the museum's educational and outreach programs as well. (SBM/ DA)*

LEFT: *Concord Coach on display at Strawbery Banke in 1972 (PER)*

covered everything from tips on fundraising and museum display to notes on the colonial costumes worn by guides (which the Overseers felt added an unnecessary "light comic touch") and the sale of plastic fruit at the Dunaway Store. Overseers grew increasingly concerned with the lack of available funds and the board's growing tendency to stray from its historic guidelines to pursue unrelated projects. They encouraged the board to start building an endowment for the future and to restore some buildings for rental to bring in more cash.

When in 1968 one Overseer suddenly asked, "What is the true purpose of Strawbery Banke?" no one seemed to know. Unhappy with the vague mission as described by the incorporation documents, the group decided to draft its own Statement of Purpose that it submitted to the board of directors in the fall of 1968. At least three of the points became instantly controversial. Strawbery Banke, they said, should emphasize "preservation as distinct from restoration, reconstruction and re-creation." Secondly, the group suggested sticking to work "within the project area." Then came the shocker. All work should be conducted, the Overseers agreed, "under the direction of professionals in the fields of historic preservation." No one working at Strawbery Banke, with the exception of young Jim Garvin, who was away at college, was a professional in the field of historic preservation.

The battle lines were quickly drawn between board members who thought it was time to hire trained administrators and the largely veteran members who favored the status quo. According to the "new" view, Strawbery Banke could only mature, gain respect, and attract large donations and grants by stepping up to a professional level. The "old" view, in brief, was that Captain Johnson had done a superb job so far and that the board did not need a bunch of "high-priced talent" telling them what to do. The Captain, they argued, could simply hire a consultant when he needed one. But that approach had already failed during a small fracas over how to rebuild the chimney in the 1695 Sherburne House. Through the Society for the Preservation of New England Antiquities, the Captain had hired the nation's most respected seventeenth-century expert, but then neglected to follow his advice. In response SPNEA, for a time, severed all ties with The Banke.

OPPOSITE: *Joiner Henry Madden (left to right), Strawbery Banke curator James Garvin and Strawbery Banke restoration carpenter Norman Clark prepare to restore the damaged balustrade of the 1796 Keyran Walsh House in 1972. The Walsh House was the first to be restored under the direct supervision of Strawbery Banke staff. (SBM/ DA)*

By far the most popular addition to Strawbery Banke during this era was the active Lowell Boat Shop. Here master boatbuilders Aubrey Marshall (left and in insert) and Ralph Lowell work on a rowing skiff. (SBM / DA)

The next blow came when Overseer Richard Howland, who had supported the project since 1958, informed the board that he was "diametrically opposed" to the reconstruction of the Old Statehouse. Howland did not believe there was enough data from which to accurately rebuild the structure to professional museum standards. Any such reconstruction, he said, "would be two-thirds phony and one-third conjectural."[18] When the directors ignored his plea and moved a portion of the statehouse building to Strawbery Banke, Dr. Howland resigned. Then Howland invoked the dreaded D-word. The whole project, he wrote in his resignation letter, was becoming "a kind of Disneyland." Thayer Cumings, chairman of the Overseers, also resigned in protest.

It was time for action. In an effort to solve its "family problems" from within, the Board of Directors asked an "outsider," B. Allen Rowland, to take the helm. A highly successful industrial real estate owner and philanthropist, Rowland had moved with his wife and family from Boston to New Castle five years earlier. As president of the Board of Directors, Rowland quickly appointed a committee to determine what kind of professional staff Strawbery Banke needed. Just as quickly, in March of 1969, the committee reported back: The Banke needed a trained director, curator, and business administrator. But the devil was in the details. Fearing that the "Special Report" of the committee was designed to oust Captain Johnson, loyal members of the "Old Guard" simply refused to deal with the topic. Employing the same strategy that the Portsmouth Planning Board had used eleven years earlier to block the creation of Strawbery Banke in Puddle Dock, the opposition simply tabled the Special Report again and again.

Nothing could bridge the impasse. Months of impassioned speeches, lengthy debate, legal wrangling, and harsh words only brought the board of directors back to where they had started. The deadlock over professional management continued into May. With the annual stockholders meeting just two months away, pressure to break the stalemate increased. When one director argued that The Banke could never afford costly professionals, President Rowland announced that he had already located $54,000 in pledges, enough to cover three salaries for two years. Another director then chastised Rowland for raising funds

ABOVE: *Overseer Ralph May (left) is the likely creator of the unique spelling of Strawbery Banke adapted from his book on the early history of Portsmouth. He is seen here with Bertram K. Little, executive director of SPNEA. Muriel Howells photo. (SBM)*

on his own without notifying the board. Someone else suggested that it might be possible to create the new positions, as long as Captain Johnson was guaranteed the top job and veto rights over his future colleagues. Each proposal brought a counter proposal.

Suddenly, in the middle of a parliamentary debate, a slight, quiet woman who rarely spoke at meetings, collapsed forward onto the conference table. She was carried from the room and quickly attended by Dr. Frederick Gray, one of the board members. The meeting recessed. When President Rowland called the meeting back to order, his face was ashen. Their colleague had suffered a heart attack and died. The group stood as each member offered up a private prayer. Then solemnly, silently, they filed out.

Getting Professional Help

For the directors at Strawbery Banke, 1969 was not the Summer of Love. The season opened on a high note when folksinger Pete Seeger floated into town on the maiden voyage of the Maine-built, seventy-five-foot, 100-ton sloop *Clearwater*. Although Seeger arrived an hour late and was hampered by laryngitis, the benefit concert, sponsored by Strawbery Banke, offered a perfect example of how authentic maritime history could be taught with flair aboard a living museum. When a slick replica of the 104-foot racing yacht *America* also stopped at The Banke, locals again suggested that Portsmouth needed its own tall ship. The local Navy Club, it was rumored, had plans to remake the Continental ship *Raleigh*. Built at Portsmouth by John Langdon in 1775, the 32-gun frigate is depicted on the New Hampshire state seal. But nothing, with the exception of an official *Raleigh*-shaped liquor decanter, ever came of the plan.

In June the local daily predicted a Strawbery Banke season "Bigger, Better This Year Than Ever Before." But not even the specter of death in the boardroom was warning enough for the entrenched directors. What happened next turned a private family feud into a "legal donnybrook" that captured headline news for months. The annual stockholders meeting on July 8 erupted into a "floor fight" when former president Donald Margeson

ABOVE: *Rosamond Thaxter of Kittery Point with architect William Perry in 1970 outside the Joshua Wentworth House. Muriel Howells photo. (SBM)*

attempted to depose President B. Allen Rowland—who was up for re-election—and replace him with Dorothy Vaughan. Such insurrection is rare among nonprofit agencies where electing the upcoming slate of officers is typically a "rubber stamp" process. Margeson, however, grabbed the opportunity to nominate an alternative set of officers from the floor of the meeting hall. President Rowland calmly told the seventy-six stockholders assembled at the restored Old Meetinghouse that Mr. Margeson had turned the evening into "a very unusual happening." Because most of the stockholders were not present and had submitted proxy votes by mail, Rowland decided it was unfair to proceed with the election and, despite a rousing protest, he adjourned the meeting until August. The protesting group then filed a court injunction, alleging that President Rowland had illegally blocked the July vote. That move shut down the August meeting too.[19] In protest of the "proxy steal," Cynthia Raymond, founder of the Guild, removed her name from nomination for a position on the board.[20]

The Puddle Dock revolution was hardly the top news story in a world turned upside down. July and August of 1969 also saw the Chappaquiddick tragedy with Senator Edward Kennedy, the Charles Manson Family murders in Los Angeles, the first human footsteps on the surface of the moon, the three-day Woodstock rock and roll festival in New York and, although no one knew it

BELOW: *A youthful and independent-minded group of volunteers and artisans were attracted to Strawbery Banke in the early 1970s, bringing new energy and revolutionary ideas to the campus. (SBM)*

at the time, the final recording session of The Beatles in London. The spat at the stockholders meeting only proved, as the community had long suspected, that Strawbery Banke was deep in the middle of a power struggle.

Portsmouth Herald editor Ray Brighton offered a running commentary reminiscent of sportscaster Howard Cosell at a prizefight, a fight that dragged on for over two years. Brighton, who was then contemplating what became his own eight hundred-plus-page history of Portsmouth, managed to frame the complex events with uncharacteristic optimism. "It's healthy," he wrote the day after the July stockholder's meeting, "to see some of the laundry hanging out on the line and rediscover that mere human beings, not demigods, are trying to run the show."[21] Clearly in favor of President Rowland's push to professionalize The Banke, Brighton referred to the opposition as a "mummified" and "parochial" in-group that wanted to perpetuate their view of "the stuffy past" for "its own aggrandizement." The time had come, he advised "to fish or cut bait."

The battle of words almost turned physical as the beleaguered directors struggled to work through their philosophic differences. Would college trained "professionals" gain control of Puddle Dock, or would it remain in the hands of a grassroots movement? The final decision, everyone knew, would define the future of Strawbery Banke. Both groups feared that, in the hands of the opposition, the waterfront project was doomed. At the end of one long, humid meeting in August, Captain Johnson stood to make an announcement. Someone, he said with undisguised anger, had sent an anonymous and provocative letter to Miss Vaughan. Then, to the astonishment of the entire group, the Captain proceeded to read portions of the inflammatory letter aloud and dispute it, point for point, as a matter of honor.

"For goodness sake! WAKE UP!" the two-page typed memo began. The unknown author warned Vaughan not to be "one of those small town yokels" who opposed bringing in museum professionals, and accused Captain Johnson of attempting to block the hiring of new trained staff members in order to keep his own job. Mr. Rowland, according to the note, was working his heart out to fulfill, not demolish Vaughan's dream. Appealing to Vaughan as "THE ORIGINATOR," the writer concluded: "All

ABOVE: *A young craftsman working while visitors tour the shop. (SBM)*

those other people who are so hell-bent for the advancement of
Strawbery Banke can't ALL be dopes—they really are very intelligent people."[22]

The former commander, according to one of the directors
in attendance, then thundered a challenge. Whoever wrote the
letter should stand up and confront him directly, he said. For a
long time no one moved or spoke. Eventually the storm clouds
dispersed and the meeting broke up. In an age of swords and
pistols, as naval hero Stephen Decatur had discovered in a deadly
duel, things might have ended differently.

In an effort to cool down after a hot summer, the stockholders
elected a compromise president in October. Charles L. Kaufman,
a former Chicago bank president and lawyer, was another "come-
from-away." An entirely new position, third vice-president, was
created for Rowland, who himself had been a compromise can-
didate two years before, but was now considered a firebrand. The
directors also elected to rehire James Garvin, now back with a
master's degree in Early American Culture, at first under the

ABOVE: *Benefactor Nellie McCarty (left)
presents Dorothy Vaughan with stock certificates
worth $100,000 toward the restoration of the
Chase House. (SBM /DA)*

title "curatorial consultant," and eventually as curator. The fall meeting was so peaceful by comparison to the heady summer reporter, Brighton quipped, that the only excitement came when one of the stockholders was stung by a hornet.

Despite the lull that followed, there were more hornet nests to tackle. The Special Report was still "off the table" and, although Garvin was back at work, the decision over a professional director and manager was hotter than ever. President Kaufman threw himself into his new job as peacemaker with vigor, soothing old wounds and studying up on the field of historic preservation. He immediately attended a two-week course for administrators in Virginia sponsored by the National Trust. He stopped to make amends with ex-Overseer Dr. Richard Howland, then at the Smithsonian Institution in Washington, DC. An excited President Kaufman returned to New Hampshire with a notebook crammed with new strategies. A quiet search for a professional director dragged on and on throughout 1970 and into the fall of 1971. The Special Report, which everyone knew recommended a change in administration from the top down, still had not been officially acknowledged. Captain Johnson had now been at the helm for ten years and, to the casual observer, it appeared that the "Old Guard" had won and the status quo reigned.

What goes around, comes around. It was fitting, in the end, that the "Founder's Last Stand" took place at the 1762 Chase House, the first restored building on the Strawbery Banke campus. Philanthropist Nellie McCarty, the first major donor to the preservation of Puddle Dock, had clear opinions on how the restored rooms should be furnished. Curator James Garvin had other ideas. Garvin based his interpretation on two detailed house inventories, one written in 1805 at the death of owner Stephen Chase, the second at the death of his widow Mary fifteen years later. These documents identified the contents of each room and provided a revealing new view of life among the wealthy in Portsmouth by 1820. Fewer carpets and curtains were used, for example, than in later years. The parlor was then used only for entertaining and held only a few straight-back chairs. Miss McCarty's tastes, however, leaned toward the more decorative, later Victorian era that followed. It was her money, and she wanted beautiful rooms. In 1965 McCarty had picked architect

OPPOSITE: *Lottie McLaughlin acted as hostess for the Chase House in the museum's opening years and lived in a top floor apartment there. Her son Robert McLaughlin was a Portsmouth bank president, Strawbery Banke administrator, and the author of the potboiler historical novel* Water Street. *Mrs. McLaughlin is seen here in the parlor with items that were later removed from the house, since they did not align with its early nineteenth-century interpretation. (SBM/DA)*

William Perry to select the furnishings for the house and assigned Vaughan and furniture storeowner Donald Margeson to monitor the task. Most of the work of selecting and purchasing the items fell to Robert E. McLaughlin, president of Piscataqua Savings Bank, who likely relied on a local antique dealer to select items that matched the restored era of the Chase House. McLaughlin also installed his mother in the third floor apartment of the house and she acted as hostess and interpreter.

"He [Mr. Perry] knows my feelings regarding this matter," McCarty wrote to Vaughan. "that the house should be well furnished in keeping with the period, but not overcrowded. You know how much I dislike overcrowded rooms!"[23]

The clash between colonial revival and professional museum cultures had been going on at nonprofit historic locations across the Atlantic seaboard for decades. It continues to this day. It struck Strawbery Banke like a bolt of lightning at the annual stockholders meeting on July 13, 1971. The meeting had gone smoothly. President Kaufmann, now sporting a funky pair of long sideburns, had been re-elected for another term without incident and was winding things up when he asked if there was any more business to consider. A man in the audience rose to speak. The man stated bluntly that he had just come from New York with Miss Nellie McCarty, who had recently toured the Chase House. The benefactor was extremely displeased with the way some items in her pet project had been "rearranged" or "hidden away" by curator Garvin. Then the spokesman dropped his bombshell. Miss McCarty, he said, had planned to bequeath an additional quarter million dollars to Strawbery Banke, but she was now withdrawing her bequest and all future support.

President Kaufman had seen the trouble brewing when the curator submitted his proposed changes to the Chase House for approval by the board of directors months earlier. Kaufman was aware that members of his own staff had alerted Miss McCarty in New York to what was going on in Portsmouth. When McCarty wrote to ask "how far the curator's powers went as to furnishings," Kaufman stood by the changes, then offered to travel to New York to explain the evolving professional policies. Instead, New York came to Portsmouth; Miss McCarty was in town.[24]

Editor Ray Brighton once more framed the public debate. Strawbery Banke was again at the "crossroads" he wrote in the *Portsmouth Herald*.[25] This was not simply about taking $250,000 "to let Miss McCarty hang drapes in the Chase House the way she wants them." This was about one generation handing over the reins of power to another. At the dawning of the Age of Aquarius, with the media awash in student protests, sex, drugs, and rock and roll, sixty-seven-year-old Dorothy Vaughan and her Originators were understandably reluctant to return the largest bequest ever offered to The Banke and simply step aside. For Vaughan, who had built her reputation as the unimpeachable source of historic research in Portsmouth with only a high school degree, and who was being slowly edged into retirement as city librarian, retreat was not an option. Brighton wrote:

> The power struggle centers around the issue of whether or not the colonial restoration project shall be operated in a professional manner, by professionals, or revert to the coziness and exclusivity of its early days that saw a tiny conclave in control . . . This is no time to temporize or compromise.

President Kaufman did not shrink from his convictions. Soon after the "bombshell" disclosure at the stockholders meeting, he addressed the Portsmouth Rotary Club, where Dorothy Vaughan, Richard Howland, Jeremy Waldron, and others had sown the seeds of the colonial village idea more than a decade earlier. Kaufman did not mention the Chase House incident in his speech, but the topic quickly arose from the audience.

"I'm glad to have at least one loaded question," Kaufman joked, then laid it all on the line. He favored a professional leadership. Benefactors were not curators. Everyone had a role to play. "I think it's time to stand up and be counted. Either Strawbery Banke is going to be known throughout the country or level off as a tourist amusement," Kaufmann declared.

When one Rotarian suggested that he might find a way to compromise with Miss McCarty in order to keep her as a benefactor, Kaufman shot back, "Do you compromise your intellectual honesty? I don't."

ABOVE: *Special guest Prince Charles of England visited The Banke in 1973, seen here with museum board chairman Arthur Brady, also a Portsmouth mayor. (SBM)*

Then Kaufman dropped a bombshell of his own by announcing plans to appoint the first professional museum director at Strawbery Banke within two weeks. A committee had been searching for eighteen months and after interviewing thirty candidates, they had found their man at last. The only question remaining was whether Kaufman had the moxie—and the proxies—to push his professional director past the "Old Guard" faction of the board and into the hearts of the stockholders.

"As in so many human endeavors," Brighton editorialized, "it apparently boils down to philosophic difference between the old and the new, with highly concerned and principled people on both sides."

President Kaufman was "a carpetbagger, pure and simple," Brighton noted, which is "the harshest indictment that can be made of a man" in Portsmouth, where anyone from out of town with new ideas was looked upon with suspicion. But truth be told, almost all of the Originators, right down to Vaughan herself, as well as Captain Johnson, were born elsewhere and had no genealogical ties to the city or the neighborhood they so energetically sought to preserve. To the Puddle Dockers who lost their homes to urban renewal, Strawbery Banke itself was often considered the carpetbagger—and yet few of those residents either could trace their Portsmouth lineage back more than a generation. The fact that benefactors Muriel Howells and Rosamond Thaxter actually were descended from old Portsmouth families carried little weight because they had the misfortune to live in Kittery.

So this was less a battle of new versus old than it was a turf war between "newer" and "newest." Like so many rural towns, Portsmouth has always had issues with strangers, or with what one local refers to as "the new-newcomers." When Captain Walter Neale arrived at Strawbery Banke in 1631, he immediately took over the 1623 settlement built by David Thomson. When Neale abandoned The Great House, the encroaching Puritans muscled their way in. When early "squatters" feared the loss of their lands in 1652 to the heirs of Captain Mason, they gathered at George Walton's tavern and rewrote the town history to suit their tastes. Human nature is immune to history. The last one in the door, according to local tradition, is not to be trusted. Residents no longer accuse newcomers of witchcraft, but an abiding fear that the next guy will ruin everything—and profit in the process—is still in play. Often the very opposite is true. History teaches that the city's largest donors to historic preservation are inevitably people from out of town, either summer visitors to the seacoast region, residents of nearby towns, or financially successful newcomers who discover Portsmouth later in life and willingly invest in its cultural resources.

In September, after being tabled for two years, the half-feared, much-anticipated Special Report finally saw the light of day. The report spelled out the qualifications and duties of a professional director, curator, and business administrator. Captain Johnson, in anticipation of the passage of the report, had already resigned his job.[26] Without pausing, President Kaufman nominated Edmund A. Lynch to be the first Director of Strawbery Banke, to begin work on November 1, 1971. The vote was unanimous.

Which Way Ought We to Go?

Ed Lynch brought a fresh perspective and a bucket of new ideas. After four years as curator at Mystic Seaport in Connecticut, Lynch saw Strawbery Banke, not as an urban renewal project, but as a maritime museum with an educational mission. Portsmouth, in a word, he said, was a "classroom." He quickly established an Educational Department under Peggy Armitage, his future successor, who immediately began a series of cultural programs in local schools. The new director reached out to the University of New Hampshire, drew in top-notch resident artisans, established the first annual budgets, beefed up accounting systems, hired a new curator of collections, expanded the exhibits, linked to the local theater troupe, and made inroads with neighbors in the South End waterfront. More than anything, Lynch knew, his job was to soothe what Brighton called the "soreness of spirit" that had developed between The Banke and the Portsmouth community. Exclusion was out. Inclusion was in.

A regime change among the board of directors helped Lynch push forward new policies. For the first time, none of the Originators were among the officers. The newest board president,

ABOVE: *B. Allen and Barbara B. Rowland were typical of the new wave of Strawbery Banke volunteers who became deeply involved soon after the "project" opened to the public. Successful in business, well educated, and attracted to the seacoast region, the Rowlands became active in many local nonprofit causes and remained active supporters of Strawbery Banke for over thirty years. Mr. Rowland was instrumental in the campaign to hire museum professionals. (SBM)*

Mrs. Warren "Libby" Delano was a former Overseer. Born in New York, Delano earned a degree in archaeology at Bryn Mawr College in 1937 and was fluent in art, historic preservation, and fundraising. Although she was, herself, one of the dreaded "Kittery Pointers," Delano and Lynch sang from the same hymnal.

The new goal at The Banke, Delano announced, "is to bridge the gap between different lifestyles, between rich and poor, native and newcomer, and to build a mutual understanding and appreciation for the past with which all groups can identify."[27]

Addressing his first stockholder's meeting at the opening of the 1972 summer season, Lynch quoted an apt passage from *Alice in Wonderland* in which Alice asked a grinning Cheshire Cat for directions: "Would you tell me please, which way I ought to go from here?" asked Alice.

"That depends a good deal on where you want to get to," said the Cat.

To go anywhere at all, Strawbery Banke needed money. The founders had known, instinctively, that the project could not be "bootstrapped" forever. Programs and professionals were costly, and they had done their best to forestall the inevitable, living off the proceeds from social functions and souvenirs, always hoping for an economic miracle. Now, with museum overhead rising and a recession raging, Lynch was on the verge of a fiscal meltdown. Corporate and private donors were drying up and, with gas prices at a new high, fewer tourists might take to the roads. To survive, Lynch told stockholders, it was time to clean up and rent some of the Puddle Dock buildings. Tenants would enliven the empty campus and generate working capital. Riding with the tide, slowly renovating more structures into museum-quality exhibits, was no longer feasible. Again, editor Brighton spoke out in favor of the New Guard:

> What Lynch did, with the precision of a highly skilled surgeon, was strip away the skin of self-delusion we have all allowed to pervade our thinking when it comes to Strawbery Banke, a coating of belief that from somewhere, somehow will come a fairy godmother to turn the Strawbery Banke pumpkin into a golden coach. It isn't going to happen.[28]

By the next annual meeting in 1973, stockholders had warmed to the concept of "adaptive rehabilitation" housing at The Banke, but Lynch had still tougher measures in mind. Richard Nixon was fending off the Watergate scandal and the economy had worsened. With an $18,000 deficit, Lynch was forced to plead for funds from the Overseers, the Guild, and a handful of staunch benefactors. Having dashed the myth of the fairy godmother, the director proceeded to sever the final cord at Strawbery Banke Inc. The original investors, he believed. had become a boat anchor. Major changes at the Internal Revenue Service enacted in 1969, Lynch said, threatened Strawbery Banke's tax exemption. Nonprofit agencies governed by "members" rather than "stockholders," according to new regulations, now enjoyed

BELOW: *A publicity photograph shows the new wave of professional craftspeople working from shops at Strawbery Banke. They include (back row, left to right) weaver Anita Rosencrantz, blacksmith Peter Happny, potter Jerry Beaumont, boatbuilder Douglas Martin (seated in chair) Windsor chair maker Michael Dunbar and leatherworker Rod Neumer. (SBM)*

a better tax advantage. For the good of the corporation, he proposed, the stockholders must vote themselves out of existence.

Dorothy Vaughan was highly displeased. The move that Lynch considered merely another step in a strategic plan to keep Strawbery Banke afloat, for Vaughan, was a "devious and very calculated" conspiracy. Lynch, with former board presidents Rowland, Kaufman, and others, she believed, wanted total ownership of The Banke.[29] "They want to buy up the project," Vaughan wrote in desperation to an ally. "The former president is feeding this tripe to the *Herald* and he is very much in the picture." There were even rumors, Vaughan suggested, that Portsmouth's new Historic District Commission, a city committee formed to promote preservation, had secret plans to gain control of all the historic house museums and rule them from a central body that would profit from the long-anticipated tourism boom. It was a scenario hauntingly similar to what Vaughan and the Originators themselves had been accused of when they took over Puddle Dock in 1958. Imagining enemies at every turn, Vaughan called Captain Johnson out of retirement to assist in a counterattack. In a last ditch effort to protect The Banke from the conspiratorial carpetbaggers, they contacted stockholders and collected their proxies for a final showdown at the 1973 annual meeting.

Roughly one hundred stockholders gathered at the South Meetinghouse on July 10, 1973. President Delano laid out the cold facts. Out of thirty thousand original corporate shares, only 5,026 were sold. They belonged to twelve hundred total stockholders. More than half of those stockholders owned a single share, making their investment in Strawbery Banke just $10 in more than a decade. Fully sixty-five percent of those stockholders were not even members of the museum and did not pay the $15 annual fee. The mailing and printing costs of communicating with these one-vote "investors" already outweighed their investment, Delano pointed out. Meanwhile, over one thousand loyal, dues-paying museum members had no vote at all. It was time, Delano said, to change the bylaws. It was time, the *Herald* echoed, to recycle all those stock certificates into wallpaper.

"It wasn't as bloody as it sounds," Ed Lynch recalls today. "It was all very polite and courteous."[30] The counter-revolution was over before it started. With one vote per $10 share, wealthier

stockholders easily overwhelmed the smaller grassroots investors, some of whom still believed that their stocks had a cash
trade-in value. Voting members, at one vote per membership,
replaced stockholders and the board of directors became a board
of trustees. Captain Johnson, loyal to the end, stood to protest
this "unnecessary" change in the bylaws. But he was not unhappy
with the goals of the new administration. Back in 1964, he too
had suggested that Strawbery Banke should become a classroom
for the study of maritime history—and now it was. Dorothy
Vaughan was elevated to the permanent but non-voting position of honorary chairman of the board of trustees. Soon after,
at age seventy, her contract as city librarian was not renewed
and she received another honorary position. Believing that she

ABOVE: *A gift of former Puddle Docker and
benefactor Harry Winebaum, the 1770-era
Joshua Wentworth House floats by barge from
north to south waterfront. It was the last of the
historic houses moved to the museum campus.*
(SBM)

ABOVE: *A commemorative coin from Portsmouth's 350th anniversary celebration decorated with the image of a strawberry.* (JDR)

had been "kicked out" of her two favorite institutions, Vaughan withdrew for a time from Portsmouth activities. But she reappeared as president of the Wentworth-Gardner and Tobias Lear House Association, just down the road from Strawbery Banke. For much of the next three decades she greeted visitors, often sitting in a folding metal chair at the door of the colonial mansion once owned by two of Portsmouth's wealthiest and most powerful aristocrats.

Strawbery Banke, meanwhile, enjoyed a burst of creative freedom. Curator Jim Garvin compiled a book of rare Portsmouth photographs, now part of the museum collection, then moved on to become curator at the New Hampshire Historical Society and later state architectural historian at the New Hampshire Division of Historic Resources. Ed Lynch was especially proud to launch the Lowell Boat Shop project that brought skilled wooden boat builders back to the Piscataqua. Dozens of hand-crafted wooden skiffs and "Strawbery Banke dories" were constructed for sale as visitors watched. Other top-notch artisans, including Windsor chair-maker Michael Dunbar, blacksmith Peter Happny, and cabinet-maker Thomas Moser, plied their trades as both businessmen and living history museum exhibits. Lynch collaborated with Theatre-by-the-Sea, a tiny grassroots stage built in the basement of a grain warehouse on Ceres Street. The troupe re-animated an eighteenth-century farce called "The Toothache" and presented free shows in the recently completed park across the street. Strawbery Banke's next president, Arthur Brady, owner of an auto dealership, nourished the theatre project. The tiny experimental Children's Art Festival of Strawbery Banke, evolved into the thriving summer Prescott Park Arts Festival that now entertains up to five thousand summer visitors nightly with concerts, dance, and musical theater from a sophisticated outdoor stage on the Piscataqua River.

The summer of 1973 marked the three hundred fiftieth anniversary of David Thomson's arrival at "Piscataway." Unable to match the expansive 1923 pageant, Portsmouth held a variety of parades and re-enactments, welcoming an odd list of dignitaries that included the Lord Mayor of Portsmouth, England, Smokey the Bear, Ronald McDonald, the Budweiser Clydesdales, and "Bonnie" Prince Charles of England. That summer also marked the arrival of the final historic house transported to Puddle Dock. Its original owner, Joshua Wentworth, was related to all three Wentworth governors, but unlike his Loyalist kin, Joshua sided with the patriot cause. Unable to move the enormous Joshua Wentworth house with its elaborate wood-paneled rooms through the narrow streets from the North End in one piece, engineers shipped it down the Piscataqua by barge. Throngs watched the amazing journey. The 1770 structure was a gift of Harry Winebaum, a city newspaper distributor and Strawbery Banke founder, who had used the building as an office. Winebaum waited nervously ashore as tugboats nudged the floating house dramatically under the upraised section of Memorial Bridge. The journey was especially poignant for Winebaum, who had begun his career in Portsmouth as a "newsie" while living in the Jewish community at Puddle Dock.

When Ed Lynch moved on to another post in 1974, director Peggy Armitage kept the emphasis on dramatic educational projects. Since many of the Wentworth-era merchants grew rich in the timber trade in the eighteenth century, someone suggested re-enacting the felling and delivery of a "mast tree" from the New Hampshire woods. It was indeed a learning experience. While early New Hampshire artisans felled entire forests, a modern team of specialists dedicated weeks to collecting a single tree. Historians reproduced two ancient axes and, after extensive scouting, found a stout straight pine in Rollinsford, not far from John Mason's only successful Indian trading post down river at Newichawannock. A film crew from New York arrived to help document the felling of the stately mast tree, but dangerous winds postponed the symbolic event to the next day. Then with five cameras rolling and photographers poised, the lumberjacks struck their final blows. The great tree hung impossibly still, then coaxed by a sudden breeze, fell exactly in the wrong direction. It landed with a thundering crash perilously close to a stunned observer. "Damn!" a voice rang out. "It missed!" Hauling the great mast tree onto its sled by oxen and eventually to Strawbery Banke brought on more trial and more error. Rediscovering Portsmouth's past was more exciting—and more difficult than anyone had imagined.

Last Rampage of Urban Renewal

The bulldozers of urban renewal did not stop with Puddle Dock. Even as Strawbery Banke struggled to define itself, historic Portsmouth sites were being ravaged largely to create parking space for a faded downtown. The post-World War II arguments for tearing down large blocks of old buildings remained the same into the mid-1970s—clean out the "blight," erect modern structures, increase industry and commerce, improve traffic flow, revive city centers, and move the poor and elderly into better housing. These modernization efforts now obliterated the Italian North End and almost took the rest of the old South End waterfront.

At first blush, Strawbery Banke seemed to solve Portsmouth's preservation problem by providing a sizeable spot dedicated entirely to saving colonial buildings. With The Banke accepting other buildings threatened by downtown urban renewal, like the Daniel Webster and Joshua Wentworth houses, plus nine additional independent house museums, an athenaeum, two Civil War memorial parks, ancient graveyards, and several historic churches, progressives asked—how much more history could Portsmouth afford to preserve?

The early success of The Banke helped Portsmouth see itself as a legitimate "player" in the heritage tourism business. Somewhat threatened by the new kid on the block, the nine separate house museums finally began promoting themselves cooperatively in 1966 under the Historic House Associates Committee of the Chamber of Commerce. Strawbery Banke was inevitably seen as "the wealthiest and largest" in a family of poor cousins.[31] Despite frequent discord and jealousy, the museums projected a united front by painting a bright red line on the downtown sidewalk connecting the historic house museums with Strawbery Banke. A new Portsmouth Historic District Commission also appeared in the late-1960s, after the opening of The Banke, bringing with it new zoning laws designed to promote preservation—laws Muriel Howells had lobbied for a decade earlier.

History museums were considered a popular lure for tourists, but Portsmouth's citizens had yet to fully embrace the notion that the future of the entire city was intimately tied to its historic

*As a project born from urban renewal,
Strawbery Banke was largely powerless to
respond to the destruction of "Little Italy"
in the North End. In this rarely seen image
from 1963, a tenement in Puddle Dock is
demolished. The same house is visible in
the photo on the left by Doug Armsden at
what is now the museum campus. Hundreds of buildings in the North End and
Vaughan Street later suffered the same fate.
(SBM/DA)*

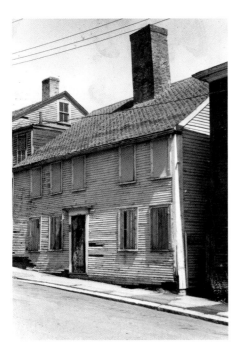

preservation. When urban renewal projects again savaged the equally historic Deer, Russell, and Vaughan streets in the North End, preservationists slowed, but could not stop, the federally funded incursion. A *Portsmouth Herald* reader pointed out that this area was arguably more important than the buildings salvaged in Puddle Dock. Portsmouth should stop saving mediocre buildings, he wrote, "while her aristocratic splendor is crushed in her face."[32]

Distant newspapers like the *Manchester Union Leader* and the *Worcester Sunday Telegram*[33] offered detailed articles on the historic architecture of the North End. Both papers lobbied for preservation. But even though citizens opposed to the project outnumbered proponents two to one, the story never caught fire in the *Portsmouth Herald*. Instrumental in promoting the preservation of buildings in Puddle Dock, the *Herald* now changed course. Even as the newspaper championed the cause of professional management at Strawbery Banke, it pushed for the blanket demolition and total modernization of the North End waterfront neighborhood. This turnaround, one historian points out, coincided with the relocation of the newspaper offices from Congress Street downtown to a three-acre parcel of freshly cleared land in the North End. Facing the extended Maplewood Avenue directly across from the ancient North Cemetery, the *Herald* positioned itself on the future city access road leading from the planned Interstate to the rerouted downtown access.[34] Again, as in Puddle Dock, the *Herald* was all but mute to the cries of poor residents forced out of their homes through the federal power of eminent domain. In his voluminous history of Portsmouth, published at the height of the project, editor Ray Brighton, a part-owner of the newspaper, was unapologetic. Referring to the "wonderful people" of Little Italy in a footnote, Brighton acknowledged without emotion that three hundred long-time residents were "involved" in the removal of the neighborhood. But their situation was overshadowed by "the great changes urban renewal has wrought in the North End," he concluded.[35]

While avoiding the human interest angle, the *Herald* promoted plans to build a glorious new industrial center to replace the shabby ethnic neighborhood. Front-page articles featured an artist's conception of a gleaming glass $2 million complex

ABOVE: *About 200 homes, including this very early colonial, were lost in the North End and Vaughan Street urban renewal. (RMC)*

proposed for the North End site. It included a hundred-room motor hotel, swimming pool, underground parking, offices and a two-story shopping mall. City councilors, hoping to locate new city offices in the complex, passed the urban renewal plan with only one dissenting vote. Mayor Eileen Foley, daughter of former mayor Mary Dondero, favored the project even as she noted proudly that her father had grown up in Little Italy.

Born out of urban renewal, Strawbery Banke was in no position to protest, especially against the combined forces of the city, the media, the business community, and the Portsmouth Urban Renewal Authority. The Banke's own Originators were split, with attorney Jeremy Waldron opposed to demolishing the North End, and former President Donald Margeson, whose store within the North End was miraculously spared, in favor. Portsmouth Housing Authority chief executive Walter J. Murphy vehemently insisted that all houses in the identified region were "substandard" and that "a program of total renewal" was the only sensible avenue. You preservationists have your end of town, "progressive" forces implied—now we will get ours. Once the heart of the British colony of New Hampshire, Puddle Dock was spared the full trauma of urban renewal, possibly because the public had come to perceive it as "distant" from downtown and its waterfront activity faded. The commercial New Hampshire State Pier was by now located in the North End just across from the doomed Little Italy. Positioned along the tracks of the old train station, the neighborhood was considered blighted, a weak source of tax revenue, closer to the commercial heart of the city and ripe for economic revival. Earlier redevelopment projects closer to the center of town had resulted in a small pedestrian "mall" and a two-story municipal parking garage that was later found to be of substandard quality, and had to be torn down and rebuilt. Now the city wanted to wield its demolition hammer in the North End.

Because the small city was already supporting some forty house museums, including Strawbery Banke, and other non-profit uses of historic buildings, preservationists had to try a unique tactic. Only a use that would keep houses in the North End on the tax roles, they knew, had any chance to win over a city starved for tax dollars. Robert Chase, then working at Strawbery

ABOVE: *Portsmouth Preservation Inc. set out to save up to a hundred pre-1830 North End houses by employing "adaptive rehabilitation" but succeeded in preserving only about a dozen on The Hill. (RMC)*

LET 250 YEARS OF HISTORY
SELL YOUR GOODS.

Banke, resigned his position to form Portsmouth Preservation Inc. Like Strawbery Banke, the new organization sold stock to quickly build capital to bid on old houses and land for preservation as the city acquired urban renewal parcels in the North End. But this time investors paid $500 per share, instead of $10, and the profit-making corporation planned to restore and return the buildings to private use, not to create more house museums. It was an idea ahead of its time. Federal tax law still greatly favored new construction over rehabilitation. But Portsmouth Preservation Inc. had friends in high places, including supporters in the newly expanded National Register of Historic Places, plus a strong local board of businessmen, lawyers, and new-comers. Girded for battle, the little corporation took on the Vaughan Street Urban Renewal "modernists" in the North End.

In 1969, Portsmouth Preservation, Inc. quickly raised $200,000 and aggressively lobbied to save the North End waterfront. But Portsmouth Housing Authority chief executive Walter Murphy, while acknowledging the concept of preservation, had no room for historic structures in his all-consuming vision of Portsmouth's future. Preservationists hoped to save up to one hundred structures. As the project dragged on, the number diminished. Eventually, in partnership with its architect and developer, Nelson Aldrich of Boston, Portsmouth Preservation Inc. was able to purchase and "moth-ball" just over a dozen buildings on "The Hill," adjacent to the Parade shopping mall. Most of the saved structures were moved from the North End demolition area, while a few were saved on their foundations. When the Boston developer failed, the cluster of historic buildings were sold to a local property manager at a loss and later adapted for use as office space. The recession at the close of the Nixon era was a tough time for adapting old buildings. It wasn't until the "Reagan Revolution" that the federal government came to favor preservation by for-profit companies and adapted tax laws accordingly.

And so the sledge hammer fell again. Close to four hundred buildings were torn down and all 221 families and seventy-eight individuals in the largely Italian neighborhood were relocated to new apartment houses, or they moved away. The promised space age complex, however, never materialized. Instead Portsmouth got a large vacant lot that stood empty, as preservationists had warned, for more than a decade until the arrival of the Portsmouth Sheraton hotel. Just across the street the Parade Mall, a stark, new twenty-five thousand square foot industrial building that included an A&P supermarket, quickly went bankrupt. The new brick *Portsmouth Herald* office "plant" sat alone on the edge of a weedy lot that had once been a lively neighborhood.[36]

Like the close-knit Puddle Dockers, residents of Little Italy remember only an idyllic time. Delfo Cominati, born in the North End in 1911, spoke to friends at a reunion gathering in 1986. "We were all very poor," he said, "but we had a great life." Mary Succi Ciotti shared stories of vendors delivering ice and live chickens to her tenement home, and learning to dance the jitterbug in the hot streets in summer. Despite the easy-going nostalgia, an undercurrent of sadness and anger still runs just beneath the surface for a neighborhood vaporized by federal and local decree.

"We were all happy people," resident 'Mundo' Zoffoli said. Then pausing, he added, "When urban renewal came through and took our houses, they put us all in debt, because they didn't pay us enough."[37] Today standing in The Hill, within the small enclave of Georgian and Federal homes just below a towering modern hotel complex, imaginative visitors can catch a glimpse of the lost Italian neighborhood.[38]

Back at Strawbery Banke, director Ed Lynch could only "sit by and watch helplessly," he says today, as the North End was broken up and carried away. But when the housing authority turned its sights on the rest of the South End waterfront, The Banke rose up in defense of its neighbors. Based on a 1971 study by a Connecticut company, the residential South End below Strawbery Banke was blighted beyond salvation and had to go. City planning director Robert A. Thoresen, who would soon have a major impact on redesigning downtown Portsmouth and sparking an economic renaissance, did not believe the report was accurate. He hired Strawbery Banke curator Jim Garvin and three interns to conduct a second South End survey during the summer of 1972. Garvin's field assessment of three hundred fifty structures came to a wholly different conclusion. By using more appropriate measurement standards, Garvin found less than

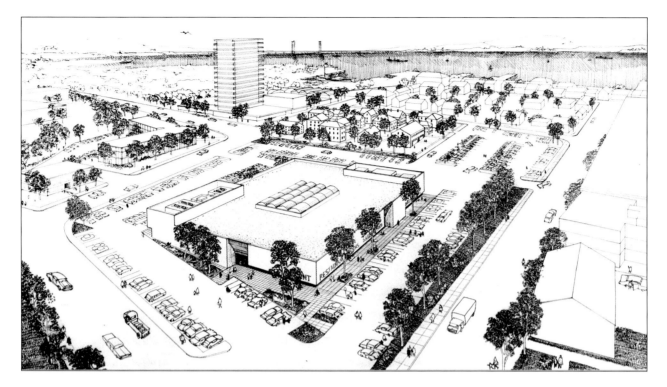

TOP: *The promised high-rise hotel in a modernized North End did not materialize after the destruction of "Little Italy." The Sheraton Harborside arrived a decade later and the planned office space remains a parking lot today. The Parade Mall (bottom of sketch) is being replaced, and the extensive preservation project (top) was limited to only about a dozen buildings. (RMC)*

RIGHT: *Adaptive re-use of restored historic houses from "Little Italy" are commercial offices on The Hill today (JDR)*

one percent of the structures were in poor shape. Plans to begin another urban renewal project there were abandoned. As a result, Jim Garvin recalls:

> South Enders were elated. They had seen and thwarted a threat directed at the essential character of their neighborhood. Perhaps for the first time, residents of the area perceived themselves as a unique part of the city, an area with an identity rooted in its architectural distinctiveness. Out of this perception came the founding of the South End Association, an organization focused on neighborhood preservation and improvement in 1972. Strawbery Banke was a partner both in awakening the self-awareness of the neighborhood and in shielding the area from harm.[39]

The Strawbery Banke "project" was growing up. Conceived as a Rotary study group, incubated as a mayoral committee, the little nonprofit agency was maturing into a professional museum. The city came to The Banke for guidance and the result in the South End, unlike the fearsome project at the other end of town, was cause for celebration. Today South End homes near Strawbery Banke are among the most valuable and sought after in the city. A revolutionary change had begun, but like all revolutions, what came next did not come easily.

Portsmouth Reborn 1975–1985

I f Strawbery Banke, Inc. began its days like a ship adrift in the swirling Piscataqua River, the arrival of professional managers helped tether that ship to the dock. But with water rising and falling eight feet or more at every Portsmouth tide, even a secured ship has its ups and downs. Through nine directors and two interim directors the museum has struggled to define itself and stay afloat.

But a funny thing happened on the way to the twenty-first century. Portsmouth changed too. Reacting, in part, to the early success of Strawbery Banke, the city began polishing its image in the 1970s with an eye toward preservation. In the same way it had welcomed back its errant sons and daughters in the nineteenth century, Portsmouth now concentrated on welcoming tourists. This time, however, instead of decorative arches, bunting, and flags, the changes were more concrete. The entire downtown got a facelift. Thanks largely to federal funding, real money went into real improvements to streets and sidewalks, trees and parking, signs, and buildings.

Two things quickly happened. The combination of a reviving downtown, historic sites, summer festivals, and funky waterfront arts and dining drew more tourists, but it also attracted a wave of young new Portsmouth residents who fueled the metamorphosis. In response, many long-time locals fought against the changing tide in an effort "to keep Portsmouth Portsmouth." But

ABOVE: *A limner paints a subject's face into a previously prepared portrait. The '70s and early '80s marked the peak of the crafts era at Strawbery Banke. (SBM)*

OPPOSITE: *Created in 1978 to celebrate the tourist-friendly redesign of the city center, Market Square Day in June continues to be a popular annual festival in Portsmouth. (RMP)*

what exactly did that mean? If Strawbery Banke preserved the oldest part of town, why did it represent, for some, the worst that modern gentrification had to offer?

Packaging the past with the present, a common Portsmouth sales tool, was finally beginning to succeed economically—or it was failing horribly, according to members of the Old Guard. Modern thinking planted into the re-animated body of the ancient city became, for some, a sort of Frankenstein's monster, laying waste to familiar working-class seaport traditions. Natives protested as cafes and boutiques blossomed and traffic snarled along the newly paved sidewalks, while back at Strawbery Banke, an increasingly mature museum struggled through its turbulent adolescent years.

The Crosstown Renaissance

Master Chef James Haller came to Portsmouth via Chicago and New York City. He recalls sitting in his car outside the Rockingham Hotel on a wintry evening in 1969. Snowcaps formed on the bronzed lions guarding the doors of Frank Jones's ancient hotel and on the curved wooden fence surrounding the John Paul Jones House next door. An out-of-work television writer and part-time waiter, Haller was smitten, like so many before him, by the city's tumbledown charm.

"I didn't know what I was going to do with my life, but I knew I was going to do it here," Haller recalls today.[1]

A friend suggested he open a restaurant in Portsmouth and Haller first proposed the idea to the director at Strawbery Banke. Captain Carl Johnson told Haller about plans to adapt Stoodley's Tavern into just such an eatery, using the wooden panelling salvaged from Sparhawk Mansion in Kittery Point. Unable to afford the lease, Haller scraped together $2,700 to outfit the basement of a battered warehouse across from the tugboats on Ceres Street. Opened in November 1970, the tiny Blue Strawbery restaurant, with its many-course formal sittings, quickly gained regional, national, then international recognition for creative cuisine and for Haller's bestselling cookbooks.

ABOVE: *The revival of the north waterfront as a dining, shopping, and theatre area combined with the evolution of Prescott Park and Strawbery Banke to inspire a downtown renaissance. (RMC)*

LEFT: *James Haller stands outside his newly opened Blue Strawbery restaurant one door down from Theatre-by-the-Sea across from the tugboats on Ceres Street. Haller briefly considered a location at Stoodley's Tavern in Strawbery Banke. (HAL)*

At first Haller's restaurant on the docks was an anomaly. Locals stayed away in droves. Only three percent of his early clientele were Portsmouth residents, Haller notes, and yet the Blue Strawbery was often fully booked. At first the nearest competitors were two topless bars, but the classy Dolphin Striker and Oar House restaurants soon followed. The site of the old Kittery ferry became, appropriately, the Old Ferry Landing restaurant. Salamandra Glass, a craft shop featuring live glass blowing, opened on the same block and other unique businesses quickly appeared.[2]

This microscopic theatre district grew up around the ninety-two-seat Theatre-by-the-Sea that had opened in 1965, the same year as Strawbery Banke. Four years later, actor Jon Kimball joined the troupe of starving artists there. Born in South Dakota, educated at the London Academy of Music and Drama, Kimball experienced the same revelation as Haller at roughly the same moment.

"When I drove into Portsmouth in 1969, I felt—I'm home," Kimball says. "Somehow I knew this was where I would live."[3]

After a stint in New York City, Kimball returned in 1974 to manage the new summer theatre program at Prescott Park

ABOVE: *The Strawbery Banke Chamber Orchestra defined the heritage project as a serious cultural entity. Founder Frank Dodge is at right. Plays and concerts sponsored by The Banke and performed at Prescott Park helped spark the annual summer arts festival that continues to this day. (SBM)*

on Marcy Street. Kimball combined local talent with New York equity actors. The cultural experiment, launched with funds bequeathed by the Prescott sisters, really pumped life into the waterfront park for the first time since it was enlarged and expanded in the 1950s. It not only provided Portsmouth with year-round professional stage productions, but magically linked the south and north ends, creating the first step in a waterfront "culture zone." The family-friendly summer programs also created a seamless blend with Strawbery Banke across the street. But it took a third "come-from-away" to connect the dots between the two evolving waterfront districts and the city's downtown.

Bob Thoresen was anything but a starving artist. In 1972, at age twenty-eight, he became Portsmouth's new city planner, just as urban development was taking its final bite out of the North End. Although not trained to focus on preservation, Thoresen quickly found himself working with Strawbery Banke curator Jim Garvin in the successful effort to stop further urban renewal destruction in the South End. He also worked with members of Portsmouth Preservation, Inc. as they struggled to save a few buildings in the demolition of Little Italy. "I got it right away," Thoresen recalls. "The way we were going to revitalize this town is not through demolition."[4]

Thoresen organized a study group to rethink the city center with an eye toward tourism. The first step was to redesign the storefronts of thirty-four downtown buildings. Based on early photographs, store and building owners were asked to return their old buildings to the way they had originally looked, at their own expense. Although the voluntary process was "like pulling teeth" at first, Thoresen admits, most businesses complied. The restoration, which usually meant stripping off modernized layers rather than recreating old storefronts, was exactly what Dorothy Vaughan and Muriel Howells had campaigned for in the 1950s that evolved into Strawbery Banke, Inc. The first phase coincided nicely with the city's three hundred fiftieth anniversary celebration in 1973.

Having recently toured Denmark, Thoresen was intrigued by the highly "walkable" city of Copenhagen. Early plans for Market Square proposed rerouting traffic entirely to create a pedestrian area stretching from Pleasant Street, around the old central

ABOVE: *The final expansion of Prescott Park with its gardens and outdoor stage was completed forty years after the dedication of the park by Josephine Prescott. This expansion coincided with the flowering of the "maritime neighborhood" interpretation of Strawbery Banke. (JDR)*

"Parade," and down two blocks to Fleet Street. But the volume of traffic was too great to make such drastic changes. Pedestrian-friendly improvements instead included wider brick sidewalks, granite curbs and crosswalks, rows of trees, a small fountain, park benches, clearer signs, and a host of subtler details.

Ironically, because Portsmouth had suffered through so many urban renewal projects, the city was now eligible for more federal funding. These entitlements provided "community improvement" money that allowed the city to bring in professional consultants and pay for much of the work. In early June of 1978, to celebrate their improved downtown, Portsmouth citizens held the first Market Square Day. The summer block party is now one of dozens of festivals and events that draw millions of visitors annually.

Those who joined the cultural upheaval in Portsmouth from the mid-1960s to the early 1980s still speak of it in glowing terms. Politically the seacoast region was becoming a liberal hub in a perennially Republican state. Dubbed "the San Francisco of the East" and "the Cambridge of the North," Portsmouth's revolutionary spirit seemed to gain momentum during the presidency of Richard Nixon, mellow under Jimmy Carter, and smolder through the days of Ronald Reagan and George Bush. Jon Kimball of the Prescott Park Arts Festival sums it up like this:

There was something about the town back in the 1970s that fostered these grassroots entrepreneurs. Young people were trying to make their mark. A group of people interested in ideas and the expression of ideas—through visual and performing arts or politics—they all converged on this little sleepy town and changed it. It didn't have anything to do with money. It had to do with fun.[5]

Preservation alone had not revived the economy or turned Portsmouth into a tourist Mecca as the Originators of Strawbery Banke had promised. Instead, historic buildings throughout the city created a romantic backdrop that attracted a new generation of players. For now the money-makers focused on the malls rather than the evolving downtown and waterfront areas. The 460,000 square foot Newington Mall on the outskirts of town already offered seventy-two stores when the Fox Run Mall opened next door in the early 1980s. With one hundred additional stores on 676,500 square feet, this shopping "Godzilla" was the largest mall in New Hampshire.[6] Outlet malls, superstores, twenty-four-hour gas pavilions and "miracle mile" fast food chain restaurants would follow. Dorothy Vaughan's nightmare vision of Portsmouth as Anywhere USA eventually came to pass.

Unlike many cities, however, Portsmouth did not entirely sell its downtown soul to progress. The sacrifice came largely along the sprawling outskirts of town. As early as 1983, noting that eighty percent of the license plates at the mall were from out-of-state, some downtown merchants were optimistic. Perhaps mall shopping was the final lure that might entice tourists in large numbers. Attracted by mega-malls, liquor stores, and New Hampshire's famous lack of a sales tax, tourists might also drive the last few miles to sample the cultural attractions of historic downtown Portsmouth. Nestled along the scenic Piscataqua, not far from sandy beaches, the city was finally on its way to becoming a full-blown destination point—and Strawbery Banke was at its very heart.

Self Discovery

Having escaped the protective grasp of its original incorporators, Strawbery Banke spent the 1970s and early 1980s, in the vernacular of the times, "getting its head together." As director for five years beginning in 1974, Peggy Armitage was more "mom" than "captain of the ship." Years earlier, as education director, she had watched Captain Johnson welcome busloads of arriving students. He stood high on a wooden milk crate in the parking lot, Armitage recalls, and sternly informed children of the rules to "minimize their impact" on the museum—no running, no loud noises, no touching things. Armitage, by contrast, asked the children to please jump up and down and shout. "Ready?" she would ask when their burst of energy had faded. "Now, let's go have some fun.[7]"

A warm patriotic and preservationist wave washed through the city as the 1976 American Bicentennial met the downtown renaissance project. In 1977, Armitage continued her predecessor's move to "tear down the fences," metaphorically at least. Strawbery Banke was "rejoining the living world" of Portsmouth. As a bonus, residents of the city could visit the museum free on special days. More historic buildings, she announced, would be adapted to private and business use, bringing much-needed revenue to the museum and putting three structures back on the city tax rolls.[8] Portsmouth residents still talk enthusiastically about the Puddle Dock Reunion that same year. Scores of former Puddle Dockers and friends gathered for an emotional tour of their neighborhood-turned-museum. Interviews and photos collected here and at a similar event in 1982 were then assembled into an exhibit honoring those who had lived in Puddle Dock before they were evicted by urban renewal. The healing process had begun.[9]

Mary Pietsch Harding, who orchestrated the 1977 reunion, says the atmosphere was festive. She heard no tales of former Puddle Dockers mistreated or traumatized by events, but says there was a deep sense of nostalgia for the loss of a proud community that no one outside the neighborhood seemed to respect. The worst impact, Harding says today, came years after urban

ABOVE: *Making a connection between the past and the present has been the one strongest and most consistent mission of Strawbery Banke since its creation. (MJB)*

OPPOSITE: *Peter Happny in the Dinsmore Blacksmith Shop. (SBM)*

ABOVE AND OPPOSITE: *Tamarind jar discovered during Puddle Dock dig. Archaeologist Martha Pinello helped Strawbery Banke distinguish itself during the 1980s and '90s for the number and quality of its archaeological programs. (SBM)*

renewal. Puddle Dockers grew increasingly embarrassed by the widening public view that they were somehow "substandard" people because they had lived in dilapidated buildings and done nothing to improve their own living conditions.

"There was a perception that they didn't take care of their houses, but they did, on the inside. They were not the junk piles; they simply lived next to a junk pile," Harding says. "Later they wondered—if their houses were so bad that they had to move out—then why weren't the buildings torn down too?"[10]

More educational exhibits telling more Portsmouth stories quickly followed. The 1695 Sherburne House kicked off a new exhibit showing how early timber frame structures were built. Then in a move that surprised no one, Portsmouth's very first historic house museum, the Thomas Bailey Aldrich Memorial, officially became part of Strawbery Banke.[11] The long-anticipated display of 1,267 early woodworking tools then opened in the restored 1810 Lowd House. The exhibit goes to the very soul of the question— "What makes Portsmouth Portsmouth?" It was the abundance of wood in colonial days that drew the ship builders, house builders, and furniture makers for whom the city is now famous. Early maritime builders or "housewrights" and interior wood "joiners" were skilled at creating wooden joints without nails. A timber frame building was so tightly constructed, local carpenters still boast, that it could be moved or even flipped intact on its side. Some of the Piscataqua joiners, employed to build sturdy watertight ships from New Hampshire trees, also built local homes. Early Piscataqua-made furniture is among the most prized and pricey in the nation. Some of the tools on display at the Lowd House had been used by local craftsmen to create the decorative elements in the city's finest eighteenth-century mansions. Peter Lowd, who owned the Puddle Dock house where the exhibit resides, was a successful cooper and carpenter in the early nineteenth century.

No longer distracted by moving houses across town, Strawbery Banke was finally beginning to discover itself. Despite the often-disapproving presence of founder and honorary board member Dorothy Vaughan, museum researchers were digging far beyond Brewster's flawed *Rambles*. The more they dug into old deeds, letters, and records, the more interesting the Puddle

Dock houses became. To create historically accurate gardens, the museum had to educate the ladies of the local garden clubs, who as museum benefactors, had considerable clout when it came to "beautifying" the campus, often in the same flowery way Lady Bird Johnson had beautified America's highways. Late nineteenth-century gardens, a horticulture scholar explained in 1977, were a "happy conglomeration of everything." Authentic period gardens did not look like modern gardens or match modern tastes in landscaping.[12] The difficulty, according to one staff member from the period, was to convince the ladies of the supportive garden clubs not to plant petunias all around the campus.

Digging into the earth also changed the way Strawbery Banke defined itself. For example, a ceramic tamarind jar from the West Indies, discovered in Puddle Dock, might have been owned by a freed or enslaved Black resident. Excavations into the refuse tossed into an old privy at the Rider-Wood House (1790) suggested that "poor" widow Mary Rider had not been as poor as many imagined. A lengthy study of artifacts from the site of Samuel Marshall's early eighteenth-century pottery shop on Horse Lane revealed a wealth of information. Turning up everything from custard cups to chamber pots, archaeologists were able to learn that Marshall worked with local clays and used highly toxic lead glazes when firing his pottery. Marshall died at age forty-four.[13]

Archaeology has been part of the Strawbery Banke experience from the museum's earliest days. In 1964, as workers bulldozed land, moved houses, and dug trenches for sewer and utility lines, amateur historians sifted the disturbed soil and collected shards of pottery, metal pots, and broken glass. Lawrence Straus, a fifteen-year-old Portsmouth boy, attracted headlines when he asked permission to organize his own "dig." Wearing a pith helmet and wading boots, and carrying a pickaxe and shovel, Straus searched for the outline of the ancient piers and docks along the tidal inlet.[14] (Dr. Lawrence Straus grew up to be a leading scholar in northern Paleolithic archaeology.) In the 1960s in New Hampshire, all archaeology was amateur, but modern techniques have advanced from using bulldozers and pickaxes to the use of digital measurements and soft bristle brushes; the lion's share of the data comes from carefully documenting the digging

process. As the discipline itself developed, Strawbery Banke kept pace and hired professionals, sometimes extending its expertise to projects in other parts of the city. In 1979, with over a hundred thousand artifacts collected, the museum opened a public exhibit and research laboratories at the museum's Archaeology Center in the restored Joshua Jones House.

Ceramics expert Louise Richardson points out that archaeological work completed by Strawbery Banke is on par with that at Williamsburg and has gained scholarly attention internationally. Because ceramics can be identified and dated with great accuracy, and because such items survive longer than metal, wood, or bone, excavations in Portsmouth have yielded a wealth of data that sometimes contradicts existing knowledge. By discovering what people in Portsmouth discarded, Richardson says, historians not only learn about Portsmouth, but they create a reference point for scholars everywhere.[15]

Active in the original Prescott Park Arts Festival and a co-founder of Market Square Day, director Peggy Armitage was also at the helm when Strawbery Banke first received accreditation from the American Association of Museums. Only two other New Hampshire institutions, the Currier Art Gallery in Manchester and Dartmouth College, had then achieved certification. Despite this new status, its addition to the National Registry of Historic Places and other professional credits, the Puddle Dock museum was still known to many as "the project."

Peggy Armitage's most lasting contribution is the one for which she is perhaps least known. In 1979, with restaurateur Dick Gallant, University of New Hampshire marine docents, and an eager group of seacoast craftspeople, she announced that Strawbery Banke would host the recreation of a seventy-foot, flat-bottomed gundalow, complete with retractable sail. These rugged "Mack trucks of the Piscataqua" could carry up to fifty tons of cargo and were common along the estuary here from the mid-1600s. Bricks, cotton, timber, farm animals—anything that went up or down these tidal rivers was likely to go by gundalow. The last gundalow successfully launched in this region was the *Fannie M.* in 1886. The grassroots Gundalow Project planned to build a floating museum that was unique to the Piscataqua region. And unlike all the other well-touted attempts to reconstruct the

Ranger, the *Raleigh*, and other wooden sailing ships—this one really happened.

As with the symbolic felling of the mast tree years earlier, the creation of the *Captain Edward H. Adams*, named for the region's last gundalow skipper, brought renewed respect for the workmen of the past. Built from four New Hampshire-grown logs, each forty feet long, the gundalow took twice the time to complete at twice the estimated cost. As tempers rose and funds dwindled, the $100,000 project, on the brink of completion, sat idle on the museum campus for an entire winter. Then, in fits and starts, a team of oxen hauled the ocean-going barge the last muddy quarter mile from one end of Strawbery Banke to the other, across Marcy Street, and through Prescott Park to the river.

For many residents, 5 P.M. on June 13, 1982, ranks among the most stirring moments in Portsmouth history. Ten gigantic oxen, one weighing thirty-eight hundred pounds, hauled the *Captain Adams* along on wooden rollers in the pelting rain. A full day passed as over three thousand onlookers urged the gundalow team ahead. Historian Richard Winslow captured the splashdown:

> "Gee up! Gee up! Gee up!" the drovers yelled frenziedly, cracking their whips on the backs and shoulders of the oxen. The beasts dug their hooves into the turf. They plodded forward. The cable pulled taut. The gundalow slid ahead on its log rollers. "Whoa! Whoa! Whoa!" the drovers yelled as the gundalow approached the edge of the logs. With tongs and peaveys the crew brought the rear logs to the front in preparation for another pull.[16]

This was truly maritime history come alive. Modern viewers saw first hand what was once a common sight along the Piscataqua—a ship taking to the sea. The crowd roared its approval when, after a last tug, the first gundalow launched in a century slid down the embankment toward the river. The crowd groaned in unison at the crunching sound of wood against wood as the heavy ship veered suddenly, crashed into the pier. and ripped out one of its sturdy pilings, then settled back peacefully in the waves. A quarter century later, the *Captain Edward H. Adams* still plies the waters, but instead of bricks and lumber, it carries stories of

ABOVE AND OPPOSITE: *This early Mickey Mouse doll was discovered in a bricked-up oven at the Winn House. Archaeological field schools for adults and children are a popular museum activity. (SBM)*

Strawbery Banke became a partner in the building of the gundalow Captain Edward H. Adams. *The flat-bottomed sailing ship is seen here under construction in a photo by Peter Randall and during its 1982 launch captured by photographer Ralph Morang.* (RMP / PER)

the sea and the region's fragile ecosystem to the towns of the tidal river basin. Strawbery Banke, meanwhile, was shifting with the wind. By the launch of the gundalow, director Peggy Armitage had moved on and, within the next four years, three more directors would follow.

The Identity Crisis

By 1980 Strawbery Banke was beginning to figure out what it was not. It was no longer the "parking lot of history" that its founders had planned, where endangered Portsmouth structures could be stored and re-animated. It was not a poor man's Colonial Williamsburg or a Sturbridge Village copycat. Continuing scholarly research into Puddle Dock itself was turning up fascinating data. National interest in ordinary working people of all ethnic groups was growing. History was no longer just about rich, remote, and heroic white figures. The key to the success of Strawbery Banke was hidden somewhere within the ten-acre campus itself, waiting only to be discovered. American colleges and universities, meanwhile, were graduating more and more "social history" majors interested in the lives of ordinary people. With fewer academic positions available, this army of underemployed scholars turned to outdoor history museums like Strawbery Banke. Interested in getting history right, warts and all, many in this new wave of historians were eager to explore the gritty realities of life. Some turned away from the freshly painted homes and clean streets of idealized reconstructions like Williamsburg.[17] Puddle Dock, with half its ramshackle buildings still largely untouched and the Portsmouth youth culture booming, was a grad student's dream.

Hired at first to revise the museum guidebook, James Vaughan and others found a host of inconsistencies. The Clark House (now the Wheelwright House), for example, was restored to one historic period, its gardens to another period, and it was named after a family from a third period.

"We've got a research gold mine here that's been virtually untapped," James Vaughan enthusiastically told the *Portsmouth Herald* in his first major press conference as the newest Strawbery Banke director in 1980. "The potential is almost unmatched." It

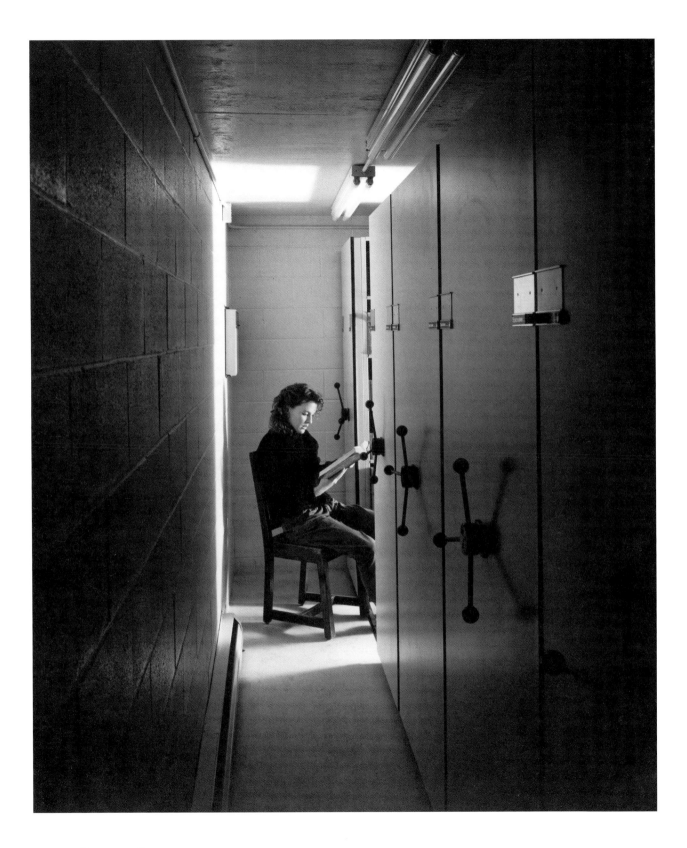

was time, Vaughan (no relation to Dorothy Vaughan) declared, for the museum to stop apologizing for what it had not accomplished and start taking credit for the great work completed to date. Besides, he noted, visitors had the advantage of seeing, not just restored buildings and exhibits, but work in progress. It was time, he said, for Strawbery Banke to move "from being on the defensive to going on the offensive."[18]

This marketing approach was not entirely new. In truth, as far back as 1958, Richard Howland had also referred to Portsmouth history as "a gold mine," both "metaphorically as well as realistically." (Even Captain John Mason was looking for gold mines in 1630.) And from the early 1960s, Captain Carl Johnson aggressively reminded visitors that they enjoyed the rare privilege of watching the colonial village being built. But this time the marketing campaign came with new clarity and a new strategy. Strawbery Banke now saw itself as an "urban neighborhood" and its goal was to tell the story of that community through time. Instead of sticking to a fixed time period like Sturbridge (originally 1790–1840, and later focused on 1836) or Plimoth Plantation (1627), Strawbery Banke decided to celebrate its entire three-hundred-fifty-year history.

"We were a little ahead of the curve," Jim Vaughan says today, comparing Portsmouth to other outdoor museums of the time. "We didn't start the multigenerational idea at Strawbery Banke. The Sherburne House exhibit had already stepped outside the original post-Revolutionary War-era plan. We were just trying to hang it all together, to find a way to rationalize what had already been done and move into a new direction that was more people oriented."[19]

Driving the point home, Vaughan rolled out a new museum logo featuring silhouettes of four museum buildings depicting three centuries of architectural design. The fifth image was a

OPPOSITE: *A movement toward scholarly study of Puddle Dock in the late 1970s and early 1980s redefined the Strawbery Banke interpretation. Here a woman reviews archived documents in the vault at the Thayer Cumings Library. (SBM)*

LEFT: *The updated Strawbery Banke logo appeared in the early '80s with the new marketing slogan "an historic waterfront neighborhood," signifying the demise of the original "colonial village" concept. (SBM)*

ABOVE: *Fashion meets history as museum visitors observe a spinning demonstration during the "Craft Era" in the 1970s. (SBM)*

RIGHT: *With a quarter century of experience as interpreter and craftsman, cooper Ron Raiselis continues to teach the art of barrel-making to Strawbery Banke visitors. (SBM)*

sailing ship looking vaguely like a gundalow. Below the images were the words "an historic waterfront neighborhood."

Museum consultant John Durel was among those graduate students and also education director in the '70s and early '80s when he helped craft the museum's new, non-defensive identity. He discovered that visitors to Strawbery Banke enjoyed themselves more when they could participate in the learning process. They volunteered for archaeology work, wanted to touch and use objects, liked to draw their own interpretation from open-ended exhibits, and liked to go behind the scenes whenever possible. Weaned at Disneyland, members of the "Me Generation," now grown and with kids of their own, demanded more interactivity for their money, Baby Boomers' kids were equally willing to be educated but less willing to be bored than their parents, preferring the "hands-on" approach popularized by newer science museums and children's "discovery centers." This idea of museum exhibits as "learning laboratories," rather than as static displays or as props used by guides or interpreters, began to seep into the design of a series of new Strawbery Banke exhibits that would open years later. But even at a museum now dedicated to showing "change through time," change did not come easily. Breaking from the tried and true house museum model—in which people pay money to look at old buildings and old objects and listen to interpreters dressed in period costumes—was easier said than done. Writing in 1986 about the concept of museum visitors as "active participants," Durel noted:

> The full potential of this approach has yet to be realized at Strawbery Banke . . . There is still sentiment within the museum for taking the more traditional living history approach, which tends to be less scholarly oriented (at least on the surface) and less demanding on visitors. At this point it is uncertain as to whether the museum-as-laboratory approach will grow or simply become another feature in a varied presentation.[20]

New programs, however, cost money, and Strawbery Banke was again running on empty. Youthful Jim Vaughan held high hopes that aggressively marketing a "single, cohesive philosophy" would increase attendance, and it did. A total of 65,600 visitors

showed up during 1981, and attendance figures held steady through the following economic recession that forced a decline at most historic sites. But, by opening two weeks earlier and closing two weeks later, the new season also tapped additional resources. The increase was less than Vaughan predicted, however, and only a tiny portion of the gate generated by more established outdoor history museums.

The new marketing plan was designed, in part, Vaughan told the *Herald*, to make the museum less reliant on outside contributors. This attempt at financial independence never materialized. The Banke remained beholden to its major benefactors who inevitably hailed, not from Portsmouth, but from New Castle, Rye, and Kittery Point and "The Yorks" in Maine. The deep undercurrent of distrust over money, class, and education that had always separated Portsmouth from its wealthy neighbors continued to simmer during the rise of what some have labeled the "Craft Era" or "Folkie Period" of Strawbery Banke in the 1970s and early 1980s. Muriel Howells, a founder of both the museum and the Guild, expressed her concern that the youthful staff of the museum might "run amok." Former board president Arthur Brady joked publicly about reducing the number of "LOLIS" (Little Old Ladies in Sneakers) on campus. Relations with the Guild of Strawbery Banke were sometimes strained. Guild earnings, Banke officials complained, largely went back into supporting Guild buildings, store advertising, and inventory. The new museum logo served, in part, to indicate that Strawbery Banke and the Guild were two separate organizations.

The bottom line, according to John Durel, who is today a museum consultant, is that the money comes from three sources—permanent endowments that yield annual interest income, museum attendance and programs, and constant fundraising. Healthy nonprofit organizations are successful at all three. Strawbery Banke was failing in every category. But while many grassroots nonprofits foundered or failed, he notes, this museum marched on, fueled in large part by "naiveté and passion."

"We were so excited about what we were doing," Durel says, "coming out of graduate school studying social history. We were going to tell the story of ordinary people. There was a real sense of excitement and breaking ground."[21]

"We didn't know it at the time," Jim Vaughan says today "but we were really at the peak of the nation's interest in its own history." An overabundance of historic sites, a generational shift in attitude, the way people travel—scholars continue to debate the elements that led to a drop in attendance at history museums across the country beginning around this time.

Meanwhile, there were more immediate changes to address. A woman's health organization located in an historic house at the corner of Court and Pleasant streets downtown was attracting front-page news. Owned by Strawbery Banke, the building had been exhibited briefly in 1960 and was now leased to the New Hampshire Feminist Health Center. "10 Abortions a Week Planned at Clinic" one headline shouted. Initial reports incorrectly announced that the clinic would be located "in Strawbery Banke," and letters of protest and support poured in. Anti-abortion picketers carrying graphic signs shouted at women entering the clinic in a pitched battle that lasted years.

"Strawbery Banke has come of age and stands on sturdy ground." That was the opposing view of museum president Mary Ann Esposito as another young professional, David Donath, replaced Vaughan as director in 1984. Donath's mission was to raise money and "bind up some very old wounds." He immediately launched a $2.5 million capital campaign. His fundraising efforts were aided, he recalls, by the fact that President Esposito was a gourmet Italian chef, best known today for her many cookbooks and long-running public television series *Ciao Italia*. Fund raising progressed deliciously, Donath says, when Esposito offered to cook something up for a meeting.[22]

Raised in Wisconsin, the son of a corporate executive, Donath was equally comfortable at cocktail party fundraisers and backyard barbecues. He was decidedly uncomfortable, however, when Muriel and William White Howells turned up one December afternoon to discuss renewing their financial commitment to the museum. Dressed as a nineteenth-century Father Christmas for the museum's annual Candlelight Stroll, Donath was wearing a plush green suit, boots, and a fake beard when the Howells arrived. "I had to look totally ridiculous," Donath says, but the long-time museum patrons were gracious and heartily amused. After touring the newest museum exhibits and improvements with the vintage Santa, the Kittery Pointers enthusiastically donated toward the capital campaign. It would not be their largest or their last contribution. David Donath, however, got an offer he could not refuse—to launch a new museum in Vermont with millionaire Lawrence Rockefeller. His sudden departure after little more than a year left the ship rudderless again.

BELOW: *Revolution within and without: Patriots battle the British at Strawbery Banke during the turbulent early 1980s in Portsmouth. (SBM)*

Karma Chameleon

The warm vibe of the '70s had long drifted out to sea by the time deputy director Vince Lombardi joined the museum team early in 1985. "It was pretty contentious when I got there," Lombardi says. But he was used to tough situations. As a park ranger in "Southie" on the Boston Freedom Trail, he had successfully quelled a racially explosive situation in Dorchester Heights, the same site where Henry Knox drove off the British under General Washington in the Revolution. Hired to assist David Donath, Lombardi quickly found himself in charge of the embattled Strawbery Banke, an odd job for a biology major from New Jersey.[23]

While the trustees searched for a new director, Lombardi threw himself into the upkeep of Puddle Dock's long-neglected buildings. The successful $2.5 million capital campaign initiated by Donath had been targeted to that purpose. Lombardi credits trustee Jameson French with bridging the gap between the disaffected benefactors and the newcomers now running the museum. French was in his twenties when he joined the board of directors and had been a child when his grandparents, members of the York "upper crust," had begun donating funds to the museum in the early 1960s. Growing up, French observed first-hand how philanthropy worked, and how the most generous benefactors were very often the most discreet; a sponsor bequeathing a million dollars or more might give the money anonymously. French's social connections and fundraising savvy, Lombardi says, helped get The Banke back on its feet financially more than once.

As during its tense transition to professional leadership in the early 1970s, the board was again on pins and needles. A rarely seen 1983 consulting report commissioned by the trustees identified the major problem, once again, as growing pains. All of the issues among staff, board, and administration, the report stressed, were not unique. It noted:

> [The problems] are common to almost every major museum effort . . . as they evolve from a small but important historical endeavor that was a vision of a dedicated few into a major national or regional institution requiring

inordinately larger financial services, a stronger and more qualified board leadership, a broadened and more diversified membership, and a highly professional staff.[24]

Despite the tumultuous times, the report implied, things were actually going quite well at Strawbery Banke. Membership had plateaued, but attendance was holding steady. Fully ninety percent of museum visitors came from outside New Hampshire, a statistic that mirrored the early customer base at Jim Haller's Blue Strawbery restaurant on the other side of town. The number and quality of museum exhibits were extraordinary, the report concluded, despite "grossly inadequate funding" and a severe lack of support staff. Then the consultants laid it on the line. The new residents of the Puddle Dock neighborhood, like so many evolving nonprofit companies, were one big dysfunctional family. Executive directors had to get tougher. Staff members had to stop bickering. There was too much talking and not enough communicating. There was, exactly as there had been in 1962, too many generals, not enough soldiers.

But the consultants reserved their strongest criticism for the board of trustees. With a solid professional staff in place, the "adolescent" Strawbery Banke was on the verge of maturing into a major museum. But many of the trustees, overly cautious and procrastinating, were in denial of the museum's potential, the report said. Some were dragging their feet, and others were trying to push the butterfly back into the cocoon—and possibly for good reason. A bigger, better museum was going to cost more money and the institution was already running on fumes through slow economic times. The result was panic at the board level, and the trustee's solution, as is so often the case in nonprofit agencies, was to find a new director who could make all the bad things go away. A more effective, long-term strategy, the consultants suggested, was to avoid panic, create clearer goals, improve communication, avoid assigning blame, pull together, stop micromanaging, raise more money, and train trustees to be more effective leaders. Easier said than done.

As in 1969, the crisis in the Strawbery Banke boardroom in the first half of the 1980s seemed to come from the chaotic world outside the fence. Controversy among Portsmouth fire, police,

ABOVE: *Two irascible figures from history meet beneath a tree at Strawbery Banke. A Mark Twain re-enactor at a Chautauqua presentation entertains as the real First Lady Barbara Bush looks on during Strawbery Banke's 25th anniversary celebration in 1983. (SBM)*

and city government, five years of anti-abortion pickets outside the woman's health center, the sale of the local hospital to a for-profit corporation—all stirred public debate. Attempts to create a new maritime museum in the North End stalled when the USS *Albacore* submarine literally got stuck in the mud as engineers tried to haul it to dry land. Angry protestors fought to save the historic Portsmouth Music Hall from condominium developers. Theatre-by-the-Sea president Arthur Brady, formerly of Strawbery Banke, announced tearfully that the troupe could no longer afford its summer park program. Even preservationists were angry with Strawbery Banke when the museum was unable to come to the aid of an historic structure that was threatened with demolition by a bank that also happened to be one of the museum's benefactors.[25]

This era also saw a burst of unexplained murders as shocking as the Water Street crime wave in 1912. Portsmouth police called 1982 "the year of the bodies." It began in 1981 when twenty-three-year-old Laura Kempton was found beaten to death in her downtown apartment. Six months later Valerie Blair, also twenty-three, was killed while walking her dog at Odiorne's Point. Michael Bouchard, twenty-five, Dennis Chase, forty-six, and Tammy Little, twenty, were all killed in their Portsmouth apartments over the next few months. Thefts, burglaries and robberies tripled from 1967 to 1981. Police blamed drugs.[26]

As always, Portsmouth blamed the "carpetbaggers." The more Portsmouth spiffed itself up, the more newcomers arrived to exploit and degrade the city, longtime residents pointed out. It was a simple case of cause and effect; the crime wave had to be connected to the influx of visitors, they said. National magazines and travel guides put Portsmouth on their "best small city" and "undiscovered treasure" lists. The tourists were bad enough, but more and more visitors were moving into the region permanently—Jim Haller, Bob Thoresen, Jon Kimball, and thousands more. Entire corporations like Congoleum, Liberty Mutual, Data General, Fisher Scientific, and Wheelabrator-Frye were transplanting their employees to the tiny seventeen-mile New Hampshire seacoast. Housing prices were up, and escalating property taxes threatened to force long-time residents out of their homes, and low-income families out of the city altogether. The

ABOVE: *Protestors rally against nuclear power in Seabrook, New Hampshire, in the 1980s. (JAN)*

new carpetbaggers came in a variety of forms—artistic, upwardly mobile, urban, entrepreneurial, childless, educated, gay, professional, ethnic, young, retired, liberal, and corporate. For those who believed their lifestyle was threatened by rising taxes, crime, crowded streets, and changing values, the newcomers arrived like locusts in a plague called "gentrification."

To find the culprit, one only had to pick up the latest national and regional publications where Portsmouth was suddenly chic and trendy. To explain this phenomenon, journalists checked newspaper clip files and rediscovered Dorothy Vaughan, now moving into her eighties, but as full of quotable quips as ever. Distilled through time, Vaughan's 1957 speech to the business leaders at the Portsmouth Rotary was now seen as the first shot fired in a revolution to preserve history that culminated in the creation of the waterfront museum. "They heard the cash registers ringing," Vaughan told *US News & World Report* in a 1981 interview. As a result, the magazine concluded, "the Strawbery

Banke project touched off a spirit of revolution that spread across much of Portsmouth."[27]

But many locals wanted "an evolution, not a revolution," according to the *Boston Globe*. The early 1980s in Portsmouth was too much, too fast. In a detailed study of the Portsmouth identity crisis in its color Sunday magazine, the *Globe* pitted Vaughan against her arch-rival Evelyn Marconi. Twenty years earlier, Marconi had lost her home to eminent domain in a federal urban renewal project sparked by Vaughan. Now it was payback time.

"The Revitalization of Portsmouth was a big flop," Marconi told the *Globe*. "Plastic City, USA. All revitalized downtowns look the same. They all have brick and granite."[28]

Strawbery Banke, according to the *Sunday Globe*, became a target of much of the "Old Guard" bitterness. Vaughan, still a proponent of keeping all things in Portsmouth old, but now disenfranchised from the museum she had founded, shared many of Marconi's fears and was able to straddle both sides of the fence. Preservation was good, she said, but not when it brought harmful changes to local residents. Calling historic districting "hysterical districting," Marconi, who served for years as a city councilor and assistant mayor, continued to remind anyone who would listen that urban renewal had "disemboweled Portsmouth." Referring to the Strawbery Banke occupation of Puddle Dock, she said, "They cut out the heart . . . It is missing the people, the ethnic groups."

But time heals all wounds—and, unfortunately, creates new ones. Although New Hampshire remains one of the least ethnically diverse states in America, Portsmouth today is increasingly diverse. People again leave their doors unlocked. Rising housing costs and taxes, however, continue to take their toll on elder and lower income residents, while others have profited handsomely. Over the next two decades, by any measure, the carpetbaggers won the battle. Portsmouth became a twenty-first-century city with a thriving high-tech base. But the dynamic tug-of-war between preservation and progress, between old and new, between rich and poor, is never far below the surface.

ABOVE: *A look over the fence toward the Daniel Webster House and the garden of the Goodwin Mansion where the wisteria are in bloom. (PET)*

LEFT: *A happy cyclist in the annual Fourth of July parade that winds through the streets of the Strawbery Banke campus. (MJB)*

Back to the Future
1985–2008

Communities have a history ... and for this reason we can speak of a real community as a "community of memory," one that does not forget its past. In order not to forget that past, a community is involved in telling its story ... And if the community is completely honest, it will remember stories not only of suffering received but of suffering inflicted... The communities of memory that tie us to the past also turn us to the future as communities of hope. They carry a context of meaning that can allow us to connect our aspirations for ourselves and those closest to us with the aspirations of a larger whole and see our own efforts as being, in part, contributions to a common good.
—From *Habits of the Heart*[1]

Williiam Shakespeare defined seven ages of man, from the infant "mewling and puking in the nurse's arms" to "mere oblivion." Nonprofit consultants often compare corporations to the human life cycle in five stages—infant, growing, prime-of-life, aging, and dying.[2] Based on that model, the second quarter century at Strawbery Banke Inc. marks the museum's passage from its "growing stage," where the searching adolescent gained a clearer sense of purpose and identity, into the early "prime stage" of maturity. Then again, there are those

OPPOSITE: *Portsmouth stays closely connected to its past through its many historic houses, sites, and institutions. During the annual Candle-light Stroll at Strawbery Banke, thousands of visitors join volunteers in celebrating holiday traditions centuries old. (RAF)*

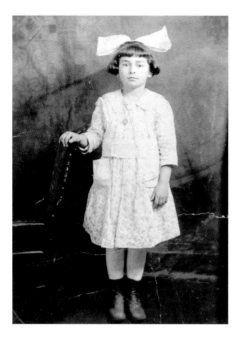

who define consultants themselves as people who ask to borrow your watch in order to tell you what time it is—and then keep the watch.

With ten years before the mast, Captain Carl Johnson still holds the record as longest running Strawbery Banke "director," although his title at the time was "executive vice president." Five leaders quickly followed him. Then, beginning in the mid-1980s, under the new title of "president," the smooth transition between Jane Nylander (1986-92) and Dennis O'Toole (1992-98) finally gave the museum time to shake off its youthful and experimental ways, and get down to business. Both were seasoned and well-respected museum professionals. Formerly director at the New Hampshire Historical Society, Nylander then worked fifteen years as a curator at Sturbridge Village, while O'Toole had served fourteen years as a museum educator at Colonial Williamsburg. The board of directors was "ecstatic," according to a witness, when each took on the job.

Trained as a curator, Jane Nylander instinctively turned her attention as president to the state of the museum structures and collections. "I was very unhappy with the way the place looked," she recalls. "I was trying to improve its appearance."[3] An authority on New England interiors and textiles, Nylander was a published author, and a member of the Colonial Dames and the American Antiquarian Society. The emphasis now shifted once again, this time from a recent focus on social history to an appreciation of the decorative arts, a move Nylander reinforced by officially renaming the organization Strawbery Banke Museum. Benefactor dollars from the recent capital campaign transformed building after building. Even those as-yet-unrestored were scraped and painted or stained. The campus began to look colorful, less abandoned, and more uniformly cared for. The extreme makeover culminated in a full-color supplement to the prestigious *Antiques Magazine* that showcased the museum gardens, houses, furniture, interiors, ceramics, metalwork, glassware, and paintings.[4]

"People sometimes forget that the founding purpose of a preservation project like Strawbery Banke is to keep its historic buildings in good repair," says architectural historian Richard Candee, author of *Building Portsmouth*, and a frequent consultant and former board member at the museum. "In trying to be all things to all people, outdoor museums can often tend only to buildings that are in the worst shape. They never get to the stage where they can keep the buildings, once restored, in good working order."[5]

The facts, Candee says, are the facts. Historic buildings are expensive to maintain. Costs only go up and they never end. The more buildings the museum owns, the more dollars are required just to keep pace. Regular cyclical maintenance programs are more cost efficient than crisis management. Evidence over decades now shows, Candee adds, that the comparatively small income from outdoor museum admissions, especially in recent years, is inadequate to cover all the sagging beams, leaky roofs, and peeling paint that Nature can deliver. Without a substantial endowment of millions of dollars, he says, Nature will eventually win out.

Ironically, the best advice about the fiscal risk of launching the Puddle Dock preservation project came from the project's most powerful opponent. Former New Hampshire governor Charles Dale had warned as early as 1958 that the "bargain" purchase of twenty-seven original buildings for roughly $28,000 was no bargain at all, since the total paid was far less than would be required to restore even a single house.

Restoration carpenter John Schnitzler, the boy who broke windows at Strawbery Banke in the 1960s when he was only eight, is today the museum's longest-surviving employee. As a teen fascinated by old houses, Schnitzler joined the project under director Peggy Armitage as part of a government employment-training program in 1977. Back then carpenter Norm Clark was the one-man maintenance team.

"And here I am today," Schnitzler laughs. "It's still just me and one half-time guy." Despite the ups and downs of three decades, his affection for the Puddle Dock project is undiminished. Everything he knows, Schnitzler says, he has learned here on the job, amassing knowledge of early American construction that he could never have learned in any formal school. Like Candee, Schnitzler sees the preservation of historic buildings as job one. "The buildings are really the reason we're here," he says gesturing around the campus. "It's what created all this. It's our backbone, it's our base. These are the nonrenewable resources."[6]

Restoration carpenters Norm Clark (top) and John Schnitzler at work. Their two careers combined span almost the entire life of Strawbery Banke during its first half-century. (SBM & JDR)

Meanwhile president Nylander's campaign to clean house was curtains for the Old Statehouse, at least at Strawbery Banke. Although it had a new roof, by the late 1980s the building was an eyesore, Nylander recalls, and an affront to the beautified campus. A homeless man was living under the building, drawing electricity from an extension cord plugged into a nearby craft shop. Jim Garvin, the original Strawbery Banke curator and now the state architectural historian, had by this time proven that the remaining one-third of the eighteenth-century statehouse was indeed the real McCoy. But having suffered the rebuke of its Overseers regarding the statehouse reconstruction twenty years earlier, museum planners opted out for good.

Although plans to build a Strawbery Banke "welcome center" were still under discussion, museum administrators could not reconcile the imagined Market Square statehouse with their new emphasis on authentic everyday life in Puddle Dock. A 1988 bill introduced by state senator Elaine Krasker of Portsmouth would have appropriated $1.75 million to restore the building. When that bill failed to pass, Strawbery Banke officials ordered that the shabby structure be labeled as "Property of the State of New Hampshire" and promptly removed from museum grounds. During the spring and summer of 1990, every surviving original piece of the Old Statehouse was marked and recorded on architectural drawings, and the structure was dismantled. The marked pieces were packed into a used, forty-foot trailer and towed to Concord, New Hampshire, to await future state plans for preservation and interpretation. Dorothy Vaughan's dream of a colonial village at Puddle Dock was fully and permanently off the table.

Some remember this "decorative arts" era at Strawbery Banke as less soulful, even sterile, when compared to the "hippie" seventies. A mature museum-like decorum and professional formality proved to many that the kids were no longer in charge of the candy shop. Critics point out that the museum's official newsletter, previously filled with action images of local craftspeople and costumed re-enactors, was now more likely to feature empty rooms and historic objects. Not a single human figure appears in the sixty-eight-page Strawbery Banke supplement to *Antiques Magazine* released in July 1992. The stark architectural photographs were reminiscent of those found in historic house

OPPOSITE: *Attention to regional decorative arts has always been at the core of the Strawbery Banke mission, but flowered in the 1980s under president Jane Nylander. A few items selected from thousands in the collection include (top to bottom) a portrait of Rev. Samuel Haven (1790–1780), a tin-glazed English earthenware punch bowl (1740–1750), a Portsmouth-made mahogany and maple side chair (1760–1790), a black basalt stoneware teapot (1820–1849), and a silver cann stamped with the crest of Tobias Lear (1770–1780), and a rope and earthenware storage jar (1725–1775). (SBM)*

guides from the early twentieth century. Like the aristocratic merchants of bygone days, Strawbery Banke now seemed to be living in a material world. And with memories of empty Puddle Dock and North End streets during urban renewal still fresh in the public mind, some suggested that the museum had lost the common touch.

For many others, however, the new improved Strawbery Banke was finally on target. A series of education symposia attracted a widening membership interested in historic renovation and the decorative arts. Nylander's tenure reassured the small but fiercely loyal philanthropic "base" that their millions of donated dollars were not being frittered away. People in the museum world, local corporations, and major granting agencies were increasingly impressed with the Puddle Dock transformation. The ladies of the Guild of Strawbery Banke were so impressed that in 1990 the independent nonprofit closed its shop and disbanded after donating a total of $600,000 to the museum over thirty years. Now that the museum had "achieved national, as well as international status, it seems unnecessary to continue the Guild," its final president announced. [7]

Despite blue-collar criticism, the mid-1980s and 1990s were actually a breakthrough era for the common man and woman at Strawbery Banke. Freed from the need to interpret a narrow band of history, an exciting new series of exhibits opened under Nylander and O'Toole that dramatized the lives of ordinary and diverse citizens on the Portsmouth waterfront. An exhibit honoring the "everyday life" of English immigrants John and Mary Rider opened in 1990. The Riders, who sold rum and molasses in their neighborhood shop, were able to help nine nieces and nephews make a new start in early nineteenth-century America. All the way across campus, the 1766 William Pitt Tavern finally opened its doors, following extensive renovation funded by the New Hampshire Grand Lodge of Free and Accepted Masons. John Stavers' famous tavern, once home to the "Flying Stagecoach" to Boston, had been a hub of both Tory and Revolutionary society in the Granite State. Stoodley's Tavern too, at long last, was renovated. The original idea of converting it to a restaurant was dropped and the tavern featured in the novel and

ABOVE: *Mrs. Goodwin trims the flowers outside the governor's mansion. (DSS)*

film *Northwest Passage* was adapted for public use as a learning center in 1996.

But the real revolution was taking place in three lesser-known structures. Tapping the scholarship that percolated up from earlier years, the Drisco and Shapiro houses, along with the Abbott Store exhibit, pushed the bounds of traditional museum thinking by setting restorations in the "recent past" of the twentieth century. Visitors entering the nondescript Drisco House today see a dramatic comparison of domestic life on the Portsmouth waterfront spanning two hundred fifty years. The duplex is restored on the right side to the year 1795 when the original owner John Shapley ran a small shop in the front room. A modest sitting room behind the shop had to accommodate wife Catherine Shapley, at least three teenaged daughters, and various boarders. The Shapley's sold their house to John Drisco five years later, but the second half of the exhibit leaps much further forward. The left entrance welcomes visitors into the cozy 1955-era living room and kitchen of its last occupants. Former Portsmouth librarian Sherm Pridham says the reconstruction, with its early black and white television set, linoleum floor, post World War II furniture, and "vintage" kitchen appliances, looks just as he remembers from childhood. Pridham's family members were the last tenants there prior to urban renewal. In the Drisco House, the daily worlds of the Shapleys and the Pridhams carry on, side-by-side under one roof, leaving what is changed and unchanged through centuries for the museum visitor to explore.

Although Bertha and Walter Abbott opened their store in one of the oldest buildings in Puddle Dock, it was their lives that museum planners found most compelling. Funded in part by a $200,000 grant from the National Endowment for the Humanities in Washington, DC, the "Little Corner Store" on Jefferson Street was impeccably restored to its World War II appearance and opened to an enthusiastic public in 1994. The "real flesh and blood" tales of the Abbotts and their neighbors greatly intrigued president Dennis O'Toole, who was a "social historian" and former director of education at Williamsburg. He immediately revived the concept of the museum as a "Historic Waterfront Neighborhood" popularized a decade before. He welcomed the foundering Gundalow Project to merge with Strawbery Banke,

ABOVE: *Mrs. Tucker entertains visiting children outside the Abbott store. (RMP)*

and reinstated the image of a sailing ship, erased for six years, back into the museum logo. While continuing to honor the material culture of the Piscataqua region, O'Toole appeared more attuned to the metaphysical than the physical. Keeping the "living heart" of Puddle Dock beating through narrative, he says today, is also an important form of historic preservation. On accepting the presidency, he said, "I'm looking forward to telling the story of a community of people and the changes, trials, triumphs, pain, work, celebrations, and feuds that they knew."[8] Putting "people" back into the museum's mission, he says, was his personal agenda—more role players, more staff, more visitors, more festive, and educational events.[9]

The history pendulum had crossed over. Not only were the common Puddle Dock residents now interesting and worthy of serious study, but they themselves were becoming working class heroes. It was while volunteering for the Abbott Store project that Valerie Cunningham wondered why no local African Americans had been included among the oral history interviews. No one knew. Cunningham was inspired to interview Portsmouth's "Black elders," and discovered seacoast African American families going back nine generations. O'Toole encouraged her and Strawbery Banke education director Mark Sammons to collect information for what became both the Portsmouth Black Heritage Trail and an influential book on Portsmouth's African American history. Enslaved and freed men and women, formerly the invisible residents of Portsmouth and now identified, have since become the central characters in local walking tours, television features, Web sites, even two novels, and a play.[10]

Interest in the neighborhood's Jewish heritage, likewise, turned the spotlight on Abraham Millhandler and Sarah Tapper. Both Ukrainian immigrants fled to America after the assassination of Russian Czar Nicholas II that resulted in a wave of deadly pogroms against Russian Jews. Abraham, who changed his last name to Shapiro, and his new wife Sarah were only two of twenty-three million immigrants who came to America between 1880 and 1920. But in Portsmouth, New Hampshire, fully half of the six hundred residents living in Puddle Dock early in the twentieth century were foreign-born. The Shapiro House exhibit, opened in 1997, tells their story as honestly and enthusiastically

ABOVE: *Mrs. Shapiro lights a menorah to celebrate Hanukkah. (RAF)*

OPPOSITE TOP: *Cooper Ron Raiselas inspects his work on a new barrel for a group of visitors to his cooperage. (RMP)*

OPPOSITE BOTTOM: *The opening of the Tyco Visitors Center in 2006 was the culmination of decades of planning. It was the first new building constructed on campus in four decades. (RMP)*

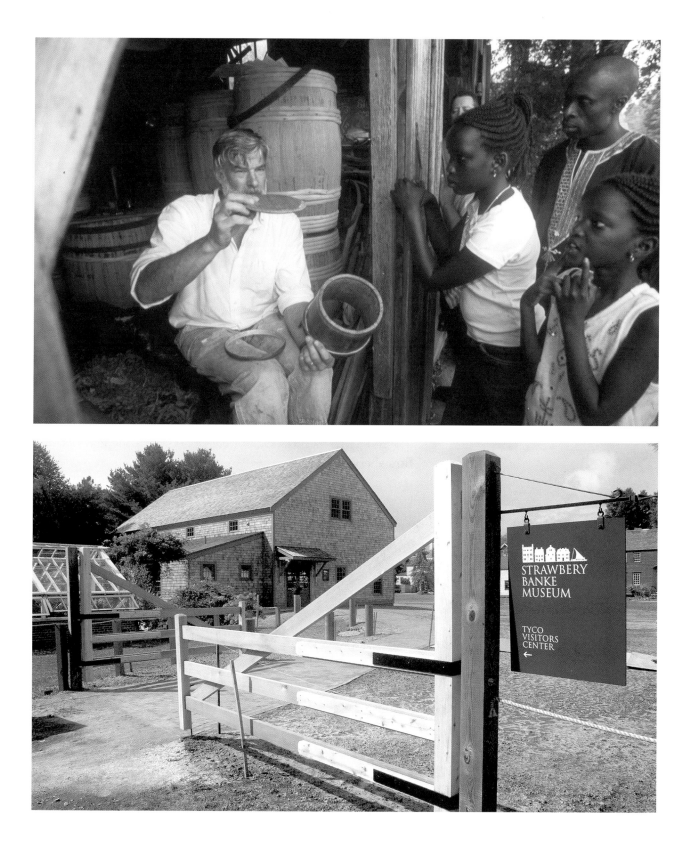

ABOVE: *The gundalow built at Strawbery Banke and launched at Prescott Park still visits Piscataqua sites as a traveling maritime museum. (GUN)*

as if they were George and Martha Washington. Their lives have been studied and their home as carefully reconstructed as that of wealthy Portsmouth merchant Stephen Chase and his wife Mary, or Governor Ichabod Goodwin and his wife Sarah. The museum now truly represents its neighborhood without regard to time, gender, race, religion, age or social status. Strawbery Banke, seen for its unique gardens, its historic buildings and artifacts, its diverse people, and its cultural programs, was truly becoming more than the sum of its parts.

For decades, in all weather, museum patrons had purchased their entrance tickets from a volunteer sitting inside a converted garden shed. It was time to trade up.[11] As the twenty-first century approached, Strawbery Banke developed plans to build a much-needed $2.1 million welcome center on Marcy Street across from the Liberty Pole and gardens at Prescott Park. Funded by local corporations and designed to look like an early waterfront warehouse, the structure would include an important orientation area, displays, a gift shop, rest areas, and function rooms. Sketches of the proposed building first appeared early in the 1990s, not long after the Old Statehouse had been removed. Work on an 8,100 square foot facility was about to begin in the spring of 1998, and the ceremonial groundbreaking had already taken place, when museum archaeologists raised a red flag. Remnants of an ancient timber wharf built on the old creek and now buried in the tidal muck were too precious to destroy, they said. Following considerable debate and public excitement over the first major archaeological discoveries at Puddle Dock since the 1970s, O'Toole agreed. The construction project ground to a halt, which is where it remained through two more museum leaders and into the next millenium.

If adversity really does build character, this was the ideal time for a transformation. The stalled visitor center and the demise of the twentieth century once again had museum board members asking the fundamental question—what is Strawbery Banke? It had begun, to be painfully honest, as a city-wide effort to rid the South End of five scrap metal yards and a few dilapidated homes at federal expense. It became, in the process, an attempt to revive a fading seaport by attracting tourists to a nostalgic village made up of preserved colonial buildings. With no central founding theme, it evolved and matured as one professional manager after another shaped the available resources to match his or her personal vision of the Puddle Dock campus. Each separate idea stuck, but had yet to fully fuse. Asking ten people what Strawbery Banke did best might bring ten separate replies. Keeping all its parts moving, was like watching an acrobat precariously spinning too many plates on sticks.

"Everyone came with the best intentions and everyone made a contribution," Kathleen Stiso Mullins says of her fellow administrators, curators, staff, and volunteer army. Mullins replaced O'Toole as president in 1999 and launched a major "visioning" study designed to re-invent the museum from the ground up. The fundamental struggle, and therefore the challenge, Mullins says today, is that, unlike other museums, Strawbery Banke was not born with its story already idealized and its message conceived. "It is so real," she says, "that nobody can quite get their arms around it."[12]

BELOW: *Members of the New Hampshire Wheelmen are guests on the campus of Strawbery Banke Museum during the annual Fourth of July celebration. (RMP)*

ABOVE: *Since the early days of Strawbery Banke, the winter Candlelight Stroll has been the most popular event on the historic Puddle Dock campus. (RMP)*

With the deficit still high and maintenance costs rising, trustees were concerned that attendance at outdoor history museums across the nation had begun to flag. The rise of the Internet, the increased number of hyperactive family theme parks, giant family "home entertainment" TV theaters, and the busy lifestyles of a whole new hi-tech generation were taking a toll on traditional historic destinations. "Downsizing" the campus, some suggested, was the only solution. Museum presidents, it was clear, needed to be both informed about history and adept at business management.

Then the terrorist attacks of September 11, 2001, sent shockwaves through the nation. Americans saw America differently. The effects of a long-running foreign war, a new awareness of global issues, shifting definitions of patriotism, the fearsome culture of terrorism changed the country. Air travel would never be the same. Everything was being redefined, even the way people plan, visit, and support historic places. The result, today, is a nation in search of its identity. That is a search Strawbery Banke knows well—from abandoned British plantation, to a thriving seaport, a combat zone, a low-income ethnic community, a preservation project, and a history museum. It may turn out that New Hampshire's oldest neighborhood, by successfully adapting itself time and again, has something important to teach the world. If history tells us how people change, or don't change through time, then the ten-acre museum at Puddle Dock is the perfect observation point.

"Being perpetually on the edge of change can be exhausting for an institution," says New Hampshire state senator Martha Fuller Clark. "Out of crisis comes strength, but out of constant crisis comes a nervous breakdown." A second-generation supporter and leader of Strawbery Banke, Clark began as a volunteer in the late 1960s when her family was among the original benefactors. Having seen the museum's full fifty-year story play out, Clark is convinced that doing things the hard way builds character, and that every knock and bruise came with a lesson learned. By exploring each new trend in the evolving history museum field, she says, Strawbery Banke was able to discover its own path and, through that journey, gained incredible self-reliance. The museum's ability to be flexible and "turn on a dime," she says, is among its greatest assets. Its next half century, she believes, is going to be even more exciting.[13]

"Try to imagine the last fifty years in Portsmouth without a Strawbery Banke," says former director Jim Vaughan. Vaughan is currently a vice-president at the National Trust for Historic Preservation in Washington, DC, the organization from which Richard Howland made his all-important visit to Portsmouth in 1957. "Strawbery Banke has had a unifying effect on this city."

"Strawbery Banke is one of those places people in the museum field can't stop talking about," says former director David Donath. "It's fascinating. It's a case study in all the things that bedevil the field. It's a rich, concentrated microcosm, and that makes it even richer and saltier. You can't help loving it. I was charmed by the place."[14]

"I have an even more sanguine perception," Charles Bickford says. As acting-president in 2004, he took the tiller just prior to president Lawrence Yerdon, who arrived the following year. A medievalist by education, Bickford knew Strawbery Banke for its "stellar reputation." As the former director of the New

Hampshire Humanities Council, Bickford knew the museum as a widely respected repository for history, for great ideas, and for great educational programs. Watching the museum campus come alive with thousands of visitors during a summer Fourth of July muster, a fall Halloween bonfire or a winter Candlelight Stroll, he says, no one can question what this museum means or why its role is so vital today.

"This place is wonderful," Bickford says. "My only question is how are we going to keep this great show on the road?" In his first days on the job, Bickford recalls, his picture appeared in the newspaper. Walking home that afternoon, he says, someone stopped him on the street, not with congratulations, but to recount a lengthy, animated tale about urban renewal forty years earlier. Bickford listened. "Sometimes people just need to be heard," he says.[15]

Portsmouth has a long memory. It remains proud of its great moments and embarrassed by its failures, long after all those who were great or who failed have gone to dust. It is a city that sometimes forgets to forgive those who trespass against it. Portsmouth

BELOW: *To study and conserve its collections, Strawbery Banke opened the new Carter Center in the summer of 2007 just prior to its 50th anniversary celebration.* *(SBM)*

is a city, many have said, just small enough to be charming and just big enough to be dangerous. Its founder, Captain John Mason, has no monument in Portsmouth, his Great House has no marker. The city's most beloved native-born leader, Governor John Wentworth, was driven out of town by an angry mob. These stories are told and told again in large part because telling stories is what Portsmouth does so well. Tourism is now New Hampshire's largest industry. And it is easy to talk about the past in the state's only seaport where so much of New Hampshire history took place and where so many ancient buildings still stand. Old Portsmouth and New Portsmouth are twin dimensions vibrating in the same space, but at different times. Visitors step from one dimension to the next and back without even knowing.

But change happens. Despite its old appearance, Portsmouth is changing rapidly. In the 1980s, some local citizens protested the building of a downtown hotel in the cleared North End, fearing it would destroy the character of the city center—a city, by the way, that had previously included a dozen downtown hotels and taverns. Today, in contrast, many see Portsmouth's future tied to a number of new hotels and conference centers delivering thousands of visitors to shops, restaurants, and cultural sites. In the 1990s, the closing of Pease Air Force Base, some said, spelled doom. Thousands of military and civilian jobs were lost, and Portsmouth's population dropped sharply for the first time since the end of the West India Trade in the nineteenth century. The Air Force left behind toxic dumpsites, and early attempts to convert the area to a private airport and industrial park did not go smoothly. Today the flourishing Pease International Tradeport is considered a major American success story. Recently, after a rancorous twenty-year public debate, Portsmouth decided to sacrifice one small turn-of-the-century brick armory in order to gain a dynamic new state-of-the-art library.

Change happens. The Blue Strawbery is gone, but the iconic spire of the Old North Church is back after a $2 million restoration. The "immutable" Old Man of the Mountain tumbled down a Granite State hillside and disappeared in 2003, but the historic Wentworth by the Sea hotel reappeared the same year after two decades in ruins, and the Portsmouth Music Hall has been lovingly restored to its late-nineteenth-century glory. The

Created by so many, Strawbery Banke depends on the continued support of thousands of benefactors, members, volunteers and staff. The combined and very different voices of Dorothy Vaughan, Muriel Howells, and Richard Howland created the perfect harmony in 1958. It can still be heard today. The Vaughan portrait (above left) is by Rich Beauchesne. (HOW and SBM)

once-forgotten African Burying Ground, rediscovered below the city streets in 2003, will again become a hallowed grave site, the traffic rerouted, and a memorial installed. The art of preservation, Portsmouth has learned is not about saving everything. Preservation is about knowing when to hold on and when to let go. Preservation is about sailing the ship, not stopping the tide.

In September 2005, Strawbery Banke opened the Tyco Visitor Center, the first new building on campus in forty years. At one half the size and one third the cost of the original plan, the new facility is situated far from the ancient wharf archaeology site, and not far from where museum Originators had planned their gateway to a colonial village. Compromise, says president Larry Yerdon, is essential to managing change. "You've got to have a mixed bag today. We want to combine different types of exhibits—some narrated, some self-guided or using the latest technology, some with role players, some experiential. Our motto is—we preserve so that we can educate."

Born in upstate New York, educated in New England, Yerdon holds advanced degrees in both history and business administration. He came to Portsmouth after eighteen years at Hancock Shaker Village. His first task on arrival, he says, was to balance the budget and eliminate the nagging deficit. He believes in building a team of professionals who know where they are headed and why. Yerdon measures success partly in terms of "visitor experience." People come to historic museums these days for "delight, discovery, and learning," he says. And he is not afraid to speak the other dreaded D-word. "Anybody who does what I do and hasn't been to Disneyland, doesn't know the competition," Yerdon says. That does not mean animated Puddle Dockers or Piscataqua water slides, he adds, but it does mean thinking about Strawbery Banke as a place modern visitors want to see, and in the process, smoothing out the fiscal roller coaster ride that museum administrators have been on for so long.[16]

Change happens. Yerdon is the first manager in the museum's history who did not know Dorothy Vaughan. "The Originator" died in 2004 just shy of her one hundredth birthday. But he encounters her spirit everywhere. In 2006, at the opening of the visitor center, Yerdon dedicated a plaque in memory of the late Muriel Howells. Her husband of seventy-three years attended, then passed away three months later at age ninety-seven. Richard Hubbard Howland, the third strong voice in the call to arms that preserved Puddle Dock, died the following year at age ninety-six.

The torch has passed, but fifty years after its imagining, Strawbery Banke runs on. Each summer, in a new Portsmouth tradition, proud immigrants gather here, raise their right hands, and officially become citizens of the United States of America. Each fall as the leaves sweep down Jefferson Street and up Horse Lane, strangely costumed children encounter long-lost Portsmouth characters wandering familiar paths. Each winter the neighborhood disappears, but only momentarily, in the blinding grip of a New England storm. But weather changes. And when the outdoor candles are lit along the paths, and the scent of wood smoke and mulled cider drift by, and the carolers hit their harmony just right—no one wonders why Portsmouth clings so earnestly to the past or why the buildings of Strawbery Banke still stand. We preserve the past because we need it. It is here—in these hallowed places where the winds of change grow calm—that we chart the wisest future for our nation and ourselves.

OPPOSITE: *Watercolor of houses at Strawbery Banke by Wikie Rowland. (SBM)*

ABOVE: *Four costumed junior role players march forward into Portsmouth's past at a Strawbery Banke Museum Fourth of July festival. (RMP)*

Photo Credit Abbreviations

ARM   Douglas Armsden

BAK   Prof. Emerson Baker

BCP   Back Channel Press, John and Nancy Grossman

CER   Jim Cerny

COL   The National Society of the Colonial Dames in the State of NH, Moffatt Ladd House

DSS   Deiter Stark-Strong

DUN   John Dunkle

GUN   The Gundalow Company

HAL   James Haller

HOW   Gurdon Howells Metz and William Dean Howells

HUB   Jonathan Hubbard, Rosamond Thaxter Papers

JAN   Jan Harney

JDR   J. Dennis Robinson

KEC   Kimberly E. Crisp

MAR   Evelyn Marconi and family

MEB   Maryellen Burke

MJB   Mary Johanna Brown

NHDHR   NH Division of Historical Resources

NHHS   NH Historical Society

PAAR   William Tenny Paarlberg

PEC   Robert Pecunies and all those attending the 1982 Puddle Dock Reunion at Strawbery Banke

PET   Fred Pettigrew

PHS   Portsmouth Historical Society

PIR   Wendy Pirsig

PNS   Portsmouth Naval Shipyard

PPL   Portsmouth Public Library

RAF   Rafi Landau

RMC   Richard M. Candee

RMP   Ralph Morang Photography

SBM   Strawbery Banke Museum Collections

SBM/DA   Douglas Armsden Collection at Strawbery Banke Museum

WAR   The Warner House Museum

WGTL   Wentworth Gardner & Tobias Lear House Assoc.

WOOD   The Woodman Institute, Dover, NH

Selected Bibliography

Adams, Nathaniel. *Annals of Portsmouth* (1825). Hampton, NH: Peter E. Randall Publisher, reprinted 1971.

Aldrich, Mrs. Thomas Bailey. *Crowding Memories.* Boston: Houghton Mifflin Company, 1920.

Aldrich, Thomas Bailey. *The Old Town by the Sea.* Boston: Houghton Mifflin Company, 1917.

_____. *The Story of a Bad Boy.* Boston: Houghton Mifflin Company, 1922.

Baker, Emerson. *The Devil of Great Island*: *Witchcraft & Conflict in Early New England.* New York: Palgrave Macmillan, 2007.

_____. "Finding the Almouchiquois: Native American Families, Territories and Land Sales in Southern Maine." *Ethnohistory* 51, no. 1 (Winter 2004).

Belknap, Jeremy. *The History of New Hampshire. Boston:* Belknap and Young, 1892.

Bolster, Jeffrey W. (editor) *Cross-Grained & Wiley Waters: A Guide to the Piscataqua Maritime Region.* Portsmouth, NH: Peter E. Randall Publisher LLC, 2002.

Bouton, Nathaniel. *Provincial Papers: Documents and Records Relating to the Province of New-Hampshire 1623-1680.* Concord, NH: George E. Jenks, 1867.

Brewster, Charles W. *Rambles About Portsmouth.* 2, vols., originally 1859 and 1869. Somersworth, NH: New Hampshire Publishing Company, 1972.

Brewster, Edith Gilman. *Some Three Hundred Years Ago.* Concord, NH: W.B. Ranney Company, 1922.

Brighton, Raymond A. *The Prescott Story.* New Castle, NH: The Portsmouth Marine Society, 1982.

_____. *They Came to Fish.* Portsmouth, NH: Peter E. Randall, Publisher, 1994.

Buell, Augustus C. *Paul Jones, Father of the American Navy.* Vol. 1. New York: Charles Scribner's Sons, 1901.

Caduto, Michael J. *A Time Before New Hampshire: The Story of a Land and Native Peoples.* Hanover, NH: University Press of New England, 2003.

Caldwell, Bill. *Islands of Maine: Where America Really Began.* Camden, ME: Downeast Books, 1981.

Calloway, Colin G., ed. *Dawnland Encounters: Indians and Europeans in Northern New England.* Hanover, NH: University Press of New England, 1991.

Candee, Richard. *Building Portsmouth: The Neighborhoods and Architecture of New Hampshire's Oldest City* (Revised). Portsmouth, NH: Back Channel Press, 2006. (First edition published Portsmouth, NH: Portsmouth Advocates, 1992.)

_____. "The 1823 'Centennial' Celebration of New Hampshire's Settlement." *The Dublin Seminar for New England Folklife* (Boston University 2000):47-61.

_____. "Millwright and Merchant: Water-powered Saw-milling in Seventeenth-century Maine and New Hampshire." *Old-Time New England* 60, no. 4 (Spring, 1970):131-149.

_____. " 'Old Portsmouth . . . Home of the Stocking Business': A Forgotten Nineteenth-century Industry and its Inventors." *Historical New Hampshire* 57, no. 3 & 4 (Fall/Winter 2002):85-107.

_____. *Wallace Nutting's Portsmouth: Photographs of the "Colonial" Past 1908–1918.* Portsmouth, NH: Back Channel Press, 2007.

_____. "Social Conflict and Urban Rebuilding: The Portsmouth, New Hampshire Brick Act of 1814." *Winterthur Portfolio* 32, no. 2 & 3 (Summer/Autumn 1997):119-146.

_____. *Wooden Buildings in Early Maine and New Hampshire: A Technical and Cultural History 1600-1720.* University of Pennsylvania, dissertation, 1976.

Charlton, Edwin A. *New Hampshire As It Is.* Claremont, NH: Tracy and Sanford, 1855. (Reprinted Westminster, MD: Heritage Books Inc., 1997):4.

Clark, Charles E. *The Eastern Frontier: The Settlement of Northern New England 1610-1763.* New York: Alfred A. Knopf, 1970.

Crisp, Kimberly E. "Water Street Remembered." University of New Hampshire, honors thesis, May 15, 1996.

Cumings, Thayer. *Strawbery Banke: The First 25 Years.* Unpublished manuscript. Strawbery Banke Museum Archives.

Drake, Samuel Adams. *A Book of New England Legends and Folklore.* Roberts Brothers,1884. Reprinted Vermont: Charles E. Tuttle Company, 1971.

Drown, Daniel Augustus. *Idyls of Strawberry Bank.* Portsmouth, NH: privately printed, 1873.

Dupre, Mary Bentley. "The History of Archeology at Strawbery Banke Museum." *The New Hampshire Archeologist* 35, no. 1 (1995):12-28.

Durel, John W. *From Strawbery Banke to Puddle Dock: The Evolution of a Neighborhood.* University of New Hampshire, dissertation, May 1986.

_____. " 'Historic' Portsmouth: The Role of the Past in the Formation of a Community's Identity." *Historical New Hampshire* 31, nos. 3 &4 (Fall/Winter 1986):97-117.

_____. "The Past: A Thing to Study, a Place to Go," in *Public History: An Introduction*, Barbara J. Howe and Emery L. Kemp, eds. Malabar, FL: West Virginia University, Robert E. Krieger Publishing Company, 1986: 229-240.

Fields, Mrs. James T. *James T. Fields.* Boston: Houghton, Mifflin and Company, 1881.

Foster, Sarah Haven. *The Portsmouth Guide Book.* Portsmouth, NH: Joseph H. Foster, 1884.

Garvin, James L. and Susan Grigg. *Historic Portsmouth: Early Photographs from the Collections of Strawbery Banke.* Portsmouth, NH: Strawbery Banke, Inc., 2006.

Garvin, James L. "Blanchard's Balloon: First Flight in New Hampshire." *New Hampshire Profiles* (June 1976): 66-68.

_____,ed. "Preservation History of New Hampshire." *New Hampshire's State Historic Preservation Plan.* Concord, NH: New Hampshire Division of Historical Resources (July 2006).

_____. "Strawbery Banke: Agent of Change, Agent of Preservation in Portsmouth." *Strawbery Banke Newsletter* (Fall 1998).

_____. "Strawbery Banke, the First Decade." Unpublished report presented at the thirtieth anniversary of the Strawbery Banke Board of Overseers, September 30, 1995.

Gilmore, Robert C. and Ingmire, Bruce C. *The Seacoast New Hampshire: A Visual History.* Virginia Beach, VA: The Donning Company, 1989.

Giffen, Sarah L. and Murphy, Kevin D. *A Noble and Dignified Stream: The Piscataqua Region in the Colonial Revival, 1860–1930.* York, ME: Old York Historical Society, 1992.

Gold, Jack Anthony. "Case Study: The Evolution of Historic Preservation in Portsmouth, N.H.: Strategies for Improved Preservation Planning Services." Cornell University Graduate School Master of Arts thesis, January 1978.

Grossman, Nancy W. *The Placenames of Portsmouth.* Portsmouth, NH: Back Channel Press, 2005.

Hackett, Frank W. *Portsmouth Records 1645–1656: A Transcript of the First Thirty-Five Pages of the Earliest Town Book.* Portsmouth, NH: privately printed, 1886.

Hazlett, C.A. "Reminiscences of Portsmouth Authors." *Granite Monthly* (March 1915).

Hayes, H. Wilbur. *Attractive Bits Along the Shore.* Portland, ME: H. Wilbur Hayes, circa 1895.

Hill, Ralph Nading. *Yankee Kingdom: Vermont and New Hampshire.* New York: Harper & Brothers, 1960.

Hosmer, Charles B. Jr. *Preservation Comes of Age: From Williamsburg to the National Trust, 1926-1949.* Charlottesville, VA: University Press of Virginia, 1981.

Howells, Mrs. William White (Muriel). "The Story of Strawbery Banke Restoration." *Bulletin of the Garden Club of America* 55, no. 3 (May 1967):4-9.

Howells, Mr. William White Howells and Muriel Howells. Interview by Deborah S. Gardner, August 16, 1994.

Howells, Muriel. Interview by Judith Moyer for Strawbery Banke Museum, September 21, 1990.

_____. Scrapbooks relating to the founding of Strawbery Banke Museum, 1957–1982. Strawbery Banke Museum Collection.

Jacobson, Marcia. *Being a Boy Again: Autobiography and the American Boy Book.* Tuscaloosa, AL: University of Alabama Press, 1994.

Jobe, Brock. *Portsmouth Furniture: Masterworks from the New Hampshire Seacoast.* Society for the Preservation of New England Antiquities, 1993.

Kelly, Margaret Whyte. *Sarah–Her Story: The Life Story of Sarah Parker Rice Goodwin.* Portsmouth, NH: Back Channel Press, 2006.

Lawson, Russell, M. *Passaconaway's Realm: Captain John Evans and the Exploration of Mount Washington.* Hanover, NH: University Press of New England, 2002.

May, Ralph. *Early Portsmouth History.* Boston: C.E. Goodspeed & Co., 1926.

McLaughlin, Robert E. *Water Street: A Novel.* New York: Carlton Press, Inc., 1986.

Morison, Elizabeth Forbes and Elting E. *New Hampshire: A Bicentennial History.* New York: W.W. Norton & Company, Inc., 1976.

Morrill, H. Bartlett. "The Windings of the Piscataqua." *The Granite Monthly* XXIV, no. 3 (March 1898):124-134.

Moses, J.M. "John Mason's Three Great Houses." *Granite Monthly* 50, 1918: 116-110.

Nutting, Wallace. *New Hampshire Beautiful.* Framingham, MA: Old America, 1923.

Osgood, Herbert L. *The American Colonies in the Seventeenth Century.* New York: Columbia University Press, 1904-07. (Available online.)

Pendery, Steven R. "Urban Process in Portsmouth, New Hampshire..." *New England Archaeology Dublin Seminar for New England Folklife Annual Proceedings 1977* (Boston University, 1978).

Piscataqua Pioneers: Selected Biographies of Early Settlers in Northern New England. Portsmouth, NH: Peter E. Randall, Publisher, 2000.

Portsmouth Book, The. Boston: Geo. H. Ellis, Printer, 1899.

Roberts, Paige W. "The Politics of Preservation: Historical Consciousness and Community Identity in Portsmouth, New Hampshire." George Washington University dissertation, May 21, 2000.

_____. "The Floral Architect: Rules and Designs for Processions." *The Dublin Seminar for New England Folklife* (Boston University 2000):29-46.

Robinson, Brian and Charles Bolian. "A Preliminary Report on the Rocks Road Site." *The New Hampshire Archaeologist* 28, no. 1 (1987):19-51.

Robinson, J. Dennis. Various articles from www.SeacoastNH.com archive.

Rogers, Mary Cochran. *Glimpses of a Social Capital.* Boston: Printed for the Subscribers, 1923.

Sammons, Mark J. and Valerie Cunningham. *Black Portsmouth: Three Centuries of American-American Heritage.* Hanover, NH: University Press of New England, 2004.

Saltonstall, William G. *Port of Piscataqua.* Cambridge, MA: Harvard University Press, 1941.

Seavey, Mrs. Frances N. "The Graffort Club of Portsmouth." *Granite Monthly* (September 1901):202-207.

Sherman, George. *History of Temple Israel Portsmouth, New Hampshire 1893–1997.* Privately printed, 1997.

Shillaber, B. P. *The Double-Runner Club or The Lively Boys of Rivertown.* Boston: Lee and Shepard Publishers, 1882.

Stanley, Raymond W. *The Four Thompsons of Boston Harbor 1621–1965.* Boston: Thompson Academy, 1966.

Szasz, Ferenc. "John Lord's Portsmouth." *Historical New Hampshire* 44, no. 3 (Fall 1989):138-149.

Thompson, Ralph E. and Matthew R. *First Yankee: The Story of New Hampshire's First Settler.* Privately printed, 1979. Reprinted Portsmouth, NH: Peter E. Randall, Publisher, 1997.

Twain, Mark. *Mark Twain in Eruption: Hitherto Unpublished Pages about Men and Events.* Bernard DeVoto, ed. New York: Harper & Brothers Publishers, 1922.

Vaughan, Dorothy. The Papers of Dorothy Vaughan Archive at the New Hampshire Historical Society (unprocessed).

_____. The Dorothy Vaughan Collection, Strawbery Banke Museum (unprocessed).

_____. Vertical Clipping File, Portsmouth Athenaeum.

Volk, Joyce. "Going to Blazes." *Piscataqua Decorative Arts Society*, Vol. 1 (2002–2003), 12–21.

_____, ed. *The Warner House: A Rich and Colorful History.* Portsmouth, NH: The Warner House Association, 2006.

Ward, Barbara McLean, ed. *Produce & Conserve, Share & Play Square: The Grocer & the Consumer on the Home-Front Battlefield During World War II.* Portsmouth, NH: Strawbery Banke Museum, 1994.

Wilderson, Paul W. *Governor John Wentworth and the American Revolution: The English Connection.* Hanover, NH: University Press of New England, 1994.

Weaver, Robert C., ed. *Preserving Historic America*. Washington, DC: Department of Housing and Urban Development, June 1966.

Willoughby, Elaine Macmann. *The Story of Strawbery Banke in Portsmouth New Hampshire*. Booklet published by the author, 1970.

Winslow, Olga Elizabeth. *Portsmouth: The Life of a Town*. New York: The MacMillan Company, 1966.

Winslow, Richard E. III. *Do Your Job!: An Illustrated Bicentennial History of the Portsmouth Naval Shipyard 1800-2000*. Portsmouth, NH: Portsmouth Marine Society, 2000.

_____. *The Piscataqua Gundalow*. Portsmouth, NH: Portsmouth Marine Society, 1983.

_____. *Wealth and Honour: Portsmouth During the Golden Age of Privateering 1775–1815*. Portsmouth, NH: Portsmouth Marine Society, 1988.

Zeidman, Jack and Ida. Interviewed by Mary Pietsch, Strawbery Banke Museum Archives, August 24, 1977.

ENDNOTES

Chapter 1: Opening Ceremonies (1965)

1 A letter from John F. Rowe, Commissioner, New Hampshire Dept. of Resources and Economic Development, *Portsmouth Herald* (June 16, 1965).

2 *Portsmouth Herald* (July 21, 1965).

3 "City Must Sell Itself," *Portsmouth Herald* (July 21, 1965).

4 *Ibid.*

5 "Strawbery Banke Project To Have First Phase Opening Memorial Day," *Carroll County Pioneer* (February 19, 1965).

6 "The Merchant's Review," *Seacoast News* (May 13, 1965).

7 Bruce Fuller, conversation with author (December 2006).

8 "Colonial Restoration Project to Open in Portsmouth," *Sunday Register* (New Haven, CT: February 14, 1965).

9 Robert C. Weaver, ed., *Preserving Historic America* (Washington DC: Department of Housing and Urban Development, June 1966):14-15.

10 "Strawbery Banke," *Portsmouth Herald* (May 28, 1965): special section.

11 "Foul Weather Dampens Seacoast Opening of Strawbery Banke in Portsmouth," *Sunday Telegram* (Portland, ME: May 30, 1965).

12 Thayer Cumings, *Strawbery Banke: The First 25 Years*, unpublished manuscript (Portsmouth, NH: Strawbery Banke Museum Archives):30.

13 "Strawbery Banke, It's Not Finished!" *Portsmouth Herald* (May 28, 1965): special section sidebar.

14 George Washington does not mention the Chase incident in his own journal of his New England tour (the entire Washington diary is available online at the Library of Congress Web site), nor does Elwin L. Page mention it in his short book (*Washington in New Hampshire*, 1932). Dorothy Vaughan's assertion while she was president of Strawbery Banke that Washington dined at the Chase House is certainly not true. ("The Chase House" by Dorothy Vaughan, Chase House files, SBM archives. May 1, 1962). One source references a January 5, 1799 article in the *Portsmouth Oracle*; however that article could not be located in that paper.

15 Nellie McCarty's original $100,000 gift to the Chase House was given in memory of Dr. Charles Green, MD, who was a former Portsmouth native. The reason for this memorial remains unclear. Green, like McCarty, was a collector of Victorian Parian ware and had donated many items to the American Wing of the Metropolitan Museum that McCarty admired. Miss McCarty's

OPPOSITE: The Daniel Webster house waits for its new foundation after being moved across the city during the formative years of Strawbery Banke, Inc. (SBM/DA)

own collection, placed in the Chase House was, according to Dorothy Vaughan, "as good but not as extensive" as Dr. Greene's collection. "She [McCarty] feels," Vaughan reported around 1969, "that because this is her Memorial Gift, she wants to be responsible for everything that goes into the house. If others contribute gifts or loans of furniture, it will cease to be her memorial gift." (Vaughan re: Chase House Collection, undated note in Chase House files at SBM.)

16 The house was obtained by Harry Winebaum, an early supporter of the museum, who purchased and held it for Strawbery Banke Inc.

17 Carl A. Johnson to Harold J. Anderson, February 13, 1964 (Chase House files at SBM).

18 Memorandum from Carl A. Johnson, December 2, 1963 (Chase House files at SBM).

19 James Garvin notes that the architectural "team" consisted primarily of William Perry and Walter Rosenfeld of his firm. Most unforeseen issues were disclosed by local contractor John Paterson of E. L. Paterson & Sons as work progressed. The main problem was that the contract drawings had been completed prior to much physical investigation of the house, so the onset of actual work revealed much previously undetected physical evidence.

20 Carl A. Johnson to Harold J. Anderson, February 13, 1964 (Chase House files at SBM).

21 Carl. A. Johnson to Ernest Colprit, May 22, 1965 (Chase House files at SBM).

22 Chase House Committee memo to board members, May 18, 1970 (Chase House files at SBM).

Chapter 2: Left Behind: The Orphaned Plantation (1600–1635)

1 Emerson Baker, interview with the author (2006). Baker notes that Captain John Walker explored Maine's Penobscot River in 1579-80 and reported seeing Native Americans twenty years before Gosnold's better known visit. See also: Colin Woodard, *The Lobster Coast* (New York: Penguin Books, 2004), 66. Woodard notes that Walker robbed the Natives of three hundred dried moose hides, one of many European acts of aggression against local Indians prior to colonization.

2 Scholars disagree as to the location of Savage Rock. Cape Elizabeth has also been suggested as the site. Naval historian Samuel Eliot Morison, who was also an Overseer of Strawbery Banke Museum, has suggested that the location might be nearby Cape Neddick in Maine.

3 For more on this tale, see Ralph May's *Early History of Portsmouth* (Boston: C.E. Goodspeed and Co. 1926), 29-31.

4 Ralph May, 35.

5 For more on this era, see Michael J. Caduto, *A Time Before New Hampshire* (Hanover NH: University of New Hampshire, 2003).

6 For reference to Seabrook, New Hampshire, skeletal remains see Brian Robinson and Charles Bolian, "A Preliminary Report on the Rocks Road site," in *The New Hampshire Archaeologist* 28, no. 1 (1987):19-51. For information on the Eliot, Maine, site see Douglas Kellogg, "The Neal Garrison Paleoindian Site, York County, Maine" in *Archaeology of Eastern North America* 31 (2003):73-131. Also for a coastal site of the same era look for Bull Brook in Ipswich, Massachusetts, circa 11,000 radiocarbon years or 12,000-13,000 real years. See also Betrand G. Pelletier and Brian S. Robinson, "Tundra, Ice and a Pleistocene Cape on the Gulf of Maine: A Case of Paleoindian Transhumance," *Archaeology of Eastern North America* 33 (2005):163-176.

7 See Michael J. Caduto, *A Time Before New Hampshire* (2003).

8 Nathaniel Bouton, ed. *Provincial Papers: Documents and Records Relating to the Province of New Hampshire, From the Earliest Period of Its Settlement: 1623-1686*, vol. 1 (Concord, NH: George E. Jenks, State Printer, 1867), 106. This entry is dated October 10, 1633. Hereafter referred to as *The Provincial Papers.*

9 Emerson Baker, "Finding the Almouchiquois: Native American Families," *Ethnohistory* 51, no. 1 (Winter 2004).

10 Ralph May, 74-75.

11 Amazingly, two of the Native Americans, Manteo and Wanchese, had first traveled to England earlier with Captain Arthur Barlowe in 1584 on a mission to explore the possibilities of colonization in the Americas for Sir Walter Raleigh.

12 Maine historians held proudly to the legend of the first English settlement at Maine, but the Popham Colony was not discovered until 1994 when a researcher following an early drawing, "the John Hunt map," located the ruins of the fort. See the Web site for Popham Colony, "the first English colony in New England," www.pophamcolony.org.

13 A reproduction of the letter, along with the English translation, can be found in Henry O. Thayer, "The Sagadahoc Colony" (Portland, ME: Gorges Society, 1892), 115-119. This line quoted is on page 119. The original letter is at the Maine Historical Society.

14 Emerson Baker notes that, in one instance, early explorers approaching a town called Lachine, Quebec, just up river from

Montreal, believed they were getting close to "La Chine," or China. Emerson Baker, conversation with the author (2006).

15 Others have suggested that by changing the Indian names to European names, he was effectively hoping to obscure the native claims to ownership, a practice historians have labeled "imperialism of the map." Emerson Baker, conversation with the author (2006).

16 Herbert Osgood, *The American Colonies in the Seventeenth Century* (New York: Columbia University Press, 1904). The full name was the "Council established at Plymouth in the County of Devon for the Planting, Ruling, and Governing of New England in America." The group was limited to 40 members of the nobility who intended to rule the region like feudal barons. The group actually divided up New England in a lottery although only 11 of then 28 members showed up for the meeting. Gorges had a difficult time getting members to gather and to pay dues. (Osgood source found online, page 102-121.) Even the foremost scholar of Mason's land grants blames the five-year "aimless floundering existence" of the Council on the decades of confusion that followed in New Hampshire. See Otis Grant Hammond, "The Mason Title and Its Relations to New Hampshire and Massachusetts" in *The Proceedings of the American Antiquarian Society* (October 1916): 245-246.

17 This battle over seniority led to separate Dover and Portsmouth centennial celebrations in 1823, helped launch the New Hampshire Historical Society, and shaped the way Portsmouth and Dover have separately defined and preserved their history ever since. See more on this in Chapter 5 of this book.

18 Nathaniel Adams, *Adams Annals* (Portsmouth, NH: Peter Randall Publisher, 1971 reprint), 17. Adams notes a Laconia grant to Mason and Gorges on November 3, 1631, and includes the other grantees as John Cotton, Henry Gardner, George Griffith, Edwin Gay, Thomas Wannerton, Thomas Eyre, and Eliezer Eyre who had reportedly already spent £3,000 to establish the settlement at Pascataway. These investors later sold off their failed New Hampshire investment to Mason, as did Gorges.

19 Osgood, 124. Ralph May notes that the English held a "superlatively erroneous picture" of the region at the time and believed that the headwaters of the Piscataqua were about 90 miles from Lake Champlain, page 85.

20 Nathaniel Adams, 18. Adams's sources say the Little Harbor in 1631 included "six great shallops, five fishing boats with sails, anchors, and cables, and 13 skiffs."

21 Olga Elizabeth Winslow, *Portsmouth: The Life of a Town* (New York: The MacMillan Company, 1966), 36.

22 Nathaniel Adams, 10. Hilton Point, also known as Dover Point, was first known to settlers by the Indian name Winnichahannat, renamed Northam and eventually to become a part of Dover.

23 Bruce E. Ingmire, "A Famous Seacoast Non-battle Was at Bloody Point," *Portsmouth Press* (March 10, 1991).

24 Exactly who accompanied Neale has fascinated and frustrated north country historians for centuries. For a discussion of Neale's journey and the Darby Field exploration in 1642 see Russell M. Lawson's *Passaconaway's Realm: Captain John Evans and the Exploration of Mount Washington* (Hanover, NH: University Press of New England, 2002), 16.

25 Provincial Papers, vol. 1, 90 (correspondence dated May 5, 1634).

26 Provincial Papers, vol. 1, 92.

27 Local historians have long argued over the names and locations of Mason's original manor houses, also called "Mason's Hall," the "Manor House," "Rendezvous," "The Great Hall," "Mason's Manor House," etc. For one view see Appendix A of Everett S. Stackpole's *The History of New Hampshire*, vol. 1 (1916), 373-376, and the Moses references that follow. Currently the "Great House" is used most often to refer to the site on the Portsmouth waterfront at Strawberry Bank.

28 J.M. Moses, "John Mason's Three Great Houses," *Granite Monthly* 50 (1914):116-119. Moses raises even more complexities about the original Piscataqua settlements in "Sander's Point," *Granite Monthly* XLVIII, no. 6 (June 1916):167-171.

29 Now in the British Museum, the map of the Piscataqua River by "I.S." was produced in the 1660s and has proven quite accurate based on historic records and archaeological digs in the region. See a detail of this map in Chapter 3.

30 Emerson Baker, members of the Chadbourne Family, and the Old Berwick Historical Society have unearthed over 30,000 artifacts at the 1640-1690 Chadbourne site in Maine. Modern descendents of the Chadbourne family have taken a strong interest in the South Berwick excavation. For more information see their Web site.

31 Steven R. Pendory, "Urban Process in Portsmouth, New Hampshire..." in *New England Archaeology Dublin Seminar for New England Folklife Annual Proceedings 1977* (Boston, MA: Boston University Press, 1978), 27-28.

32 Moses, 117.

33 Charles Brewster, *Rambles About Portsmouth*, vol.1 (Somersworth, NH: New Hampshire Publishing Company, 1971), 18. Nathaniel

Adams offers his list that includes first names as well. Spellings vary in different accounts, but for the sake of genealogy, Adams' list from page 18 is reproduced here: "The names of the stewards and servants, sent by Mason into his province of New Hampshire, were Walter Neal, Ambross Gibbins, Thomas Camocks, William Raymond, Francis Williams, George Vaughan, Thomas Warnerton, Henry Jocelyn, Francis Norton, Sampson Lane, Renald Fernald, Ralph Goe, Henry Goe, William Cooper, William Chadborn, Francis Matthews, Humphrey Chadborn, William Chadborn, Jun.(sic), Francis Rand, James Johnson, Anthony Ellins, Henry Baldwin, Thomas Spencer, Thomas Furral, Thomas Herd, Thomas Chatherton, John Crowther, John Williams, Roger Knight, Henry Sherborn, John Goddard, Thomas Fernald, Thomas Withers, Thomas Canney, John Symonds, John Peverly, William Seavey, Heanry Langstaff, William Berry, Jeremiah Walford, James Wall, William Brakin, Thomas Walford, Thomas Moore, Joseph Beal, Hugh James, Alexander Jones, John Ault, William Brackett, James Newt.

34 Tracking what ships arrived when remains tricky, but settlers may have also arrived at Strawberry Bank around this time aboard the *John* and the *Lyon's Whelp;* see Ralph May, 100.

35 Historians do not generally agree which side of the street the Great House inhabited. The 1720 Oracle House now sits on the lot bordering Strawbery Banke Museum, but it was moved there in 1937.

36 Various accounts refer to "The Cove" and "The Creek" interchangeably as well as to that shift over time. Since "The Creek" is also used to denote other locations in Portsmouth (Witch Creek, Sagamore Creek, Islington Creek, etc.) I chose to simply use "The Cove" here to refer to the body of water at Puddle Dock, sometimes using the phrase the "tidal inlet." The name "Puddle Dock" technically does not appear until the eighteenth century.

37 Provincial Papers, vol. 1, 62.

38 *Ibid.*, 81.

39 Nathaniel Adams, 293-4.

40 J. Dennis Robinson, *Lord Baltimore: Founder of Maryland* (Mankato, Minnesota: Compass Point Books, 2006).

Chapter 3: Portsmouth at Rivermouth (1635–1700)

1 The author's key regret in researching this book was the lack of time available to track down this theory that the origin of the name Strawberry Bank may come from an English location of the same name. I was unable to find a single person or source that

suggested this in my research, so I turned to my favorite research tool—Ebay. Repeatedly typing the phrase into the online auction Web site frequently led to postcards and references to English sites and structures named Strawberry Bank. The only other reference that appeared after months of repeated searching, besides those connected with New Hampshire, was a turn of the twentieth-century book for children entitled *Strawberry Bank; or, Home From India*. The book is published in London, but does not list an author or publication date. It is my sincere hope that someone will follow-up on this footnote in a more scholarly and productive manner.

2 Local historians tend to agree that the strawberry patch, if it existed, was near the current St. John's Episcopal Church. The obsession with this story, promoted by local historians Ralph May and Dorothy Vaughan, culminated with the release of the first Strawbery Banke Museum brochure. The opening text (see Chapter 9) implies that the scent of fresh strawberries attracted the passing ships into Portsmouth Harbor in 1630. A modern researcher has speculated, but not on the record, that settlers might have discovered strawberries cultivated by Native Americans, but not recognized them as such due to differences in cultivation practices. Another archaeologist, again not on the record, suggested that the above is unlikely.

3 Frank W. Hackett, *Portsmouth Town Records 1645–1656: A Transcript of the First Thirty-Five Pages of the Earliest Town Book* (Portsmouth: Privately printed, 1886), 22.

4 Nathaniel Adams, 44.

5 Provincial Papers, vol.1, 217-219.

6 The story survives largely due to a detailed nineteenth-century newspaper article by Charles W. Brewster, editor of the *Portsmouth Journal*. His account on witchcraft was among the essays collected in the second volume of Brewster's *Rambles About Portsmouth* (Ramble #144).

7 J. Dennis Robinson, "Attack of the Rock-Throwing Devil," www.SeacoastNH.com (April, 2003); versions also appeared in *Foster's Daily Democrat* and the *New Hampshire Gazette*.

8 The full title of the pamphlet published in London by Richard Chamberlain in 1698 was: *Lithobolia: or, the Stone-Throwing Devil. Being an Exact and True Account (by way of Journal) of the various Actions of Infernal Spirits, or (Devils Incarnate) Witches, or both; and the great Disturbance and Amazement they gave to George Waltons Family, at a place call'd Great Island in the Province of New-Hampshire in New-England, chiefly in Throwing about (by an*

Invisible hand) Stone, Brick s, and Brick-bats of all Sizes, with several other things, as Hammers, Mauls, Iron-Crows, Spits, and other Domestick Utensils, as came into their Hellish Minds, and this for the space of a Quarter of a Year.

9 Emerson Baker, *The Devil of Great Island: Witchcraft & Conflict in Early New England* (New York: Palgrave Macmillan, 2007).

10 Ralph May, 100.

11 Provincial Papers, vol. 1, 180. See also *Black Portsmouth* by Mark Sammons and Valerie Cunningham (Hanover, NH: University Press of New England, 2004) for more on slavery in colonial Portsmouth.

12 Libby, 718.

13 *Ibid.*, 259.

14 Provincial papers, vol. 1, 384.

15 Frank W. Hackett, 50-66. Although Belknap says the original records were "destroyed," Hackett argues that there is no evidence of this. After the book was again recopied, Hackett notes a reference in 1677 to two earlier books still surviving.

16 Provincial Papers, vol. 1, 208.

17 Candee, Richard, "Millwright and Merchant: Water-powered Saw-milling in Seventeenth-century Maine and New Hampshire," *Old-Time New England*, 60, no. 4 (Spring 1970):131-149. See also by Candee, Chapter 3 in *Wooden Building in Early Maine and New Hampshire: 1600-1720* (Univ. of Pennsylvania dissertation, 1976), 103-196.

18 See William Saltonstall, *Ports of Portsmouth* (Cambridge, MA: Harvard University Press, 1941), Chapter 2.

19 *Ibid.*, 17.

20 *Ibid.*, 14.

21 Commission of John Cutt, 1680, The Avalon Project Online, Yale Law School, originally found in The Federal and State Constitutions Colonial Charters, and Other Organic Laws of the States, Territories, and Colonies Now or Heretofore Forming the United States of America Compiled and Edited Under the Act of Congress of June 30, 1906, by Francis Newton Thorpe (Washington, DC: Government Printing Office, 1909).

22 Jeremy Belknap, as cited in Elizabeth Forbes Morison and Elting E. Morison, *New Hampshire: A History* (New York: W.W. Norton, 1976), 31. They cite Belknap's *History of New Hampshire*, vol. 1, 137.

23 Jeremy Waldron, a descendent of the murdered Dover leader, was among the founders of Strawbery Banke Inc. in 1958 and is one of its longest surviving supporters.

Chapter 4: On the Waterfront (The 1700s)

1 Research suggests that the back staircase was donated to Strawbery Banke in the 1980s and is currently in storage.

2 Richard Candee, *Wooden Buildings in Early Maine and New Hampshire: A Technological and Cultural History* (Philadelphia: University of Pennsylvania, 1976, dissertation), 188.

3 Richard Candee, "Warner House Origins: The Merchant House in Early Eighteenth-century London & New England," *The Warner House: A Rich and Colorful History*, edited by Joyce Volk (Portsmouth, NH: Warner House Association, 2006). This book, with its series of scholarly essays and color photographs, provides an extraordinary study of the house, its furnishings, family, renovation, and history as an independent house museum in Portsmouth.

4 Now known as the Wentworth Coolidge Mansion on Little Harbor Road, Portsmouth, New Hampshire.

5 Clark, Charles E., *The Eastern Frontier: The Settlement of Northern New England 1610-1763* (New York: Alfred A. Knopf, 1970), Chapter 7.

6 *Ibid.*, 100.

7 *Ibid.*, 99.

8 See the Web site www.colonialancestors.com for lists of Harvard graduates by year.

9 James L. Garvin, longtime New Hampshire scholar of the Wentworth-Coolidge Mansion at Little Harbor, points out that it is important to be wary of the myth of the "unlimited greed" of the Wentworths, and especially of Benning Wentworth. Eighteenth-century colonial officers were expected to provide their holders with certain emoluments, and Wentworth's creditors wanted him to have the offices of governor and Surveyor of the King's Woods so that he could become wealthy enough to honor his debts. Wentworth's promotion of settlement on the frontiers, Garvin notes, was in keeping with his instructions from George II, which are published in the State Papers. For more on Benning Wentworth and his land grant policies, see John Francis Looney, "The King's Representative: Benning Wentworth, Colonial Governor, 1741-1767," dissertation (Lehigh University, 1961).

10 The popular romantic and historically inaccurate story of "Lady Wentworth" is told in a ballad by Henry Wadsworth Longfellow in his poem by the same name. The poem appeared in the bestselling collection *Tales of Wayside Inn* that also includes the romantic and inaccurate ballad of the midnight ride of Paul Revere. Another

Victorian ballad also entitled "Lady Wentworth" by Nora Perry fictionalizes the life of Frances Atkinson, wife of New Hampshire Governor John Wentworth.

11 Paul W. Wilderson, *Governor John Wentworth and the American Revolution: The English Connection* (Hanover, NH: University Press of New England, 1994), introduction.

12 In a later television version of *Northwest Passage*, the role of Hunk Mariner was played by Buddy Ebson, later known for the television series "The Beverly Hillbillies" and for his role as detective Barnaby Jones.

13 According to the official Strawbery Banke guidebook, Stoodley's first Portsmouth tavern, the King's Arms, was built about 1753, but burned to the ground in 1761. Therefore, the tavern depicted as Stoodley's Tavern in the film would have been the King's Arms. James Stoodley's tavern moved to Strawbery Banke from Daniel Street late in 1965 was Stoodley's second tavern, constructed a few years after the time set in the novel.

14 Strawbery Banke Official Guidebook, 42.

15 Mark J. Sammons and Valerie Cunningham, *Black Portsmouth: Three Centuries of African-American Heritage* (Hanover, NH: University Press of New England, 2004), 19.

16 *Ibid.*, 38-39.

17 Nathaniel Adams, 222–223.

18 Paul W. Wilderson, 184.

19 *Ibid.*, 179.

20 *Ibid.*, 173.

21 *Ibid.*, 212.

22 Adams, 271.

23 Adams, 290.

24 See Chapter 1.

25 At least according to Elwin Page, author of *George Washington in New Hampshire* (1932, page 56 in reprinted edition), who cites a local newspaper account placing Washington at the Wentworth mansion.

26 John W. Durel, *From Strawbery Banke to Puddle Dock: The Evolution of a Neighborhood* (Durham, NH: University of New Hampshire, dissertation, 1986), 12-37.

27 Clark, 104.

28 Reverend William Shurtleff, letters published in *Church History of New England.* (Boston?: 1743), 383 ff.

29 For more on consuming culture in early America, see Richard L. Bushman's *The Refinement of America: Persons, Houses, Cities* (New York: Vintage Books, 1992).

30 As quoted in the acknowledgements of Brock Job's *Portsmouth Furniture* (Boston, MA: Society of New England Antiquities, 1993).

31 J. F. D. Smyth, *A Tour in the United States of America*, vol. II (London: 1784; reprinted New York: New York Times and Arno Press, 1968), 371. Thanks to Richard Candee for this and the previous reference.

32 James L. Garvin, "Blanchard's Balloon: First Flight in New Hampshire," *New Hampshire Profiles* (June 1976): 66-68.

Chapter 5: The Birth of Puddle Dock (The 1800s)

1 Thomas Bailey Aldrich, *The Story of a Bad Boy* (Boston, MA: Houghton Mifflin Company, 1922 reprint), 28.

2 Dona Brown, "Purchasing the Past: Summer People and the Transformation of the Piscataqua Region in the Nineteenth Century," in *A Noble and Dignified Stream: The Piscataqua Region in the Colonial Revival, 1860-1930* (York, ME: Old York Historical Society, 1992), 3-14.

3 From Julian Ursyn Niemcewicz, in "Under the Vine and Fig Tree: Travels through America in 1787–1799" as quoted in Richard M. Candee, "Social Conflict and Urban Rebuilding: The Portsmouth, New Hampshire, Brick Act of 1814," *Winterthur Portfolio*, 32, nos. 2 & 3 (Summer/Autumn 1997):119.

4 Richard E. Winslow III, *Do Your Job!: An Illustrated Bicentennial History of the Portsmouth Naval Shipyard 1800-2000* (Portsmouth, NH: Portsmouth Marine Society, 2000), 1.

5 Durell, 36.

6 Richard M. Candee, "Social Conflict and Urban Rebuilding: The Portsmouth, New Hampshire, Brick Act of 1814," *Winterthur Portfolio* 32, nos. 2 & 3 (Summer/Autumn 1997): 125.

7 William G. Saltonstall, 120.

8 *Ibid.*, 155.

9 Ray Brighton, *Rambles About Portsmouth* (Portsmouth, N.H.: Portsmouth Marine Society, 1994), 151-153.

10 The complete quote from Samuel Adams Drake. *A Book of New England Legends and Folk Lore* (Rutland, VT: Charles E. Tuttle Company, 1981 edition), 332. It reads: "Its commercial importance waned, progress was arrested, and the place came to a standstill; and it is today more remarkable for what it has been than for what it is."

11 Richard M. Candee, " 'Old Portsmouth . . . Home of the Stocking Business': A forgotten Nineteenth-century Industry and its

Inventors," *Historical New Hampshire* 57, nos. 3 & 4 (Fall/Winter 2002):85-107.

12 Kenneth E. Shewmaker, ed., *Daniel Webster, "The Completest Man": Documents from the Papers of Daniel Webster*, as cited online at the Dartmouth Web site for Webster speeches.

13 These words were penned by William P. Adams as cited in Richard M. Candee, "The 1823 'Centennial' Celebration of New Hampshire's Settlement," *The Dublin Seminar for New England Folklife* (Boston, MA: Boston University, 2000), 57.

14 Kenneth E. Shewmaker, 94-99.

15 Richard M. Candee, "The 1823 'Centennial' Celebration of New Hampshire's Settlement," 55.

16 Nathaniel Adams, 255.

17 Ferenc Szasz, "John Lord's Portsmouth," *Historical New Hampshire* 44, no. 3 (Fall 1989):138-149.

18 *Ibid.*, 148.

19 John Durel, " 'Historic' Portsmouth: The Role of the Past in the Formation of a Community's Identity," *Historical New Hampshire* 31, nos. 3 & 4 (Fall/Winter 1986):102.

20 Charles Brewster, *Brewster's Rambles*, vol. 2 (Somersworth, NH: New Hampshire Publishing Company, 1972), 365.

21 For much more see J. Dennis Robinson, *Wentworth by the Sea: The Life and Times of a Grand Hotel* (Portsmouth, NH: Peter E. Randall Publisher, LLC, 2004).

22 *The Reunion of '73* (Portsmouth, NH: Charles W. Gardner, 1873), 29, as quoted in John Durel.

23 H. Wilbur Hayes, *Attractive Bits Along the Shore* (Portland, ME: circa 1895), no page numbers.

24 Sarah Foster, *Portsmouth Guide Book* (Portsmouth, NH: Joseph H. Foster, 1884).

25 H. Wilbur Hayes, no page numbers

26 H. Bartlett Morrill, "The Windings of the Piscataqua," *The Granite Monthly* XXIV, no. 3 (March 1898):130.

27 See Paige Roberts, *The Politics of Preservation: Historical Consciousness and Community Identity in Portsmouth, New Hampshire* (Washington, DC: George Washington University, 2000, dissertation). Hereafter referred to as *Preservation*.

28 Richard Candee, "Brick Act of 1814," 137.

29 *Ibid.*, 139.

30 As quoted in Nancy Grossman's *Placenames of Portsmouth* (Portsmouth, NH: Back Channel Press, 2005), 21.

31 Sarah Foster, 23.

32 John Durel, *From Strawbery Banke to Puddle Dock . . .* , Chapter 6.

33 Parts of *An Old Town by the Sea* were serialized earlier in *Atlantic Monthly* making the dates of Aldrich's observations difficult to attribute to a specific year.

34 Thomas Bailey Aldrich, *An Old Town by the Sea* (Boston, MA: Houghton Mifflin Company, 1917); all quotes here are from Chapter 2, "Along the Water Side."

35 Mrs. James T. Fields, *James T. Fields* (Boston, MA: Houghton, Mifflin and Company, 1881), 1.

36 B.P. Shillaber, *The Double-Runner Club or The Lively Boys of Rivertown* (Boston: Lee and Shepard Publishers, 1882), 44-45.

37 Aldrich, *The Story of a Bad Boy*, 139.

38 J. Dennis Robinson, "Blood on the Snow in Portsmouth," www.SeacoastNH.com (2002).

39 John W. Durel, "'Historic' Portsmouth," 107.

40 Paige W. Roberts, *The Politics of Preservation*, 29.

41 Daniel Augustus Drown, *Idyls of Strawberry Bank* (Portsmouth, NH: privately printed, 1873), 8.

42 *Ibid.*, 261.

Chapter 6: Red Lights and White Gloves (1900–1935)

1 R. Clipston Sturgis, "Architecture of Portsmouth," *The Portsmouth Book* (Boston, MA: Geo. H. Ellis, Printer, 1899), 6.

2 Mrs. Frances N. Seavey, "The Graffort Club of Portsmouth," *Granite Monthly* (September 1901):202-207.

3 *Ibid.*

4 Lilian (Mrs. Thomas Bailey) Aldrich, *Crowding Memories* (Boston, MA: Houghton Mifflin Company, 1920), 2.

5 *Ibid.*, 132.

6 *Ibid.*, 145.

7 *Ibid.*, 110-111.

8 In his review of *The Story of a Bad Boy* in the *Atlantic Monthly* in January 1870, William Dean Howells wrote of Aldrich: "No one seems to have thought of telling the story of a boy's life, with so great desire to show what a boy's life is, and so little purpose of teaching what it should be; certainly no one has thought of doing this for the life of an American boy." As quoted in Marcia Jacobson, *Being a Boy Again: Autobiography and the American Boy Book* (University of Alabama Press, 1994). It is notable that the first four editors of the *Atlantic* had connections to the Piscataqua region. James Russell Lowell (editor, 1857-1861) was among the visitors to the Appledore Hotel salon at the Isles of Shoals, and James Thomas Fields (1861-1871) grew up in Portsmouth's South End. They were followed by editors William Dean

Howells (1871–1881) and Thomas Bailey Aldrich (1881-1890), thus ensuring that *Atlantic* readers continually learned about the Portsmouth scene during three critical decades during the rise of colonial revival tourism.

9 All Twain quotes on Portsmouth and Lilian Aldrich here come from page 292-295 of *Mark Twain in Eruption: Hitherto Unpublished Pages about Men and Events*, edited by Bernard DeVoto (New York: Harper & Brothers Publishers, 1922).

10 "Many People Daily Visit Aldrich Home," *Portsmouth Times* (August 1, 1912).

11 Hazlett, C.A., "Reminiscences of Portsmouth Authors," *Granite Monthly* (March 1915).

12 Key references to prostitution on Water Street are drawn from research by Kimberly Crisp, a descendant of Alta Roberts. This quotation comes from page 18 of Kimberly Crisp, *Water Street Remembered* (Durham, NH: University of New Hampshire, 1996), masters thesis.

13 For more information also see Chapter 23 of Ray Brighton's book *They Came to Fish*, titled "The Red Lights are Turned Off" (Portsmouth, NH: Peter E. Randall, 1973, reprinted 1994), 212-233. Details here come from Brighton and a study of the murders in Portsmouth newspaper articles from the summer and fall of 1912. The information also appears in "The Deadly Summer of 1912" by J. Dennis Robinson, published in various newspapers and online at www.SeacoastNH.com. Some key articles are also noted here.

14 "Woman is Charged With Serious Crime," *Portsmouth Times* (August 16, 1912) and "Ethel Duffy Tells Story of Her Experience," the following day.

15 "Has Become a Nuisance," *Portsmouth Herald* (September 12, 1912).

16 "City Marshal Entwistle Resigns," and "City Marshal Entwistle Will Hold the Fort," *Portsmouth Herald* (September 21, 1912) and "Marshal Entwistle Says He Has Not Resigned," two days later.

17 Saltonstall, 39.

18 Mark Sammons and Valerie Cunningham, *Black Portsmouth: Three Centuries of African-American Heritage* (Hanover, NH: University of New England Press, 2004), 17. (See also www.SeacoastNH.com.) John Moffatt's ship, the *Exeter*, returned from Africa in 1755 with 61 slaves: 20 men, 15 women, seven "man boys," two "women girls," ten boys and seven girls. The ship's carpenter, John Winkley, had contracted with Moffatt to receive in exchange for his labor on the trip free passage and his choice of "a prime slave"

at the price paid "on the coast of Guinea." John Moffatt acquired one slave by stealing him from his Massachusetts owner and taking him on a voyage to Portugal; Moffatt was convicted in 1725 for the kidnapping. Thirty-six slaves also were available from brokers at major American auction centers from Boston to New Orleans.

19 Richard M. Candee, *Building Portsmouth: The Neighborhoods & Architecture of New Hampshire's Oldest City* (Portsmouth, NH: Back Channel Press, 2006), 27. Originally published by the Portsmouth Advocates, 1992.

20 A quote from Wallace Nutting written in 1936. See the Web site of the Wallace Nutting Library.

21 Paige Roberts, *Preservation*, 68.

22 The tree still stands today.

23 Augustus C. Buell, *Paul Jones, Father of the American Navy*, vol. 1 (New York: Charles Scribner's Sons, 1901), 244-245.

24 The monument can be found today in Jones Park in Kittery, Maine, just over the Memorial Bridge.

25 It is unclear how much of the funds were given to Cappy Stewart for the house, and how much for the actual land, once the unpopular brick building project was abandoned by Jones executors.

26 J. Dennis Robinson article, "The Many Stories of Paul Jones House," on www.SeacoastNH.com.

27 Quoted in Paige Roberts, *Preservation*, 64.

28 Charles B. Hosmer, Jr., *Preservation Comes of Age: From Williamsburg to the National Trust, 1926–1949*, vol. 1 (Charlottesville: University Press of Virginia, 1981), 177.

29 For much more on the colonial revival on the Piscataqua see Sarah L. Giffen, and Kevin Murphy, *A Noble and Dignified Stream: The Piscataqua Region in the Colonial Revival, 1860–1930* (York, Maine: Old York Historical Society, 1992).

30 Joyce Geary Volk, ed., *The Warner House: A Rich and Colorful History* (Portsmouth, NH: The Warner House Association, 2006), 127.

Chapter 7: The Maritime Village Idea (1935–1955)

1 Wallace Nutting, *New Hampshire Beautiful* (New York: Bonanza Books, 1923), 78.

2 Information in this section from *The Prescott Story* by Raymond Brighton (Portsmouth, NH: Portsmouth Marine Society, 1982).

3 All references to this report, unless otherwise indicated, are from the documents delivered to Strawbery Banke Museum in the 1960s and recently transcribed by James Garvin for this book from: Donald Corley (compiler), *Maritime Portsmouth,*

New Hampshire, Portsmouth Restoration Project (Tentative), Architectural Research Section, 1300 Rye St., Washington, DC, W.P.A., 1936-37.

4 The idea to reconstruct the Old Statehouse, adapted by the founders of Strawbery Banke, eventually became a watershed issue in the professionalization of the museum. See future chapters for more.

5 John W. Durel, "The Past: A Thing to Study, a Place to Go," *Public History: An Introduction*, edited by Barbara J. Howe and Emery L. Kemp (Malabar, FL: West Virginia University, Robert E. Krieger Publishing Company, 1986), 230.

6 Hosmer, vol. 1, 334.

7 *Ibid.*, vol. 1, 339.

8 This profile assembled from various newspaper obituaries and articles in the Stephen Decatur file in the Portsmouth Athenaeum.

9 Howells to Cram letter (December 16, 1936), Wendell Collection, Portsmouth Athenaeum.

10 Information from newspaper clippings from "Mr. Howells in Kittery," *Boston Herald* (Saturday, May 15, 1920) and "William Dean Howells: The Kittery Years," transcript of a speech by Don L. Cook delivered at the Portsmouth Athenaeum (July 22, 1989).

11 Public—No. 292—74th Congress, S. 2073

12 Quoted in Hosmer, 334.

13 *Ibid.*, 335.

14 Howells to Cram (December 16, 1936), Wendell Collection, Portsmouth Athenaeum.

15 Quoted line is from Howells to Wendell (February 20, 1937), Wendell Collection, Portsmouth Athenaeum.

16 Barbara McLean Ward, ed., *Produce & Conserve, Share & Play Square: The Grocer & the Consumer on the Home-Front Battlefield During World War II* (Strawbery Banke Museum, 1994), 57.

17 Paige Roberts, *Preservation*, 101.

18 Corley, Introduction.

19 This information on Mayo is drawn largely from Hosmer (335-340) and Roberts (*Preservation*, Chapter 3).

20 Clark to Vaughan (January, 1940), Dorothy Vaughan Collection at New Hampshire Historical Society. NOTE: portions of this collection most relevant to Strawbery Banke Museum have been given to the Museum by the New Hampshire Historical Society. These are referenced as part of the Dorothy Vaughan collection at SBM, not yet accessioned at this writing.

21 Hosmer, 335.

22 "To Study Historic Portsmouth," *Portsmouth Herald* (July 6, 1938).

23 Roberts, *Preservation*, 94.

24 1936-1937 WPA Proposal.

25 Howells to Cram (December 16, 1936).

26 Roberts, *Preservation*, 106.

27 Zeidman, Jack and Ida, interviewed by Mary Pietsch Harding (August 24, 1977), SBM.

28 All material on the Abbott Store abridged from: Barbara McLean Ward, ed., *Produce & Conserve, Share & Play Square: The Grocer & the Consumer on the Home-Front Battlefield During World War II* (Portsmouth, NH: Strawbery Banke Museum, 1994).

29 Information here on WWII Puddle Dock is drawn from another essay in *Produce & Conserve, Share & Play Square* by Gregory C. Colati and Ryan H. Madden, entitled "Victory Begins at Home: Portsmouth and Puddle Dock During World War II," 57-78.

30 *Ibid.*, 77.

31 Sherman Pridham, conversation with the author at Strawbery Banke (August 2006).

Chapter 8: Three Strong Voices (1955–1958)

1 Clare Kittredge, "Remembering a pioneer of preservation," *The Boston Globe* (July 22, 2004).

2 Dorothy Vaughan, conversation with the author at Tobias Lear House, Portsmouth, NH (July 4, 1998).

3 George Bartter, "Ask Dorothy," *New Hampshire Profiles* (April, 1962).

4 Clare Kittredge, "History honors one who honors its history," *The Boston Globe* (May 27, 1990).

5 John Mead Howells, likely with Vaughan's assistance, called this the Cutter-Langdon Mansion, in part after its 1817 owner, Dr. Ammi Cutter. *Architectural Heritage of the Piscataqua*, figures 106-109.

6 Muriel Howells to Wenberg (October 4, 1956), *Howells Scrapbook*, SBM.

7 Wenberg to Howells (October 16, 1956), *Howells Scrapbook*, SBM.

8 Charles Brewster refers to the house at Middle and Congress Street as the "Storer" house and tells the story of Mary Treadwell in Ramble #24, 136.

9 Dorothy Vaughan speech to Portsmouth Rotary Club (October 6, 1983), Dorothy Vaughan Collection, SBM.

10 Ray Brighton, *They Came to Fish*, 353-354

11 Dorothy Vaughan, transcript of speech to Portsmouth Rotary Club (June 20, 1957). The notes to the central part of the speech, according to Vaughan, were lost. Dorothy Vaughan Collection, SBM.

12 Jeremy Waldron interview with the author (April 2007).

13 All quotations here from Muriel Howells interviewed by Judith Moyer (September 21, 1990), SBM.

14 *Ibid*.

15 Howland to Kimball (June 26, 1957) *Howells Scrapbook*, SBM.

16 "Waldron Urges City Project to Save Colonial Heritage," *Portsmouth Herald* (October, 1957).

17 "Colonial Village Challenge to Portsmouth," *Portsmouth Herald* (October 29, 1957).

18 Thayer Cumings, 4.

19 Richard Howland, public lecture at Rockingham Ballroom (February 6, 1958), Dorothy Vaughan Collection, SBM.

20 Muriel Howells interviewed by J. Moyer.

21 Muriel Howells, letter to her family (February 7, 1968), *Howells Scrapbook*, SBM.

22 All references to the content of this speech are from a typed manuscript of Richard Howland's address to Portsmouth Rotary Club (February 6, 1958), Dorothy Vaughan Collection, SBM.

23 Muriel Howells, letter to her family (February 7, 1968), *Howells Scrapbook*, SBM.

24 Howland to Muriel Howells (February 8, 1957), *Howells Scrapbook*, SBM.

Chapter 9: Strawbery Banke Inc. (1958–1965)

1 As quoted by James L. Garvin in "Strawbery Banke: Agent of Change, Agent of Preservation in Portsmouth," *Strawbery Banke Newsletter* (Fall 1995).

2 Minutes of Portsmouth Housing Authority meeting (February 19, 1958), *Howells Scrapbook* and author conversation with Jeremy Waldron (April 2007).

3 Minutes of Colonial Portsmouth Committee, Portsmouth City Council (March 26, 1958).

4 Ralph May, 139.

5 "Council Okays Bonds for Urban Renewal," *Portsmouth Herald* (June 8, 1958).

6 "Strawbery Banke to Pay Its Own Way," *Portsmouth Herald* (October 10, 1958).

7 Sumner Winebaum as told to him by his father Harry Winebaum, conversation with the author (October 2005).

8 Author interview with Jeremy Waldon (April 2007) and from reports previously written by Waldron loaned to the author.

9 "Regarding the Marcy Street Area," *Portsmouth Herald* (August 15, 1959).

10 "Planners Still Stall Action on Village Project," *Portsmouth Herald* (October 1959), *Howells Scrapbook,* SBM.

11 "Planning Board Delays Action," *Portsmouth Herald* (September 4, 1958).

12 "Planners Still Stall Action on Village Project," *Portsmouth Herald* (October 1959).

13 "Legal Difficulty Stymies Final Okay for Banke," *Portsmouth Herald* (November 20, 1959).

14 Cynthia Raymond, speech to directors of the Strawbery Banke Guild (October 20, 1981). All references in this section come from the speech on the history of the Guild.

15 "Portsmouth's Chance to Sell Its History," *Portsmouth Herald* (February 10, 1959).

16 Strawbery Banke brochure, SBM.

17 Jeremy Waldron, who continues to advocate for a reconstruction of the Old Statehouse on the Portsmouth waterfront, does not recall the Howells-Decatur plan being an influence on the colonial village concept. It was, however, very much in the mind of Dorothy Vaughan who had worked with John Mead Howells and later Captain Chester Mayo on the South End maritime village plan. Muriel Howells learned about the plan from Stephen Decatur and both women frequently referred to the WPA project in articles and speeches.

18 Daniel F. Ford, "Portsmouth Slum Clearance Marks New Era," *The Christian Science Monitor* (May 25, 1959).

19 Thayer Cumings, Strawbery Banke: The First 25 Years (unpublished manuscript, SBM), 9.

20 Cynthia Raymond, conversation with the author (November 2006).

21 Thayer Cumings, 16.

22 J. Dennis Robinson, "Daniel Webster Lost in Portsmouth," appeared in *Fosters Daily Democrat*, *New Hampshire Gazette,* and www.SeacoastNH.com.

23 Raymond Brighton, *Portsmouth Herald* (November, 1961).

24 Jeremy Waldron to Dorothy Vaughan, private memo (undated), Dorothy Vaughan Collection, SBM.

25 Sources include Linnea Staples, "Says Governor Goodwin Home Fund OK'd 'Regrettable,'" *New Hampshire Sunday News* (November 4, 1962); "Governor Goodwin House in Portsmouth

to be Restored" (November 1, 1962); memo from Russell B. Tobey, Director, New Hampshire Division of Parks to Governor Wesley Powell (October 3, 1962); Dorothy Vaughan Collection, SBM.

26 While Dorothy Vaughan and others spoke of Perry in reverential tones, others saw him as a representative of the colonial revival style, less concerned with historic accuracy than with creating a nostalgic and patriotic vision of an imagined colonial past.

27 "Top Architect Plans Strawbery Banke," *Portsmouth Herald* (August 1, 1964).

28 Shawne K. Wickham, "Her Perseverance to Preserve Port City's History Paid Off," *Manchester Union Leader* (1987).

29 Clare Kittredge, "The Woman Who Saved Portsmouth," *Seacoast Woman* vol. 5, no. 40 (January 12, 1982).

30 "Librarian's Talk Started Restoration," The *Portsmouth Herald* (May 23, 1965).

31 John Schnitzler, conversation with the author (March 2007).

32 "Memorial Day in '65 Set for Banke Opening," *Portsmouth Herald* (July 28, 1964).

33 "Renewal Head Praises Banke Development," *Portsmouth Herald* (September 25, 1965).

34 The official number of displaced families comes from the Portsmouth Housing Authority Collection as referenced in Paige Roberts' dissertation, *Preservation*, 125.

35 "A Place for History to Hang Its Hat," *The New Hampshire Town Crier* (undated, estimated 1963), supplement to the *Derry Star* and other regional newspapers.

36 Mae Johnson, interviewed by Mary Pietsch Harding (August 17, 1997), SBM.

37 Comments by Evelyn Marconi come from interviews with the author (November 2006) and from Elizabeth Dinan, "A Nonsense Case of Eminent Domain," *Portsmouth Herald* (August 7, 2005).

38 Paige Roberts, *Preservation*, 147.

Chapter 10: Shifting Foundations (1965–1975)

1 "Strawbery Banke, Inc., Summary of a Report and Survey," presented to the Board of Directors, Newsome & Company, Inc., Boston, MA, April 14, 1964. This initial report was paid for by a grant from the Spaulding Potter Fund, a philanthropic group that later evolved into the New Hampshire Charitable Foundation.

2 Movie producer Louis de Rochemont, best known for his *March of Time* documentaries showed the building was still solid when he staged a party scene in Kittery Point for his controversial "race film," *Lost Boundaries,* in 1948. Horace Mitchell, who was born in

Sparhawk and inherited it, played a role in the de Rochemont film. Always intending to restore the mansion, Mitchell died without achieving his goal. His widow was paid $1,500 by Strawbery Banke for the rights to remove portions of the interior.

3 See "Sparhawk to Become Part of Banke," *York Coast County Star* (December 29, 1965) and Rita Perry, "Sparhawk Hall to Fall," *Portsmouth Herald* (December 21, 1966).

4 Johnson to Thaxter (January 21, 1966) and Johnson to William Perry (February 4, 1966), Rosamond Thaxter Papers, courtesy of Jonathan Hubbard.

5 Wallace Murphy, Jr. (Portsmouth Savings Bank) to Jeremy Waldron (November 8, 1967) and John L. Frisbee III (National Trust) to President of Portsmouth Savings (November 27, 1967), Rosamond Thaxter Collection, courtesy Jonathan Hubbard; see also "Society Seeks to Save Whipple House," *Portsmouth Herald* (August 13, 1968).

6 Lady Bird Johnson's purchase was higher than the average sale. During its first three months the Dunaway Store grossed an income of $20,000 from 12,250 sales, for an average of $1.63 per customer, according to the August 1967 notes of the Board of Directors.

7 "Old Port City Thrilled Lady Bird," *Portsmouth Herald* (June 11, 1967) and other news clippings from the week.

8 "Strawbery Banke Stands on the Verge of Still Another Crucial Decision," *Portsmouth Herald* (June 13, 1973).

9 "City 'Needs Bath' in Visitor's Opinion," *Portsmouth Herald* (May 7, 1966).

10 "Banke Scorned," *Portsmouth Herald* (January 6, 1967).

11 "Banke's Charm Lost," *Portsmouth Herald* (March 31, 1966). The Dunaway Store was later run by the Guild of Strawbery Banke until the Guild was dissolved in 1990. It continued as the museum gift shop until the creation of the Tyco Visitor Center in 2005 when the Dunaway Store was leased as a restaurant.

12 From Gurney quoted by Garvin in his history of the Old Statehouse. "The Colonial Statehouse Through Time," www.SeacoastNH.com

13 At this writing, the timbers are again being studied with federal funding to determine the final disposition of New Hampshire's original statehouse.

14 The names of buildings have changed over time at Strawbery Banke. The Wheelwright House during its initial restoration was called the John Clark House and the Walsh House was then the Benjamin Bigelow House, notes Jim Garvin.

15 Justine Flint Georges, "A New Look at an Old Town; Strawbery Banke . . . as its restorers see it," *New Hampshire Profiles* (July 1967).

16 Former Portsmouth head librarian Sherman Pridham recalls being kicked out of one of the buildings at this time. Raised in Puddle Dock, Pridham had returned from college to visit his former home (now the Drisco House) when his party of trespassers was broken up by "a man with a flashlight" who he now thinks might have been Jim Garvin, whom he later came to know.

17 James L. Garvin, "Strawbery Banke, the First Decade," presented at the Thirtieth Anniversary of the Strawbery Banke Board of Overseers (September 30, 1995).

18 Howland to Carl A. Johnson (February 15, 1969); Howland to Rowland (August 5, 1969); collection of Rosamund Thaxter and recounted in Thayer Cumings's history of Strawbery Banke.

19 Details drawn from Thayer Cumings's history and local newspaper accounts.

20 Raymond to Margeson (July 10, 1969), collection of Rosamond Thaxter, courtesy of Jonathan Hubbard.

21 "Strawbery Banke Gets All Shook Up," *Portsmouth Herald* (July 10, 1969) and "Strawbery Banke, a Great Local Asset, Stands on the Brink of Decision," *Portsmouth Herald* (July 31, 1969). See also "Power Struggle Breaks Into Open," *Portsmouth Herald* (July 9, 1969); "Strawbery Banke Hit by Court Injunction," *Portsmouth Herald* (August 1, 1969).

22 Anonymous letter to Dorothy Vaughan (undated), Dorothy Vaughan Collection, SBM.

23 Nellie McCarty to Dorothy Vaughan [unsigned] (March 11, 1965), Dorothy Vaughan Collection, SBM.

24 Thayer Cumings, 112.

25 Articles quoted in this section include: "Strawbery Banke Is Once Again at a Crossroad Important to its Future," *Portsmouth Herald* (July 16, 1971); "Strawbery Banke Rift Laid Open," *Portsmouth Herald* (July 1971); and "Strawbery Banke Is on Threshold of a Real Philosophic Crisis," *Portsmouth Herald* (July 1971).

26 After announcing his potential retirement, Captain Johnson appeared to change his mind. He later submitted a fourteen-point memo arguing that, although he had announced plans to retire, he had not officially and technically tendered his resignation.

27 Cumings, 134.

28 "Lynch Offers Strawbery Banke Realistic Plans for Use of Houses," *Portsmouth Herald* (July 13, 1972).

29 Dorothy Vaughan typed memo to "Tom" (May 8, 1973), Dorothy Vaughan Collection, SBM, includes all comments in this paragraph. Collection also includes a memo from a stockholder who had changed her vote after a telephone call from Vaughan, plus a number of proxies signed over to her by stockholders for the July 1973 meeting.

30 Edmund C. Lynch, conversation with the author (December 2006).

31 Thayer Cumings manuscript. This sentiment was popularized by the idea that Strawbery Banke was going to generate money for the local economy. See also "Banke Seen Key to Mint Dollars," *Portsmouth Herald* (August 17, 1963), and "Money in the Banke," *The Beacon* (June 1964).

32 "Portsmouth Stands to Lose Heritage," letter from Joseph W. Hammond, *Portsmouth Herald* (August 14, 1968).

33 "Can Portsmouth, New Hampshire save these historic houses and reap a profit too?," *Worcester Sunday Telegram* (September 14, 1969).

34 Paige Roberts, *Preservation*, 168.

35 Raymond Brighton, *They Came to Fish*, vol. 1, 369; vol. 2, 425-6.

36 In 2007 *The Portsmouth Herald*, now a member of the Seacoast Media Group, moved its facility out of the city center to the Pease International Tradeport on the outskirts of Portsmouth. At this writing a large portion of the former Little Italy neighborhood is still undeveloped and serves as a hotel parking lot. The Parade Mall is being replaced by a hotel complex.

37 J. Dennis Robinson, "Russell Street Reunion," videotape (1986) and Robinson's "Urban Renewal Takes Little Italy," www.SeacoastNH.com and in various local newspapers.

38 For a complete inventory of houses on The Hill, see Richard Candee, *Building Portsmouth: The Neighborhoods and Architecture of New Hampshire's Oldest City* (Revised, Portsmouth, NH: Back Channel Press, 2006), 18-24.

39 Garvin, James L., "Strawbery Banke: Agent of Change, Agent of Preservation in Portsmouth," *Strawbery Banke Newsletter* (Fall 1995).

Chapter 11: Portsmouth Reborn (1975–1985)

1 James Haller, conversation with the author (February 2007). Although Haller adopted the colonial spelling of "strawbery," the name Blue Strawbery was not, as many still assume, a reference to Strawbery Banke. It came, instead, from a small blue piece of lapis that Haller wore around his neck, he says, because it reportedly

held the power to dispel the fear of success. When asked—"Why are you wearing a blue strawberry?" —the idea for the restaurant was born. Haller is currently a master chef, consultant, and teacher.

2 Another key figure in the "renaissance" was Richard Morton who purchased the brick buildings on Ceres Street and encouraged, supported, and volunteered at Theatre-by-the-Sea. Morton made it possible for start-up companies to revive the waterfront and was a benefactor to Strawbery Banke, the Historical Society, and other groups.

3 Jon Kimball, conversation with the author (February 2007). Kimball was director of the North Shore Music Festival from 1983 to 2007. He lives in seacoast New Hampshire.

4 Bob Thoresen, conversation with the author (February 2007).

5 Kimball, conversation with the author (February 2007).

6 "Portsmouth Faces a Fox in the Henhouse," *Boston Sunday Globe* (February 20, 1983).

7 Peggy Armitage, conversation with the author (January 2007).

8 "Strawbery Banke Adapting New 'Dual-Role' in Portsmouth," *Portsmouth Herald* (November 19, 1976); "Banke is Living," *Portsmouth Herald* (March 26, 1977); and "Strawbery Banke Plans to Rejoin 'Living' World," *Portsmouth Herald* (March 31, 1977).

9 Historian Paige Roberts offers an alternative view of the Puddle Dock display currently in the "tiny and decrepit" Joshua Jackson House at Strawbery Banke. Roberts writes: "Sensitive to the bitterness still felt by many former residents, the exhibit's description of Puddle Dock is infused with nostalgia about the bygone days of the neighborhood during the early twentieth century. Much as Native Americans became noble figures for turn-of-the-century Americans, Puddle Dockers likewise became attractive just as they (seemed to) disappear (through dispersion). The same language has been used to describe both groups and their culture once they had been evicted. Now Strawbery Banke has appropriated Puddle Dockers as an interesting ethnic other." *Preservation*, 145-146.

10 Mary Pietsch Harding interview with author (April 2007).

11 The real Aldrich would likely have been displeased with the joining of his family estate to what he considered a lower class neighborhood just over the fence. Like many of his contemporaries, he was largely intolerant of other races, religions, and classes as exhibited by many of his letters, essays, and poems.

12 "Historic Garden Dedicated at Strawbery Banke," *Manchester Union Leader* (June 21, 1977). Also, Peter Happney, conversation with the author (February 2007).

13 For more information see Mary Bentley Dupre, "The History of Archeology at Strawbery Banke Museum," *The New Hampshire Archeologist* 35, no. 1 (1995):12-28.

14 "Young Straus Seeks Puddle Dock Rim," *Portsmouth Herald* (July 18, 1964).

15 Louise Richardson interview with author (April 2007).

16 Winslow, Richard E. III, *The Piscataqua Gundalow* (Portsmouth, NH: Portsmouth Marine Society, 1983 and 2002), 136.

17 John W. Durel, "The Past: A Thing to Study, a Place to Go," *Public History: An Introduction*, edited by Barbara J. Howe and Emery L. Kemp (Malabar, FL: West Virginia University, Robert E. Krieger Publishing Company, 1986), 233.

18 "New Banke Director Sparking Changes," *Portsmouth Herald* (April 15, 1980) and "History Springs to Life at Strawbery Banke," *Portsmouth Herald* (December 27, 1980).

19 James Vaughan, conversation with the author (March 2007).

20 Durel, *The Past*, 239.

21 John Durel, conversations with the author (Winter 2007).

22 David Donath, conversation with the author (February 2007).

23 Vince Lombardi, conversation with the author (March 2007).

24 "Evaluative Study of Management and Operation of Strawbery Banke," Edward L. Protz Associates, Inc., Galveston, Texas (May 1983), Dorothy Vaughan Collection, SBM.

25 In 1980 a separate nonprofit agency, The Portsmouth Advocates, was formed to promote the preservation of the historic and architectural character of Portsmouth. Launched by Richard Candee and Martha Fuller Clark, who also served as Strawbery Banke trustees, the new organization allowed Strawbery Banke to withdraw from controversial lobbying except for its own buildings, and to increase its role as an educational rather than an advocacy institution.

26 Sue Hertz, "Time and Tide in Portsmouth," *The Boston Sunday Globe* (1983).

27 "Old New England Port Rescues Its Vanishing Charm," *US News and World Report* (October 19, 1981).

28 *Ibid.*

Chapter 12: Back to the Future (1985–2008)

1 As quoted by Dennis O'Toole on his arrival at the Strawbery Banke Museum in 1992, from *Habits of the Heart: Individualism and Commitment in American Life*, by Robert Bellah, Richard Madsen, William M. Sullivan, Ann Swidler, and Steven M.

Tipton (Berkeley, CA: University of California Press, 1986), page 153 in 1996 paperback edition.

2 See for example Ichak Adizes, *Corporate Lifecycles* (Englewood Cliffs, NJ: Prentice Hall, 1988).

3 Jane Nylander, conversation with the author (March 2007).

4 "Strawbery Banke Museum, Portsmouth, New Hampshire," reprinted from *The Magazine Antiques* (July, 1992).

5 Richard Candee, conversation with the author (March 2007).

6 John Schnitzler, conversation with the author (March 2007).

7 "Guild of Strawbery Banke Closes It's Doors Forever," *Strawbery Banke Newsletter* 22, no. 3 (Fall 1990).

8 *Strawbery Banke Newsletter* 24, no. 2 (Winter 1992-93).

9 Dennis O'Toole, conversation with the author (February 2007).

10 A play entitled *Thirst for Freedom*, by Emory Wilson, dramatized the life of the historical Ona Judge Staines who escaped from George and Martha Washington and lived out her life in seacoast New Hampshire. *A Child Out of Place* by Patricia Wall offers a fictional account for children of slaves living in the Warner House. In the novel *Patriot's Reward*, by Stephen Clarkson, an educated enslaved man from Portsmouth, New Hampshire, fights in the American Revolution.

11 The shed was attached to a former four-stall garage that had served as Strawbery Banke's carpentry shop and had then been converted to an "orientation center."

12 Kathleen Stiso Mullins, conversation with the author (March 2007).

13 Martha Fuller Clark, conversation with the author (March 2007).

14 David Donath, conversation with the author (February 2007).

15 Charles Bickford, conversation with the author (March 2007).

16 Lawrence Yerdon, conversation with the author (March 2007).

Index

About the Author

J. Dennis Robinson is editor and owner of the popular regional Web site SeacoastNH.com. An educator, audio and video producer, lecturer, and columnist, Robinson has published over a thousand articles on local history and culture. His most recent books include juvenile biographies of outlaw Jesse James and Maryland founder Lord Baltimore, and *Wentworth by the Sea: The Life and Times of a Grand Hotel*. He lives in Portsmouth, New Hampshire, with his wife Maryellen Burke.

About The Photographers

Richard Haynes Jr. earned a Master of Fine Arts from Pratt Institute in New York. Born in the South, he is currently a noted New Hampshire painter, educator, and activist. Ralph Morang grew up in Rye, and his family has been involved with Strawbery Banke since the 1960s. He has been a freelance photographer and photojournalist in the seacoast for thirty years. Douglas Armsden photographed Strawbery Banke in its founding years. Born in 1920, he lives in Kittery Point, Maine.

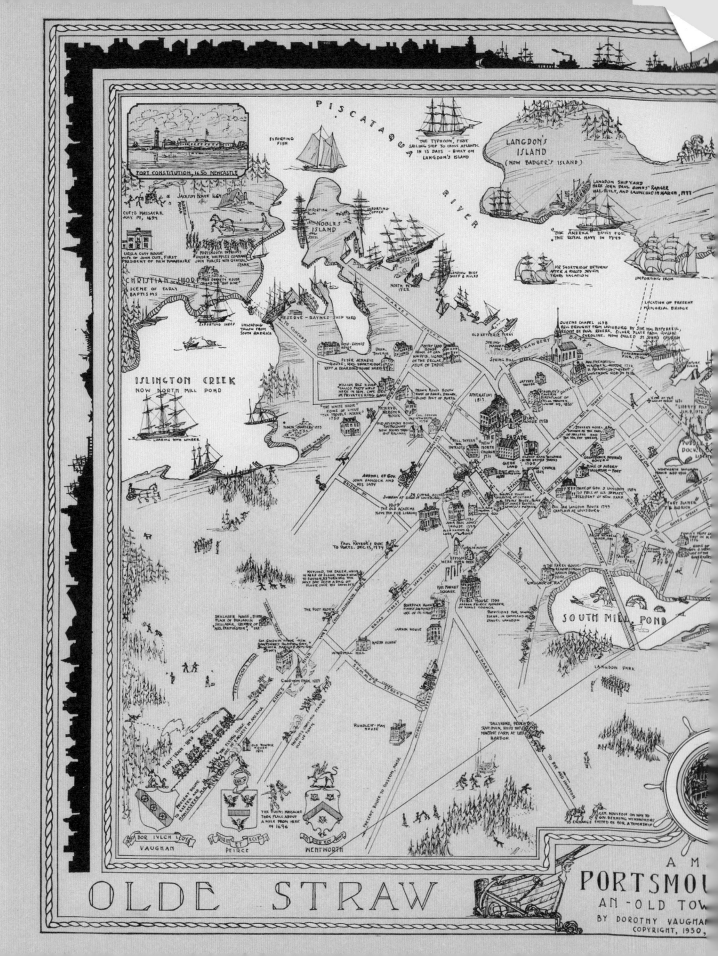